PURE & SIMPLE

HOMEMADE INDIAN VEGETARIAN CUISINE

First published in 2009 by
Interlink Books
An imprint of Interlink Publishing Group, Inc.
46 Crosby Street, Northampton, Massachusetts 01060
www.interlinkbooks.com

ISBN: 978-1-56656-770-1

Editor: Neeta Datta
American edition editors: Hiltrud Schulz, Sara Rauch, Leyla Moushabeck
Design: Supriya Saran
American edition cover design: Juliana Spear
Production: Naresh Nigam

Printed and bound in Singapore

To request our free 40-page full-color catalog, please call us toll free at
1-800-238-LINK; visit our website at www.interlinkbooks.com,
or send us an email: info@interlinkbooks.com

PURE & SIMPLE

HOMEMADE INDIAN VEGETARIAN CUISINE

VIDHU MITTAL

Photography by
SANJAY RAMCHANDRAN

Interlink Books

An imprint of Interlink Publishing Group, Inc.
Northampton, Massachusetts

For every vegetarian food lover

ACKNOWLEDGEMENTS

Sanjay Ramchandran who very patiently took photographs. His creativity reflects in this book.

Jagdish Babu DK who systematically rearranged selected photographs and text. It was a boon for a non-tech savvy person like me to have him around.

Sujatha Puranik Rakhra, an invaluable sounding board, who was always there for me whenever I needed her.

Abhishek Poddar, who has a creative eye, gave several ideas for the layout and the cover page.

William GK who assisted in the final styling of each dish before it was shot.

And, most importantly, my husband, **Som**, our children, **Nidhi, Tarang,** and **Siddharth**, my sister, **Anu**, and my domestic help, **Madamma**, who supported me as I journeyed through this book.

CONTENTS

FOREWORD

Even before our father's job took us to Bangalore, our parents were great hosts. They loved having friends and family over for vivacious gatherings. Aside from the great company, the hallmark of these events was, undeniably, food.

The spreads were highlighted with Indian classics like *dal makhani* and *methi paneer,* as well as continental gems like corn with spinach, casseroles, and potato with mixed vegetable cakes.

As our parents' social circle grew larger and more eclectic, so did the opportunity for the two of them to hone their entertaining skills.

It was during this time that a close friend of our mother's, and a regular at these gatherings, encouraged her to consider sharing her culinary skills. Our family jumped onboard, making posters for "Fancy Chef Cookery Classes."

Her first course – Party Cooking – spanned five days, during the work week, and had two simple tenets: vegetarianism and delighting a crowd. For three hours every day, our dining room was transformed into a working kitchen, complete with a portable stove, notebooks, and raw ingredients. Five housewives made up the first class. My mother's tasty, yet easy-to-prepare recipes, along with her straightforward teaching style lead to all five returning for the sequel: Party Cooking 2.

With these humble beginnings in culinary pedagogy, Mom expanded her selection of classes to include international cuisine. When dining at the newest eatery in Bangalore, she always tried to figure out how to recreate the dishes. And then we'd return home to be guinea pigs for her experiments.

Nobody ever heard the two of us complain. For sixteen years, we have watched her make many aspiring cooks (and as a consequence, their families) very happy. This book is a culmination of what she's learned and is sure to spread that joy to many more.

Nidhi and Tarang

INTRODUCTION

Around the globe, popularity in both Indian cuisine and vegetarianism is rising steadily. This book will introduce you to the joys of cooking and even show how it can actually be a relaxing activity. Arming you with simple methods, this book will allow you to recreate the intricate flavors, intoxicating aromas, and succulent textures of homestyle Indian food.

I have been conducting cookery classes in Bangalore, India, for over 15 years and it has been one of my most rewarding experiences. My many students have been the source of encouragement and inspiration for writing this book.

The recipes in this book have the characteristic flavor of my native province – Uttar Pradesh. My emphasis has been on crafting delicately spiced dishes, contrary to the hot flavors stereotypically associated with Indian cuisine.

Combinations of these recipes make for delicious menus that are also very well-balanced meals. You will find many ways to pick and choose various courses like soups, salads, refreshing drinks, entrées, and scrumptious desserts.

I have had the opportunity to perfect these recipes over the years. With these dishes, I have also tried to illustrate the immense visual appeal of Indian food and highlight the natural colors of the freshest ingredients. The preparations for these recipes involve very simple and easy-to-understand steps. Photographs accompany all the recipes and highlight each step of the process.

I hope you and your loved ones enjoy cooking these dishes as much as I have enjoyed writing this book.

Vidhu Mittal

DISCOVER SPICES

Spices are essential food additives enhancing the flavor, aroma, and also color of the food. These are natural and dried and used either whole or ground. Some of these can be sprinkled but the true flavors are enhanced when roasted, preheated in a cooking medium, or added during cooking. Spices must be stored in airtight containers to retain freshness.

 **Asafetida** (*hing*): It is a resin from a tree and has a strong smell when raw, but when cooked it imparts a smooth flavor. This spice aides in digestion and is used in food as a condiment. It must be stored away from other spices because of its strong odor.

 Bay leaf (*tej patta*): It is a dried leaf of the bay laurel tree, and has a pleasant flavor. Normally a dish is seasoned with 2-3 leaves. The fragrance of bay leaf is more obvious than the taste in cooked food. Leaves can be removed before serving.

 Black cardamom (*badi elaichi*): It is a hairy brown pod which is used whole or crushed to add flavor to a dish. Black cardamom can be used in soups, rice, and savory dishes and is discarded while eating. It is also used in the preparation of the Indian spice mixture *garam masala*.

 Black peppercorn (*sabut kali mirch*): It is a sun-dried berry of a pepper plant. Black peppercorn is sometimes used whole, but is more often ground. It is also the main ingredient in the Indian spice mixture called *garam masala*.

 Black salt (*kala namak*): It is an unrefined mineral salt, greyish in color. It is used extensively in Indian cooking as it enhances the flavor in *chaats* and savories.

 Carom (*ajwain*) **seeds**: Carom seeds are greyish brown in color; they are aromatic and slightly pungent in taste. Only a small quantity added to clarified butter (*ghee*) or oil is enough to flavor the dish. This helps reduce flatulence.

 Chili powder (*lal mirch*): It is a hot spice prepared from ground red chilies and the spiciness varies with the type of chili used. Small quantity of chili powder is added to oil while cooking curries. It can also be sprinkled over *chaat* and *raita* to add an extra zing. Kashmiri red chilies are often used as they add color and are less spicy.

 Cinnamon (*dalchini*): This is a bark of a tree, which is rolled and then dried. Cinnamon has an aromatic and sweet flavor. Ground cinnamon is widely used in soups, desserts, and stews. Cinnamon sticks are used for indirect flavoring in a dish and may be removed while eating.

 Clove (*laung*): It is an aromatic dried flower bud. It is used for both sweet and savory dishes. Rice and soups seasoned with cloves in ghee or oil infuse a soothing flavor.

 Coriander (*dhaniya*) **seeds**: These are dried fruits of the cilantro plant, greenish brown in color with a slight savory flavor. Ground coriander is widely used in Indian curries.

 Cumin (*jeera*) **seeds**: These are small, elongated seeds which have a distinctive aroma and flavor. Cumin seeds emit their own flavor after browning in oil for curries. They can also be roasted and ground and are used for flavoring yogurt dishes.

 Fennel (*saunf*) **seeds**: These are small, elongated, aromatic, and light green in color. They have a sweet taste. Ground fennel seeds are used in curries and pickles. Whole seeds are often chewed in India as a mouth freshener.

 Fenugreek seeds (*methi dana*): These are hard and pale yellow in color with a bitter taste. Only a few seeds are added for seasoning and flavoring. Ground or whole seeds are used in Indian pickles and emit a pleasant aroma.

Green cardamom (*choti elaichi*): These are light green in color with tiny, black seeds inside. The cardamom seeds are groundd and used in sweet dishes, tea, and some exotic dishes. Green cardamom has a distinctive, refreshing flavor and is also a good mouth freshener.

 Jaggery (*gur*): This is boiled and solidified raw sugarcane juice, used extensively in Indian cooking. It has a unique flavor and is used in both sweet and savory dishes. It is considered healthier than sugar as it retains more mineral salts.

 Mango powder (*amchur*): This is the sun-dried powdered form of raw mangoes. It is generally added to cooking vegetables toward the end to give a tangy flavor to the dish. Adding earlier can delay the cooking process.

 Mint (*pudina*) **powder**: This is the sun-dried powdered form of fragrant mint leaves. It adds a refreshing flavor to drinks, dry vegetables, Indian breads, and curries. Mint powder can be stored for up to a month.

 Mustard seeds (*rai*): These are the small, round seeds of the mustard plant. The color varies from black to brown to yellow. Savory dishes are tempered with mustard seeds, and powdered mustard is used in pickles to give a sour taste. Bottled mustard paste is used for salad dressing and accompaniments.

 Nutmeg (*jaiphal*): It is oval with a spicy flavor and aroma and is always used grated. It is used to flavor vegetables, soups, cakes, and puddings.

 Saffron (*kesar*): Saffron strands are dried stigmas of the saffron crocus flower. It is an expensive and exotic spice. Saffron strands are generally infused in hot water or hot milk to extract its color and delicate flavor.

 Sesame (*til*) **seeds**: These are generally found in two colors: white and brown. It has a nutty taste and emits more flavor when roasted. Roasted seeds are ground and mixed to prepare desserts and savory dishes.

 Turmeric (*haldi*) **powder**: It is a root which resembles fresh ginger. It is bright yellow in color. Powdered turmeric is an important ingredient in Indian curries and has an earthy, bitter flavor. It also acts as an antibacterial agent.

KNOW YOUR VEGETABLES

LEAFY GREENS

Spinach (*palak*): Spinach has dark green, smooth leaves and is generally cooked, but the young leaves are often used in salads. It has a bitter-sweet flavor. The most common way to prepare spinach is by sautéing with other vegetables or lentils.

Scallion (*hara pyaz*): Also known as green onion, this vegetable normally has small white bulbs at the tip and is ideal for stir-fry dishes. Scallion has a mild flavor and is, therefore, relished in salads.

Mint (*pudina*): The leaves have a fresh aromatic, sweet flavor with a menthol after taste. Mint leaves are also used in beverages and ice creams.

Fenugreek (*methi*): Fenugreek leaves have a strong, bitter flavor with a characteristic aroma.

Curry leaves (*kadhi patta*): Curry leaves come from the curry tree, a short tree whose leaves resemble those of the neem plant. The leaves are commonly used for seasoning. They can also be used in the dried form, but fresh leaves have a superior aroma.

Cilantro (*dhaniya*): All parts of this leafy plant are edible. Heat diminishes the flavor of cilantro leaves very quickly and hence they are most commonly used in the final step of preparing a dish, typically as a garnish. The leaves are best stored refrigerated, in airtight containers.

Lemon grass: Lemon grass has a strong lemon-like flavor and is the main ingredient in Thai cuisine. The stems of fresh lemon grass are tough. The chopped grass can be bruised to release its flavor, if used whole in cooking then remove before serving.

GREEN VEGETABLES

Zucchini: Zucchini is a variety of squash, with shiny, edible outer skin. The flesh is white inside with a delicate flavor. Yellow zucchini is also available.

Raw mango (*kairi*): It is a large tropical fruit found in many varieties; raw mango is oblong and greenish. It is primarily used for making pickles and chutneys.

Okra (*bhindi*): Also known as lady's finger, okra is fairly popular in Indian cuisine. It looks like a capsule about 2-5 inches long. Its big white seeds are tender when cooked and contribute a lot to the flavor of the vegetable.

Green peas (*hara mattar*): Also known as garden peas, these are bright green pods. The peas inside are glossy, crunchy, and sweet. Shell just before using. Green peas are a fair source of vitamins A and C and iron.

Green chili: The most commonly used vegetable in Indian cooking is the small green chili. A good substitute for this could be the Thai green chili. It has a very sharp and pungent spiciness, and is frequently used to flavor a dish right from the start.

Green banana (*kacha kela*): Green banana is used in many parts of India. It is hard and crunchy when raw. It softens when heated or pressure cooked and has a fibrous texture.

Green beans: These are mostly fat and fleshy, and firm when fresh. Steamed and sautéed, beans can also be used in salads. Green beans contain a fair amount of vitamins A and C.

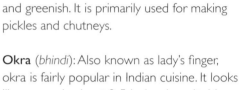

Broccoli: Broccoli belongs to the cabbage family, and has fleshy, dark green flower heads. It is quick and easy to prepare, and can be eaten boiled or steamed or raw with a dip of your choice. Broccoli is also used in soups and side dishes.

Bell pepper (*Shimla mirch*): Bell pepper and chilies are members of the capsicum family. Green bell pepper has a fresh raw flavor, whereas the red, yellow, and orange ones are sweeter. Pepper can be fried with onion and garlic, braised with tomatoes, combined with potatoes, and used raw in salads.

ROOT VEGETABLES

Potato: Potato is a starchy, tuberous root vegetable. It is an important source of carbohydrates. It also contains potassium, iron, and vitamins B and C. Potato can be boiled, baked, deep-fried, sautéed, mashed, or roasted.

Sweet potato (*shakarkandi*): Sweet potato is a starchy and sweet-tasting root vegetable. The skin color ranges from white to pink to reddish brown. Sweet potato can be baked or boiled and has a distinct sweet and savory flavor. It is used in savory and salad dishes.

Carrot (*gajar*): Carrot is a root vegetable, either orange or red in color, with a crisp texture when fresh. It has a sweet and fragrant flavor when eaten raw. Carrot can be cooked in many ways. Carrot juice is a healthy drink and can also be blended with salad dressing. It is rich in carotene and vitamin A.

Colocasia (*arvi*): Colocasia is a round or elongated tuberous, hairy root vegetable. It is boiled like potato, peeled, and then used. It has a sticky flesh.

Ginger (*adrak*): Fresh ginger is pale in color with knobbly roots. Ginger's flavor is peppery and slightly sweet, while its aroma is pungent and spicy. Ginger enhances and complements both sweet and savory food. It is used to spice cookies, cakes, tea, coffee, jams, and pickles.

Radish (*mooli*): Radish can be found in multiple varieties. The one most commonly used in Indian cooking is in the Daikon family. It has long, white, elongated, and smooth roots. The raw flesh of these roots has a crisp and crunchy texture. The taste is pungent and sharp – almost peppery.

GOURDS

Bitter gourd (*karela*): Also known as bitter melon, this is a fruit with a warty texture on the outside. The flesh part is thin and the entire fruit is almost hollow with large seeds. It is best cooked when it is green and unripened. This vegetable has a strong bitter flavor. Salting, followed by washing, can mitigate the bitterness a little.

Bottle gourd (*lauki*): Also known as calabash, bottle gourd is large and hollow. The freshest samples have a light green skin and white flesh. It is cooked most often like a squash. It can be the main ingredient in a lot of recipes but also complements other dishes like lentils very well.

Ridge gourd (*turai*): Ridge gourd has even ridges running down the exterior at regular intervals. It is typically harvested before maturity. At that stage it is light green in color and has tender flesh.

Cucumber (*khira*): Cucumber is a long, green, cylindrical fruit of the gourd family with edible seeds and crisp flesh. It is normally eaten raw in salads. The young cucumber is used for making pickles.

MISCELLANEOUS VEGETABLES

Cauliflower (*phool gobi*): While cauliflower is available in many colors, the most popular among these is the white variety. It can be prepared in a number of ways: boiled, roasted, fried, steamed or even eaten raw. It is low in fat and high in dietary fiber and vitamin C.

Cabbage (*bandh gobi*): Cabbage is widely used in Indian cooking. The part of the plant normally consumed is the immature bunch of leaves that are light green in color. It is most often prepared by sautéing and also complements other vegetables such as peas and potatoes.

Onion (*pyaz*): Onion is an integral part of Indian cuisine. It adds a delicate aroma when cooked and a sharp taste when used raw as a garnish.

Pearl onion: Pearl onion is most commonly used in stews. However, it can just easily be used in saucy and dry dishes alike. The flavor is sweeter than normal onions.

Garlic (*lasan*): Garlic is widely used for its pungent flavor. It is typically paired with ginger for a richer, aromatic taste. It has a very long shelf life and is typically stored in warm dry conditions.

Tomato: The tomato found in India is very similar to the Italian Roma tomato. It is widely used in Indian cooking, especially as a base for sauces. It is also frequently consumed in its raw form.

Cherry tomato: Cherry tomato is the smaller variety of the traditional tomato. It is a little sweeter in taste and is most commonly served raw in salads.

Lemon (*nimbu*): Freshly squeezed lemon juice adds great flavor to most foods. The acidity it provides can really enrich the taste of an otherwise bland dish.

Pumpkin (*kaddu, kaashiphal*): The pumpkin found in India is typically dark orange and sometimes almost red. It tends to have a thick flesh but is otherwise mostly hollow and contains a mesh of seeds. The seeds aren't typically used in cooking but the flesh is consumed widely.

Baby corn (*bhutta*): Baby corn is harvested premature corn, which is typically 2-4 inches long. It is consumed whole on the cob. It is tender and provides a nice crunchiness.

GOODNESS OF LEGUMES

Legumes are the edible seeds of peas and beans. Highly nutritious, legumes can be used in soups, curries, or as an accompanying vegetable. A variety of legumes exist with colors that range from yellow to red-orange to green, brown, and black. They are sold in many forms, with or without the skins, whole or split. They contain high levels of proteins, vitamin B1, dietary fiber, and minerals.

Yellow Lentil
(*arhar dal*)

Whole Red Lentil
(*kale masoor*)

Red Gram Lentil
(*malka masoor*)

Dehusked Split Bengal Gram
(*chana dal*)

Chickpeas
(*kabuli chana*)

Split Green Gram
(*chilka moong dal*)

Kidney Beans
(*rajmah*)

Dehusked Split Black Lentil
(*dhuli urad dal*)

Split Green Lentil
(*dhuli moong dal*)

White Peas
(*safed mattar*)

Black-eyed Pea
(*lobhia*)

Black Gram
(*kala chana*)

Green Lentil
(*sabut moong dal*)

Dry Lentil Dumplings
(*magori*)

KITCHEN EQUIPMENT

Pressure cooker

Skillet

Grater (*kaddu kas*)

Griddle (*tawa*)

Deep-frying wok (*kadhai*)

Deep strainer

Saucepan

Measuring cup

Idli stand

Colander (*chalni*)

Spice box (*masala dani*)

Tongs (*chimta*)

Strainer (*chai ki chalni*)

Sieve / Sifter (*chhanni*)

Tempering ladle
(*chouk ki kalchi*)

Rolling board and rolling pin
(*chakla-belan*)

Chopping board

Mortar and pestle (*moosal*)

Potato masher

Wire whisk

Vegetable peeler

Melon scoop

Knives (*churi / chaku*)

Pancake turner (*palta*)

Spatula (*jharni*)

Ladle (*kalchi*)

Slotted spoon (*Boondi* ladle)

DRINKS, SOUPS & SALADS

SPICED YOGURT DRINK
Mattha

Serves: 4

INGREDIENTS
1 cup Yogurt (*dahi*)
½ tsp Roasted cumin (*jeera*) powder (see p. 184)
Salt to taste
¼ tsp Mint (*pudina*) powder (see p. 11)
¼ tsp Black salt (*kala namak*)
2 cups Water
Cilantro (*dhaniya*) leaves, chopped for garnishing

METHOD
• Whisk the yogurt. Add roasted cumin powder, salt to taste, mint powder, and black salt. Stir to mix well.

• Add water and mix well.

• Serve chilled garnished with cilantro leaves.

• Spiced yogurt drink gives a cool refreshing feeling during summer.

ICED TEA
Sharbati Chai

INGREDIENTS

For the tea syrup:

1¼ cups Sugar
1 cup Water
6 tbsp Lemon grass, chopped
5 tsp Tea leaves
2 tbsp Lemon (*nimbu*) juice

For each serving:

2 tbsp Prepared tea syrup
2 tsp Lemon juice
2 tsp Honey
Ice cubes
2 Lemon, slices
8 Mint (*pudina*) leaves
½ cup Chilled water

METHOD

- **For the tea syrup**, mix sugar, water, and lemon grass in a pan. Boil on low heat till the sugar dissolves. Add tea leaves and turn off the heat. Leave covered for 20 minutes.

- Strain the tea mixture, cool and add 2 tbsp lemon juice. Set aside.

- In each serving glass, put 2 tbsp tea syrup, 2 tsp lemon juice, 2 tsp honey, and fill with ice cubes.

- Add lemon slices and mint leaves. Fill with chilled water and serve.

- Iced tea is an unusually flavored substitute for aerated drinks.

MANGO MOCKTAIL
Aam Panna

INGREDIENTS

2 Raw mangoes (*kairi*), medium-sized, pressure cooked, peeled, pulp removed
(see p. 183)
Salt to taste
4 tbsp Mint (*pudina*) leaves
2 tbsp Confectioners' sugar
1 tsp Roasted cumin (*jeera*) powder (see p. 184)

For each serving:
Gram flour granules (*boondi*, see p. 168), crushed ice and mint sprigs

METHOD

• Blend the mango pulp with 4 cups water, salt to taste, and mint leaves.

• Strain the mixture in a sieve.

• Add sugar and roasted cumin powder to the mango mixture; mix well and chill.

• Put crushed ice in each glass, pour the drink, and serve garnished with 2 tsp gram flour granules and mint sprigs.

• Two mangoes will give approximately 1½ cups of pulp.
• Mango mocktail is a good summer drink as it prevents heat stroke.

• Gram flour granule (*boondi*) packets are available in any Indian grocery store.

ORANGE GLORY
Narangi Savera

INGREDIENTS
3-4 Oranges (*santara*), peeled, broken into segments, chilled
5 oz Papaya (*papita*), cut into medium-sized cubes, chilled
2 tbsp Confectioners' Sugar
¼ tsp Black salt (*kala namak*)
1½ cups Water
1 tsp Lemon (*nimbu*) juice
Crushed ice for serving

METHOD
• Blend the chilled oranges and cut papaya with sugar, black salt, and water in a mixer.

• Strain and add lemon juice.

• Put crushed ice into individual glasses, pour the fruit mixture, and serve.

• Red papaya tastes better in this drink.

• This is a delightful and healthy breakfast drink.

TENDER COCONUT COOLER
Daab Shikanji

INGREDIENTS
2 cups Tender coconut water (*daab*), chilled
2 cups Lemon soda, chilled
½ tsp Black salt (*kala namak*)
2 tsp Honey
For the garnishing:
1 tbsp Tender coconut flesh (*malai*), chopped
1 tsp Cilantro (*dhaniya*) leaves, chopped
¼ lb Papaya (*papita*)

METHOD
- Scoop out 8 papaya balls with a fruit scooper and keep aside.

- Mix coconut water, lemon soda, black salt, and honey together.

- Pour into individual glasses. Serve garnished with chopped tender coconut flesh, cilantro leaves, and papaya balls.

- Tender coconut water is rich in mineral salts.
- It acts as a coolant for the digestive system.

- The flesh of the tender coconut has a soft creamy texture and can be easily scooped out and chopped.

MINTY LEMONADE
Hara Bhara Nimbu Pani

INGREDIENTS
1 tbsp Lemon (*nimbu*) juice
1½ tbsp Sugar
¼ tsp Black salt (*kala namak*)
4-6 Mint (*pudina*) leaves
¾ cup Water
Ice for serving

METHOD
- Put lemon juice, sugar, black salt, mint, and water into a jar and mix well.
- Pour into a tall serving glass.
- Serve with ice.

- Minty lemonade is a healthy substitute for carbonated drinks.
- Calorie watchers can use sugar substitutes.

TOMATO CUCUMBER MELODY
Tamatar Khira Lajawab

INGREDIENTS
4 Tomatoes, medium-sized, cut
into 8 pieces
2 cups Water
Salt to taste
¼ tsp Black pepper (*kali mirch*)
2 tsp Confectioners' Sugar
For serving: mix together
2 tbsp Cucumber (*khira*), finely
chopped
1 tbsp Bell pepper (*Shimla
mirch*), finely chopped
½ tbsp Mint (*pudina*), chopped
½ tbsp Cilantro (*dhaniya*)
leaves, chopped

METHOD
• Heat 5 cups water for 4
  minutes, turn off the heat.
  Add the tomatoes and leave
  them covered for half an
  hour. Remove and chill the
  tomatoes.

• Blend the chilled tomatoes
  with 2 cups water and strain.

• Add salt, black pepper, and
  sugar. Mix and chill.

• **For serving**, put 1 tbsp
  chopped vegetable mixture
  into individual glasses, fill with
  tomato juice and serve.

• Do not liquify the tomatoes without blanching, to ensure that the pulp and liquid do not separate.

• Tomato Cucumber Melody makes a healthy, refreshing lunch-time drink.

CARROT SOUP
Gajar Shorba

Serves: 4

INGREDIENTS

4 Carrots (*gajar*), medium-sized,
cut into cubes
1 Potato, medium-sized, cut into
cubes
2 tsp Butter
2 tsp Cilantro (*dhaniya*) leaf
paste
Salt to taste
6 Black peppercorns (*sabut kali
mirch*), crushed
½ tsp Sugar

METHOD

- Heat 1 tsp butter in a
  pressure cooker for 30
  seconds; add carrots and
  potato and cook for a
  minute. Add 3½ cups water
  and pressure cook until one
  whistle. Cool, blend and
  strain. Set aside.

- Grind the cilantro leaves in a
  mortar to a fine paste.

- Heat 1 tsp butter in a pan;
  add cilantro leaf paste and
  sauté for 10 seconds. Add the
  strained vegetable mixture,
  salt, black pepper, and sugar;
  bring to the boil, and simmer
  for 2 minutes. Serve hot.

- Carrot soup is a quick healthy soup which can be prepared with red
  or orange carrots.

- This soup can be garnished with cream or freshly ground pepper,
  if desired.

GREEN PEA SOUP
Mattar Shorba

Serves: 4-6

INGREDIENTS

For the soup stock:
2 cups Green peas (*hara mattar*), shelled
2 cups Spinach (*palak*), chopped
1 tbsp Mint (*pudina*), chopped

Other Ingredients
2 tsp Butter
1 cup Milk
Salt and black pepper (*kali mirch*) to taste
¼ tsp Sugar
¼ tsp Ground nutmeg (*jaiphal*)
2 tsp Lemon (*nimbu*) juice
Fried bread croutons for garnishing

METHOD

• **For the soup stock**, melt 1 tsp butter in a pressure cooker, add green peas, spinach, and mint; cook for 30 seconds. Add 2½ cups water and pressure cook until one whistle. Simmer for 2 minutes.

• Remove, cool, blend and strain.

• Melt 1 tsp butter in a pan; add strained soup stock, milk, salt, black pepper to taste, sugar, and ground nutmeg. Bring to a boil, simmer for 2 minutes and then remove from heat.

• Add lemon juice and croutons just before serving.

• Mint adds a unique flavor to the soup.
• To retain the green color of the soup, remove the lid from the pressure cooker after the pressure drops and cover the soup with a wire mesh.

SPINACH SOUP
Palak Shorba

Serves: 4

INGREDIENTS

8 cups Spinach (*palak*),
chopped, washed
½ tsp Sugar
1 tsp Butter
1 cup Milk
Salt and black pepper (*kali mirch*) to taste
¼ tsp Ground nutmeg (*jaiphal*)
Cream for garnishing

METHOD

• Boil 5 cups water; add spinach and ¼ tsp sugar; cook for 4 minutes and drain. Cool and blend with 2½ cups water.

• Melt 1 tsp butter in a pan; add blended spinach, milk, salt, black pepper to taste, nutmeg, and ¼ tsp sugar.

• Bring the mixture to a boil, simmer for 2 minutes and remove from heat.

• Serve hot garnished with cream.

• Spinach soup is enriched with iron and is very good for growing children.

• The calorie conscious can omit the cream.

TOMATO SOUP
Tamatar Shorba

INGREDIENTS

6 Tomatoes, medium-sized, ripe,
cut into 8 pieces
2 Carrots (*gajar*), medium-sized,
cut into cubes
1 tsp Butter
Salt to taste
½ tsp Sugar
1 tsp Roasted cumin (*jeera*)
powder (see p. 184)
¼ tsp Black peppercorns (*sabut
kali mirch*), freshly ground
For the garnishing:
1 cup Fried bread croutons
Cilantro (*dhaniya*) leaves,
chopped
Heavy cream

METHOD

- Pressure cook the tomatoes
  and carrots with 2 cups
  water until one whistle.

- Set aside to cool. Blend and
  strain.

- Melt 1 tsp butter in a pan;
  add strained tomato mixture,
  salt to taste, sugar, roasted
  cumin powder, and ground
  black pepper. Bring to a boil
  and simmer for 5 minutes.

- Serve hot garnished with
  fried bread croutons, cilantro
  leaves, and heavy cream.

- Tomato soup is a popular and all-time favorite soup.
- Carrots give this soup its body and additional flavor.

- Bread croutons are ½" cubes, deep-fried or sautéed until crisp.

VEGETABLE GARDEN SOUP
Sabz Baghan Shorba

INGREDIENTS

2 tbsp Green gram (*dhuli moong dal*), washed, soaked for 30 minutes

2 Tomatoes, large, cut into 8 pieces

1 Carrot (*gajar*), medium-sized, cut into cubes

1 tsp Butter

½ cup Carrots, grated

½ cup White cabbage (*bandh gobi*), shredded

½ cup Tomatoes, chopped

Salt and black pepper (*kali mirch*) to taste

¼ tsp Sugar

2 tsp Lemon (*nimbu*) juice

½ cup Spinach (*palak*), finely chopped

METHOD

• Pressure cook the soaked green gram, tomatoes, and carrot with 3 cups water until one whistle. Cool, blend and strain.

• Melt 1 tsp butter in a pan; add grated carrots, shredded cabbage, and chopped tomatoes; sauté for 30 seconds. Add the strained tomato mixture, salt, black pepper to taste, and sugar.

• Bring the mixture to a boil and simmer for 5 minutes. Remove from heat.

• Add lemon juice and chopped spinach, mix and serve hot.

• This soup can be garnished with fried bread croutons.

• This is a healthy soup with a combination of lentil and vegetables.

CHICKPEA SOUP
Kabuli Chana Shorba

INGREDIENTS
1 cup Chickpeas (*kabuli chana*), boiled (see p. 193)
1 cup Potatoes, chopped
2 tsp Butter
¼ cup Onion, chopped
½ tsp Ground cumin (*jeera*)
½ tsp Garlic (*lasan*), chopped
½ tsp Ginger (*adrak*) paste (see p.191)
1 cup Spinach (*palak*), finely chopped
Salt to taste
Black peppercorns (*sabut kali mirch*) freshly ground to taste
Lemon (*nimbu*) juice to taste

METHOD
• Melt 1 tsp butter in a pressure cooker; add onion and cook for a minute. Add the potatoes and cook for 30 seconds. Add 3 cups water and pressure cook until one whistle, cool, blend, and strain.

• Melt 1 tsp butter in a pan; add cumin, garlic, ginger paste, and spinach. Cook for 30 seconds.

• Add boiled chickpeas, strained onion-potato mixture, salt and black pepper to taste; bring to a boil, and simmer for 2 minutes.

• Add lemon juice to taste and serve hot.

• This is a wholesome soup with a good combination of proteins and carbohydrates.

• All soups taste best when served fresh.

CHICKPEA SALAD
Kabuli Chana Salaad

INGREDIENTS

¾ cup Chickpeas (*kabuli chana*),
boiled, strained
(see p. 193)

For the dressing:
1½ tbsp Lemon (*nimbu*) juice
2 tsp Confectioners' Sugar
1 tbsp Cilantro (*dhaniya*) leaves,
chopped
½ tsp Salt
¼ tsp Red chili flakes

For the tempering:
1 tbsp Vegetable oil
¼ tsp Mustard seeds
12 Curry leaves (*kadhi patta*)

For the garnishing:
2 tbsp Coconut (*nariyal*), grated
1 tbsp Cilantro leaves, chopped

METHOD

- **For the dressing**, combine all
  the ingredients together.

- Mix the dressing with the
  boiled chickpeas. Cover with
  plastic wrap and chill for an
  hour.

- **For the tempering**, heat
  1 tbsp oil in a pan for 30
  seconds; add mustard seeds
  and curry leaves. Pour over
  chilled salad, just before
  serving.

- Serve garnished with grated
  coconut and cilantro leaves.

- This unusual salad, with the delicate flavor of coconut, is tempered
  with south Indian spices.

CORN SALAD
Makai Salaad

INGREDIENTS

1¾ cup Sweet corn (*makai*)
½ cup Yellow bell pepper,
chopped into medium-sized cubes
½ cup Red bell pepper, chopped
into medium-sized cubes
¼ cup Scallions (*hara pyaz*),
chopped
2 tsp Vegetable oil
½ cup Fried noodles for
garnishing

For the dressing:

1½ tbsp Vegetable oil
1 tbsp White / Balsamic vinegar
(*sirka*)
¼ tsp Salt
¼ tsp Black peppercorns (*sabut
kali mirch*), freshly ground
1 tsp Confectioners' sugar

METHOD

- Heat 2 tsp oil in a pan; add the corn and cook for a minute. Set aside to cool (see p. 197). Refrigerate corn and chopped vegetables until further use.

- **For the dressing**, mix all the ingredients together and set aside.

- Mix the corn and vegetables with the dressing just before serving.

- Serve chilled garnished with fried noodles.

- Cut vegetables for salad should always be covered with plastic wrap before chiling.
- Olive oil and refined peanut oil can also be used for the dressing.
- Noodles are always deep-fried after boiling.

CUCUMBER SALAD WITH YOGURT DRESSING
Dahi Kakdi

INGREDIENTS

2 Cucumber (*khira*), medium-sized

1 tbsp Peanuts (*moongphalli*), coarsely powdered (see p.185)

For the dressing:

½ cup Yogurt (*dahi*), thick (see p.198)

2 tsp White / Balsamic vinegar (*sirka*)

2 tsp Confectioners' sugar;

¼ tsp Salt

1 tsp Mint (*pudina*), chopped

METHOD

- Cut cucumber into slices and chill.

- **For the dressing**, mix all the ingredients together and refrigerate.

- Layer the dressing over the cucumber slices just before serving.

- Serve chilled garnished with peanuts.

- Drain 1½ cups yogurt in a strainer for 30 minutes to make ½ cup thick yogurt.

- Use baby cucumber or English cucumber for better taste.

POTATO AND PICKLED ONION SALAD
Aloo Pyaz, Sirkewale

INGREDIENTS

6 Potatoes, medium-sized
1¼ cups Pickled onions (see p. 164)
½ cup Scallions (*hara pyaz*), chopped
1½ tbsp Vegetable oil

For the dressing: mix and set aside

¾ tsp Salt
½ tsp Black peppercorns (*sabut kali mirch*), freshly ground
2 tsp Confectioners' sugar
2 tsp Mint (*pudina*) leaves, coarsely pounded
½ tsp Mustard (*sarson*) powder
1 tbsp White / Balsamic vinegar (*sirka*)
½ tsp Ginger (*adrak*) paste
2 tsp Lemon (*nimbu*) juice

For the garnishing:

1 tbsp Cilantro (*dhaniya*) leaves, chopped
2 tbsp Peanuts (*moongphalli*), skinned

METHOD

- Apply ½ tbsp oil on the potatoes. Bake at 400° F for 25-35 minutes or until soft (see p. 182). Peel and cut the potatoes into 1" cubes.

- Heat 1 tbsp oil in a pan; add the potatoes and sauté on medium heat until light golden brown. Remove and set aside to cool.

- Mix the sautéed potatoes, pickled onions, and scallions with the dressing, just before serving.

- Serve garnished with cilantro leaves and peanuts.

- Baked and sautéed potatoes seasoned with *chaat masala* can be served as a tasty snack with drinks.

SALAD MEDLEY WITH JAGGERY DRESSING
Mila Jula Salaad

INGREDIENTS

2 Cucumbers (*khira*), medium-sized, cut into medium-sized cubes
1 Carrot (*gajar*), cut into medium-sized cubes
1 Tomato, cut into medium-sized cubes
1 Apple (*seb*), cut into medium-sized cubes
¼ cup Sweet corn (*makai*)

For the dressing:
1 tbsp Vegetable oil
¼ tsp Red chili flakes
2 tsp Jaggery (*gur*)
2 tsp Lemon (*nimbu*) juice
¼ tsp Mint (*pudina*) powder (see p. 11)
¼ tsp Salt

METHOD

- Cut the vegetables, cover with plastic wrap, and chill in the refrigerator.

- **For the dressing**, heat 1 tbsp oil in a pan for 30 seconds. Add red chili flakes and cook for 10 seconds. Add jaggery and mix well.

- Turn off the heat, and cool the mixture. Add lemon juice, mint powder, and salt; keep aside.

- Mix the dressing with the chilled vegetables and cut apple just before serving.

- Jaggery is made by boiling raw sugarcane juice and is used extensively in Indian cooking. It gives a unique flavor to the salad.

- Sprinkle 1 tsp lemon juice on cut apple to prevent browning.

SWEET POTATO AND BEAN SPROUT SALAD
Chatpata Shakarkandi Salaad

Serves: 4-6

INGREDIENTS

1 lb Sweet potatoes (*shakarkandi*)
1 oz Bean sprouts
4 oz Iceberg lettuce
1-2 tbsp Vegetable oil for shallow-frying

For the dressing: mix and set aside

1½ tbsp Lemon (*nimbu*) juice
3 tsp *Chaat masala*
2 tbsp Cilantro (*dhaniya*) leaves, chopped
½ tsp Salt

METHOD

- Apply oil to the sweet potatoes. Bake at 400°F for 20-30 minutes until soft (see p. 182). Peel and cut into ¼" discs.

- Heat 2 tbsp oil in a pan for 60 seconds and shallow-fry the discs on medium heat until light golden brown.

- Remove from the heat and place onto a plate.

- Add dressing just before serving.

- Arrange the discs on a serving plate and garnish with bean sprouts and lettuce.

- Applying oil to the sweet potatoes helps to peel the skin easily.
- Instead of baking, sweet potatoes can also be pressure cooked.

- Sweet potato discs with dressing can also be served as an appetizer.

TOMATO AND COTTAGE CHEESE SALAD
Tamatar aur Masala Paneer Salaad

INGREDIENTS

4 Tomatoes, firm, medium-sized, quartered, pulp removed (see p.186)
5 oz Masala cottage cheese (*paneer*) (see p.188), cut into small cubes, chilled
4 Lettuce leaves, large

For the seasoning:
1 tbsp Olive / Vegetable oil
2 tsp White / Balsamic vinegar (*sirka*)
2 tsp Confectioners' Sugar
¼ tsp Mustard (*sarson*) powder
¼ tsp Mint (*pudina*) powder (see p. 11)
¼ tsp Black peppercorns (*sabut kali mirch*), freshly ground
¼ tsp Salt

METHOD

- **For the seasoning**, mix all the ingredients together.

- Apply ¾ of the seasoning to the tomato skins.

- Mix the remaining ¼ of the seasoning with the cubed masala cottage cheese.

- Arrange the seasoned tomato skins on a serving plate. Put 1 tbsp cottage cheese mixture on each tomato skin.

- Serve chilled garnished with a fan formation of lettuce leaves.

- Masala cottage cheese, cut into larger cubes, can also be served, along with toothpicks as an appetizer.

SNACKS & APPETIZERS

CORN ON TOAST
Karare Makai Pav

INGREDIENTS

4 Bread slices
¾ cup Sweet corn (*makai*)
1 tbsp Celery, chopped
¼ cup White sauce (see below)
Vegetable oil for deep-frying
Cilantro (*dhaniya*) leaves
and Tomatoes, chopped for
garnishing
For the white sauce:
2 tsp Vegetable oil
1 tsp All-purpose flour (*maida*)
½ cup Milk
Salt and black pepper (*kali mirch*) to taste
¼ tsp Sugar
2 tsp Processed cheese, grated

METHOD

- **For the white sauce,** heat 2 tsp oil in a pan for 30 seconds; add flour and sauté for 10 seconds, turn off the heat. Add milk and the remaining ingredients for white sauce and mix well. Turn on the heat again and bring mixture to a boil, stirring constantly. Remove and set aside.

- Mix the corn and celery in the white sauce and set aside.

- Cut each slice of bread into 4 triangles and remove the crusts.

- Heat 1"-deep oil in a shallow pan; deep-fry the bread triangles in hot oil until light golden brown. Remove with

a slotted spoon.

- Put 1 tsp of corn mixture on each piece of bread, garnish with tomatoes and cilantro leaves and serve hot.

- Use day-old bread, as it absorbs less oil.
- Use milk that is room temperature and be sure to turn off the heat, as instructed in the white sauce preparation, to avoid lumps.

- Calorie watchers can toast the bread instead of frying.
- This snack makes a good appetizer with drinks.
- Serve with tomato sauce and red chili sauce.

CRISPY BABY CORN
Chhote Karare Bhutte

INGREDIENTS

12 Baby corn (*bhutta*)
Vegetable oil for deep-frying

For the batter:

2 tbsp All-purpose flour (*maida*)
2 tbsp Cornstarch
2 tsp White sesame (*til*) seeds
1 tbsp Celery, chopped
¼ tsp Baking powder
¼ tsp Black pepper (*kali mirch*)
¼ tsp Salt
¼ tsp Sugar
Water to make semi-thick batter

METHOD

- **For the batter**, mix all the ingredients mentioned and prepare a semi-thick batter with water.

- Coat each baby corn with the prepared batter.

- Heat 1"-deep oil in a shallow pan; deep-fry baby corn in medium-hot oil, until light golden brown.

- Remove with a slotted spoon and serve hot.

- If the baby corn are thick, slit them into two, vertically.
- This snack makes a good appetizer for parties.

- This snack can be half-fried ahead of time and re-fried for a minute in hot oil, just before serving.

COTTAGE CHEESE FRITTERS
Paneer Pakodi

INGREDIENTS

1 lb Cottage cheese (*paneer*) (see p. 188), cut into 2" X 2" block, ½" thick
Vegetable oil for deep-frying
Chaat masala to sprinkle

For the filling: mix together

3 tsp Ginger (*adrak*) paste (see p. 191)
1½ tsp Green chili paste (see p. 191)
2 tsp Cilantro (*dhaniya*) paste
½ tsp *Chaat masala*
¼ tsp Salt
1 tsp Lemon (*nimbu*) juice mix

For the batter:

1½ cups Gram flour (*besan*)
¼ tsp Baking powder
¼ tsp Carom (*ajwain*) seeds
½ tsp Salt
½ cup Water (approx.) to make semi-thick batter

METHOD

- Slit ½" -thick blocks of cottage cheese horizontally into 2 slices. Put ½ tsp layer of filling on one slice and cover with the second slice.

- **For the batter**, mix all the ingredients together and prepare a semi-thick batter with water.

- Press the filled 2 slices of cottage cheese together and coat with the batter on all sides. Heat 1"-deep oil in a shallow pan; deep-fry cottage cheese in medium-hot oil until light golden brown.

- Remove with a slotted spoon.

- Cut each into 2 pieces, place the cut side up on the serving plate, sprinkle *chaat masala* and serve hot.

- Use fresh cottage cheese.
- Serve as an appetizer to a meal or as an afternoon snack.

FLORET FRITTERS
Gobi Pakodi

Serves: 4-6

INGREDIENTS

1 Cauliflower (*phool gobi*), medium-sized, cut into 20 florets
Vegetable oil for deep-frying
Chaat masala and Cilantro (*dhaniya*) leaves, chopped for garnishing

For the batter:

1½ cups Gram flour (*besan*)
¼ tsp Baking powder
¾ tsp Carom (*ajwain*) seeds
⅛ tsp Asafetida (*hing*)
¾ tsp Salt
2 tsp Ginger (*adrak*) paste (see p. 191)
1 tsp Green chili paste (see p. 191)
2 tbsp Cilantro leaves, chopped
1 tbsp Coriander (*dhaniya*) seeds, crushed
¾ cup Water (approx.) to make semi-thick batter

METHOD

- Boil 5 cups water, add ½ tsp salt and cauliflower florets and cook for a minute. Remove and drain.

- **For the batter**, mix all the ingredients together and prepare a semi-thick batter with water.

- Coat the cooked cauliflower florets with the batter. Heat 1"-deep oil in a shallow pan; deep-fry the florets in medium-hot oil for 30 seconds; remove and cool.

- Press it slightly, re-fry in hot oil until light golden brown.

- Sprinkle *chaat masala* and cilantro leaves. Serve hot.

- Be careful not to over-boil the cauliflower as this will increase its oil absorption.
- Floret fritters are an excellent accompaniment to any meal and can also be served as a snack.
- Serve with green chutney (see p. 154) / sweet chutney (see p. 157) and tomato sauce.

POTATO FRITTERS
Aloo Pakodi

INGREDIENTS

2 Potatoes, medium-sized, cut into discs, immersed in water
Vegetable oil for deep-frying
Chaat masala and Cilantro (*dhaniya*) leaves, chopped for garnishing

For the batter:

1½ cups Gram flour (*besan*)
½ tsp Carom (*ajwain*) seeds
a pinch Asafetida (*hing*)
1 tsp Ginger (*adrak*) paste (see p. 191)
½ tsp Green chili paste (see p. 191)
½ tsp Red chili powder
½ tsp Salt
¼ tsp Baking powder
¾ cup Fenugreek (*methi*) leaves, chopped
½ cup Water (approx.) to make semi-thick batter

METHOD

- **For the batter**, mix all the ingredients together and prepare a semi-thick batter.

- Coat the potato slices with batter on both sides.

- Heat 1"-deep oil in a shallow pan; deep-fry the potato slices in medium-hot oil until light golden brown. Remove with a slotted spoon.

- Sprinkle *chaat masala* and cilantro leaves, and serve hot.

- Serve with green chutney (see p. 154), sweet chutney (see p. 157) or tomato sauce.

- This is a perfect snack to eat with hot tea on a rainy afternoon.
- Potato fritters are quick to prepare when unexpected guests drop in.

STUFFED CHILI FRITTERS
Bharwa Mirchi ki Pakodi

INGREDIENTS

12 Light green chilies, large
Vegetable oil for deep-frying
Chaat masala and Cilantro
(*dhaniya*) leaves, chopped for
garnishing

For the stuffing:
2 tsp Vegetable oil
1½ cups Sweet corn (*makai*)
Salt to taste
½ tsp *Chaat masala*
2 tbsp Cilantro leaves, chopped
½ tsp Mint (*pudina*) powder
(see p. 11)
1 tsp Lemon (*nimbu*) juice

For the batter:
1½ cups Gram flour (*besan*)
¼ tsp Baking powder
¼ tsp Carom (*ajwain*) seeds
a pinch Asafetida (*hing*)
½ tsp Salt
¾ cup Water to make a semi-thick batter

METHOD

• **For the stuffing**, heat 2 tsp oil in a pan; add sweet corn, salt to taste, *chaat masala*, cilantro leaves, and mint powder; cook for a minute. Add lemon juice and mix well. Set aside.

• Slit each green chili vertically with a sharp knife, keeping its shape intact. Fill with the corn stuffing.

• **For the batter**, mix all the ingredients together and prepare a semi-thick batter with water. Coat each chili evenly with batter.

• Heat 1"-deep oil in a shallow pan; deep-fry the green chilies in medium-hot oil until light golden brown. Remove with a slotted spoon.

• Sprinkle *chaat masala* and cilantro leaves and serve hot.

• They can be semi-fried ahead of time, refrigerated and re-fried in hot oil before serving.

• Chilies can be filled with any stuffing of your choice.

SPICY SPINACH FRITTERS
Palak Chaat

INGREDIENTS

20 Spinach (*palak*), leaves
Vegetable oil for deep-frying

For the batter:
1 cup Gram flour (*besan*)
1½ tbsp Rice flour
½ tsp Carom (*ajwain*) seeds
1 tsp Red chili powder
a pinch Asafetida (*hing*)
¼ tsp Baking powder
½ tsp Salt
½ cup Water (approx.) to make semi-thick batter

For serving:
1 cup Potatoes, boiled, chopped (see p. 183)
½ cup Green chutney (see p. 154)
¾ cup Sweet chutney (see p. 157)
1¼ cups Yogurt (*dahi*), beaten
Salt to taste
Red chili powder to taste
Roasted cumin (*jeera*) powder to taste (see p. 184)
Thin *sev* and Cilantro (*dhaniya*) leaves, chopped for garnishing

METHOD

- **For the batter**, mix all the ingredients together and prepare a semi-thick batter with water.

- Coat each spinach leaf with batter, on both sides.

- Heat 1"-deep oil in a shallow pan; deep-fry the spinach leaves in medium-hot oil to light golden brown. Set aside.

- **For serving**, place 2 spinach fritters on each serving plate. Add 2 tsp chopped potatoes, 1 tsp green chutney, 2 tsp sweet chutney, and 1 tbsp yogurt on each spinach fritter. Sprinkle salt, red chili powder, and roasted cumin powder to taste. Garnish with thin *sev* and cilantro leaves. Serve immediately.

- Spices can be adjusted as per taste.
- This can also be served as a side dish at meal times.

- All *chaats* should be arranged just before serving, otherwise they tend to get soggy.

CRISPY LENTIL FINGERS
Mast Dal Paare

INGREDIENTS

¾ cup Green gram (*dhuli moong dal*), washed, soaked for 2 hours
2 tsp Ginger (*adrak*), chopped
2 tsp Green chilies, chopped
1½ cups Water for grinding
2 tbsp Vegetable oil
1½ tsp Cumin (*jeera*) seeds
½ tsp Salt
2 tbsp Cilantro (*dhaniya*) leaves, chopped
Vegetable oil for deep-frying

METHOD

• Drain the green gram and grind to a smooth paste with ginger, green chilies, and water.

• Heat 2 tbsp oil in a non-stick pan for a minute; add cumin seeds and turn off the heat when the seeds turn brown. Add the lentil paste, salt, and cilantro leaves; mix well.

• Turn on the heat and cook the mixture, stirring constantly, until it leaves the sides of the pan.

• Pour the mixture, evenly, into a greased 8" square dish and cool it completely (3 hours). Cut into rectangular fingers 1½" × ½".

• Heat 1"-deep oil in a shallow pan; deep-fry the fingers in medium-hot oil until light golden brown. Serve hot.

• Turning off the heat after adding lentil paste is important otherwise the lentil mixture will become lumpy.
• Serve this snack at a party with a dip of your choice.

• The lentil mixture can be set ahead of time, refrigerated and fried when required.

DRY GREEN LENTIL
Sookhi Moong Dal

Serves: 4

INGREDIENTS

¾ cup Green gram (*dhuli moong dal*), soaked for 2 hours, drained
1 tbsp Vegetable oil
a pinch Asafetida (*hing*)
1 tsp Cumin (*jeera*) seeds
1½ tsp Ginger (*adrak*) paste (see p. 191)
1 tsp Green chili paste (see p. 191)
$\frac{1}{8}$ tsp Turmeric (*haldi*) powder
¾ cup Water (approx.)
Salt to taste

For the garnishing:

½ cup Tomatoes, chopped
2 tbsp Cilantro (*dhaniya*) leaves, chopped

METHOD

• Heat 1 tbsp oil in a pan for 30 seconds; add asafetida, cumin seeds, ginger and green chili pastes, and turmeric powder; cook for 10 seconds.

• Add soaked lentil, ¾ cup water, and salt.

• Cook, covered, on low heat for 10-15 minutes or until done.

• Serve hot, garnished with tomatoes and cilantro leaves.

• Be sure to reduce the heat while cooking since lentils loose water very rapidly.
• This can be served for all meals including breakfast.

• Serve with green chutney (see p. 154) and sweet chutney (see p. 157).

LENTIL PANCAKES
Moong Dal Cheela

INGREDIENTS

1¼ cups Green Gram (*dhuli moong dal*), dehusked, split, soaked for 2 hours, drained
2 tbsp Bengal gram (*chana dal*), dehusked, split, soaked for 2 hours, drained
2 tsp Green chilies, chopped
2 tsp Ginger (*adrak*), chopped
Salt to taste
a pinch Asafetida (*hing*)
2 tbsp Cilantro (*dhaniya*) leaves, chopped
Vegetable oil for frying

For the filling:

1 cup Cottage cheese (*paneer*), chopped (see p. 188)
2 tbsp Cilantro leaves, chopped
Salt to taste

METHOD

- Grind both the soaked lentils, green chilies, and ginger with just enough water to form a smooth batter. Mix the batter with salt, asafetida, and cilantro leaves in a bowl. Keep aside.

- **For the filling**, mix all the ingredients together and set aside.

- Heat a non-stick pan and brush with oil; add 1½ tbsp batter and spread until 6" wide. Add 2 tsp oil around the sides of the pancake and cook until light golden brown. Flip and leave for 30 seconds. Flip again.

- Place 1 tbsp cottage cheese filling, fold and serve hot.

- This is a good breakfast dish, high in protein and carbohydrates.
- It is served as an accompaniment at *chaat* parties.

- Calorie watchers can make oil-free pancakes.

SAVORY LENTIL CAKES
Chatpata Dhokla

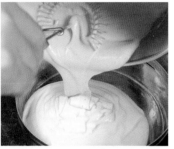

INGREDIENTS

1½ cups Gram flour (*besan*)
1 tsp Sugar
1 tsp Salt
1 tsp Citric acid
1 tbsp Vegetable oil
1 cup Water (approx.) to prepare the batter
1 tsp Baking soda

For the tempering:

1 tbsp Vegetable oil
1 tsp Mustard seeds (*rai*)
5 Green chilies, slit
2 tbsp Cilantro (*dhaniya*) leaves, chopped
¼ tsp Turmeric (*haldi*) powder
½ cup Water

For the garnishing:

2 tbsp Coconut (*nariyal*), grated
2 tbsp Cilantro leaves, chopped

METHOD

- Place a greased 8" round steel container (empty) in a double boiler. While the container is being heated, mix gram flour, sugar, salt, citric acid, oil and prepare a batter with water. Add baking soda and keep stirring until it rises to double the quantity. Remove the container from the double boiler and put the batter into the container.

- Place the container back into the double boiler and cook, covered, on high heat for 10 minutes or until done (test with a toothpick). Remove the container from the double boiler and cool the mixture in the container. Cut into large cubes and temper (see below) within the container.

- **For the tempering**, heat 1 tbsp oil in a pan for 30 seconds; add mustard seeds, green chilies, cilantro leaves, turmeric powder, and water. Bring to a boil, remove and pour over the prepared cubes.

- Garnish with coconut and cilantro leaves and serve after a minimum of 15 minutes.

- To ensure lightness, add baking soda just before cooking.
- Insert a toothpick in the center of the pan; if the mixture sticks to the toothpick, cover and cook on low heat for 5 more minutes.

- *Dhokla* can be served for breakfast or at tea time and is a favorite of calorie watchers.
- Smear 2 tsp oil on a round steel container for greasing.

MUSHROOM CROQUETTES
Khumb ke Cutlet

INGREDIENTS
1 Potato, large, boiled, grated
2 Bread slices
1½ tbsp Processed cheese, grated
¼ tsp Salt
Vegetable oil for deep-frying

For the filling:
2 tsp Vegetable oil
2 tbsp Mushrooms (*khumb*), chopped
1 tbsp Bll pepper (*Shimla mirch*), chopped
Salt and black pepper (*kali mirch*) to taste

METHOD
- Dip the bread slices in water and squeeze (see p. 199). Mix bread, potato, cheese, and salt together. Set aside

- **For the filling**, heat 2 tsp oil in the pan; add mushrooms, bell pepper, salt and black pepper to taste. Cook for 30 seconds and remove.

- Divide the potato dough into 15 equal-sized balls. Stuff each ball with ¼ tsp filling, fold to seal the filling inside and reshape.

- Heat 1"-deep oil in a shallow pan; deep-fry the croquettes in medium-hot oil until light golden brown. Serve hot.

- The proportion of bread and potato has to be right otherwise the croquette will break while frying.

- Refrigerate after filling to avoid cheese from fermenting.
- Deep-fry 3-4 croquettes at a time.

MUSHROOM CHEESE TOAST
Khumbi Toast

INGREDIENTS

1 French loaf, cut into 10 thin slanted slices
4 Button mushrooms (*khumb*), cut into thin vertical slices
1 Onion, medium-sized, chopped
2 tsp Soft butter
½ cup Cheddar cheese, grated
Salt and black pepper (*kali mirch*) to taste
1 Bell pepper (*Shimla mirch*), medium-sized, chopped
Red chili flakes to sprinkle

METHOD

- Apply soft butter on each slice of French loaf and place mushroom and onion slices along the length.

- Sprinkle cheese, salt and black pepper to taste. Garnish with bell pepper and red chili flakes.

- Bake at 350°F for 5-8 minutes or until brown.

- Always pre-heat the oven for 15 minutes before baking.
- This makes a good appetizer to serve with drinks.

- Mushroom cheese toast is a favorite among kids.

TOASTED GARDEN SANDWICHES
Hara Bhara Toast

INGREDIENTS

12 Bread slices

For the filling:

6 Beans, cut into 1" pieces
1 Carrot (*gajar*), medium-sized,
cut into 1" pieces
1 cup Cabbage (*bandh gobi*), cut
into 1" pieces
6 Baby corn (*bhutta*), cut into
1" pieces
1 Bell pepper (*Shimla mirch*),
medium-sized, cut into 1" pieces
2 tsp Butter
Salt and black pepper (*kali
mirch*) to taste
2 tsp All-purpose flour (*maida*)
¼ cup Milk
Soft butter for applying on both
sides of the bread

METHOD

- **For the filling**, heat 2 tsp butter in a pan for 30 seconds; add all
  the cut vegetables, salt and black pepper. Cover and cook for a
  minute.

- Add flour to the vegetables and cook for 30 seconds. Add milk,
  cook for a further 30 seconds and set aside.

- Pre-heat the toaster. Apply soft butter on one side of each bread
  slice. Take two slices of bread, place a portion of the filling on the
  buttered side and cover with the second slice, buttered
  side down.

- Apply butter on top surface of the sandwich, turn over and place
  sandwich in a toaster, now apply butter on the other surface.

- Close the toaster, and toast until golden brown.

- Garden sandwiches can be made with all kinds of bread — white,
  brown, and multi-grain.
- This snack can be served for breakfast or as an afternoon snack.

- Remove butter from fridge half an hour before preparing to soften.

55 || SNACKS & APPETIZERS || Pure & Simple

SAGO CUTLETS
Sabu Dana Vada

INGREDIENTS

½ cup Sago (*sabu dana*),
washed, soaked, drained, kept
covered for 8 hours
4 Potatoes, medium-sized boiled
(see p. 183), peeled, grated
2 Bread slices, wet, squeezed
(see p. 199)
2 tsp Ginger (*adrak*), chopped
½ tsp Green chilies, chopped
2 tbsp Cilantro (*dhaniya*) leaves,
chopped
¼ cup Peanuts (*moongphalli*),
skinned, coarsely ground
(see p. 185)
½ tsp Salt
Vegetable oil for deep-frying

METHOD

- Mix the grated potato with
  sago, squeezed bread, ginger,
  green chilies, cilantro leaves,
  ground peanuts, and salt into
  a smooth mixture.

- Divide the mixture equally
  into 12-15 portions and
  shape into round, flat cutlets.

- Heat 1"-deep oil in a shallow
  pan; deep-fry the cutlets
  in hot oil until light golden
  brown and serve hot.

- Sago cutlets can be served with green chutney (see p. 154) and
  sweet chutney (see p. 157).

- Do not fry more than 3-4 cutlets at a time to avoid breaking.
- Sago cutlets make an excellent party snack.

SPICY POTATO PATTIES
Chatpati Aloo Tikki

INGREDIENTS

10 Potatoes, boiled (see p. 183), peeled, grated
2 Bread slices, wet, squeezed (see p. 199)
1½ tbsp Cornstarch
½ tsp Salt
Vegetable oil for shallow-frying

For the filling:
1 cup Green peas (*hara mattar*), boiled, ground coarsely in a food processor
1 tbsp Vegetable oil
a pinch Asafetida (*hing*)
¾ tsp Cumin (*jeera*) seeds
1 tsp Ginger (*adrak*) paste (see p. 191)
1 tsp Green chili paste (see p. 191)
1 tsp Red chili powder
½ tsp *Garam masala* (see p. 184)
½ tsp Mango powder (*amchur*)
1 tbsp Cilantro (*dhaniya*) leaves, chopped
Salt to taste

METHOD

- **For the filling**, heat 1 tbsp oil in a pan for 30 seconds; add asafetida, cumin seeds, ginger paste, green chili paste, and ground green peas; mix. Add red chili powder, *garam masala*, mango powder, cilantro leaves, and salt to taste; cook on low heat for 2 minutes. Remove and set filling aside.

- Mix the potato, squeezed bread, corn flour, and salt into

a smooth mixture.

- Divide the potato mixture into 20 equal-sized balls. Stuff each potato ball with 1 tsp pea filling and shape into a flat round patty.

- Shallow-fry the patties in hot oil until light golden brown. Serve immediately.

- Potato patties can be served with lunch and dinner as well as a snack.

- Serve the patties with sweet chutney (see p. 157), green chutney (see p. 154), and tomato sauce.

SPICY POTATO PRISMS
Samosa

INGREDIENTS

For the dough:
2½ cups All-purpose flour (*maida*)

½ tsp Salt

3 tbsp Clarified butter (*ghee*), melted

Lukewarm water to make the dough

Vegetable oil for deep-frying

For the stuffing:
4 Potatoes, medium-sized, boiled (see p. 183), peeled, coarsely mashed

1 tbsp Vegetable oil

a pinch Asafetida (*hing*)

1 tsp Cumin (*jeera*) seeds

1 tsp Ginger (*adrak*) paste (see p. 191)

½ tsp Green chili paste (see p. 191)

3 tsp Ground coriander (*dhaniya*)

1 tsp Mango powder (*amchur*)

1 tsp Red chili powder

½ tsp *Garam masala* (see p. 184)

Salt to taste

2 tbsp Cilantro (*dhaniya*) leaves, chopped

METHOD

- Sieve the flour and salt together. Add melted clarified butter and prepare a semi-hard dough with lukewarm water. Cover and set aside for 10 minutes.

- **For the stuffing**, heat 1 tbsp oil in a pan for 30 seconds; add asafetida, cumin seeds, ginger and green chili pastes, and mashed potato; mix well. Add ground coriander, mango powder, red chili powder, *garam* masala, salt to taste, and cilantro leaves; mix well. Cook on low heat for 5 minutes, turning occasionally. Remove and cool.

- Divide the dough equally into 20 balls. Roll each ball evenly with a rolling pin, into a disc of 5" diameter and cut in half.

- Apply water to each semi-circle and make a hollow cone.

- Fill each cone with potato stuffing and seal the ends.

- Heat 1"-deep oil in a shallow pan; deep-fry the prisms in medium-hot oil until light golden brown and serve hot.

- To avoid bubbles in the flour covering of the *samosa*, fry in lukewarm oil first then turn up the heat after 2 minutes and deep-fry until light golden brown.

- *Samosa* is an all-time favorite snack among adults and children alike.
- Serve with green chutney (see p. 154) and sweet chutney (see p. 157).

SAVORY RICE FLAKES
Poha

INGREDIENTS

1 cup Beaten rice (*chiwda*), washed, drained in a colander
1-2 tbsp Vegetable oil
¼ tsp Mustard seeds (*rai*)
2 tsp Ginger (*adrak*), chopped
1 tsp Green chilies, chopped
12 Curry leaves (*kadhi patta*)
1 tbsp Raisins (*kishmish*), chopped
2 tbsp Cashew nuts (*kaju*), chopped
¾ cup Green peas (*hara mattar*), boiled
Salt to taste
½ tsp Sugar
1 tsp Lemon (*nimbu*) juice
2 tbsp Cilantro (*dhaniya*) leaves, chopped

METHOD

• Heat 1-2 tbsp oil in a pan for 30 seconds; add mustard seeds, ginger, green chilies, curry leaves, raisins, and cashew nuts. Cook for 30 seconds. Add green peas and cook for a minute.

• Add washed and drained beaten rice, salt to taste, sugar, lemon juice, and cilantro leaves; mix well.

• Cook on low heat, covered, for 2 minutes. Serve hot.

• Savory rice flakes are mainly served as a breakfast dish.
• Roasted peanuts can be substituted for cashew nuts.

• It can also be served with toasted bread.

SAVORY SEMOLINA CAKES
Rawa Idli

INGREDIENTS

1 cup Semolina (*rawa*), dry roasted (see p. 185)

1½ cups Yogurt (*dahi*), sour

1 tsp Salt

1½ tbsp Vegetable oil

2 tsp Bengal gram (*chana dal*), dehusked, split

2 tsp Black gram (*dhuli urad dal*), dehusked, split

1 tsp Mustard seeds (*rai*)

2 tsp Curry leaves (*kadhi patta*), chopped

1 tsp Baking soda

2 tbsp Cilantro (*dhaniya*) leaves, chopped

2 tsp Vegetable oil for greasing

METHOD

- Mix the roasted semolina with yogurt and salt to prepare a batter.

- Heat 1½ tbsp oil in a pan; add both the lentils and cook until light brown. Add mustard seeds and curry leaves; mix well. Remove and mix with the semolina batter. Add baking soda and stir in the batter. Mix well.

- Grease the semolina cake / *idli* stand with 2 tsp oil, add 1½ tbsp batter to each mold and steam for 8-10 minutes or until done (test with a toothpick).

- Remove the semolina cakes with the help of a knife.

- Serve hot with coconut chutney (see p. 156).

- Baking soda should be added in the end, to ensure that *idlis* are light.
- For better taste use slightly sour yogurt, preferably 1-2 days old.
- An *idli* stand is a stainless steel utensil with steaming compartments.

The stand is placed in a large vessel containing water to steam the semolina or rice cakes.

SPICY SEMOLINA
Rawa Upma

INGREDIENTS

1 cup Semolina (*rawa*)
2 tbsp Vegetable oil
1 cup Onions, cut into medium-sized cubes
2 tsp Ginger (*adrak*), chopped
1 Green chili, slit
2 tsp Bengal gram (*chana dal*), dehusked split
2 tsp Black gram (*dhuli urad dal*), dehusked, split
¾ tsp Mustard seeds (*rai*)
12 Curry leaves (*kadhi patta*)
2½ cups Water
Salt to taste
1 tbsp Clarified butter (*ghee*)
2 tbsp Cilantro (*dhaniya*) leaves, chopped
1 tbsp Lemon (*nimbu*) juice
2 tbsp Peanuts (*moongphalli*), fried

METHOD

- Heat 1½ tbsp oil in a pan for 30 seconds; add onions, ginger, and green chili. Cook until light brown. Add semolina and cook until light brown. Remove and keep aside.

- In the same pan, heat ½ tbsp oil; add the lentils and fry until light pink in color. Add mustard seeds and curry leaves; mix well.

- Add 2½ cups water and salt to taste and bring to a boil. Add roasted semolina, little by little, stirring constantly. Cook until semi-thick.

- Add clarified butter, cilantro leaves, lemon juice, and peanuts. Turn off the heat and leave covered for 2 minutes. Mix and serve hot.

- Spicy semolina is relished at breakfast or tea time with coconut chutney (see p. 156).
- The preparation of semolina with onion can be done in advance.

- Seasoning with lentils and mixing with water should be done just before serving.

VEGETABLE VERMICELLI
Sabzdar Sewai

Serves: 2-4

INGREDIENTS

1 cup Vermicelli (*sewai*)
¼ tsp Clarified butter (*ghee*)
¼ cup Beans, cut diagonally into
1" pieces
¼ cup Carrot (*gajar*), cut
diagonally into 1" pieces
2 tbsp Vegetable oil
½ tsp Mustard seeds (*rai*)
1 tsp Bengal gram (*chana dal*),
dehusked, split
1 tsp Black gram (*dhuli urad dal*),
dehusked, split
2 tsp Ginger (*adrak*), chopped
1 tsp Green chilies, chopped
15 Curry leaves (*kadhi patta*)
1 cup Onions, sliced
1 cup Water
Salt to taste
2 tsp Cilantro (*dhaniya*) leaves,
chopped
1 tsp Lemon (*nimbu*) juice

METHOD

• Melt ¼ tsp clarified butter in a pan; add vermicelli and cook on low heat until light golden brown (see p. 185). Remove and keep aside.

• Boil 2½ cups water; add cut carrot and beans and cook for a minute. Remove and drain.

• Heat 2 tbsp oil in a pan for 30 seconds; add mustard seeds and both lentils, fry until light brown. Add ginger, green chilies, curry leaves, and onions; cook until light brown.

• Add roasted vermicelli, 1 cup water, and salt to taste. Mix well. Cook covered, on low heat, until the water evaporates.

• Add the vegetables, cilantro leaves, and lemon juice. Mix and serve hot.

• Cook vermicelli in a flat pan for better texture.
• Soak the lentils in ½ cup water to soften. Drain before use.

• Serve with coconut chutney (see p. 156) or green chutney (see p. 154).

SPICY INDIAN PUFFS
Pani Puri

INGREDIENTS

For the puffs (*puri*):
50 gm Semolina (*rawa*)
50 gm All-purpose flour (*maida*)
Water to make the dough
Vegetable oil for deep-frying

For the liquid filling:
2 Raw mangoes (*kairi*), medium-sized
2 cups Mint (*pudina*) leaves, chopped
1 tbsp Ginger (*adrak*), chopped
2 tsp Green chilies, chopped
4 cups Water
¼ tsp Asafetida (*hing*)
1 tsp *Garam masala* (see p. 184)
4 Cloves (*laung*), roasted, ground
2 tsp Roasted cumin (*jeera*) powder (see p. 184)
½ tsp Red chili powder
1 tbsp Lemon (*nimbu*) juice
Salt to taste
1 tsp Black salt (*kala namak*)

For the filling mixture:
1 cup Potatoes, boiled, chopped (see p. 183)
1 cup Horse gram (*kala chana*), boiled (see p. 192)
Salt, red chili powder, and cumin powder to taste
1 tbsp Cilantro (*dhaniya*) leaves, chopped

METHOD

- **For the puffs (*puri*)**, sieve the semolina and flour together and prepare a semi-hard dough with water. Cover and set aside for 15 minutes. Divide the dough equally into 50 balls and roll with a rolling pin into thin round discs of 1¼" diameter. Place the discs on a moistened cloth napkin and leave covered with another moistened cloth napkin for 30 minutes. Turn upside down holding the napkin edges.

- Heat 1"-deep oil in a shallow pan; deep-fry the discs in medium-hot oil, one at a time, until light golden brown. Remove, cool, and store in an airtight container for later use.

- **For the liquid filling**, pressure cook the mangoes with 2½ cups water to one whistle. Then simmer for 2 minutes. Remove and cool. Peel and mash the mangoes with the palm and discard seeds.

- Blend the mango pulp with mint, ginger, green chilies, and 4 cups water; strain. Add asafetida, *garam masala*, roasted clove powder, cumin powder, red chili powder, lemon juice, salt to taste, and black salt; stir well.

- **To serve**, mix together all the filling ingredients. Fill the puffs with 1 tsp filling mixture and pour liquid filling into the puff. Serve immediately.

- For a sweeter taste add 1 tsp sweet chutney (see p. 157) into the puff.

- *Pani puri* is a must for *chaat* parties.
- Ready-made puffs can often be bought from any Indian savory store.
- Mango can be replaced with 2 cups of tamarind water (see p. 83).
- These are also known as *gol gappa* in North India and *puchka* in Eastern India.

SPICY CHAAT BOWLS
Chaat Katori

INGREDIENTS

2 cups All-purpose flour (*maida*)
½ tsp Salt
1 tbsp Vegetable oil
½ tsp Carom (*ajwain*) seeds
Lukewarm water to make the dough
Vegetable oil for deep-frying

For the filling:

1¼ cups White peas (*safed mattar*), soaked for 6-8 hours, boiled (see p. 193)
2 Potatoes, medium-sized, boiled (see p. 183), peeled, chopped
1 cup Green chutney (see p. 154)
2 cups Sweet chutney (see p. 157)
2 cups Yogurt (*dahi*), beaten (see p. 198)
Salt to taste
Red chili powder and roasted cumin powder (see p. 184) to taste
Thin *sev* and Cilantro (*dhaniya*) leaves chopped for decoration
20 Steel molds (*katori*) (size 2¼")

METHOD

- Sieve the flour with salt. Add oil and carom seeds and prepare a hard dough with lukewarm water. Cover and set aside for 10 minutes. Divide the dough into 20 equal balls. Roll each ball evenly with a rolling pin, into a disc 4½" in diameter.

- Stick each disc on the outer surface of a mold (*katori*), crimp the edges and prick with a fork.

- Heat 1"-deep oil in a shallow pan; fry in medium-hot oil for 2 minutes.

- Gently pry away the steel molds from the flour base after 2 minutes. Continue to fry separated flour "bowl" (*chaat katori*) until light golden brown.

- To serve, take each flour bowl (*chaat katori*) and fill it with 1½ tbsp white peas, 1 tbsp chopped potatoes, 1 tsp green chutney, 2 tsp sweet chutney, and 1 tbsp beaten yogurt. Sprinkle with salt, red chili powder, and roasted cumin powder to taste and garnish with thin *sev* and cilantro leaves. Serve immediately.

- You may vary the quantities of green chutney and sweet chutney to taste.
- This can be served for an afternoon snack or at *chaat* parties.

- *Safed mattar* is also called *ragada* in Hindi.
- Remove the steel molds (*katori*) with the help of tong and spoon when the bowls are half done.

70 Yellow Lentil || 71 Brown Lentil || 72 Tempered Mixed Lentil || 73 Spiced Green Bananas in Yogurt Curry || 74 Dumplings in Spicy Yogurt Sauce || 76 Bengal Gram with Bottle Gourd || 77 Lentil Dumplings and Spinach in Yogurt Sauce || 78 Split Green Lentil with Spinach || 79 Curried Kidney Beans || 80 Fenugreek Flavored Lentil || 81 Spicy Green Lentil || 82 Potatoes and Pepper || 83 Tamarind Flavored Potatoes || 84 Potatoes and Peas || 85 Sesame Potatoes || 86 Minty Potatoes || 87 Cumin Potatoes || 88 Cauliflower and Potatoes || 89 Spicy Colocasia || 90 Roasted Spiced Eggplant || 91 Crispy Eggplant || 92 Okra with Pearl Onions || 93 Stuffed Okra || 94 Beans with Baby Corn || 95 Baby Corn and Pepper || 96 Corn a la Cilantro || 97 Bean Sprouts with Pepper || 98 Stuffed Green Chilies || 99 Baby Carrots with Fenugreek Leaves || 100 Cabbage and Peas || 101 Gram Flour Coated Zucchini || 102 Healthy Leafy Vegetable || 103 Curried Lotus Stems || 104 Sweet Pumpkin || 105 Stuffed Bitter Gourd || 106 Mixed Vegetables with Cottage Cheese || 107 Tomato Flavored Mixed Vegetables || 108 Hot Potato Curry || 109 Potatoes in Tomato Gravy || 110 Curried Colocasia || 111 Chickpeas with Spinach Gravy || 112 Spicy Chickpeas || 113 Tangy Bottle Gourd || 114 Bottle Gourd Dumplings in Tomato Gravy || 115 Lemon Flavored Ridge Gourd || 116 Black-eyed Beans in Gravy || 117 Cottage Cheese with Peas in Gravy || 118 Lentil Dumplings with Fenugreek and Peas || 119 Bitter Sweet Creamy Peas

MAIN COURSES

YELLOW LENTIL
Arhar Dal

Serves: 4

INGREDIENTS

1 cup Yellow lentil (*arhar dal*),
washed, soaked for 30 minutes
2 Tomatoes, medium-sized, 1
grated, 1 roasted, peeled, cut into
cubes (see p. 186)
¾ tsp Salt
½ tsp Turmeric (*haldi*) powder
2 tsp Ginger (*adrak*), chopped
2 tbsp Cilantro (*dhaniya*) leaves,
chopped

For the tempering:
1 tbsp Clarified butter (*ghee*)
a pinch Asafetida (*hing*)
1 tsp Cumin (*jeera*) seeds
½ tsp Red chili powder

METHOD

- Pressure cook the soaked lentil with 1½ cups water, salt, and turmeric powder to one whistle and simmer for 4 minutes.

- Open the lid when the pressure drops, add the grated and cubed tomato, ginger, and cilantro leaves; bring the mixture to a boil. Transfer to a serving bowl and season with the tempering.

- **For the tempering**, heat 1 tbsp clarified butter in a pan; add all the ingredients in the same order as mentioned (see p. 194). Remove and pour over the lentil. Serve hot.

- To give a fresh look to the lentil, always add the tempering just before serving.

- *Arhar dal* is also called *toor dal*, and is one of the most popular lentils used in Indian cuisine. It is the main ingredient of *sambar*.

BROWN LENTIL
Kale Masoor ki Dal

INGREDIENTS

1 cup Whole red lentil (*kale masoor*), washed, soaked for 30 minutes
Salt to taste
½ tsp Turmeric (*haldi*) powder
¼ tsp Sugar
¼ *Garam masala* (see p. 184)
¼ tsp Mango powder (*amchur*)
2 tsp Ginger (*adrak*), chopped
1 tbsp Cilantro (*dhaniya*) leaves, chopped

For the tempering:
1 tbsp Clarified butter (*ghee*)
a pinch Asafetida (*hing*)
¾ tsp Cumin (*jeera*) seeds
½ tsp Red chili powder

METHOD

- Pressure cook the soaked lentil with 2½ cups water, salt, and turmeric powder to one whistle, simmer for 10 minutes.

- Open the lid when the pressure drops. Add sugar, *garam masala*, mango powder, ginger, and cilantro leaves; bring the mixture to a boil. Transfer to a serving bowl and season with the tempering.

- **For the tempering,** heat 1 tbsp clarified butter in a pan; add all the ingredients mentioned in the same order (see p. 194). Remove and pour over the lentil. Serve hot.

- Lentils are normally served at lunch time with one or two dry vegetables.

TEMPERED MIXED LENTIL
Dal Tarka

Serves: 4-6

INGREDIENTS

$1/_8$ cup Split green gram (*chilka moong dal*), washed, soaked for 30 minutes

$1/_3$ cup Bengal gram (*chana dal*), dehusked, soaked for 30 minutes

½ cup Red gram (*malka masoor*), washed, drained

Salt to taste

¼ tsp Turmeric (*haldi*) powder

2 Tomatoes, medium-sized, roasted, de-skinned, cut into small cubes (see p. 186)

2 tsp Ginger (*adrak*), chopped

1 tsp Green chilies, chopped

¼ tsp Mango powder (*amchur*)

¼ tsp *Garam masala* (see p. 184)

1 cup Fenugreek (*methi*) leaves, chopped, cooked (see p. 196)

2 tbsp Cilantro (*dhaniya*) leaves, chopped

For the tempering:

1 tbsp Clarified butter (*ghee*)

a pinch Asafetida (*hing*)

½ tsp Cumin (*jeera*) seeds

¼ tsp Red chili powder

METHOD

• Pressure cook the soaked lentils (see p. 192) with 2½ cups water, salt to taste, and turmeric powder to one whistle, simmer for 4 minutes.

• Open the lid when the pressure drops. Add chopped tomatoes, ginger, green chilies, mango powder, and *garam masala*; bring the mixture to a boil. Add cooked fenugreek and cook for a minute. Transfer to a serving dish and season with the tempering.

• **For the tempering**, heat 1 tbsp clarified butter in a pan; add all the ingredients mentioned in the same order (see p. 194). Remove and pour over the lentil. Serve hot.

• Red gram cooks very fast so avoid soaking it.

SPICED GREEN BANANAS IN YOGURT CURRY
Kele ki Kadi

INGREDIENTS

2 Green bananas (*kela*), medium-sized
1¼ cups Yogurt (*dahi*), sour
1½ tbsp Gram flour (*besan*)
1½ cups Water
2 tbsp Cilantro (*dhaniya*) leaves, chopped

For the basic seasoning:
2 tsp Clarified butter (*ghee*)
a pinch Asafetida (*hing*)
¼ tbsp Fenugreek seeds (*methi dana*)
¼ Cumin (*jeera*) seeds
4 Dry red chilies (*sookhi lal mirch*)
½ tsp Red chili powder
½ tsp Turmeric (*haldi*) powder

For the tempering:
1 tbsp Clarified butter
a pinch Asafetida
¼ tsp Mustard seeds (*rai*)
6 Curry leaves (*kadhi patta*)
¼ tsp Red chili powder

METHOD

- Pressure cook the bananas (see p. 183). Peel and cut into semi-circles.

- Mix the yogurt with gram flour and 1½ cups water and make a smooth paste. Set aside.

- **For the basic seasoning**, heat 2 tsp clarified butter in a pan for 30 seconds; add all the ingredients mentioned in the same order and mix.

- Add the cut bananas, yogurt mixture, and salt; bring to a boil, stirring constantly. Reduce heat and simmer for 10 minutes.

- Add cilantro leaves and transfer to a serving bowl and season with the tempering.

- **For the tempering**, heat 1 tbsp clarified butter in a pan; add all the ingredients mentioned in the same order (see p. 194). Pour over the prepared dish.

- Green banana, also called cooking banana, is available in most supermarkets.

- This dish can be served for both lunch and dinner.

DUMPLINGS IN SPICY YOGURT SAUCE
Kadi Pakodi

INGREDIENTS

For the gram flour balls (*pakodi*):

1 cup Gram flour (*besan*)
2 tsp Ginger (*adrak*), chopped
1 tsp Green chilies, chopped
Vegetable oil for shallow-frying

For the yogurt curry:

2 cups Yogurt (*dahi*), sour
½ cup Gram flour
3½ cups Water

For the basic seasoning:

1 tbsp Clarified butter
a pinch Asafetida (*hing*)
¼ tsp Fenugreek seeds (*methi dana*)
½ tsp Cumin (*jeera*) seeds
4 Dry red chilies (*sookhi lal mirch*)
1 tsp Turmeric (*haldi*) powder
½ tsp gm Red chili powder

For the tempering:

1 tbsp
a pinch Asafetida
½ tsp Cumin seeds
¼ tsp Red chili powder
1 tbsp Cilantro (*dhaniya*) leaves, chopped

- This recipe is very typical of Uttar Pradesh, a state in north India. *Kadi pakodi* is always served with steamed rice.
- It is often served as a family treat on Sundays.
- 2-day-old refrigerated yogurt is considered sour enough for this dish.

METHOD

- **For the gram flour balls (*pakodi*)**, prepare a semi-thick batter with gram flour and water. Add chopped ginger and green chilies. Beat until light and fluffy. (To test if the batter is fluffy drop ¼ tsp batter in ½ cup water, if batter floats it assures soft gram flour balls.)

- Heat ½"-deep oil in a shallow pan on medium heat; drop small portions of batter with your fingers and fry until light golden brown. Remove and immediately immerse in salted water; dip and remove. (For salted water, take 3¾ cups water and mix with 1½ tsp salt.)

- **For the yogurt curry**, mix the yogurt and gram flour with 3½ cups water to a smooth texture. Set aside.

- **For the basic seasoning**, heat 1 tbsp clarified butter in a pan; add all the ingredients mentioned in the same order.

- Add the yogurt mixture and salt to taste; bring to a boil. Add soaked gram flour balls and bring to a boil. Reduce heat and simmer for 15 minutes. Serve hot with the tempering.

- **For the tempering**, heat 1 tbsp clarified butter in a pan; add all the ingredients mentioned in the same order (see p. 194). Pour over the prepared dish.

- The process of dipping and removing the *pakodi* from water helps to remove the excess oil but still keeps it firm.

BENGAL GRAM WITH BOTTLE GOURD
Lauki Chane ki Dal

INGREDIENTS

¾ cup Bengal gram (*chana dal*), de-husked, washed, soaked for 30 minutes
1½ cups Bottle gourd (*lauki*), peeled
2 tsp Ginger (*adrak*), chopped
1 Green chili, slit
Salt to taste
½ tsp Turmeric (*haldi*) powder
2 tbsp Cilantro (*dhaniya*) leaves, chopped
2 tsp Lemon (*nimbu*) juice

For the tempering:
1 tbsp Clarified butter (*ghee*)
a pinch Asafetida (*hing*)
½ tsp Cumin (*jeera*) seeds
½ tsp Red chili powder

METHOD

- Peel and cut bottle gourd into 1" cubes.

- Pressure cook the soaked lentil, bottle gourd, ginger, green chili, salt, and turmeric powder with 2 cups water, to one whistle; simmer for 10 minutes.

- Open the lid when the pressure drops. Add cilantro leaves and bring the mixture to a boil. Reduce heat and simmer for 2 minutes. Add lemon juice and mix well. Transfer to a serving bowl and season with the tempering.

- **For the tempering**, heat 1 tbsp clarified butter in a pan; add all the ingredients in the same order mentioned (see p. 194). Pour over the prepared lentil.

- Avoid adding lemon juice while cooking, as the preparation may get bitter.
- Bengal gram and bottle gourd complement each other.

LENTIL DUMPLINGS & SPINACH IN YOGURT SAUCE
Magori Palak ki Kadi

Serves: 4-6

INGREDIENTS

1 cup Sun-dried green gram
dumplings (*magori*) (see p. 185)
2 cups Spinach (*palak*), chopped,
cooked (see p. 196)
Vegetable oil for deep-frying
1½ cups Yogurt (*dahi*), sour
2 tbsp Gram flour (*besan*)
1 tsp Ginger (*adrak*) paste
(see p. 191)
1 tsp Green chili paste
(see p. 191)
1½ cups Water

For the seasoning:
½ tbsp Clarified butter (*ghee*)
a pinch Asafetida (*hing*)
1 tsp Cumin (*jeera*) seeds
¾ tsp Turmeric (*haldi*) powder
½ tsp Red chili powder

For the tempering:
1 tbsp Clarified butter
a pinch Asafetida
¼ tsp Cumin seeds
¼ tsp Red chili powder

METHOD

- Heat ½"-deep oil in a shallow pan; deep-fry the *magori* in medium-hot oil until light golden brown. Remove, crush them lightly and set aside.

- Mix yogurt, gram flour, ginger paste, and green chili paste with water to a smooth paste; set aside.

- **For the seasoning**, heat the pressure cooker for 30 seconds; add ½ tbsp clarified butter and the remaining ingredients in the same order; mix. Add fried and crushed *magori*; mix. Add 1½ cups water and ¼ tsp salt; cook to one whistle, and simmer for 5 minutes. Turn off the heat.

- Open the lid when the pressure drops. Add yogurt mixture and salt to taste; bring to a boil. Reduce heat and simmer for 10 minutes.

- Add cooked spinach and bring to a boil. Remove and transfer to a serving bowl and season with the tempering.

- **For the tempering**, heat 1 tbsp clarified butter in a pan; add all the ingredients in the same order mentioned (see p. 194). Pour over the prepared dish.

- *Magoris* are prepared by soaking and grinding split green gram, shaping into small dumplings and then drying them in the sun. They are available in most Indian food stores.

- Mix spinach just before serving as this gives a fresh appetizing look.
- Mash the cooked spinach before adding.

SPLIT GREEN LENTIL WITH SPINACH
Moong Dal Palak

Serves: 4-6

INGREDIENTS

1 cup Green gram (*moong dal*), washed, soaked for 15 minutes
1½ cups Spinach (*palak*), chopped, cooked
(see p. 196)
¼ tsp Clarified butter (*ghee*)
Salt to taste
½ tsp Turmeric (*haldi*) powder
1½ tsp Ginger (*adrak*), chopped
1 Tomato, medium-sized, chopped

For the tempering:
1 tbsp Clarified butter
a pinch Asafetida (*hing*)
1 tsp Cumin (*jeera*) seeds
2 Cloves (*laung*)
¼ tsp Black pepper (*kali mirch*)

METHOD

• Heat the pressure cooker for 30 seconds; add ¼ tsp clarified butter, green gram, salt to taste, turmeric powder, ginger, tomato, cooked spinach, and 2 cups water. Cook to one whistle, remove from heat.

• Open the lid when the pressure drops. Bring the mixture to a boil. Transfer to a serving dish and season with the tempering.

• **For the tempering**, heat 1 tbsp clarified butter in the pan; add all the ingredients in the same order mentioned (see p. 194). Pour over the lentil. Serve hot.

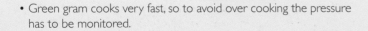

• Green gram cooks very fast, so to avoid over cooking the pressure has to be monitored.

• It can be served to those who require an iron-rich diet

CURRIED KIDNEY BEANS
Rajmah

INGREDIENTS

1 cup Kidney beans (*rajmah*),
washed, soaked for 8 hours
½ tsp Salt
1 tsp Turmeric (*haldi*) powder
(¾ + ¼)
3 tbsp Vegetable oil
2 Bay leaves (*tej patta*)
2 Black cardamom (*badi elaichi*),
crushed
3 Onions, medium-sized, grated
2 tsp Ginger (*adrak*) paste
(see p. 191)
½ tsp Green chili paste
(see p. 191)
¼ tsp Garlic (*lasan*) paste
(see p. 191)
¾ tsp Red chili powder
4 Tomatoes, large, liquidized
(see p. 187)
½ tsp *Garam masala*
(see p. 184)
2 tbsp Cilantro (*dhaniya*) leaves,
chopped

METHOD

- Pressure cook the soaked beans with 4½ cups water, salt, and
  ¼ tsp turmeric powder to one whistle. Reduce heat and simmer
  for 30 minutes. Turn off the heat.

- Heat 3 tbsp oil in a pan for 30 seconds; add bay leaves, black
  cardamom, onions, ginger, green chili and garlic pastes; fry until
  light golden brown. Add ¾ tsp turmeric powder and red chili
  powder; mix.

- Add liquidized tomato and fry until oil separates.

- Add cooked kidney beans along with the water and salt to taste;
  bring to a boil. Reduce heat and simmer for 10 minutes.

- Add cilantro leaves and *garam masala*. Turn off the heat.
  Serve hot.

- Curried kidney beans tastes best with steamed rice.
- This is a popular north Indian dish.
- 2 tsp clarified butter can also be added to the dish to enhance the
  flavor.

- Beans are available in two colors, light brown and dark brown. The
  dark brown beans take 10 minutes more to pressure cook than the
  light brown beans.

FENUGREEK FLAVORED LENTIL
Urad Chana aur Methi Dal

Serves: 4-6

INGREDIENTS

½ cup Split black gram (*dhuli urad dal*), dehusked
¹/₃ cup Bengal gram (*chana dal*), dehusked, split
Salt to taste
¾ tsp Turmeric (*haldi*) powder
2 tsp Ginger (*adrak*), chopped
1 tsp Green chilies, chopped
1 cup Fenugreek (*methi*) leaves, chopped
1 tsp Clarified butter (*ghee*)
3 Tomatoes, medium-sized, liquidized (see p. 187)
1½ cups Water

For the tempering:
1 tbsp Clarified butter
a pinch Asafetida (*hing*)
1 tsp Cumin (*jeera*) seeds
½ tsp Red chili powder

METHOD

- Wash and soak both the lentils together for 30 minutes. Pressure cook with salt to taste, turmeric powder, ginger, green chilies, and 1½ cups water to one whistle. Reduce heat and simmer for 4 minutes. Turn off the heat.

- Heat the pan for 30 seconds; add fenugreek leaves and cook covered for 30 seconds. Set aside.

- Heat 1 tsp clarified butter in a pan for 30 seconds; add liquidized tomato and salt to taste; cook for 2 minutes on medium heat. Remove and set aside.

- Add cooked fenugreek and tomato to the cooked lentil and bring the mixture to a boil. Remove and transfer to a serving bowl and season with tempering.

- **For the tempering**, heat 1 tbsp clarified butter in a pan; add all the ingredients in the same order mentioned (see p. 194). Pour over the lentil. Serve hot.

- Ensure that the tempering does not burn. To keep this from happening remove the pan from the heat after adding asafetida and cumin seeds. Add red chili powder later.

SPICY GREEN LENTIL
Sabut Moong ki Dal

INGREDIENTS

1 cup Whole green gram (*sabut moong dal*), washed, soaked for 30 minutes
¾ tsp Turmeric (*haldi*) powder
Salt to taste
1 tbsp Ginger (*adrak*) chopped
1 Green chili, slit
½ cup Tomatoes, grated (see p. 186)
½ tsp Mango powder (*amchur*)
½ tsp Sugar
¼ tsp Garam masala (see p. 184)
2 tbsp Cilantro (*dhaniya*) leaves, chopped

For the tempering:

1½ tbsp Clarified butter (*ghee*)
a pinch Asafetida (*hing*)
1 tsp Cumin (*jeera*) seeds
¾ tsp Red chili powder

METHOD

• Pressure cook the soaked lentil with 3 cups water, turmeric powder, salt, ginger, and green chili to one whistle. Reduce heat and simmer for 12 minutes. Turn off the heat.

• Open the lid when the pressure drops. Add grated tomato, mango powder, sugar, *garam masala,* and cilantro leaves; bring the mixture to a boil. Remove and transfer to a serving dish. Season with the tempering.

• **For the tempering**, heat 1½ tbsp clarified butter in a pan; add all the ingredients mentioned in the same order (see p. 194). Remove and pour over the lentil. Serve hot.

• This dish can be served with *besan methi roti* (see p. 138) and *khasta roti* (see p. 139).

• It is high in protein.
• Soaking the lentil for 30 minutes helps them to cook faster.

POTATOES AND PEPPER
Aloo Shimla Mirch

Serves: 4

INGREDIENTS
2 Potatoes, medium-sized,
boiled (see p. 183) peeled, cut
lengthwise into fingers
1 Pepper (*Shimla mirch*),
medium-sized, cut lengthwise
into fingers
1½ tbsp Vegetable oil
a pinch Asafetida (*hing*)
½ tsp Cumin (*jeera*) seeds
2 tsp Gram flour (*besan*)
2 tsp Ground coriander
(*dhaniya*)
½ tsp Red chili powder
Salt to taste

METHOD
- Heat 1 tbsp oil in a pan for
  30 seconds; add asafetida,
  cumin seeds, and gram flour;
  cook for 10 seconds.

- Add cut pepper and cook for
  a minute. Add cut potatoes,
  cilantro powder, red chili
  powder, and salt to taste;
  cook on low heat for 2
  minutes, stirring occasionally.
  Serve hot.

- Gram flour gives a unique flavor to this dish.
- All varieties of bell peppers can be used.

TAMARIND FLAVORED POTATOES
Imli Aloo

INGREDIENTS

6 Potatoes, medium-sized, boiled (see p. 183), peeled, cut into 1" cubes
2 tbsp Vegetable oil
a pinch Asafetida (*hing*)
1 tsp Cumin (*jeera*) seeds
¼ tsp Fenugreek seeds (*methi dana*)
¼ tsp Fennel (*saunf*) seeds
4 Dry red chilies (*sookhi lal mirch*)
1 tbsp Tamarind (*imli*) water (see below)
3 tsp Ground coriander (*dhaniya*)
1 tsp Red chili powder
½ tsp *Garam masala* (see p. 184)
½ tsp *Chaat masala*
½ tsp Mint (*pudina*) powder (see p. 11)
3 tbsp Cilantro (*dhaniya*) leaves, chopped
Salt to taste

METHOD

• Heat 2 tbsp oil in a pan for 30 seconds; add asafetida, cumin seeds, fenugreek seeds, fennel seeds, dry red chilies and tamarind water; cook for 30 seconds. Add potatoes and mix well.

• Add ground coriander red chili powder, *garam masala*, *chaat masala*, mint powder, cilantro leaves, and salt to taste. Mix well. Cook on low heat for 5 minutes, stirring occasionally. Serve hot.

• *Imli aloo* can also be enjoyed as an appetizer as well.
• Soak 1 tbsp tamarind in ½ cup hot water for 30 minutes, mash and strain in a bowl. Discard the seeds and use the tamarind water as required.

POTATOES AND PEAS
Sukhe Aloo Mattar

Serves: 4-6

INGREDIENTS

4 Potatoes, medium-sized, boiled (see p. 183), peeled, cut into 1" cubes

½ cup Green peas (*hara mattar*), boiled

2 tbsp Vegetable oil

a pinch Asafetida (*hing*)

1 tsp Cumin (*jeera*) seeds

¾ tsp Ginger (*adrak*) paste (see p. 191)

¼ tsp Turmeric (*haldi*) powder

½ tsp Red chili powder

2 Tomatoes, medium-sized, grated (see p. 186)

2 tsp Ground coriander (*dhaniya*)

¼ tsp *Garam masala* (see p. 184)

2 tbsp Cilantro (*dhaniya*) leaves, chopped

¼ tsp Cumin seeds

Salt and black pepper (*kali mirch*) to taste

METHOD

- Heat 1½ tbsp oil in a pan for 30 seconds; add asafetida, cumin seeds, ½ tsp ginger paste, turmeric powder, red chili powder, and grated tomato; cook until oil separates. Add cut potatoes and mix well.

- Add cilantro powder, salt to taste, *garam masala*, and cilantro leaves; cook for 5 minutes on low heat, stirring occasionally. Set aside.

- Heat ½ tbsp oil in a pan for 30 seconds; add cumin seeds, ¼ tsp ginger paste, green peas, salt and black pepper to taste; cook on low heat for 2 minutes.

- Mix with prepared potatoes. Serve hot.

- To retain the green color of the peas, it is advised to cook them separately from potatoes.

- Overcooking the greens generally changes their color.

SESAME POTATOES
Til Aloo

Serves: 10-12

INGREDIENTS

20 Baby potatoes, washed, wiped, make a cross with a sharp knife
2 tsp White sesame (*til*) seeds
2 tbsp Vegetable oil
½ tsp Cumin (*jeera*) seeds
½ tsp Ginger (*adrak*) paste (see p. 191)
½ tsp Green chili paste (see p. 191)
1 tsp Mint (*pudina*) paste
a pinch Asafetida (*hing*)
½ tsp *Chaat masala*
2 tbsp Cilantro (*dhaniya*) leaves, chopped

For the stuffing: mix and set aside

2 tsp Ground coriander (*dhaniya*)
¾ tsp Red chili powder
1 tsp Mango powder (*amchur*)
½ tsp *Garam masala* (see p. 184)
Salt to taste

METHOD

- Heat the pan for 30 seconds; add sesame seeds and roast on low heat, stirring constantly, until light brown. Set aside.

- Place the potatoes in a container inside the pressure cooker filled with 1½ cups water, and cook to one whistle. Reduce heat and simmer for 4 minutes. Remove and cool.

- Fill the boiled potatoes with the stuffing *masala*.

- Heat 2 tbsp oil in a pan for

30 seconds; add cumin seeds, ginger paste, green chili paste, mint paste, stuffed potatoes, and *chaat masala*; cook on medium heat for 2 minutes, stirring constantly.

- Add cilantro leaves and roasted sesame seeds; mix well. Serve hot.

- Instead of pressure cooking, potatoes can also be baked at 400°F for 20-25 minutes or until soft, or they can be cooked in a microwave.
- Roasted sesame seeds give a nice crunchy element to this dish..

MINTY POTATOES
Pudina Aloo

INGREDIENTS

10 Baby potatoes, boiled, peeled (see p. 183)
1½ tbsp Vegetable oil
a pinch Asafetida (*hing*)
½ tsp Cumin (*jeera*) seeds
1½ tsp Ginger (*adrak*) paste (see p. 191)
½ tbsp Green chili paste (see p. 191)
1 tsp Mint (*pudina*) paste
2 tsp Ground coriander (*dhaniya*)
¾ tsp Red chili powder
½ tsp Mango powder (*amchur*)
1 tsp Mint powder (see p. 11)
¼ tsp *Chaat masala*
¼ tsp *Garam masala* (see p. 184)
3 tbsp Mint, chopped
2 tbsp Cilantro (*dhaniya*) leaves, chopped
Salt to taste

METHOD

• Heat 1½ tbsp oil in a pan for 30 seconds; add asafetida, cumin seeds, ginger paste, green chili paste, and mint paste; cook for 10 seconds.

• Add potatoes and mix well. Add ground coriander; red chili powder, mango powder, mint powder, *chaat masala,* and *garam masala*; cook on low heat for 5 minutes, turning occasionally.

• Add mint, cilantro leaves and salt; mix and cook for a minute. Serve hot.

• The combination of dried and fresh mint paste makes this dish delicious.

CUMIN POTATOES
Jeera Aloo

INGREDIENTS

4 Potatoes, medium-sized,
boiled (see p. 183), peeled, cut
into 1" cubes
1½ tbsp Vegetable oil
a pinch Asafetida (*hing*)
½ tsp Cumin (*jeera*) seeds
2 tsp Ground coriander
(*dhaniya*)
½ tsp Red chili powder
½ tsp Mango powder (*amchur*)
Salt to taste
2 tbsp Cilantro (*dhaniya*) leaves,
chopped

METHOD

- Heat 1½ tbsp oil in a pan for
  30 seconds; add asafetida and
  cumin seeds.

- Add cubed potatoes, ground
  coriander, red chili powder,
  mango powder, and salt; mix
  well. Cook on low heat for 5
  minutes, stirring occasionally.

- Add cilantro leaves and cook
  for 30 seconds more. Serve
  hot.

- Cumin Potatoes is a popular dish. It is quick to prepare and can be
  served with any meal.

CAULIFLOWER AND POTATOES
Gobi Aloo

Serves: 4-6

INGREDIENTS

1 Cauliflower (*phool gobi*), medium-sized, cut into 1½" florets
2 Potatoes, medium-sized, peeled, cut lengthwise into ½" pieces
1½ tbsp Vegetable oil
a pinch Asafetida (*hing*)
½ tsp Cumin (*jeera*) seeds
2 tsp Ginger (*adrak*), chopped
1 tsp Green chilies, chopped
¼ tsp Turmeric (*haldi*) powder
½ tsp Red chili powder
Salt to taste
½ tsp *Garam masala* (see p. 184)
¼ tsp Mango powder (*amchur*)
1 tbsp Cilantro (*dhaniya*) leaves, chopped

METHOD

- Heat 1½ tbsp oil in a heavy-bottom saucepan for 30 seconds; add asafetida, cumin seeds, ginger, chilies, turmeric powder, and red chili powder; mix.

- Add cut potatoes, cauliflower, salt, and ½ cup water. Cook, covered, on high heat, stirring occasionally, until the water dries up or the potatoes are cooked.

- Add *garam masala*, mango powder, and cilantro leaves; mix well. Serve hot.

- Cut potatoes should be kept in water otherwise they turn brown.
- This dish can be served for both lunch and dinner.

- If water dries up before the potatoes are done, it is advised to cook for 5 more minutes, covered, on low heat.

SPICY COLOCASIA
Sookhi Arvi

INGREDIENTS

1 cup Colocasia (*arvi*)
1½ tbsp Mustard oil /
Vegetable oil
a pinch Asafetida (*hing*)
½ tsp Carom (*ajwain*) seeds
2 tsp Ground cor*iander*
(dhaniya)
½ tsp Red chili powder
¼ tsp Mango powder (*amchur*)
Salt to taste
2 tbsp Cilantro (*dhaniya*) leaves,
chopped.

METHOD

- Pressure cook the colocasia with water to one whistle. Cool and drain.

- Peel and press colocasia within the palm. Set aside.

- Heat 1½ tbsp oil in a pan for 30 seconds; add asafetida, carom seeds, and colocasia; mix well.

- Add cilantro powder, red chili powder, mango powder, and salt. Cook on low heat for 5 minutes, stirring occasionally. Add cilantro leaves; mix. Serve hot.

- Colocasia is sticky by nature so avoid over-boiling.

- In north India, only a few dishes are cooked in mustard oil for its unique flavor.

ROASTED SPICED EGGPLANT
Baingan Bharta

Serves: 4-6

INGREDIENTS

1 Eggplant (*baingan*), large, make 4 1" deep slits
2 tbsp Vegetable oil +
1 tsp for applying
1 Onion, large, cut into medium-sized cubes
1½ tsp Ginger (*adrak*), chopped
1 tsp Green chilies, chopped
½ cup Green peas (*hara mattar*), boiled
Salt to taste
2 Tomatoes, medium-sized, 1 grated (see p. 186),
1 chopped into 8 pieces
¼ tsp Turmeric (*haldi*) powder
½ tsp Red chili powder
1 tbsp Cilantro (*dhaniya*) leaves, chopped

METHOD

- Apply 1 tsp oil the outer surface of the eggplant. Roast over the flame until soft. Cool, peel, and mash. Set aside.

- Heat 1 tbsp oil in a pan; add onion, ginger, and green chilies; cook until light brown. Add green peas and salt to taste; cook for a minute. Add cut tomato and cook for 30 seconds. Remove.

- Heat 1 tbsp oil in the same pan; add turmeric powder, red chili powder, and grated tomato; cook for a minute. Add mashed eggplant and salt to taste; cook until semi-thick.

- Add the onion mixture and cilantro leaves; mix lightly for a minute. Serve hot.

- Applying oil to the outer surface of the eggplant helps to remove the skin easily.
- Roasting the eggplant enhances the flavor of the dish.

CRISPY EGGPLANT
Chatpate Baingan

INGREDIENTS

1 Eggplant (*baingan*), medium, cut into ¼"-thick slices
½ tsp Salt
½ tsp Turmeric (*haldi*) powder
3-4 tbsp Vegetable oil
Chaat masala and Cilantro (*dhaniya*) leaves, chopped

For coating the eggplant: mix and set aside

2 tbsp Wheat flour (*atta*)
½ tsp Salt
½ tsp Red chili powder
2 tsp Sesame (*til*) seeds
½ tsp Ground fennel (*saunf*)
¼ tsp *Garam masala* (see p. 184)

METHOD

- Sprinkle ½ tsp salt and ½ tsp turmeric powder on both sides of the eggplant and leave aside for 10 minutes. Use later for coating.

- Coat each slice of eggplant with coating mixture, on both sides, evenly.

- Heat 2 tbsp oil in a non-stick pan for 30 seconds; add 5-6 coated eggplant slices and cook until light golden brown on both sides, adding more oil if required. Repeat with the remaining slices.

- Serve hot, sprinkled with *chaat masala* and cilantro leaves.

- Crispy eggplant can be prepared for any meal.
- Sprinkling salt and turmeric powder on the eggplant slices extracts water, and hence aids in binding the coating to the eggplant.

OKRA WITH PEARL ONIONS
Bhindi aur Chhote Pyaz

Serves: 4-6

INGREDIENTS

1 cup Okra (*bhindi*), remove head and tail, cut diagonally in ¾" pieces
½ cup Baby onions, peeled
2 tbsp Vegetable oil
Salt to taste
1 tbsp Cilantro (*dhaniya*) leaves, chopped
¼ tsp Sugar
2 Green chilies, medium-sized, cut diagonally
¼ tsp Ground black pepper (*kali mirch*)

METHOD

- Heat 1 tbsp oil in a pan for 30 seconds; add the onions and fry until light brown. Add salt and cilantro leaves; mix and set aside.

- Heat 1 tbsp oil in the same pan for 30 seconds; add okra, salt, sugar, and green chilies. Cover and cook on low heat until soft.

- Add black pepper and onion mixture; cook for a minute. Remove and transfer to a serving dish.

- Adding ¼ tsp sugar while cooking okra helps to retain the green color.

STUFFED OKRA
Bharwa Bhindi

INGREDIENTS

1 cup Okra (*bhindi*), washed, wiped dry with a clean napkin

For the stuffing:

½ tsp Turmeric (*haldi*) powder

2 tsp Ground coriander (*dhaniya*)

1 tsp Red chili powder

2 tsp Ground fennel (*saunf*)

¾ tsp Mango powder (*amchur*)

Salt to taste

For the seasoning:

2½ tbsp Vegetable oil

a pinch Asafetida (*hing*)

1 tsp Cumin (*jeera*) seeds

METHOD

- Cut the top and bottom of the okra and slit vertically with a sharp knife, keeping the shape intact.

- Mix the stuffing ingredients together; fill each okra evenly.

- Heat 2½ tbsp oil in a pan for 30 seconds; add asafetida, cumin seeds, and stuffed okra; Cover and cook, on low heat, stirring occasionally, until the ends of the okra have softened. Serve hot.

- Select tender okra for better flavour.
- While cooking greens or any green vegetables, remove them from the pan as soon as they are cooked and cover them with a cloth instead of a lid to retain the green color.

BEANS WITH BABY CORN
Beans aur Chotte Bhutte

Serves: 4-6

INGREDIENTS

1 cup Green beans, cut diagonally to 1" pieces
12 Baby corn (*bhutta*), cut diagonally to 1" pieces
¼ tsp Sugar
1 tbsp Vegetable oil
2 tsp Black gram (*dhuli urad dal*), de-husked, soaked for 15 minutes
2 tsp Bengal gram (*chana dal*), de-husked, soaked for 15 minutes
½ tsp Mustard seeds (*rai*)
¼ tsp Ginger (*adrak*) paste (see p. 191)
¼ tsp Garlic (*lasan*) paste (see p. 191)
2 Dry red chilies (*sookhi lal mirch*)
15 Curry leaves (*kadhi patta*)
Salt to taste
¼ tsp Black pepper (*kali mirch*)
2 tbsp Coconut (*nariyal*), grated

METHOD

• Boil 3½ cups water; add ¼ tsp sugar and beans; cook for 4 minutes. Drain.

• Boil 2½ cups water; add baby corn and cook for a minute. Drain.

• Heat 1 tbsp oil in a pan; add the lentils and cook for 30 seconds. Add mustard seeds, ginger-garlic paste, dry red chilies, and curry leaves; mix well.

• Add beans, baby corn, salt, and black pepper; cook for a minute. Add 1 tbsp grated coconut and mix.

• Remove and serve hot garnished with remaining coconut.

• This is a quick vegetable dish to prepare.
• Soaking helps the lentils to remain soft even after cooking.

BABY CORN AND PEPPER
Mazedaar Shimla Mirch aur Chhote Bhutte

INGREDIENTS

30 Baby corn (*bhutta*), tender,
cut diagonally to 1" pieces
1 Pepper (*Shimla mirch*),
medium-sized, cut diagonally to
1" pieces
½ tbsp Corn flour
½ tbsp Gram flour (*besan*)
¾ tsp Red chili powder
(½ + ¼)
½ tsp *Garam masala* (¼ + ¼)
(see p. 184)
¼ tsp Mango powder (*amchur*)
1 tbsp Milk
Vegetable oil for cooking and
deep-frying
2 tbsp Onion, chopped
1 tsp Garlic (*lasan*) paste
(see p. 191)
½ tsp Green chili paste
(see p. 191)
Salt and black pepper
(*kali mirch*) to taste
2 tsp Honey
½ cup Scallions
(*hara pyaz*), chopped

METHOD

- Sprinkle ½ tbsp corn flour
  and ½ tbsp gram flour over
  the baby corn. Add ½ tsp
  red chili powder, ¼ tsp *garam
  masala*, mango powder, and
  milk; mix and leave aside for a
  minute.

- Heat 1"-deep oil in a shallow
  pan; deep-fry the baby corn
  mixed with spices in medium-
  hot oil for 2 minutes; set
  aside.

- Heat 1 tbsp oil in a pan for
  30 seconds; add onion, garlic
  and green chili pastes; cook

for a minute. Add pepper and
cook for 30 seconds.

- Add fried baby corn, salt,
  black pepper, honey, ¼ tsp
  red chili powder, and ¼ tsp
  garam masala; mix well. Add
  scallions; mix. Serve hot.

- Mix the baby corn with the vegetables just before serving for better
  flavor and texture.

- This is a popular party dish.
- Cut corn should measure up to 2 cups and pepper up to ¾ cup.

CORN A LA CILANTRO
Dhaniyawale Makai ke Dane

INGREDIENTS

1 cup Sweet corn (*makai*)
Vegetable oil for cooking
1 Onion, medium-sized, chopped
1 tsp Ginger (*adrak*), chopped
¼ tsp Garlic (*lasan*), chopped
¼ tsp Red chili powder
2 tsp Ground cilantro (*dhaniya*)
4 Tomatoes, medium-sized, 3 roasted and cut into cubes, 1 grated (see p. 186)
¼ tsp Sugar
Salt to taste
¼ tsp *Garam masala* (see p. 184)
2 tbsp Cilantro (*dhaniya*) leaves, chopped

METHOD

- Heat 2 tsp oil in a pan for 30 seconds, add sweet corn and cook for 2 minutes on medium heat, stirring occasionally. Remove and set aside.

- Heat 1 tbsp oil in the same pan for 30 seconds, add onion, ginger, and garlic; sauté until light pink. Add red chili powder, and cilantro mix. Add cut and grated tomatoes and sugar, cook until semi-thick.

- Add cooked corn, salt to taste, *garam masala*, and cilantro leaves; cook for a minute on high heat. Serve hot.

- Fresh cilantro leaves enhances the flavor of this dish.

BEAN SPROUTS WITH BELL PEPPER
Ankurit Moong aur Shimla Mirch

INGREDIENTS
2 cups Bean sprouts
1 Bell pepper (*Shimla mirch*), medium-sized, cut diagonally to 1" pieces
2 Tomatoes, medium-sized
½ Yogurt (*dahi*)
2 tsp Gram flour (*besan*)
1 tbsp Vegetable oil
a pinch Asafetida (*hing*)
½ tsp Cumin (*jeera*) seeds
½ tsp Ginger (*adrak*) paste (see p. 191)
¼ tsp Green chili paste (see p. 191)
¼ tsp Turmeric (*haldi*) powder
¼ tsp Red chili powder
Salt to taste
¼ tsp *Garam masala* (see p. 184)
1 tbsp Cilantro (*dhaniya*) leaves, chopped

METHOD
- Boil 3½ cups water, add bean sprouts and cook for 1½ minutes. Drain. Roast the tomatoes (see p. 186), peel and cut diagonally to 1" pieces.

- Mix yogurt with 2 tsp gram flour to a smooth paste.

- Heat 1 tbsp oil in a pan; add asafetida, cumin seeds, ginger and green chili pastes. Add turmeric powder, red chili powder, and yogurt mixture; cook for 2 minutes.

- Add sprouts and salt; cook until semi-thick.

- Add pepper and tomatoes; cook for 2 minutes. Add *garam masala* and mix well. Serve hot garnished with cilantro leaves.

- Cut pepper should measure up to ½ cup and tomatoes up to 1 cup.
- Yogurt and gram flour should be mixed properly, otherwise the mixture may curdle.
- Sprouts are high in protein.
- Boiled sprouts mixed with tomato and salt can also be served for breakfast.

STUFFED GREEN CHILIES
Bharwa Mirchi

Serves: 6-8

INGREDIENTS

8 Light green chilies (*mirchi*)
1½ tbsp Mustard (*sarson*)/
Vegetable oil
a pinch Asafetida (*hing*)
¼ tsp Cumin (*jeera*) seeds
¼ tsp Carom (*ajwain*) seeds
2 tsp Gram flour (*besan*)
For the stuffing: mix and set aside
4 Potatoes, medium-sized, boiled
(see p. 183), peeled, grated
1½ tsp Ground fennel (*saunf*)
½ tsp Ground cilantro (*dhaniya*)
½ tsp Mango powder (*amchur*)
¼ tsp *Garam masala*
(see p. 184)
¼ tsp Red chili powder
1 tbsp Cilantro (*dhaniya*) leaves,
chopped
Salt to taste

METHOD

- Slit the green chilies vertically
  with a sharp knife, keeping the
  shape intact, and deseed.

- Tightly stuff the chilies with
  the stuffing mixture tightly. Cut into 2 pieces.

- Heat 1½ tbsp oil in a pan for 30 seconds; add asafetida, cumin
  seeds, carom seeds, and gram flour; cook for 10 seconds. Add
  stuffed chilies and cook on high heat for 2 minutes, stirring
  constantly. Serve hot.

- Stuffed green chilies are spicy in taste.
- The stuffing can also vary, for example: grated *masala* cottage

cheese (see p. 189) and *sookhi moong dal* (see p. 50) mixture can also
be used.

BABY CARROTS WITH FENUGREEK LEAVES
Gajar Methi

INGREDIENTS

½ lb Baby carrots (*gajar*), peeled
2 cups Fenugreek (*methi*) leaves, chopped, washed, dried over napkins
1½ tbsp Vegetable oil
a pinch Asafetida (*hing*)
½ tsp Cumin (*jeera*) seeds
Salt to taste
¼ tsp Sugar
½ tsp Red chili powder
1 tsp Ground cilantro (*dhaniya*)

METHOD

- Heat 1½ tbsp oil in a pan; add asafetida, cumin seeds, and carrots; sauté for a minute. Add ½ cup water, salt to taste, and sugar; cook covered on low heat until done.

- Add red chili powder and cilantro; cook for 30 seconds.

- Add fenugreek leaves and cook on high heat for a minute; toss frequently. Serve hot.

- When the carrot ends are soft, the carrots are done.
- Both orange and red carrots can be used.

- Normally in India, red carrots are available during winter.
- Carrots are rich in vitamin A.

CABBAGE AND PEAS
Patta Gobi Mattar

INGREDIENTS

½ lb Cabbage (*bandh gobi*), cut into 1½" strips, rinsed, drained
¾ cup Green peas (*hara mattar*), shelled
1½ tbsp Vegetable oil
a pinch Asafetida (*hing*)
½ tsp Cumin (*jeera*) seeds
1 Green chili, slit
¼ tsp Turmeric (*haldi*) powder
Salt to taste
¼ tsp Garam masala
(see p. 184)
2 tbsp Cilantro (*dhaniya*) leaves, chopped

METHOD

• Heat 1½ tbsp oil in a pan for 30 seconds; add asafetida, cumin seeds, green chili, and turmeric powder.

• Add green peas and cook for 30 seconds. Add cabbage and salt to taste; mix and cook covered on medium heat until soft.

• Add *garam masala* and cilantro leaves; mix and serve hot.

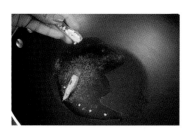

• This is a quick and healthy vegetable dish.
• Frozen peas can also be used.

GRAM FLOUR COATED ZUCCHINI
Besani Zucchini

INGREDIENTS

2 Zucchini, medium-sized, cut diagonally to 1" pieces
1½ tbsp Vegetable oil
¼ tsp Carom (*ajwain*) seeds
¼ tsp Cumin (*jeera*) seeds
1 tbsp Gram flour (*besan*)
¼ tsp Turmeric (*haldi*) powder
1 tsp Red chili powder
2 tsp Ground coriander (*dhaniya*)
Salt to taste
¼ tsp Mango powder (*amchur*)
½ tsp *Chaat masala*
2 tbsp Cilantro (*dhaniya*) leaves, chopped

METHOD

- Heat 1½ tbsp oil in a pan for 30 seconds; add carom seeds, cumin seeds, gram flour, and turmeric powder. Cook for 10 seconds.

- Add cut zucchini, red chili powder, cilantro, and salt to taste; cook for 2 minutes on high heat, stirring frequently.

- Add mango powder, *chaat masala*, and cilantro leaves; cook for a minute. Serve hot.

- Zucchini has a shiny outer skin that is edible.
- Yellow zucchini is also available.

- Zucchini, cut into fingers and served with any dressing, makes a good salad.

HEALTHY LEAFY VEGETABLE
Hara Saag

INGREDIENTS

1 lb *Hara saag*, hard threads from stalks removed, chopped into fine pieces, washed, drained
2 tbsp Mustard (*sarson*) oil / Vegetable oil
¼ tsp Fenugreek seeds (*methi dana*)
2 tsp Ginger (*adrak*), chopped
1 tsp Green chilies, chopped
2 Dry red chilies (*sookhi lal mirch*)
Salt to taste

METHOD

• Heat 2 tbsp oil in a pan for 30 seconds; add fenugreek seeds, ginger, green chilies, dry red chilies, and *saag*; mix well. Cook, covered, for 2 minutes on high heat.

• Uncover, add salt and cook open on high heat until the water evaporates, stirring occasionally. Serve hot.

• *Cholai* is a green leafy plant whose leaves and tender stems are cooked as *saag*. This *saag* is also available with a reddish tint.

• This *saag* is also called *cholai saag* or *dandi khere*.

CURRIED LOTUS STEMS
Sookhi Kamal Kakri

Serves: 4-6

INGREDIENTS
½ lb Lotus stems (*kamal kakri*), peeled
3 tbsp Vegetable oil
2 Onions, medium-sized, peeled, grated
½ tsp Ginger (*adrak*) paste (see p. 191)
¾ tsp Red chili powder
½ tsp Turmeric (*haldi*) powder
4 Tomatoes, medium-sized, liquidized (see p. 187)
Salt to taste
2 tbsp Cilantro (*dhaniya*) leaves, chopped

METHOD
- Cut the lotus stems diagonally to ¼" pieces.

- Pressure cook the lotus stems with 2 cups water to one whistle and simmer for 2 minutes. Cool and drain.

- Heat 3 tbsp oil in a pan; add grated onion and fry until golden brown. Add ginger paste, red chili powder, and turmeric powder; mix well.

- Add liquidized tomato and cook until semi-thick. Add lotus stems and salt; cook, stirring occasionally, for 10 minutes or until dry.

- Serve hot garnished with cilantro leaves.

- While buying lotus stems, select the white ones with closed ends as the open-ended ones are muddy inside.

- Boiled lotus stem can also be used to prepare a spicy *chaat*.
- Lotus stem is considered a delicacy in Indian vegetarian cooking.

SWEET PUMPKIN
Meetha Kaddu

Serves: 4-6

INGREDIENTS

½ lb Red pumpkin (*kaddu*),
peeled, cut into ¾" cubes.
Cut the peels into 1" pieces.
2 tbsp Vegetable oil
a pinch Asafetida (*hing*)
½ tsp Fenugreek seeds
(*methi dana*)
2 tsp Ginger (*adrak*), chopped
1 tsp Green chilies, chopped
½ tsp Turmeric (*haldi*) powder
½ tsp Red chili powder
Salt to taste
½ tsp Mango powder (*amchur*)
1 tbsp Jaggery (*gur*), powdered
2 tbsp Cilantro (*dhaniya*) leaves,
chopped

METHOD

- Heat 2 tbsp oil in a pan for
  30 seconds; add asafetida and
  fenugreek seeds; sauté until
  brown. Add ginger, green
  chilies, turmeric powder, red
  chili powder, and cut peels;
  cook for a minute. Add cut
  pumpkin and mix.

- Add salt to taste and ½ cup
  water; cook, covered, on high
  heat, stirring occasionally until
  the water evaporates.

- Uncover; add mango powder
  and jaggery; cook for a
  minute.

- Add cilantro leaves; mix well.
  Serve hot.

- *Meetha kaddu* is a festival dish and is accompanied with *aloo tamatar rasedar* (see p. 109) and *urad dal kachori* (see p. 140).

STUFFED BITTER GOURD
Bharwa Karela

Serves: 4-6

INGREDIENTS

½ lb Bitter gourd (*karela*),
peeled, slit vertically with a
sharp knife, keeping shape intact
Salt to apply inside bitter gourd
2 tbsp Mustard oil /
Vegetable oil
a pinch Asafetida (*hing*)
¼ Fenugreek seeds
(*methi dana*)

For the stuffing: mix together
1½ tsp Ground fennel (*saunf*)
¾ tsp Ground coriander
(*dhaniya*)
½ tsp Red chili powder
½ tsp Turmeric (*haldi*) powder
½ tsp Mango powder (*amchur*)
a pinch Asafetida
Salt to taste

METHOD

- Apply one pinch salt inside each bitter gourd and leave aside for half an hour. Wash and squeeze the water out.

- Fill each bitter gourd with the stuffing evenly. Set aside.

- Heat 1 tbsp mustard oil in a pressure cooker for 30 seconds; add asafetida, fenugreek seeds, and stuffed bitter gourd; mix. Add ¼ cup water and cook to one whistle, on high heat. Reduce and simmer for 3 minutes and cool.

- Transfer bitter gourd to a non-stick pan; cook until the water evaporates. Add 1 tbsp oil and cook for 10 minutes on low heat, turning occasionally, until light golden brown. Serve hot.

- Tender, small bitter gourd tastes better because it is seedless.

- *Bharwa karela* can be kept at room temperature for 4 days after cooking, hence it is a good traveling food item.

MIXED VEGETABLES WITH COTTAGE CHEESE
Sabz Paneer

Serves: 4-6

INGREDIENTS

½ lb Cottage cheese (*paneer*),
cut into 1" fingers (see p. 188)
8 Green beans, cut diagonally to
1" pieces
2 Carrots (*gajar*), medium-sized,
cut diagonally to 1" pieces
1 Bell pepper (*Shimla mirch*),
medium-sized, cut diagonally to
1" pieces
2 tbsp Vegetable oil
Salt to taste
¼ tsp Sugar
$^1/_8$ tsp Turmeric (*haldi*) powder
½ tsp Red chili powder
2 Tomatoes, medium-sized, cut
into cubes
1 tbsp Tomato sauce
¼ tsp *Garam masala*
(see p. 184)

METHOD

- Heat 1 tbsp oil in a pan for
  30 seconds; add cut green
  beans, carrots, bell pepper,
  sugar, and salt; cook, covered,
  on medium heat for 2
  minutes. Remove and set
  aside.
- Heat 1 tbsp oil in the same
  pan; add turmeric powder, red
  chili powder, and cut
  tomatoes; cook for a minute.
- Add tomato sauce, cottage
  cheese, and salt to taste; cook,
  covered, for a minute. Add
  cooked vegetables and *garam
  masala*; mix well and cook for
  a minute. Serve hot.

- *Sabz paneer* can be served any time with any meal.
- *Sabz paneer* is a healthy combination of protein, calcium, and fiber.

TOMATO FLAVORED MIXED VEGETABLES
Milijuli Videshi Tarkariyan

INGREDIENTS

½ lb Broccoli, cut into 1½"
florets, blanched for a minute,
drained
¼ lb Mushrooms (*khumb*), cut
into half, blanched for 20
seconds, drained
¾ cup Red pepper, seeded, cut
into fingers
¾ cup Yellow pepper, seeded,
cut into fingers
1½ tbsp Vegetable oil
2 Onions, medium-sized,
chopped
1 tsp Garlic (*lasan*) paste
(see p. 191)
½ tsp Green chili paste
(see p. 191)
2 Tomatoes, medium-sized,
chopped
½ tsp *Chaat masala*
Salt to taste

For the tomato *masala*:

2 Tomatoes, medium-sized,
liquidized (see p. 187)
2 tsp Vegetable oil
¼ tsp Red chili powder
1 tsp Ground coriander
(*dhaniya*)
1 tbsp Tomato sauce
¼ tsp *Garam masala*
(see p. 184)
Salt to taste

METHOD

- **For the tomato *masala*,** heat
2 tsp oil in a pan for 30
seconds; add red chili powder,
cilantro powder, liquidized
tomato, tomato sauce, *garam
masala*, and salt; cook on
medium heat until the
mixture thickens. Set aside.

- Heat 1½ tbsp oil in a pan for
30 seconds; add the onions
and cook for a minute. Add
garlic and green chili pastes;
cook for 10 seconds.

- Add red and yellow pepper,
tomatoes, broccoli, and
mushrooms; cook for a
minute on high heat.

- Add the tomato *masala*,
chaat masala, and salt to
taste; cook on high heat
for a minute. Serve hot.

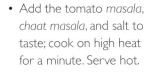

- Mixed vegetables taste best when mixed with tomato *masala* just
before serving.

HOT POTATO CURRY
Aloo ka Jhol

Serves: 4

INGREDIENTS

4 Potatoes, medium-sized,
boiled (see p. 183), peeled,
broken into small pieces
1 tbsp Vegetable oil
a pinch Asafetida (*hing*)
1 tsp Cumin (*jeera*) seeds
2 tsp Ginger (*adrak*), chopped
1 tsp Green chilies, chopped
½ tsp Turmeric (*haldi*) powder
½ tsp Red chili powder
Salt to taste
½ tsp Mango powder (*amchur*)
½ tsp *Garam masala*
(see p. 184)
2 tbsp Cilantro (*dhaniya*) leaves,
chopped

METHOD

* Heat 1 tbsp oil in a pan for
  30 seconds; add asafetida,
  cumin seeds, ginger, and green
  chilies; mix.

* Add turmeric powder, red
  chili powder, potatoes, and
  1½ cups water; mix well.

* Add salt to taste, mango
  powder, *garam masala*, and
  cilantro leaves; bring to a boil.
  Reduce heat and simmer for
  5 minutes. Serve hot.

* This potato dish is generally served with *meetha kaddu* (see p. 104), *sada paratha* (see p. 131), and *urad dal kachori* (see p. 140).

* Boiled potatoes are normally kept handy in Indian homes. They can be stored in the refrigerator for up to a week.

POTATOES IN TOMATO GRAVY
Aloo Tamatar Rasedar

Serves: 4-6

INGREDIENTS

4 Potatoes, medium-sized, peeled, cut into 1" cubes, immersed in water
3 Tomatoes, medium-sized, liquidized (see p. 187)
1½ tbsp Vegetable oil
a pinch Asafetida (*hing*)
1 tsp Cumin (*jeera*) seeds
½ tsp Turmeric (*haldi*) powder
¾ tsp Red chili powder
1 tsp Ginger (*adrak*) paste (see p. 191)
½ tsp Green chili paste (see p. 191)
Salt to taste
2 tbsp Cilantro (*dhaniya*) leaves, chopped
¼ tsp *Garam masala* (see p. 184)

METHOD

- Heat 1½ tbsp oil in a pressure cooker for 30 seconds; add asafetida, cumin seeds, turmeric powder, red chili powder, ginger paste, and green chili paste; mix well. Add liquidized tomato and cook for 2 minutes.

- Add cut potatoes, 1¾ cups water, and salt. Pressure cook to one whistle, simmer for 5 minutes and turn off the heat, cool.

- Uncover the lid, add cilantro leaves and *garam masala*; bring to a boil, simmer for 2 minutes. Remove and serve hot.

- This dish can also be prepared with boiled potatoes and cooked in a pan instead of a pressure cooker.

- Chopped ginger and chopped chilies can also be liquidized along with the tomatoes.

CURRIED COLOCASIA
Rasedar Arvi

INGREDIENTS

½ lb Colocasia (*arvi*), peeled, cut into small fingers
Vegetable oil for cooking and deep-frying
2 Onions, medium-sized, grated
½ tsp Red chili powder
½ tsp Turmeric (*haldi*) powder
½ tsp Ground coriander (*dhaniya*)
½ cup Yogurt (*dahi*), 2-day-old, beaten (see p. 198)
Salt to taste
1 tbsp Cilantro (*dhaniya*) leaves, chopped
2 tsp Mint (*pudina*), chopped
¼ tsp *Garam masala* (see p. 184)

METHOD

- Heat 1"-deep oil in a shallow pan; deep-fry colocasia fingers in medium-hot oil to light golden brown. Set aside.
- Heat 2 tbsp oil in a pan for 30 seconds; add grated onion and fry until golden brown.

Add red chili powder, turmeric powder, and ground coriander; mix.

- Add beaten yogurt and fry until oil separates.
- Add fried colocasia fingers,

1½ cups water, and salt to taste; bring to a boil and simmer for 5 minutes.

- Add cilantro leaves, mint, and *garam masala*; mix. Serve hot.

- Beat yogurt well, before adding to the gravy, to avoid separation.
- *Sada paratha* (see p. 131) is generally served with this dish.

CHICKPEAS WITH SPINACH GRAVY
Chana Palak

INGREDIENTS

1 cup Chickpeas (*kabuli chana*), soaked for 8 hours in plenty of water, drained
1 lb Spinach (*palak*), chopped, washed, drained in a colander
1 tbsp Vegetable oil
Salt to taste

Coarsely powdered:
½ tsp Cumin (*jeera*) seeds
2 Cloves (*laung*)
4 Black peppercorns (*sabut kali mirch*)

For the garnishing:
1 tbsp Vegetable oil
1 Onion, large, cut into medium-sized cubes
2 tsp Ginger (*adrak*), chopped
2 Tomatoes, medium-sized, cut into cubes
Salt to taste

METHOD

• Pressure cook soaked chickpeas with 1 ¼ cups water and ¼ tsp salt to one whistle, simmer for 20 minutes, cool. Drain.

• Heat a pan for 30 seconds; add spinach and cook covered for 2 minutes. Remove and cool. Grind coarsely in a food processor. Set aside.

• Heat 1 tbsp oil in a pan for 30 seconds; add coarsely powdered spices and cook for 10 seconds. Add boiled chickpeas and cook for a minute. Add puréed spinach and salt to taste; bring to a boil and simmer for 2 minutes. Transfer to a serving dish.

• **For the garnishing**, heat 1 tbsp oil in a pan; add onion and cook for a minute. Add ginger, tomatoes, and salt. Cook for 30 seconds. Pour this mixture evenly over the chickpeas. Serve hot.

• The same recipe can be used to make Corn and Spinach or Cottage Cheese and Spinach.

• Use 1 cup sweet corn for Corn and Spinach and ½ lb cottage cheese for Cottage Cheese and Spinach.

SPICY CHICKPEAS
Chana Masala

Serves: 4-6

INGREDIENTS

1 cup Chickpeas (*kabuli chana*), soaked for 8 hours in plenty of water, drained
¼ tsp Baking soda
2 tbsp Vegetable oil
1 tsp Cumin (*jeera*) seeds
2 Onions, large, chopped into small pieces
1 tsp Garlic (*lasan*) paste (see p. 191)
1 tsp Red chili powder
2 tsp Ground coriander (*dhaniya*)
5 Tomatoes, medium-sized, liquidized (see p. 187)
2 Green chilies, slit
1 tbsp Ginger (*adrak*), julienned
2 tsp *Chana masala*
2 tbsp Pomegranate seed (*anar dana*) powder
Salt to taste
2 tbsp Cilantro (*dhaniya*) leaves, chopped

Coarsely ground:
4 Cloves (*laung*)
2 Black cardamom (*badi elaichi*)
2 Green cardamom (*choti elaichi*)
1" Cinnamon (*dalchini*) stick

METHOD

- Pressure cook chickpeas with baking soda and 2½ cups water (see p. 193).

- Heat 2 tbsp oil in a pan for 30 seconds; add cumin seeds, onions, and garlic paste; fry until light brown. Add coarsely powdered spices and mix.

- Add red chili powder, coriander, and liquidized tomato; fry until oil separates.

- Add boiled chickpeas along with water, green chilies, ginger, *chana masala*, pomegranate seed powder, and salt. Bring the mixture to a boil and simmer for 10 minutes.

- Add cilantro leaves. Serve hot.

- Pomegranate seed powder is available in any Indian grocery store. It is basically dried and powdered pomegranate seeds. The color of the dish changes to dark brown after adding this powder.

- This dish can be garnished with cut tomatoes, onions, ginger, and chilies.
- Spicy Chickpeas is a popular Indian dish that is usually accompanied with *bhatura* (see p. 141).

TANGY BOTTLE GOURD
Lauki Tamatardar

Serves: 4-6

INGREDIENTS

1 lb Bottle gourd (*lauki*), peeled, cut into 1" cubes
2 Tomatoes, medium-sized, grated (see p. 186)
1 tsp Clarified butter (*ghee*)
a pinch Asafetida (*hing*)
½ tsp Cumin (*jeera*) seeds
2 tsp Ginger (*adrak*), chopped
½ tsp Turmeric (*haldi*) powder
Salt to taste
2 tbsp Cilantro (*dhaniya*) leaves, chopped

METHOD

• Heat 1 tsp clarified butter in a pressure cooker for 30 seconds; add asafetida, cumin seeds, ginger, turmeric powder, and bottle gourd; mix well.

• Add 1 cup water and salt and pressure cook to one whistle. Reduce heat and simmer for 5 minutes. Cool.

• Uncover, add grated tomato and cook until semi-thick.

• Add cilantro leaves and mix. Serve hot.

• Bottle gourd is a light vegetable, generally recommended to those with digestive troubles and the calorie-conscious.
• This dish can also be prepared without tomatoes.

BOTTLE GOURD DUMPLINGS IN TOMATO GRAVY
Lauki Kofta

INGREDIENTS

For the koftas:

½ lb Bottle gourd (*lauki*), peeled, grated

a pinch Asafetida (*hing*)

4 tbsp Gram flour (*besan*)

¼ tsp Salt

1 tbsp Cilantro (*dhaniya*) leaves, chopped

Vegetable oil for deep-frying

For the gravy:

1½ tbsp Vegetable oil

a pinch Asafetida

1 tsp Cumin (*jeera*) seeds

½ tsp Turmeric (*haldi*) powder

¾ tsp Red chili powder

1 tsp Ginger (*adrak*), chopped

4 Tomatoes, medium-sized, liquidized (see p. 187)

2 tbsp Yogurt (*dahi*), beaten (see p. 198)

Salt to taste

¼ tsp *Garam masala* (see p. 184)

1 tbsp Cilantro leaves, chopped

METHOD

- **For the koftas**, mix the grated bottle gourd with asafetida, gram flour, salt, and cilantro leaves. Divide the mixture equally into 20 balls.

- Heat 1"-deep oil in a shallow pan; deep-fry, 10 balls at a time, in medium-hot oil, until light golden brown. Set aside. Repeat until all are fried.

- **For the gravy**, heat 1½ tbsp oil in a pan for 30 seconds; add asafetida, cumin seeds, turmeric powder, red chili powder, and ginger; mix. Add liquidized tomato and fry until the oil separates. Add beaten yogurt and cook for a minute.

- Add the fried balls, 3 cups water, and salt. Bring the mixture to a boil reduce heat and simmer for 5 minutes. Add *garam masala* and cilantro leaves; mix well. Serve hot.

- Don't leave the bottle gourd mixed with gram flour and salt for a long time as it will become watery, making it difficult to shape into balls.

- Grated bottle gourd turns brown if left unused for a long time, so grate just before preparing.

LEMON FLAVORED RIDGE GOURD
Rasedar Turai

INGREDIENTS

2 lb Ridge gourd (*turai*), peeled, cut into ½" semi-circles
1 tsp Clarified butter (*ghee*)
a pinch Asafetida (*hing*)
½ tsp Cumin (*jeera*) seeds
$\frac{1}{8}$ tsp Turmeric (*haldi*) powder
Salt to taste
2 tbsp Cilantro (*dhaniya*) leaves, chopped
½ tsp Lemon (*nimbu*) juice

METHOD

• Heat 1 tsp clarified butter in a pressure cooker for 30 seconds; add asafetida, cumin seeds, turmeric powder, ridge gourd, and salt; mix. Pressure cook to one whistle. Cool.

• Uncover pressure cooker lid and bring the mixture to a boil.

• Add cilantro leaves and lemon juice; mix well and turn off the heat. Serve hot.

• Ridge gourd can also be cooked in a pan on low heat until soft.
• Ridge gourd is easy to digest and served as a part of a light Indian meal.

BLACK-EYED PEAS IN GRAVY
Lobhia Taridar

Serves: 4-6

INGREDIENTS

1 cup Black-eyed peas (*lobhia*), soaked for 4 hours in plenty of water, drained

Salt to taste

½ tsp Turmeric (*haldi*) powder (¼ + ¼)

1 tbsp Vegetable oil

a pinch Asafetida (*hing*)

$\frac{1}{3}$ tsp Cumin (*jeera*) seeds

½ tsp Red chili powder

3 Tomatoes, medium-sized, liquidized (see p. 187)

1 tsp Ginger (*adrak*) paste (see p. 191)

¼ tsp Green chili paste (see p. 191)

Salt to taste

¼ tsp *Garam masala* (see p. 184)

2 tbsp Cilantro (*dhaniya*) leaves, chopped

METHOD

• Pressure cook the black-eyed peas with 2 cups water, salt, and ¼ tsp turmeric powder to one whistle; simmer for 5 minutes and cool (see p. 193).

• Heat 1 tbsp oil in a pan for 30 seconds; add asafetida, cumin seeds, red chili powder, ¼ tsp turmeric powder, liquidized tomato, ginger paste, and green chili paste; fry until oil separates. Add boiled black-eyed peas along with the water.

• Add salt to taste and bring to a boil. Reduce heat and simmer on low heat until semi-thick. Add *garam masala* and cilantro leaves. Serve hot.

• Pressure cooked black-eyed peas can be used in salads, after discarding the water.

COTTAGE CHEESE WITH PEAS IN GRAVY
Mattar Paneer

INGREDIENTS

½ lb Cottage cheese (*paneer*), cut into slices (see p. 188)
2 cups Green peas (*hara mattar*), boiled
4 tbsp Vegetable oil
2 Bay leaves (*tej patta*)
2 Onions, medium-sized, grated
1 tsp Ginger (*adrak*) paste (see p. 191)
¾ tsp Red chili powder
¾ tsp Turmeric (*haldi*) powder
3 Tomatoes, medium-sized, liquidized (see p. 187)
2 tbsp Yogurt (*dahi*), beaten (see p. 198)
2 tbsp Heavy cream
a pinch Sugar
¼ tsp *Garam masala* (see p. 184)
1 tbsp Cilantro (*dhaniya*) leaves, chopped

METHOD

• Heat 1 tbsp oil in a non-stick pan for 30 seconds; add cottage cheese and fry, on medium heat, on both sides until light brown (see p. 189). Remove, cool, and cut into 1" cubes. Set aside.

• Heat 3 tbsp oil in a pan for 30 seconds; add bay leaves, grated onion, and ginger paste; fry until light golden brown, stirring occasionally. Add red chili powder and turmeric powder; mix well. Add liquidized tomato and fry until the oil separates. Add beaten yogurt and fry until oil separates.

• Add cream, green peas, and cottage cheese; cook for a minute.

• Add 1½ cups water, salt to taste, and sugar. Bring to a boil and simmer for 5 minutes. Add *garam masala* and cilantro leaves; mix. Serve hot.

• Cream adds a better texture and taste to this gravy. Calorie watchers can avoid the cream.

• This onion-tomato gravy can be used for other gravy dishes as well.

LENTIL DUMPLINGS WITH FENUGREEK AND PEAS
Methi Magori Mattar

INGREDIENTS

1 cup Dry lentil dumplings (*magori*)

1½ cups Fenugreek (*methi*) leaves, chopped, cooked (see p. 196)

¾ cup Green peas (*hara mattar*), boiled

Vegetable oil for cooking and deep-frying

Salt to taste

a pinch Asafetida (*hing*)

½ tsp Cumin (*jeera*) seeds

½ tsp Ginger (*adrak*) paste (see p. 191)

¼ tsp Green chili paste (see p. 191)

½ tsp Red chili powder

½ tsp Turmeric (*haldi*) powder

3 Tomatoes, medium-sized, liquidized (see p. 187)

¼ tsp *Garam masala* (see p. 184)

2 tbsp Cilantro (*dhaniya*) leaves, chopped

METHOD

- Heat ½"-deep oil in a shallow pan; deep-fry the lentil dumplings in medium-hot oil until light golden (see p. 185) brown. Set aside.

- Heat 2 tsp oil in a pan for 30 seconds; add boiled peas and cook for a minute. Add salt. Set aside.

- Heat 2 tsp oil in a pressure cooker; add fried lentil dumplings, 2 cups water, and salt. Cook until one whistle, then simmer for 5 minutes, cool. Set aside.

- Heat 1 tbsp oil in a pan for 30 seconds; add asafetida, cumin seeds, ginger paste, green chili paste, red chili powder, and turmeric powder; mix. Add liquidized tomato and bring to a boil. Cook for 2 minutes, on medium heat. Add fenugreek leaves and cook for a minute.

- Add pressure cooked dumplings along with water and bring to a boil, simmer for 5 minutes. Add *garam masala* and mix.

- Add cooked peas and cilantro leaves; cook for 2 minutes. Serve hot.

- This dish is relished with *sada roti* (see p. 137).

- Fenugreek leaves add a delicate bitter flavor to the dish.

BITTER SWEET CREAMY PEAS
Methi Malai Mattar

INGREDIENTS

1 cup Green peas (*hara mattar*), boiled
1½ cups Fenugreek (*methi*) leaves, chopped
Salt to taste
1½ tbsp Vegetable oil
1 Onion, large, grated
1 tsp Ginger (*adrak*) paste (see p. 191).
½ tsp Garlic (*lasan*) paste (see p. 191)
½ tsp Red chili powder
½ tsp Ground coriander
2 Tomatoes, medium-sized, grated (see p. 186)
2 tsp Butter
1 tbsp Heavy cream
2 tbsp Milk
¼ tsp Sugar
¼ tsp *Garam masala* (see p. 184)

METHOD

- Add ½ tsp salt to fenugreek leaves, mix and leave aside for 5 minutes. Squeeze and set aside.

- Heat 1½ tbsp oil in a pan for 30 seconds, add grated onion, ginger and garlic pastes; cook on medium heat until light pink. Add squeezed fenugreek leaves and cook for a minute. Add red chili powder and coriander; mix well.

- Add grated tomato and cook for a minute.

- Add boiled peas, white butter, cream, milk, salt to taste, and sugar; bring to a boil and simmer for 2 minutes. Add *garam masala* and mix well. Serve hot.

- The process of squeezing the fenugreek leaves to remove the excess water, after adding salt, reduces the bitterness.

RICE & BREADS

PEAS AND CARROT PILAF
Gajar Mattar Pulao

INGREDIENTS

1 cup Basmati rice
2 Carrots (*gajar*), medium-sized, chopped
½ cup Green peas (*hara mattar*)
1 tbsp Clarified butter (*ghee*)
2 Cloves (*laung*)
½ tsp Cumin (*jeera*) seeds
2 cups Water
Salt to taste

METHOD

- Wash and soak the rice in plenty of water for 20 minutes. Drain.

- Heat 1 tbsp clarified butter in a pan for 30 seconds; add cloves, cumin seeds, peas, and carrots. Cook for a minute on medium heat.

- Add soaked rice, 2 cups water, and salt to taste; bring to a boil and cook, covered, on low heat, till water evaporates or until rice is done. Serve hot.

- To get good textured rice, it is advised to cook it, covered, on low heat, after one boil.
- Stirring rice constantly while cooking breaks the grains.

- Any pilaf accompanied by flavored yogurt, of your choice, is a complete meal.

CORN PILAF
Bhutte ka Pulao

INGREDIENTS

1 cup Basmati rice
1 cup Corn (*bhutta*)
1 tbsp Clarified butter (*ghee*)
¼ tsp Black pepper (*kali mirch*)
1" Cinnamon (*dalchini*) stick
½ cup Spring onions (*hara pyaz*), chopped
½ cup Green pepper (*Shimla mirch*), chopped
2 cups Water
Salt to taste

METHOD

- Wash and soak the rice in plenty of water for 30 minutes. Drain.

- Heat 1 tbsp clarified butter in a pan for 30 seconds: add black pepper and cinnamon stick.

- Add chopped spring onions, pepper, and corn; cook for 30 seconds.

- Add soaked rice, 2 cups water, and salt to taste; bring to a boil. Cover and cook on low heat till water evaporates or until rice is done. Serve hot.

- The water quantity used to cook the rice should always be double the quantity of raw rice.

CUMIN PILAF
Jeera Pulao

INGREDIENTS

1 cup Basmati rice
1 tbsp Clarified butter (*ghee*)
2 Bay leaves (*tej patta*)
2 Black cardamom (*badi elaichi*)
4 Cloves (*laung*)
1" Cinnamon (*dalchini*) stick
1 tsp Cumin (*jeera*) seeds
2 cups Water
Salt to taste
1 tbsp Cilantro (*dhaniya*) leaves, chopped

METHOD

- Wash and soak the rice in plenty of water for 30 minutes. Drain.

- Heat 1 tbsp clarified butter in a pan for 30 seconds; add bay leaves, black cardamom, cloves, cinnamon stick, and cumin seeds; stir-fry.

- Add soaked rice and cook for 10 seconds.

- Add 2 cups water and salt to taste; bring to a boil. Cover and cook on low heat till the water evaporates or until rice is done.

- Serve hot garnished with cilantro leaves.

- Cumin pilaf is very safe to make as it goes with any combination of lentil and gravy dish.

- Basmati rice has a unique aroma and flavor, but any good quality long-grain rice can also be used.

MIXED VEGETABLE LENTIL RICE
Sabzion ki Kichadi

Serves: 2-4

INGREDIENTS

½ cup Rice, small grain
½ cup Split green gram (*dhuli moong dal*)
¾ cup Green peas (*hara mattar*)
¾ cup Carrots (*gajar*), chopped
¾ cup Cauliflower (*phool gobi*) florets
1 cup Potatoes, cubed
½ tsp Turmeric (*haldi*) powder
½ tsp Salt
2 tbsp Cilantro (*dhaniya*) leaves, chopped

For the tempering:

1 tbsp Clarified butter (*ghee*)
a pinch Asafetida (*hing*)
1 tsp Cumin (*jeera*) seeds
2 Cloves (*laung*)
2 Black cardamom (*badi elaichi*)
½" Cinnamon (*dalchini*) stick

METHOD

- Wash and soak the rice and green gram together in plenty of water for 30 minutes. Drain.

- Pressure cook the rice and green gram with cut vegetables, 3 cups water, salt, and turmeric powder to one whistle. Keep aside to cool.

- Uncover the pressure cooker lid and bring the mixture to a boil. Add cilantro leaves. Season with the tempering.

- **For the tempering,** heat 1 tbsp clarified butter in a pan for 30 seconds; add asafetida, cumin seeds, cloves, black cardamom, and cinnamon stick. Top it evenly over the rice mixture. Serve hot.

- *Kichadi* is always served with yogurt, pickle, and *papad*.
- *Kichadi* can also be prepared without vegetables.
- Use all forms of green gram except the whole (*sabut*) lentil.
- *Kichadi* is a complete one-dish meal.

FENUGREEK FLAVORED COTTAGE CHEESE PILAF
Methi Paneer Pulao

Serves: 2-4

INGREDIENTS

1 cup Basmati rice
1 cup Fenugreek (*methi*) leaves, chopped
7 oz Cottage cheese (*paneer*), cut into slices (see p. 188)
2 tsp Vegetable oil
1½ tbsp Clarified butter (*ghee*)
2 Onions, medium-sized, cut into cubes
½ cup Cilantro (*dhaniya*) leaves, chopped
2 Tomatoes, medium-sized, cut into 8 pieces, liquidized (see p. 187)
2 cups Water
Salt to taste

METHOD

- Wash and soak the rice in plenty of water for 30 minutes. Drain.

- Heat 2 tsp oil in a non-stick pan for 30 seconds; sauté the cottage cheese till light golden brown on both sides. (see p. 189). Remove and cut into 1" cubes. Keep aside.

- Heat 1 tbsp clarified butter in a pan for 30 seconds; add chopped onions and fry till light brown. Add fenugreek leaves and cilantro leaves; cook for a minute.

- Add liquidized tomato and cook for a minute.

- Add soaked rice, 2 cups water, and salt to taste; bring to a boil. Cover and cook on low heat.

- When the rice is half-cooked, add cottage cheese and cook till the rice is done. Serve hot.

- *Pulao* is a rice dish containing spices to which vegetables may or may not be added.

MIXED VEGETABLE PILAF
Sabz Pulao

Serves: 2-4

INGREDIENTS

1 cup Basmati rice
2 Potatoes, medium-sized, cut into cubes
1 cup Cauliflower (*phool gobi*) florets
1 cup Green peas (*hara mattar*)
1 tbsp Clarified butter (*ghee*)
1 tsp Cumin (*jeera*) seeds
½ tsp Turmeric (*haldi*) powder
2 cups Water
1½ tsp Salt

METHOD

• Wash and soak the rice in plenty of water for 30 minutes. Drain.

• Heat 1 tbsp clarified butter in a pan for 30 seconds; add cumin seeds and turmeric powder. Add potatoes, cauliflower, and peas; mix well. Cook for a minute on medium heat. Add soaked rice and mix.

• Add 2 cups water and salt; bring to a boil. Cover and cook on low heat till the water evaporates or until rice is done.

• Soft firm texture of rice checked with index finger is considered to be done.
• Soaking helps the rice to cook properly and evenly.

• Always cook rice dishes in a flat pan to get better texture.
• This *pulao* is usually prepared in winter as peas and cauliflower are in abundance.

SPICY LENTIL RICE
Dal Biryani

INGREDIENTS

1 cup Basmati rice
¼ cup Yellow lentil (*arhar dal*)
Vegetable oil for deep-frying
2 Potatoes, medium-sized, cut into cubes
2 Onions, medium-sized, cut into flakes
1 tbsp Clarified butter (*ghee*)
2 cups Water
Salt to taste
¼ tsp *Garam masala*
(see p. 184)
1 tbsp Cilantro (*dhaniya*) leaves, chopped

For seasoning 1:

½ tsp Cumin (*jeera*) seeds
½ tsp Ginger (*adrak*) paste
(see p. 191)
½ tsp Garlic (*lasan*) paste
(see p. 191)
½ tsp Green chili paste
(see p. 191)

For seasoning 2:

½" Cinnamon (*dalchini*) stick
2 Black cardamom (*badi elaichi*)
¼ tsp Turmeric (*haldi*) powder

METHOD

- Wash and soak the rice and yellow lentil separately in plenty of water for 30 minutes. Drain.

- Deep-fry the potatoes in medium-hot oil till light golden brown. Remove and keep aside.

- Deep-fry the onions in hot oil till light golden brown. Remove and keep aside.

- Heat 1 tbsp clarified butter in a pan for 30 seconds; add all the ingredients of seasoning 1 and mix well. Add seasoning 2 and mix.

- Add soaked rice and lentil; cook for 30 seconds. Add 2 cups water and salt to taste; bring the mixture to a boil. Cover and cook on low heat, till water evaporates or until rice is done.

- Add fried potatoes and onions, and *garam masala*; mix. Serve hot garnished with cilantro leaves.

- This dish is a complete meal in itself with a combination of rice and lentil together.
- *Dal Biryani* can also be accompanied with plain yogurt.

TOMATO RICE
Tamatar ke Chawal

Serves: 2-4

INGREDIENTS

1 cup Basmati rice
4 Tomatoes, medium-sized, cut into 8 pieces, liquidized (see p. 187)
1 tbsp Clarified butter (*ghee*)
¼ tsp Mustard seeds (*rai*)
¼ tsp Cumin (*jeera*) seeds
15 Curry leaves (*kadhi patta*)
2 tsp Bengal gram (*chana dal*), dehusked, split
2 tsp Black gram (*dhuli urad dal*), dehusked, split
2 Onions, medium-sized, chopped into medium-sized cubes
¼ tsp Turmeric (*haldi*) powder
¼ Red chili powder
Salt to taste
2 tbsp Cilantro (*dhaniya*) leaves, chopped
2 tbsp Peanuts (*moongphalli*), skinned

METHOD

- Wash and soak the rice in plenty of water for 30 minutes. Drain. Boil the rice (see p. 190) in water. Drain and keep aside.

- Heat 1 tbsp clarified butter in a pan for 30 seconds; add mustard seeds, cumin seeds, curry leaves, Bengal gram, and black gram; cook till light pink in color.

- Add the onions and cook till light brown. Add turmeric and red chili powders; mix. Add liquidized tomato and cook till thick.

- Add boiled rice and mix lightly.

- Add salt to taste, cilantro leaves, and peanuts; cook on low heat for 5 minutes, stirring occasionally. Serve hot.

- Leftover rice can also be used to prepare this dish.

- Tomato rice has a nutty flavor.

HEALTHY VEGETABLE PILAF
Hariyali Pulao

INGREDIENTS

1 cup Basmati Rice
1 cup Broccoli florets
1½ cups Zucchini, cut diagonally
1½ cups Spinach (*palak*), chopped
1 tbsp Clarified butter (*ghee*)
¼ tsp Black pepper (*kali mirch*)
2 cups Water
Salt to taste

METHOD

- Wash and soak the rice in plenty of water for 20 minutes. Drain.

- Heat 1 tbsp clarified butter in a pan for 30 seconds, add black pepper and spinach, cook for 30 seconds. Add broccoli and zucchini, and cook for 30 seconds more.

- Add soaked rice, 2 cups water, and salt to taste; bring to a boil. Cook, covered, on low heat till done. Serve hot.

- *Hariyali pulao* is enjoyed by everyone because of its delicate flavoring and the natural taste of vegetables.

SHALLOW FRIED PLAIN BREAD
Sada Paratha

INGREDIENTS

2 cups Whole-wheat flour (*atta*)
½ tsp Salt
¾ cup Water to make the dough
Vegetable oil for shallow-frying

METHOD

- Sieve the whole-wheat flour with salt. Knead to make a normal dough with water (see p. 190). Keep covered for 10 minutes.

- Divide the dough into 12 equal balls. Take a ball, dust and roll with a rolling pin slightly, apply ½ tsp oil, sprinkle whole-wheat flour and fold into a triangle. Dust and roll into 5½" triangle.

- Shallow-fry each *paratha* on a heated griddle (*tawa*) with 2 tsp oil until light golden brown on both sides. Serve hot.

- Fold the *paratha* first into a semi-circle and then fold the semi-circle into a triangle.
- Fresh *paratha* can be fried soft or crisp as per individual taste.

- For storing *paratha*, fry lightly so that it remains soft.

INDIAN BREAD STUFFED WITH POTATOES
Aloo Paratha

INGREDIENTS

2 cups Whole-wheat flour (*atta*)
½ tsp Salt
½ tbsp Clarified butter (*ghee*), melted
¾ cup Water to prepare dough
Vegetable oil for shallow-frying

For the filling:

4 Potatoes, medium-sized, boiled (see p. 183), peeled, mashed
1 tsp Fennel (*saunf*) powder
1 tsp Green chilies, chopped
1 tbsp Cilantro (*dhaniya*) leaves, chopped
¼ tsp Mango powder (*amchur*)
Salt to taste

METHOD

- Sieve the whole-wheat flour with salt. Add clarified butter and knead to make a normal dough with water. Keep covered for 10 minutes.

- **For the filling**, mix the mashed potato with ground fennel, green chilies, cilantro leaves, mango powder, and salt to taste. Keep aside.

- Divide the dough and the filling each into 8 portions. Roll a portion of the dough slightly, stuff with 1 tbsp filling and fold to seal the filling inside. Dust with flour and roll with a rolling pin into a 6" disc.

- Add ½ tsp oil on a heated griddle (*tawa*) and shallow-fry each disc with 2 tbsp oil until light golden brown on both sides. Serve hot.

- Stuffed *paratha* is a quick and popular meal.
- Variations can be made by changing the base of the filling to grated cauliflower, grated cottage cheese, or chopped onions.

- It can be served with yogurt, pickle, and butter.
- For calorie watchers reduce oil while shallow-frying and omit butter while serving.

DOUBLE-DECKER INDIAN BREAD
Tiranga Paratha

Serves: 2-4

INGREDIENTS

2 cups Whole-wheat flour (*atta*)

½ tsp Salt

1 tbsp Clarified butter (*ghee*), melted

¾ cup Water to make the dough

Vegetable oil for cooking

For filling 1:

7 oz Cottage cheese (*paneer*), grated (see p. 188)

½ tsp Black pepper (*kali mirch*)

2 tbsp Cilantro (*dhaniya*) leaves, chopped

Salt to taste

For filling 2:

½ tsp Green chili paste (see p. 191)

1 cup Green peas (*hara mattar*), boiled, mashed coarsely 1 tbsp / 1 tbsp Vegetable oil

½ tsp Mango powder (*amchur*)

¼ tsp *Garam masala* (see p. 184)

¼ tsp Salt

2 tbsp Cilantro leaves, chopped

METHOD

- Sieve the whole-wheat flour with salt. Add melted clarified butter and knead to make a normal dough with water. Keep covered for 15 minutes.

- **For filling 1**, mix the grated cottage cheese with black pepper, cilantro leaves, and salt to taste. Keep aside.

- **For filling 2**, heat 1 tbsp oil in a pan for 30 seconds; add green chili paste and peas, cook for a minute. Add mango powder, *garam masala*, salt to taste, and cilantro leaves; cook on low heat for 2 minutes, stirring occasionally. Remove and keep aside.

- Divide the dough into 21 balls.

- Take three balls, roll them slightly and place a portion of filling 1 on one round, cover with the second round and place a portion of filling 2 on the second round and cover with the third round.

- Press the edges, dust with flour and roll into a 7" disc. Shallow-fry each disc on a heated griddle (*tawa*) with 2 tbsp oil till light golden brown. Remove and serve hot.

   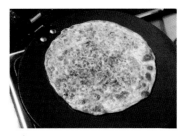

- Approximately ¾ cup water is required to make the dough.
- *Tiranga paratha* can be served with plain yogurt or *raita*.
- *Tiranga paratha* makes an ideal Sunday breakfast.

FLAKY MINT BREAD
Lachchedar Paratha

Serves: 2-4

INGREDIENTS

1 cup Whole-wheat flour (*atta*)
1 cup All-purpose flour (*maida*)
½ tsp Salt
½ cup Milk
¼ cup Water (approx.) to make the dough
Clarified butter (*ghee*) and Mint (*pudina*) powder (see p. 11) to apply inside
Vegetable oil / Clarified butter for cooking

METHOD

- Sieve both the flours with salt. Add milk and knead to make a soft dough with water. Keep covered for 15 minutes.

- Divide the dough equally into 5 balls; flatten each ball with a rolling pin, apply 2 tsp clarified butter; sprinkle ¼ tsp mint powder, and ½ tsp whole-wheat flour. Fold one end to another forming 1" pleats like a cylinder.

- Fold the cylinder to form a flat ball (*peda*). Dust and roll with a rolling pin into a 6" disc.

- Shallow-fry each *paratha* on a heated griddle (*tawa*) with 2 tbsp oil till light golden brown.

- Remove and crush along with a napkin. Serve hot.

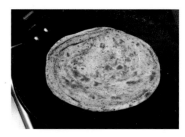
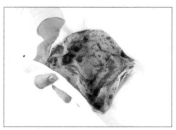

- Making a soft dough and sprinkling whole-wheat flour helps the layers to open easily.

- *Lachchedar paratha* can also be roasted directly on heat like *sada roti* (see p. 137).

CALABASH BREAD
Lauki Paratha

INGREDIENTS

1½ cups Whole-wheat flour (*atta*)
½ cup Gram flour (*besan*)
¾ tsp Salt
2 tbsp Yogurt (*dahi*)
½ lb Bottle gourd (*lauki*), grated
½ tsp Carom (*ajwain*) seeds
2 tbsp Cilantro (*dhaniya*) leaves, chopped
½ tsp Red chili powder
¼ tsp Turmeric (*haldi*) powder
Vegetable oil for cooking

METHOD

- Sieve the whole-wheat flour and gram flour with salt. Add yogurt, grated bottle gourd, carom seeds, cilantro leaves, red chili powder, and turmeric powder.

- Knead to make a normal dough with water. Keep aside covered for 5 minutes.

- Divide the dough into 12 equal balls. Dust and roll each ball slightly with a rolling pin, apply ¼ tsp oil and fold into a triangle (see p. 131).

- Dust and roll again to 4" triangle.

- Shallow-fry each *paratha* on a heated griddle (*tawa*) with 1 tbsp oil until light golden brown. Serve hot.

- Bottle gourd leaves water if left unused for a long time. Always prepare fresh dough as it is easier to roll.

SPICY INDIAN BREAD
Masala Paratha

INGREDIENTS

2 cups Whole-wheat flour
(*atta*)
½ tsp Salt
2 tbsp Yogurt (*dahi*)
¾ cup Water to make the
dough
Vegetable oil for applying inside
and for shallow-frying
4 tbsp Cilantro (*dhaniya*) leaves,
chopped

**For the masala to apply inside:
mix together**
¼ tsp Asafetida (*hing*)
¾ tsp Salt
2 tsp Red chili powder
½ tsp Carom (*ajwain*) seeds
1 tsp Cumin (*jeera*) seeds

METHOD

- Sieve whole-wheat flour with salt. Add yogurt and knead to make a normal dough with water. Keep covered for 10 minutes.

- Divide the dough into 8 equal balls, dust each ball and roll into 6" diameter. Apply 2 tsp oil, sprinkle mixed *masala*, and cilantro leaves and cut into 12 pieces with a knife.

- Place each piece on top of the other covering the last piece from masala side down, press.

- Dust and roll again with a rolling pin to 6" diameter.

- Shallow-fry each *paratha* on a heated griddle (*tawa*) with 2 tbsp oil till light golden brown on both sides. Crush with palm. Serve hot.

- *Masala paratha* served with yogurt and pickle makes a sumptuous mini meal.

- *Masala paratha* is also called 16-layered *paratha* because the dough is cut into 16 pieces before rolling for the second time.

PLAIN INDIAN BREAD
Sada Roti

Serves: 4-6

INGREDIENTS

2 cups Whole-wheat flour (*atta*)
½ tsp Salt
¾ cup Water to make the dough
Clarified butter (*ghee*) for applying

METHOD

- Sieve whole-wheat flour with salt and knead to make a normal dough with water. Keep covered for 15 minutes.

- Divide the dough equally into 12-15 balls, dust with wheat flour and roll with a rolling pin into 4" discs.

- Place on a heated griddle (*tawa*) and cook on both sides.

- Remove and roast over the flame directly till light golden brown.

- Apply ½ tsp clarified butter with a spoon and serve hot.

- Roasting can also be done on the griddle with the help of a napkin.
- Calorie watchers can omit applying clarified butter.

FENUGREEK BREAD
Besan Methi Roti

INGREDIENTS

1 cup Gram flour (*besan*)
½ cup Whole-wheat flour (*atta*)
¼ tsp Baking soda
¾ tsp Salt
½ tsp Red chili powder
½ tsp Carom (*ajwain*) seeds
a pinch Asafetida (*hing*)
2 tbsp Yogurt (*dahi*)
1 cup Fenugreek (*methi*) leaves, chopped
Clarified butter (*ghee*) for applying

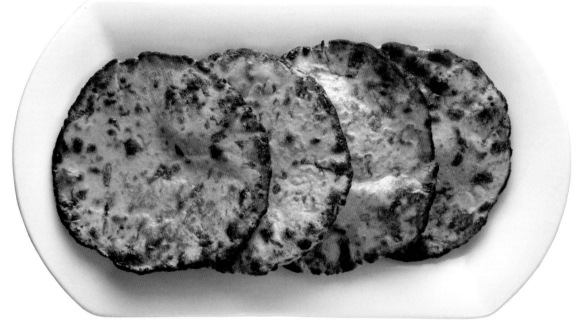

METHOD

• Sieve gram flour and whole-wheat flour with baking soda and salt. Add red chili powder, carom seeds, Asafetida, yogurt, and fenugreek leaves; mix and prepare a semi-hard dough with water. Keep covered for 30 minutes.

• Divide the dough equally into 12 balls, dust each with wheat flour and roll with a rolling pin into 2½" disc.

• Place the disc on a heated griddle (*tawa*) and cook on both sides. Remove and roast over the flame directly till light brown.

• Apply ½ tsp clarified butter on each bread and serve hot.

• Gram flour consumes less water, hence it gets difficult to handle, if the dough is too soft.

• This bread made with whole-wheat flour, gram flour, and fenugreek leaves has an unusual taste. It can be served for both lunch and dinner.

CRISP INDIAN BREAD
Khasta Roti

Serves: 2-4

INGREDIENTS

2 cups Whole-wheat flour (*atta*)
1 tsp Salt
1 tbsp Clarified butter (*ghee*), melted
¾ cup Water to knead the dough
Carom (*ajwain*) seeds to sprinkle inside
Clarified butter for applying inside and outside

METHOD

- Sieve the whole-wheat flour with salt. Add melted clarified butter and knead to make a semi-hard dough with water. Keep covered for 10 minutes.

- Divide the dough equally into 5 balls. Flatten each ball with a rolling pin, apply 1½ tsp clarified butter, sprinkle ¼ tsp carom seeds, and ¼ tsp whole-wheat flour evenly.

- Fold from one end of the disc to another like a cylinder. Press the cylinder with the palm to form a string and fold the string like a flat ball (*peda*). Dust and roll with a rolling pin into a 6" disc. Repeat with the others.

- Place the disc on a heated griddle (*tawa*), turn after 30 seconds and prick with a fork evenly. Roast over medium flame until light golden brown. Remove, apply 1 tsp clarified butter on top and serve hot.

- *Khasta roti* goes well with any variety of lentil.
- This *roti* looks flat but it is actually very crisp to taste.

LENTIL PUFFS
Urad Dal Kachori

INGREDIENTS
2 cups Whole-wheat flour (*atta*)
½ tsp Salt
Water to make the dough
Vegetable oil for deep-frying
For the filling:
1 cup Black gram (*dhuli urad dal*), de-husked, split
¼ tsp Asafetida (*hing*)
½ tsp Salt
1 tsp Red chili powder
2 tsp Fennel (*saunf*) powder
1 Potato, medium-sized, boiled, grated

METHOD
- Sieve the whole-wheat flour with salt and knead to make a normal dough with water. Keep covered for 15 minutes.

- **For the filling,** wipe the black gram with a napkin and grind to a fine powder. Mix with Asafetida, salt, red chili powder, fennel powder, and ½ water. Keep covered for 30 minutes. Add potato, mix well and keep aside.

- Divide the dough and filling each into 20 portions. Flatten the portion of the dough slightly, place 1 tsp filling and fold to seal the filling inside.

- Dust with flour and roll with a rolling pin into 3½" discs.

- Heat 1"-deep oil in a pan; fry the discs in hot oil till they puff out and become light golden brown. Serve hot.

- *Urad dal kachori*, served with *aloo ka jhol* (see p. 108) and *meetha kaddu* (see p. 104), is usually prepared on festivals like Holi and Diwali.

- Black gram consumes a lot of water. After adding water to black gram paste, it may look watery initially, but will become thick after 30 minutes.

THICK FLOUR PUFFS
Bhatura

INGREDIENTS

2 cups All-purpose flour (*maida*)

$1/_3$ cup Semolina (*suji*)

¼ tsp Baking soda

½ tsp Salt

½ tsp Baking powder

2 tbsp Yogurt (*dahi*), sour

1 tsp Sugar

Water to make the dough

Vegetable oil for deep-frying

METHOD

- Sieve the flour and semolina with baking soda, salt, and baking powder.

- Whisk yogurt with sugar and add to the flour mixture. Mix and knead to make a soft dough with water. Keep covered for 3 hours with a moist napkin.

- Divide the dough equally into 15 portions, lightly dust with flour and roll into oblong shape to 5-6" diameter.

- Heat 1"-deep oil in a pan; fry the puff in hot oil till light golden brown. Serve hot.

- All-purpose flour has an elastic texture and shrinks if not dusted with flour.
- *Bhatura* is served with *masala chana* (see p. 112), and is also accompanied with cut onions, pickle, and green chilies.
- Deep-fry the *bhatura* in hot oil otherwise they tend to consume more oil.

CAROM SPICED PUFFS
Namak Ajwain ki Puri

Serves: 4

INGREDIENTS

2 cups Whole-wheat flour (*atta*)
¾ tsp Salt
1 tsp Carom (*ajwain*) seeds
2 tsp Clarified butter (*ghee*), melted
Vegetable oil for deep-frying

METHOD

- Sieve whole-wheat flour with salt. Add carom seeds and melted clarified butter; knead to make a hard dough with water. Keep covered for 15 minutes.

- Divide the dough equally into 18 balls. Roll each ball out with a rolling pin to 3½" diameter.

- Heat 1"-deep oil in a shallow pan; deep-fry the discs in hot oil until light golden brown. Serve hot.

- *Namak ajwain ki puri* tastes best with *jeera aloo* (see p. 87), and *aam ka kas* (see p. 165).

SPICY ROASTED INDIAN BREAD
Aloo Kulcha

INGREDIENTS

2 cups All-purpose flour (*maida*)
½ tsp Salt
¼ tsp Baking soda
½ tsp Baking powder
2 tbsp Yogurt (*dahi*)
2 tbsp Milk
½ tsp Sugar
2 tbsp Vegetable oil
Water to make the dough
Butter for applying

For the filling: mix together
2 Potatoes, medium-sized, boiled, peeled, mashed
½ tsp Red chili powder
¼ tsp Mango powder (*amchur*)
¾ tsp Ground fenel (*saunf*)
¼ tsp Salt
2 tbsp Cilantro (*dhaniya*) leaves, chopped

For the topping:
2 tbsp Onion seeds (*kalonji*)= black caraway seeds
2 tbsp Cilantro leaves, chopped

METHOD

- Sieve the flour with salt, baking soda, and baking powder.

- Whisk the yogurt with milk and sugar; add to the dough along with oil and knead to make an extra soft dough with water. Keep covered for 2 hours.

- Divide the dough equally into 12 balls, flatten slightly, fill with 1 tsp filling and fold to seal the filling inside.

- Sprinkle caraway seeds and cilantro leaves on a flat surface, press each ball over it. Dust and roll with a rolling pin into 4" disc.

- Heat the gas tandoor or pressure cooker and stick the *kulcha* with the help of water on the back side and cook till light golden brown. Remove, apply butter and serve hot. Alternately, you can bake in the oven at 400°F for 4-6 minutes or until light brown.

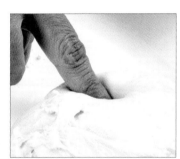

- *Aloo kulcha* can be served with any kind of lentil or vegetable.
- A soft dough gives a good texture to the *kulcha*.
- Do not apply water on the onion seeds and cilantro leaves side as this is the top side of the *kulcha*.

- *Kulcha* can be eaten with or without butter.
- This bread can also be made in a flat pan like a normal stuffed *roti*.

ACCOMPANIMENTS

POTATOES IN YOGURT
Aloo Raita

Serves: 4

INGREDIENTS
¾ cup Potatoes, boiled
(see p. 183), chopped
2 cups Yogurt (*dahi*), whisked
¼ cup Milk, chilled
Salt to taste
¼ tsp Ginger (*adrak*) paste
(see p. 191)
¼ tsp Green chili paste
(see p. 191)
¼ tsp Coriander (*dhaniya*) paste
¼ tsp Black salt (*kala namak*)
For the garnishing:
½ tsp Roasted cumin (*jeera*)
powder (see p. 184)
¼ tsp Red chili powder
1 tbsp Cilantro leaves, chopped

METHOD
• Whisk the yogurt and mix
chilled milk, salt to taste,
ginger paste, green chili paste,
cilantro paste, and black salt.

• Add potatoes and mix.

• Serve chilled garnished with
roasted ground cumin, red
chili powder, and cilantro
leaves.

• Always use chilled yogurt.
• Adding ¼ cup chilled milk checks the sourness of yogurt.

FRUITY YOGURT
Anar aur Ananas Raita

INGREDIENTS
¼ cup Pomegranate seeds
(*anar dana*)
¾ cup Pineapple (*ananas*)
pieces, canned or fresh
2 cups Yogurt (*dahi*), whisked
¼ cup Milk, chilled
Salt to taste
¼ tsp Confectioner's sugar
¼ tsp Mint (*pudina*) powder
(see p. 11) Or
½ tsp / Mint paste
¼ tsp Black pepper (*kali mirch*)
For the garnishing:
¼ tsp Roasted cumin (*jeera*)
powder (see p. 184)
1 tbsp Cilantro (*dhaniya*) leaves,
chopped

METHOD
- Whisk the yogurt and mix chilled milk, salt to taste, sugar, mint powder or paste, and black pepper.

- Add pineapple and pomegranate seeds; mix.

- Serve chilled garnished with roasted cumin powder and cilantro leaves.

- Any yogurt preparation, without cooking, mixed with herbs, fruits or vegetables, seasoned with salt, and served chilled is called *raita*.

- *Raita* has a cooling effect, hence is a good accompaniment to balance a spicy dish.

YOGURT WITH LENTIL PEARLS
Boondi Raita

INGREDIENTS
¾ cup Gram flour pearls
(*boondi*)
2 cups Yogurt (*dahi*), whisked
¼ cup Milk, chilled
Salt to taste

For the garnishing:
½ tsp Roasted cumin (*jeera*)
powder (see p. 184)
¼ tsp Red chili powder
1 tbsp Cilantro (*dhaniya*) leaves,
chopped

METHOD
- Whisk yogurt with chilled milk, salt to taste, and gram flour pearls.

- Serve chilled garnished with roasted cumin powder, red chili powder, and cilantro leaves.

- This *raita* is commonly accompanied with any kind of stuffed *paratha*.
- *Boondi* can be soaked in 2½ cups water for half an hour, squeezed and then used. This helps to remove excess oil.
- *Boondi* packets are readily available in grocery stores.
- To prepare *boondi* at home see p. 168.

LENTIL DUMPLINGS IN CREAMY YOGURT
Dahi Pakodi

INGREDIENTS

¾ cup Green gram (*moong dal*),
washed, soaked in plenty of
water for 3 hours, drained
1½ tbsp Black gram (*urad dal*),
washed, soaked in plenty of
water for 3 hours, drained
5 cups / 1 lt Yogurt (*dahi*), hung
(see p. 198)
½-1 cup Milk, chilled
Salt to taste
Vegetable oil for deep-frying
Red chili powder to taste
Roasted cumin (*jeera*) powder
(see p. 184) to taste
Cilantro (*dhaniya*) leaves,
chopped for garnishing

METHOD

- Place the yogurt in a strainer for 2 hours, discard the water, remove from strainer and whisk. Add chilled milk to get a medium-thick consistency. Add salt to taste and refrigerate.

- Grind the lentils together with minimum water to get a thick consistency. Beat the mixture until light and fluffy.

- Heat 1"-deep oil in a shallow pan; drop small portions of batter with your fingers, a few at a time, and deep-fry in hot oil to light golden brown.

- Immerse the balls in 5 cups salted water for an hour. Squeeze within the palm to remove excess water, keep aside and refrigerate.

- Place squeezed balls in a serving dish and cover with yogurt mixture. Sprinkle red chili powder, cumin powder, and cilantro leaves and serve chilled. It is served along with sweet chutney (see p. 157) and green chutney (see p.154).

- Slightly coarse ground lentil gives a better texture to *dahi pakodi*.
- For salted water, mix 1 tsp salt in 5 cups water.

- *Dahi pakodi* is an integral part of a formal family meal in north India which is served chilled.

YOGURT WITH GRATED BOTTLE GOURD
Lauki Raita

INGREDIENTS

½ lb Bottle gourd (*lauki*),
peeled, grated
2 cups Yogurt (*dahi*)
¼ cup Milk, chilled
Salt to taste

For the garnishing:

½ tsp Roasted cumin (*jeera*)
powder (see p. 184)
¼ tsp Red chili powder
1 tbsp Cilantro (*dhaniya*) leaves,
chopped

METHOD

• Pressure cook grated bottle
  gourd with 2 cups water to
  one whistle. Cool, drain, and
  squeeze.

• Whisk yogurt, add chilled milk,
  salt to taste, and squeezed
  bottle gourd; mix.

• Serve chilled garnished with
  roasted cumin powder, red
  chili powder, and cilantro
  leaves.

• For variation, grated and cooked red pumpkin can be used instead of
  bottle gourd.

LIQUID YOGURT SALAD
Kachumar Raita

INGREDIENTS
½ cup Cucumber (*khira*),
chopped
¼ cup Onion, chopped
¼ cup Tomatoes, chopped
2 cups Yogurt (*dahi*)
¼ cup Milk, chilled
½ tsp Green chili paste
(see p. 191)
Salt to taste

For the garnishing:
½ tsp Roasted cumin (*jeera*)
powder (see p. 184)
1 tbsp Cilantro (*dhaniya*) leaves,
chopped

METHOD
- Whisk yogurt, add
  chilled milk, green chili
  paste, and salt to taste; mix.

- Add cucumber, onion, and
  tomatoes; mix.

- Serve chilled garnished with
  roasted cumin powder and
  cilantro leaves.

- This *raita* can be served with any meal but it is a must with *dal biryani*
  (see p. 128).

TEMPERED LIQUID YOGURT
Tarka Mattha

Serves: 4-6

INGREDIENTS
2½ cups Yogurt (*dahi*)
¾ cup Water
Salt to taste
¼ tsp Ginger (*adrak*) paste
(see p. 191)
¼ tsp Green chili paste
(see p. 191)
1 tsp Coriander (*dhaniya*) paste
For the tempering:
2 tsp Vegetable oil
a pinch Asafetida (*hing*)
¼ tsp Mustard seeds (*rai*)
2 Dry red chilies
(*sookhi lal mirch*)
6 Curry leaves (*kadhi patta*)

METHOD
• Whisk yogurt and add ¾ cup water.

• Add salt to taste, ginger paste, green chili paste, and coriander paste; mix well.

• **For the tempering**, heat 2 tsp oil in a pan for 30 seconds; add Asafetida, mustard seeds, dry red chilies, and curry leaves.

• Pour over the yogurt mixture and serve chilled.

• Slightly sour yogurt is preferred for better taste.

• Such accompaniments make a meal interesting.

SPINACH FLAVORED YOGURT
Palak Raita

INGREDIENTS

1½ cups Spinach (*palak*), chopped
2 cups Yogurt (*dahi*)
¼ cup Milk, chilled
Salt to taste

For the tempering:

¼ tsp Clarified butter (*ghee*)
a pinch Asafetida (*hing*)
½ tsp Cumin (*jeera*) seeds
2 Dry red chilies (*sookhi lal mirch*)

METHOD

- Heat the pan for 30 seconds; add chopped spinach and cook covered for a minute (see p. 196). Remove and cool. Pound spinach to make a paste.

- Whisk yogurt and add milk, salt to taste, and spinach paste; mix.

- **For the tempering,** heat ¼ tsp clarified butter in a pan; add Asafetida, cumin seeds, and dry red chilies. Pour over the yogurt and serve chilled.

- For variation, use 2 tsp mint paste instead of spinach to make mint *raita*. Mint needs no cooking.

GREEN CHUTNEY
Hari Chutney

INGREDIENTS

2 cups Cilantro (*dhaniya*) leaves,
washed, drained in a colander
2 tsp Green chilies, chopped
½ tsp Cumin (*jeera*) seeds
a pinch Asafetida (*hing*)
½ tsp Ground coriander
(dhaniya)
1 tsp Salt
Lemon (*nimbu*) juice to taste

METHOD

• Grind cilantro leaves, green
  chilies, cumin seeds, Asafetida,
  ground coriander, and salt
  with minimum water to make
  a smooth paste.

• Transfer into a bowl.

• Add lemon juice just before
  serving.

• Lemon juice added to the chutney, just before serving, gives a fresh
  green color, but it fades after sometime because of the alkaline
  reaction of lemon.

CHERRY TOMATO CHUTNEY
Chhote Tamatar ki Chutney

INGREDIENTS

½ lb Cherry tomatoes, make a
cross on each
2 tsp Vegetable oil
a pinch Asafetida (hing)
2 tsp Ginger (adrak), chopped
1 Green chili, slit
1 tbsp Raisins (kishmish)
Salt to taste
1½ tsp Sugar
¼ tsp Black pepper (kali mirch)
½ tsp Roasted cumin (jeera)
powder (see p. 184)
1 tbsp Mint (pudina), chopped

METHOD

- Boil 3½ cups water; add tomatoes and cook for 2 minutes, uncovered. Drain in a colander. Cool and peel.

- Heat 2 tsp oil in a pan for 30 seconds; add Asafetida, ginger, green chili, and raisins.

- Add peeled tomatoes, ¼ cup water, salt to taste, and sugar; bring to a boil, and simmer for 5 minutes.

- Add black pepper, roasted cumin powder, and mint; mix well. Serve hot.

- Making a cross on the tomatoes makes it easier to peel.
- It can also be prepared with large tomatoes. In such case, cut the tomatoes into 1" cubes after peeling.

COCONUT CHUTNEY
Nariyal ki Chutney

INGREDIENTS

1 cup Coconut (*nariyal*), fresh, grated
½ cup Bengal gram (*chana dal*), dehusked, split, roasted
2 tsp Green chilies, chopped
½ tsp Salt
¾-1 cup Water to blend
2 tbsp Cilantro (*dhaniya*) leaves, chopped

For the tempering:
1 tbsp Vegetable oil
½ tsp Bengal gram, dehusked, split
½ tsp Split black gram (*dhuli urad dal*), dehusked
¼ tsp Mustard seeds (*rai*)
2 Dry red chilies (*sookhi lal mirch*)
8 Curry leaves (*kadhi patta*)

METHOD

- Blend coconut, roasted Bengal gram, green chilies, salt, and water to a smooth paste in a food processor. Add cilantro leaves and blend again for 10 seconds.

- Transfer to a bowl and keep aside.

- **For the tempering**, heat 1 tbsp oil in a pan for 30 seconds; add the lentils and cook until light brown. Add mustard seeds, dry red chilies, and curry leaves. Remove and pour over the chutney and serve.

- This chutney is generally served with south Indian snacks such as *idli*, *upma*, etc.
- Coconut chutney is always prepared fresh for authentic flavor.
- Leftover chutney should be refrigerated.
- Roasted Bengal gram is available in grocery stores.

SWEET CHUTNEY
Meethi Chutney

INGREDIENTS

1½ cups Jaggery (*gur*), broken into small pieces
2 tbsp Mango powder (*amchur*)
1½ tsp Salt

For masala A:
1 tsp *Garam masala*
(see p. 184)
2 tsp Roasted cumin (*jeera*) powder (see p. 184)
1 tsp Black salt (*kala namak*)

For masala B:
⅛ tsp Asafetida (*hing*)
2 tsp Ground coriander (*dhaniya*)
2 tsp Red chili powder

METHOD

- Mix jaggery with 1½ cups water in a pan and cook, on low heat, until it dissolves. Strain and keep aside.

- Mix mango powder in 1½ cups water.

- Mix jaggery water with mango water. Add salt and bring to a boil, simmer for 40 minutes. Remove and cool.

- Dry roast *masala* B ingredients in a pan, until light golden brown. Keep aside.

- Add *masala* A and *masala* B to the cooked jaggery and mango powder mixture and mix well.

- *Meethi* chutney can be stored in the refrigerator for up to a month.
- It can be served with any snack.

JAGGERY FLAVORED MANGO CHUTNEY
Aam ki Launji

Serves: 4-6

INGREDIENTS

1 lb Raw mangoes (*kairi*), peeled, cut into 1" cubes
2 tbsp Jaggery (*gur*), powdered
1 tbsp Vegetable oil
$1/_8$ tsp Asafetida (*hing*)
¼ tsp Fenugreek seeds (*methi dana*)
¼ tsp Cumin (*jeera*) seeds
¼ tsp Fennel (*saunf*) seeds
1 tsp Red chili powder
1 tsp Turmeric (*haldi*) powder
1 tsp Ground fennel
½ tsp Salt
¼ cup Water

METHOD

- Heat 1 tbsp oil in a pan for 30 seconds on medium heat; add Asafetida, fenugreek seeds, cumin seeds, and fennel seeds. Add red chili powder, turmeric powder, ground fennel, and cut mangoes; mix well.

- Add salt and ¼ cup water; cook, covered, on low heat, until mangoes are slightly soft. Add jaggery and cook, covered, for 2 minutes on low heat. Remove and serve.

- *Aam ki launji* has a tangy flavor.
- This *chutney* can last in the fridge for up to 15 days.

- All kinds of *paratha* can be enjoyed with this chutney.

FRESH MANGO PICKLE
Aam ka Tazaa Achaar

INGREDIENTS

2 Raw mangoes (*kairi*), cut into medium-sized cubes with skin

2 tsp Mustard seeds (*rai*)

½ tsp Fenugreek seeds (*methi dana*)

4 tsp Ground fennel (*saunf*)

2 tsp Ground coriander (*dhaniya*)

¾ tsp Turmeric (*haldi*) powder

2 tsp Red chili powder

3 tsp Salt

1 tbsp White vinegar (*sirka*)

2 tbsp Mustard (*sarson*) oil

METHOD

- Grind mustard seeds and fenugreek seeds together.

- Mix the ground seeds with fennel powder, coriander powder, turmeric powder, red chili powder, salt, white vinegar, and mustard oil to form a *masala* paste.

- Mix the *masala* paste with mango pieces and set aside for 2 hours. Serve.

- Refrigerate for later use, but consume within 30 days.

- Mixed *masala* paste can be stored for up to 6 months in the refrigerator.

LEMON FLAVORED GINGER
Nimbu ka Adrak

INGREDIENTS
¾ cup Ginger (*adrak*), peeled,
cut into 1"-long pieces
2 tsp Salt
2 tbsp Lemon (*nimbu*) juice

METHOD
• Mix the cut ginger with
  salt and lemon juice; leave
  aside for 30 minutes at
  room temperature, covered.
  Refrigerate and serve.

• Ginger turns pink in color after left mixed with lemon juice and salt.
• Refrigerate for later use.

TANGY RADISH FLAKES
Mooli ka Kas

INGREDIENTS
1 cup Radish (*mooli*), peeled, grated
2 tsp Salt
1½ tbsp Ginger (*adrak*), peeled, grated
2 tsp Green chilies, chopped
1 tbsp Cilantro (*dhaniya*) leaves, chopped
1 tbsp Lemon (*nimbu*) juice

METHOD
• Mix the grated radish with 1½ tsp salt; leave aside for 2 minutes, squeeze and discard the water.

• Mix squeezed radish with ginger, green chilies, cilantro leaves, ½ tsp salt, and lemon juice. Refrigerate and serve.

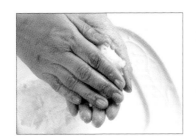

• Radish is high in water content. Adding salt and squeezing later improves the texture and prevents the radish from getting watery.

• Normally *mooli ka kas* is served during lunch time.

GREEN CHILI PICKLE
Hari Mirch ka Achaar

INGREDIENTS

¼ lb Green chilies, thick, large, washed, wiped dry, slit vertically, keeping shape intact, seeded
¾ tbsp Salt
½ tbsp Fenugreek seeds (*methi dana*)
1 tbsp Mustard seeds (*rai*)
2 tbsp Ground fennel (*saunf*)
1½ tsp Turmeric (*haldi*) powder
2 tsp Ground coriander (*dhaniya*)
1½ tbsp Lemon (*nimbu*) juice
¼ tsp Asafetida (*hing*)
2 tbsp Mustard (*sarson*) oil
2 tsp White vinegar (*sirka*)

METHOD

- Grind fenugreek seeds and mustard seeds together to a fine powder in a food processor; remove. Mix this powder with ground fennel, turmeric powder, ground coriander, lemon juice, Asafetida, 1 tbsp mustard oil, and white vinegar.

- Stuff each chili evenly with this mixed *masala*.

- Apply 1 tbsp oil on the stuffed chilies and consume after 2 days.

- *Hari mirch ka achaar* should be consumed within 7 days. For extended use, refrigerate to avoid deterioration.

QUICK GREEN CHILI PICKLE
Jhatpat Hari Mirch ka Achaar

Makes: 8-10

INGREDIENTS

4 oz Green chilies, washed, wiped-dry, slit vertically

For the filling: mix and keep aside

4 tsp *Chaat masala*

1 tsp Salt

For the seasoning:

1½ tbsp Mustard (*sarson*) oil

a pinch Asafetida (*hing*)

¼ tsp Fenugreek seeds (*methi dana*)

¼ tsp Cumin (*jeera*) seeds

2 tsp Gram flour (*besan*)

Other Ingredients

1 tsp Ground coriander (dhaniya)

2 tsp Fennel (*saunf*) powder

½ tsp Mango powder (*amchur*)

¼ tsp Salt

METHOD

• Fill each green chili evenly with the filling mixture.

• Heat 1½ tbsp oil in a pan for 30 seconds on medium heat; add Asafetida, fenugreek seeds, cumin seeds, and gram flour; cook for 10 seconds.

• Add stuffed green chilies and mix.

• Add ground coriander, fennel powder, mango powder, and salt; cook on high heat for a minute, stirring constantly. Remove and serve.

• This chili is spicy with a pungent flavor.
• Adding gram flour to this pickle brings out its true flavor.

PICKLED ONIONS
Sirkewale Pyaz

INGREDIENTS
2 Onions, medium-sized, cut into 1" cubes, layers separated
2 tbsp White / Balsamic vinegar (*sirka*)
1½ tsp Salt
½ cup Water

METHOD
• Mix the onions with white or balsamic vinegar, salt, and water; leave aside, covered, for an hour. Serve.

• Pearl onions can also be used instead of regular onions.
• Discard water before serving.

• It can be served with any meal.
• Onions turn dark pink when mixed with vinegar.

MANGO MARMALADE
Aam ka Kas

INGREDIENTS

1 kg Raw mangoes (*kairi*)
3 cups Sugar
2 tbsp Salt
¼ tsp Asafetida (*hing*)
1 tsp *Garam masala*
(see p. 184)

METHOD

- Peel and grate the mangoes.

- Mix the grated mangoes with sugar and salt. Keep covered for 30 minutes.

- Cook on medium heat, stirring occasionally, to one string consistency (see p. 200).

- Turn off the heat, add Asafetida and *garam masala*; mix well. Cool and store in an airtight jar.

- *Aam ka kas* can be stored for up to six months
- This marmalade is served with meals.

- It has a unique sweet and sour flavor.

DESSERTS

SUNRISE PUDDING
Boondi Bake

Serves: 6-8

INGREDIENTS

6 Bread slices
1 cup Gram flour (besan)
Clarified butter (ghee) for deep-frying
¾ cup Sugar
½ tsp Green cardamom (choti elaichi), ground
¼ tsp Saffron (kesar)
1½ cups Milk
1¼ cups Heavy cream (see p. 200)
2 tbsp Almonds (badam), blanched, chopped (see p. 202)
2 tbsp Pistachios (pista), blanched, chopped (see p. 202)

METHOD

• Remove the sides of the bread with a sharp knife, toast them lightly in a toaster, without browning. Keep aside.

• Combine gram flour with ¾ cup water and prepare a semi-thick batter. Heat 1½"-deep clarified butter in a shallow pan; pour the batter through a boondi ladle or a slotted spoon and fry until light golden brown. Remove and keep aside.

• Mix the sugar with ¼ cup water in a pan and cook on medium heat, stirring occasionally, to one-string consistency (see p. 200); turn off the heat. Add green cardamom and saffron powder (see p. 203); mix well.

• Add the fried boondi to the sugar syrup, mix until well coated; cool. Grind coarsely in a food processor. Keep aside.

• Arrange the bread slices in an 8" square dish, cover with boondi and pour milk evenly over it. Bake in the oven at 275°F for 10-15 minutes or until light brown.

• Remove decorate with double whipped cream, almonds, and pistachios. Serve immediately.

• This popular Indian dessert is a melody of crunchy baked boondi and chilled cream.

• Indian desserts should always be prepared in clarified butter for better taste.

FRUIT AND CUSTARD PUDDING
Thanda Phalon ka Custard

INGREDIENTS

1 cup Pulp-free orange juice
1 tbsp Agar aghar (China grass)
3 tbsp water
2 tsp Butter
6 Marie biscuit crumbs
(see p. 199)
4 tbsp Custard powder
5 cups Milk
4 tbsp Sugar
4 cups Mixed fruits, chopped
(orange, banana, apples)

METHOD

- Make the jello according to the recipe on p. 201.

- Melt 2 tsp butter in a pan, mix with biscuit crumbs. Remove and press in a 6" shallow serving dish. Leave in the refrigerator for 45 minutes to set.

- Mix the custard powder in ½ cup milk. Set aside.

- Mix the remaining 4½ cups milk with sugar in a pan and bring to a boil on medium heat. Add custard powder mixture and stir constantly to one boil. Turn off the heat, cool and chill.

- To arrange, remove the chilled biscuit crumb dish from the fridge, spoon the chilled custard over the crumbs, cover with chopped fruits and top with set jello. Serve chilled.

- Fruit and custard pudding is very popular among teenagers.
- Custard powder should be mixed in room temperature milk, or else it gets lumpy.
- Hot custard can also be served in winter with cakes.
- Set jello can be cut with a sharp knife to any size desired.

INDIAN RICE PUDDING
Chawal ki Kheer

Serves: 4-6

INGREDIENTS

2 tbsp Basmati rice

¼ tsp Saffron (*kesar*)

4 Green cardamom (*choti elaichi*), deseeded

¼ tsp Clarified butter (*ghee*)

7½ cups Milk

4 tbsp Sugar

2 tbsp Almonds (*badam*), blanched, chopped (see p. 202)

2 tbsp Pistachios (*pista*), blanched, chopped (see p. 202)

METHOD

• Wash and soak the rice in plenty of water for 10 minutes; drain. Keep aside.

• Pound saffron and green cardamom together to a fine powder (see p. 203).

• Heat ¼ tsp clarified butter in a heavy-bottom saucepan; add soaked rice and cook for a minute. Add milk and bring to a boil. Reduce heat and cook until the mixture is reduced to third its original consistency, stirring occasionally.

• Add sugar and cook for 10 minutes on low heat. Add cardamom and saffron powder and turn off the heat. Cool and refrigerate the mixture. Serve chilled garnished with almonds and pistachios.

• This is a popular easy-to-make Indian dessert.
• *Kheer* can be served either hot or cold.

• *Kheer* can be made one day in advance and kept in the fridge.
• Blanched and chopped almonds and pistachios add to the flavor.

VERMICELLI PUDDING
Sewai ki Kheer

INGREDIENTS

½ cup Vermicelli (*sewai*)
6 cups Milk
3 Green cardamom (*choti elaichi*), seeded
¼ tsp Saffron (*kesar*)
½ tsp Clarified butter (*ghee*)
2-3 tbsp Sugar
2 tbsp Raisins (*kishmish*)
2 tbsp Pistachios (*pista*), blanched, chopped (see p. 202)

METHOD

- Pound green cardamom and saffron to a powder (see p. 203). Keep aside.

- Heat ½ tsp clarified butter in a shallow pan for 30 seconds; add vermicelli and cook on low heat, stirring constantly, until light golden brown. Add milk and bring to a boil. Reduce heat and simmer for 30 minutes.

- Add sugar and raisins; cook for 5 minutes, turn off the heat.

- Add cardamom and saffron powder; mix. Serve hot or cold garnished with pistachios.

- This is a quick dessert to make on short notice.

- Vermicelli packets are easily available in Indian grocery stores.

SWEET SAFFRON RICE
Meetha Kesari Chawal

Serves: 4-6

INGREDIENTS
2/3 cup Basmati rice
½ tsp Green cardamom (*choti elaichi*), seeded
¼ tsp Saffron (*kesar*)
½ cup Sugar
¼ cup Water
½ cup Almonds (*badam*) blanched (see p. 202), cut lengthwise
2 tbsp Pistachios (*pista*) blanched (see p. 202), cut lengthwise
4 tbsp Clarified butter (*ghee*)
2 Cloves (*laung*)

METHOD
• Wash and soak the rice in plenty of water for 30 minutes, drain. Cook in boiling water until done and strain (see p. 190).

• Pound green cardamom and saffron to a fine powder (see p. 203). Keep aside.

• Mix sugar and water in a pan and cook on low heat to two-string consistency (see p. 200). Turn off the heat, add ¾ of both cut almonds and pistachios. Add powdered saffron and cardamom and cooked rice to the syrup; mix and leave covered for 2 hours. Stir occasionally.

• Heat 4 tbsp clarified butter in a pan for 30 seconds; add cloves and when it begins to change color remove and add this seasoning to the rice mixture. Mix gently.

• Serve hot or cold, garnished with remaining almonds and pistachios.

• Boiled rice added to sugar syrup leaves water initially, but soaks up after 2 hours.

• *Meetha kesari chawal* is a delicacy and is generally served along with meals.

CARROT PUDDING
Gajar ka Halwa

INGREDIENTS

2 lb Carrots (*gajar*), peeled, grated
5 cups Milk
1¼ cups Sugar
¼ lb Whole milk fudge (*khoya*) (see p. 201)
4 tbsp Clarified butter (*ghee*)
1 tsp Ground green cardamom (*choti elaichi*)
½ cup Cashew nuts (*kaju*), chopped
½ cup Almonds (*badam*), blanched, chopped (see p. 202)
¼ cup Pistachios (*pista*), blanched, chopped (see p. 202)

METHOD

- Combine the grated carrot with milk in a large pan and cook on medium heat, stirring occasionally, until the milk evaporates.

- Add sugar and cook on low heat until the mixture is semi-thick, turning frequently.

- Add grated whole milk fudge and cook on low heat for 10 minutes, turning frequently.

- Add clarified butter and cook on low heat, turning constantly for 15 minutes. Turn off the heat, add ground cardamom and chopped cashew nuts; mix well.

- Serve hot, garnished with almonds and pistachios.

- Discard the hard center portion of the carrots while grating.
- Carrot pudding can be stored in the fridge for up to a week.

- Red carrots can also be used instead of the orange ones. In fact, red carrots needs less sugar as they are sweeter in taste.

HOT SEMOLINA PUDDING
Suji Halwa

Serves: 4-6

INGREDIENTS

¾ cup Semolina (*suji*)
6 Green cardamom (*choti elaichi*), seeded
¼ tsp Saffron (*kesar*) strands
¾ cup Sugar
1¾ cup Water
5 tbsp Clarified butter (*ghee*)
2 tbsp Gram flour (*besan*)
¼ cup Almonds (*badam*), blanched, chopped (see p. 202)
2 tbsp Pistachios (*pista*), blanched, chopped (see p. 202)

METHOD

- Pound green cardamom and saffron into a fine powder (see p. 203). Keep aside.

- Prepare sugar syrup by mixing sugar and water in a pan and boiling the mixture, on low heat, until the sugar dissolves. Keep aside.

- Heat 4 tbsp clarified butter in a shallow pan for a minute; add semolina and gram flour and fry on low heat, until light golden brown, stirring frequently.

- Add sugar syrup and stir constantly, on low heat, until the mixture becomes semi-thick.

- Add cardamom and saffron powder, mix. Add the remaining 1 tbsp clarified butter and mix. Serve hot garnished with almonds and pistachios.

- Water should be added to fried semolina 30 minutes before serving, otherwise the pudding becomes too thick.

- Adding 1 tbsp clarified butter later improves the texture of the pudding.

SAFFRON PISTACHIO DELIGHT
Kesar Pista Kulfi

INGREDIENTS

10 cups Milk
5 tbsp Sugar
¼ tsp Saffron (*kesar*)
8 Green cardamom (*choti elaichi*), seeded
2 tbsp Pistachios (*pista*), blanched, chopped (see p. 202)
8 *Kulfi* molds

METHOD

- Pound saffron and green cardamom to a fine powder (see p. 203).

- Heat the milk in a shallow pan and cook on medium heat until reduced to ¼ its original consistency, stirring occasionally.

- Add sugar and cook for 2 minutes. Turn off the heat. Add saffron-cardamom powder to the condensed hot milk; mix well and cool.

- Mix the milk mixture with 1½ tbsp pistachios and blend in a mixer for 10 seconds. Pour into the *kulfi* molds, sprinkle remaining pistachios on top, cover the molds with the lid and freeze for 10-12 hours or until set.

- De-mold set *kulfi* with a sharp knife. Remove to a plate, cut into slices and serve.

- Use whole milk for better taste.
- It can also be made with skimmed milk for weight watchers.

- For easy unmolding, wash the frozen *kulfi* molds under running water.

SWEET COCONUT SQUARES
Nariyal Burfi

Serves: 8-10

INGREDIENTS

16 oz Coconut (*nariyal*), fresh, grated
2¼ cups Sugar
7 oz Whole milk fudge (*khoya*), grated (see p. 201)
1 tbsp Rose water (*gulab jal*)
Vegetarian Silver leaves (*varq*) for decoration
2 tbsp Almonds (*badam*), blanched, chopped (see p. 202)
2 tbsp Pistachios (*pista*), blanched, chopped (see p. 202)

METHOD

- Mix grated coconut with sugar and leave for 30 minutes in a shallow pan. Cook on medium heat, mixing constantly, until a sugar coating is seen on the surface, while turning.

- Add grated whole milk fudge and rose water; mix well.

- Transfer to a greased tray (8" × 4") and press down immediately. Leave to set for 4 hours.

- Decorate with silver leaves, almonds, and pistachios, and cut into square pieces. Serve.

- Select medium-ripe coconuts and scrape south-Indian style.
- Silver leaves are mainly used for decoration, and do not contribute to the taste.

- For the sugar coating to form it takes 20-30 minutes.
- This Indian sweet can be kept for up to a week. It is an ideal preparation for Holi, Diwali, and other festivals.

SWEET DIAMONDS
Shakkar Pare

INGREDIENTS

2 cups All-purpose flour (*maida*)
3 tbsp Clarified butter (*ghee*) melted
Lukewarm water to make the dough
2½ cups Clarified butter for deep-frying
1 cup Sugar
⅓ cup Water

METHOD

- Sieve the flour; add 3 tbsp melted ghee and knead to prepare a hard dough with lukewarm water. Keep aside covered for 10 minutes.

- Divide the dough into 2 equal balls, roll each ball into ¼"-thick disc and cut into ½" cubes.

- Heat 2½ cups clarified butter in a shallow frying pan until medium-hot; add the cubes and deep-fry until light golden brown. Remove and cool.

- Prepare sugar syrup with sugar and water to one-string consistency (see p. 200); turn off the heat.

- Add fried cubes into the sugar syrup and keep mixing until sugar coating is formed on the cubes. Remove, cool, and store.

- This Indian sweet is particularly made on the festival of colors, Holi.
- It can be stored for up to 20 days in a cool, dry place.

SWEET DUMPLINGS LACED IN SYRUP
Gulab Jamun

INGREDIENTS

½ lb Whole milk fudge (*khoya*)
(see p. 201)
2 oz Cottage cheese (*paneer*)
¼ cup All-purpose flour (*maida*)
2¼ cups Sugar
2¼ cups Water
2½ cups Clarified butter (*ghee*)
for deep-frying

METHOD

• Prepare sugar syrup by mixing sugar and water in a pan and boiling the mixture, on low heat, cook until the sugar dissolves, strain. Keep aside.

• Mash whole milk fudge and cottage cheese to a smooth paste separately, with a rolling stone. Mix the two pastes with flour and prepare a soft dough.

• Divide the dough equally into 20-25 portions and shape them into round balls.

• Heat 2½ cups clarified butter in a shallow pan on low heat; add 15 balls at a time, and watch until they float, increase heat to high and cook until golden brown, turning frequently and gently with the spatula.

• Remove, add them to the sugar syrup and leave for an hour. Reheat with sugar syrup and serve hot.

• *Khoya* also called *khawa* or *mawa* is a common ingredient in many traditional Indian sweets. When milk is slowly evaporated under heat, it eventually becomes a solid mass which is called *khoya*.

• *Gulab jamun* is a popular Indian dessert
• *Gulab jamun* can last for up to 10-15 days in the fridge.
• It can also be stuffed with chopped almonds and pistachios.

COOKING PROCESSES

BAKING POTATOES AND SWEET POTATOES

- Apply oil to the sweet potatoes.

- Apply oil to the potatoes.

- Bake at 400°F for 20-30 minutes or until soft.

- Bake at 400°F for 20-30 minutes or until soft.

- Cool and peel.

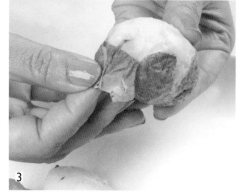

- Cool and peel.

BAKING TIP

- Applying oil to the potatoes / sweet potatoes helps to remove the skin easily.

PRESSURE COOKING POTATOES / GREEN BANANAS / RAW MANGOES

- Place raw potatoes in the pressure cooker, add enough water to cover, cook to one whistle. Simmer for 4 minutes.

- Place green bananas in the pressure cooker, add enough water to cover, cook to one whistle.

- Place raw mangoes in the pressure cooker, add enough water to cover, cook to one whistle.

- Cool and drain.

- Simmer for 4 minutes. Cool and drain.

- Simmer for 4 minutes. Cool and drain.

- Peel and use as per recipe.

- Peel or mash and use as per recipe.

PREPARING SPICE MIXES

CHANA MASALA

- Mix together 2 tbsp coriander seeds,
  2 tsp cumin seeds, 5 cloves, 1" cinnamon
  stick, 2 seeded black cardamom, 8 black
  peppercorns, and 4 dry red chilies.

- Dry roast all the spices on low heat, until
  light golden brown.
- Cool and grind coarsely.

- Store in an airtight jar.

ROASTED CUMIN POWDER

- Roast 2 tbsp cumin seeds in a pan, on
  low heat, stirring frequently, until golden
  brown.

- Cool and grind coarsely.

GARAM MASALA

- Mix together 2 tbsp black peppercorns, 8
  seeded black cardamom, and 2 tsp cloves.

- Grind to a powder.

Magori

Magoris are sun-dried split green gram dumplings. They are made by soaking and grinding split green gram, shaping them into small balls, and drying in the sun.

- Deep-fry *magoris* in medium-hot oil until light golden brown.

2

- Crush slightly if recipe requires (this releases its flavor).

Peanut Powder

- Heat 2 tbsp oil in a pan until medium-hot; add ½ cup peanuts and fry until light brown. Remove and cool.

2

- Remove the skin with fingers.

3

- Coarsely powder in a mortar and pestle, if recipe requires.

Roasting Semolina

- Dry roast semolina in a shallow pan for 5 minutes on low heat; remove.

Roasting Vermicelli

- Heat the clarified butter (as per recipe) in a pan for 30 seconds.

2

- Sauté vermicelli on low heat, stirring constantly, until light golden brown.

COOKING WITH TOMATOES

• Seeding tomatoes

1

• Cut tomato into quarters vertically, remove the seeds with a sharp knife.

2

• Cut as required in the recipe.

• Roasting tomatoes

II

• Hold the head of the tomato with a fork over direct heat, turning all over, until the skin shrinks.

2

• Cool and remove the skin.

• Grating tomatoes

1

• Cut tomato into half, vertically.

2

• Grate from the cut side down until the tomato skin.

TOMATO GRAVY / TOMATO YOGURT GRAVY

TIP
• The quantity of ingredients to be used as per recipe.

1

• Heat the oil in a pan; add asafetida, cumin seeds.

2

• Add turmeric powder and red chili powder; mix.

• Making liquidized tomato

I

• Cut tomato into 8 pieces.

2

• Blend to a smooth paste.

ONION-TOMATO GRAVY

II

• Heat the oil; add bay leaves, cinnamon, cloves.

2

• Add grated onion, and ginger-garlic paste; fry until golden brown.

3

• Add red chili powder and turmeric powder; mix.

4

• Add liquidized tomato and fry until oil separates.

3

• Add liquidized tomato, ginger, chili paste. Cook until oil separates.

4

• To make tomato-yogurt gravy, add beaten yogurt to the cooked tomato gravy.

5

• Cook until oil separates. Add water.

WORKING WITH COTTAGE CHEESE

- **Making plain cottage cheese** (*paneer*)

- Bring 5 cups milk to a boil in a pan, on medium-heat, turn off heat. Add 1-2 tbsp lemon juice, gradually, stir until milk curdles.

- Fold cloth over cottage cheese, molding, into a square shape.

- Wait for 2 minutes.

- Place a light weight over the cottage cheese for 20 minutes. Alternatively, place in a cottage cheese maker and cover with the lid for 20 minutes.

- Drain in a muslin cloth.

- Cut off any uneven edges. Use immediately or refrigerate for later use.

COTTAGE CHEESE TIP
- 5 cups milk makes 5 oz of cottage cheese.

- Making *masala* cottage cheese

- Boil 5 cups milk as above, add ¼ tsp salt, 1 tsp cumin seeds, 1 tsp chopped green chilies, and 2 tbsp cilantro leaves, turn off the heat. Add 1-2 tbsp lemon juice, gradually, stir until milk curdles.

- Wait for 2 minutes. Drain.

- Place in a cottage cheese maker and cover with the lid for 20 minutes.

- Cut off any uneven edges. Use immediately or refrigerate for later use.

- Sautéing cottage cheese

- Heat 2 tsp oil in a non-stick pan for 30 seconds; add cottage cheese and sauté on both sides, on medium heat, until light golden brown.

- Remove and cut into cubes.

BOILING RICE   MAKING DOUGH

1

1

- Wash and soak 1 cup rice in 4 cups water for 30 minutes. Drain.

- Sieve flour. Add all the ingredients (such as oil, clarified butter, yogurt, milk) given in the recipe except water.

2

2

- Boil 6½ cups water. Add soaked rice, bring to a boil and cook, covered, on low heat until the rice is soft.

- Dough may be soft, normal, or hard. Adjust the quantity of water for a soft or hard dough, as required in the recipe.

3

3

- Remove, drain in a colander, and transfer to a serving dish.

- Picture shows normal dough.

RICE TIP

- To check if the rice is cooked press with the index finger for softness.

DOUGH TIP

- Dough can be kneaded with hand or in a food processor.
- For normal dough, add 1½ cups water for 4 cups flour and knead well.

MAKING FRESH COOKING PASTES

Ginger Paste

1

- Take 2 tsp of chopped ginger.

2

- Hand pound chopped ginger to a fine paste, keep aside. Use as required.

3

Garlic Paste

1

- Take 8 garlic cloves.

2

- Hand pound chopped garlic cloves to a fine paste, keep aside. Use as required.

3

Chili Paste

1

- Take 2 tsp of chopped green chilies.

2

- Hand pound chopped green chilies to a fine paste, keep aside. Use as required.

3

PRESSURE COOKING LEGUMES

- **Pressure cooking yellow lentil** (*arhar dal*)

- Soak 1 cup in 3 cups water for 30 minutes; drain. Put in a pressure cooker.

- Add 1½ cups water.

- Add ¾ tsp salt and ½ tsp turmeric powder. Pressure cook to one whistle and simmer for 4 minutes.
- Open the lid when the pressure drops.

- **Pressure cooking horse gram** (*kala chana*)

- Soak 1 cup horse gram in 5 cups water for 8 hours; drain. Put in a pressure cooker.

- Pressure cook with 1¼ cups water and ¼ tsp salt to one whistle, simmer for 20 minutes. Open the lid when the pressure drops.

LENTIL TIP
- Make sure that the pressure drops before removing the lid to ensure that the legumes are fully cooked.

- **Pressure cooking chickpeas** (*kabuli chana*)

- Soak 1 cup chickpeas in 5 cups water for 8 hours; drain. Put in a pressure cooker.

- Add 2½ cups water.

- Add ¼ tsp salt and cook to one whistle; simmer for 30 minutes. Open the lid when the pressure drops.

- **Pressure cooking kidney beans** (*rajmah*)

- Soak ¾ cup beans in 4 cups water for 4 hours; drain.

- Put the beans in a pressure cooker and add 2 cups water.

- Add ¼ tsp turmeric powder and ¼ tsp salt; cook to one whistle and simmer for 30 minutes. Open the lid when the pressure drops.

- **Pressure cooking black-eyed peas** (*lobhia*)

- Soak ¾ cup peas in 4 cups water for 4 hours; drain. Put in a pressure cooker..

- Add 2 cups water.

- Add ¼ tsp turmeric powder and ¼ tsp salt; cook to one whistle and simmer for 5 minutes. Open the lid when the pressure drops.

TEMPERING LENTILS

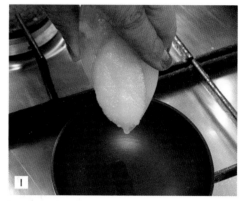

- Heat the clarified butter in a pan for 30 seconds.

- Add asafetida.

- **Variation with curry leaves**

- Heat the clarified butter in a pan for 30 seconds.

- Add cumin seeds and cook until the seeds start spluttering.

- Add mustard seeds and curry leaves.

- Remove from heat and add dry red chilies (if recipes requires) and red chili powder or ground black pepper.

- Add red chili powder.

COOKING WITH VEGETABLES

• Blanching Beans and Carrots

• Boil 5 cups water, add 1 cup beans and carrots each.

• Blanching of Bean Sprouts

• Boil 4 cups water and add 2 cups bean sprouts.

• Blanch for 2 minutes.

• Cook for 2 minutes, uncovered.

TEMPERING TIP
• Remove the pan from heat to prevent chili powder from burning as this will spoil the flavor of the dish.
• Follow quantity and ingredients in the order given in the recipe.

BLANCHING TIP
• Blanching, also called par-boiling, is lightly cooking raw vegetables for varying amounts of time in boiling water.

• Drain in a colander.

• Drain and use as per recipe.

COOKING WITH VEGETABLES

• Spinach

• Heat the pan; add 1 lb chopped spinach and ¼ tsp sugar.

• Cook covered for 2 minutes.

• Fenugreek leaves

• Heat the pan; add ½ lb chopped fenugreek leaves and ¼ tsp sugar; cover and cook for 1 minute.

• Remove and use as per recipe.

• Remove and use as per recipe.

Corn

- Heat 2 tsp oil in a pan for 30 seconds; add 2 cups corn and cook for 2 minutes, on high heat, stirring frequently.

- **Peas**

- Heat ½ tbsp oil in a pan; add 2 cups peas and ¼ tsp salt. Cook, covered, on low heat until soft.

- Remove and use as per recipe.

- Remove and use as per recipe.

TIP
- Adding ¼ tsp sugar while cooking spinach and fenugreek helps to retain the green color.

WORKING WITH YOGURT

Setting Yogurt

- Heat 5 cups milk until lukewarm.

- Add ½ tsp yogurt culture.

- Mix lukewarm milk and yogurt culture thoroughly.

- Leave to set in a warm place for 3-6 hours. Refrigerate.

- **Making hung yogurt for salad dressing:** place 2 cups yogurt in a sieve or in a muslin cloth for 2-3 hours.

- **Making yogurt for *raita* and *dahi pakodi*:** place 2 cups yogurt (as per recipe) in a sieve for 30 minutes.

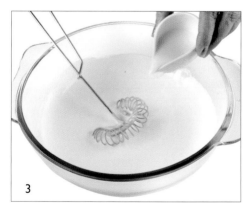

- Whisk. Add ¼-½ cup chilled milk to get a soft, creamy consistency.

WHILE MAKING DESSERTS

Biscuit crumbs

- Place 6 tea biscuits in a bag.

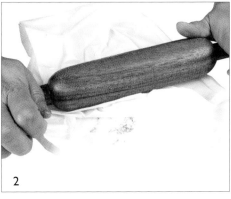

- Press with rolling pin to form crumbs.

Bread Squeezing

- Dip 2-4 slices of bread in 2½ cups water.

Yogurt TIP

- Always set yogurt using lukewarm milk (100°-110°F). Putting culture into hot milk spoils the texture and taste of the yogurt.
- Yogurt sets faster in summer while it takes longer in winter.
- Once set, refrigerate to prevent it from getting sour.

HUNG YOGURT TIP

- Milk is normally added to get the right consistency and flavor.
- Hanging yogurt removes excess water and milk gives it a fresh taste.

- Add 2 tsp melted butter, mix. Place and press in a serving dish. Refrigerate for 45 minutes until firm. Follow the recipe.

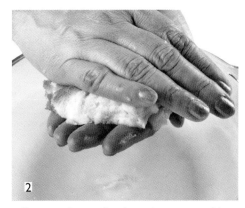

- Remove immediately and squeeze with your palms.

WHILE MAKING DESSERTS

Whipped Cream

- Mix 1¼ cups chilled heavy cream with ¼ cup chilled milk.

- Add 2 tbsp confectioners' sugar and 2 tsp rose water. Blend in a food processor until semi-thick.

- Use as required in the recipe and consume within 24 hours.

Sugar Syrup

- Mix ¾ cup sugar with ¼ cup water in a shallow pan and bring to a boil, on low heat, stirring occasionally.

- To check the string, place a drop of syrup on a plate.

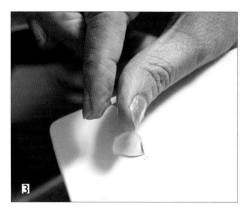

- Check between thumb and index finger.

WHIPPED CREAM TIPS
- Use chilled heavy cream and milk to avoid curdling.
- Over blending may also lead to separation of butter from cream-milk mixture.
- For variation, use ½ tsp vanilla essence instead of rose water.

CUSTARD TIPS
- Custard powder should be mixed with room temperature milk otherwise it tends to get lumpy.

SUGAR SYRUP TIPS
- **One-string consistency**: a thin string is formed when testing the sugar syrup between thumb and index finger.
- **Two-string consistency**: when testing the sugar syrup between thumb and index finger, two strings are formed.

KHOYA TIPS
- After milk is reduced to about one fourth the amount, stir constantly to avoid sticking to the bottom of the pan,, otherwise it may have a burned smell.

Custard

- Take 5 cups milk. Mix 4 tbsp custard powder in ½ cup milk.

- Boil the remaining 4½ cups milk with 4 tbsp sugar.

- Pour the custard mixture to the boiling milk, stirring constantly.

Khoya (Whole-milk Fudge)

6¼ cups Whole milk, unsweetened

Method:
Bring milk to a boil in a non-stick pan. Cook unti it reduces to a solid, soft mass over moderate heat, stirring frequently. Let cool to room temperature.

- Turn off the heat after one boil. Remove, keep aside to cool. Serve chilled.

Jello Making

- Mix 2 cups of pulp-free orange juice and 2 tbsps Agar agar (China Grass) flakes.

- Cook on low heat and bring to a boil, stirring constantly.

- Let it set in the fridge until firm. Remove with a knife or spoon. Serve chilled.

PEELING AND CHOPPING NUTS

1

- Soak ½ cup almonds in 1½ cups water for 8 hours, covered.

1

- Soak ½ cup pistachios in 1½ cups water for 8 hours, covered.

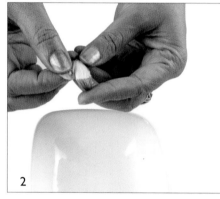

2

- Peel.

2

- Peel.

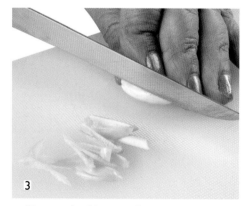

3

- Chop and refrigerate. Consume within 2 days.

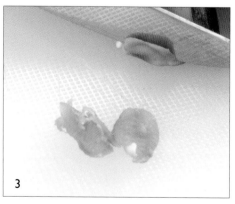

3

- Chop and refrigerate. Consume within 2 days.

TIP

- Peeled almonds and pistachios taste better than unpeeled in Indian desserts.

MAKING SAFFRON CARDAMOM POWDER

1

• Seed 8 cardamom pods.

2

• Add ¼ tsp saffron strands.

• Use quantities as indicated in each recipe.
• Saffron and cardamom can also be
  pounded individually.
• It can also be stored in the refrigerator
  for 15 days.

3

• Pound both to a fine powder.

MEAL MENUS

1

DRINK, SALAD & APPETIZER
Minty Lemonade
Hara Bhara Nimbu Pani — 25
Salad Medley with Jaggery Dressing
Mila Jula Salaad — 37
Cottage Cheese Fritters
Paneer Pakodi — 44

MAIN COURSE
Lentil Dumplings and Spinach in Yogurt Sauce
Magori Palak ki Kadi — 77
Curried Kidney Beans
Rajmah — 79
Potatoes and Bell Pepper
Aloo Shimla Mirch — 82
Corn a la Cilantro
Dhaniyawale Makai ke Dane — 96

RICE & BREADS
Cumin Pilaf
Jeera Pulao — 124
Spicy Indian Bread
Masala Paratha — 136
Plain Indian Bread
Sada Roti — 137

ACCOMPANIMENT
Tempered Liquid Buttermilk
Tarka Mattha — 152

DESSERT
Carrot Pudding
Gajar ka Halwa — 173

2

DRINKS, SALADS & APPETIZER
Tomato Cucumber Melody
Tamatar Khira Lajawab — 26
Tomato and Cottage Cheese Salad
Tamatar aur Masala Paneer Salaad — 39
Sago Cutlets
Sabu Dana Vada — 56

MAIN COURSE
Dumplings in Spicy Yogurt Sauce
Kadi Pakodi — 74
Fenugreek Flavored Lentil
Urad Chana aur Methi Dal — 80
Healthy Leafy Vegetables
Hara Saag — 102
Mixed Vegetables with Cottage Cheese
Sabz Paneer — 106

RICE & BREADS
Plain Rice
Crisp Indian Bread
Khasta Roti — 139
Plain Indian Bread
Sada Roti — 137

ACCOMPANIMENT
Plain Yogurt

DESSERT
Fruit and Custard Pudding
Thanda Phalon ka Custard — 169

3

DRINK, SALAD & APPETIZER
Iced Tea
Sharbati Chai — 21
Corn Salad
Makai Salaad — 34
Crispy Baby Corn
Chhote Karare Bhutte — 43

MAIN COURSE
Roasted Spiced Eggplant
Baingan Bharta — 90
Stuffed Green Chilies
Bharwa Mirchi — 98
Curried Colocasia
Rasedar Arvi — 110
Spicy Chickpeas
Chana Masala — 112

RICE
Fenugreek Flavored Cottage Cheese Pilaf
Methi Paneer Pulao — 126

ACCOMPANIMENT
Spinach Flavored Yogurt
Palak Raita — 153

DESSERT
Vermicelli Pudding
Sewai ki Kheer — 171

4

DRINK, SALAD & APPETIZER

Tender Coconut Cooler

Daab Shikanji   24

Chickpea Salad

Kabuli Chana Salaad   33

Floret Fritters

Gobi Pakodi   45

MAIN COURSE

Spiced Green Bananas in Yogurt Curry

Kele ki Kadi   73

Beans with Baby Corn

Beans aur Chhote Bhutte   94

Curried Lotus Stem

Sookhi Kamal Kakri   103

Cottage Cheese with Peas in Gravy

Mattar Paneer   117

BREAD

Flaky Mint Bread

Lachchedar Paratha   134

Plain Indian Bread

Sada Roti   137

ACCOMPANIMENT

Fruity Yogurt

Anar aur Ananas Raita   147

DESSERT

Sunrise Pudding

Boondi Bake   168

5

DRINK, SALAD & STARTER

Spiced Yogurt Drink

Mattha   20

Sweet Potato and Bean Sprout Salad

Chatpata Shakarkandi Salaad   38

Stuffed Chili Fritters

Bharwa Mirchi ki Pakodi   47

MAIN COURSE

Stuffed Okra

Bharwa Bhindi   93

Hot Potato Curry

Aloo ka Jhol   108

Lentil Dumplings with Fenugreek and Peas

Methi Magori Mattar   118

RICE & BREAD

Mixed Vegetable Pilaf

Sabz Pulao   127

Carom Spiced Puffs

Namak Ajwain ki Puri   142

ACCOMPANIMENT

Lentil Dumplings in Creamy Yogurt

Dahi Pakodi   149

DESSERT

Indian Rice Pudding

Chawal ki Kheer   170

6

DRINK, SALAD & STARTER

Mango Mocktail

Aam Panna   22

Potato and Pickled Onion Salad

Aloo Pyaz, Sirkewale   36

Potato Fritters

Aloo Pakodi   46

MAIN COURSE

Spicy Green Lentil

Sabut Moong ki Dal   81

Cauliflower and Potatoes

Aloo Gobi   88

Bottle Gourd Dumplings in Tomato Gravy

Lauki Kofta   114

Bitter Sweet Creamy Peas

Methi Malai Mattar   119

RICE & BREAD

Corn Pilaf

Bhutte ka Pulao   123

Plain Indian Bread

Sada Roti   137

Fenugreek Bread

Besan Methi Roti   138

ACCOMPANIMENT

Yogurt with Lentil Pearls

Boondi Raita   148

DESSERT

Saffron Pistachio Delight

Kesar Pista Kulfi   175

COMMON ACCOMPANIMENTS

Green Chutney

Hari Chutney   154

Jaggery Flavored Mango Chutney

Aam ki Launji   158

Lemon Flavored Ginger

Nimbu ka Adrak   160

Tangy Radish Flakes

Mooli ka Kas   161

Green Chili Pickle

Hari Mirch ka Achaar   162

SNACK MENUS

1

Spicy Indian Puffs
Pani Puri   64
Spicy Chaat Bowls
Chaat Katori   66
Spicy Potato Patties
Chatpati Aloo Tikki   57
Lentil Dumplings in Creamy Yogurt
Dahi Pakodi   149
Green Chutney
Hari Chutney   154
Sweet Chutney
Meethi Chutney   157

2

Lentil Pancakes
Moong Dal Cheela   51
Savory Rice Flakes
Poha   60
Sago Cutlets
Sabu Dana Vada   56
Mushroom Cheese Toast
Khumbi Toast   54
Green Chutney
Hari Chutney   154
Sweet Chutney
Meethi Chutney   157

3

Toasted Garden Sandwiches
Hara Bhara Toast   55
Potato Fritters
Aloo Pakodi   46
Spicy Semolina
Rawa Upma   62
Dry Green Lentil
Sookhi Moong Dal   50
Green Chutney
Hari Chutney   154
Sweet Chutney
Meethi Chutney   157

4

Vegetable Vermicelli
Sabzdar Sewai   63
Savory Lentil Cakes
Chatpata Dhokla   52
Corn on Toast
Karare Makai Pav   42
Savory Semolina Cakes
Rawa Idli   61
Coconut Chutney
Nariyal ki Chutney   156
Green Chutney
Hari Chutney   154

GLOSSARY OF FOOD AND COOKING TERMS

Bake — To cook in the oven by dry heat.

Batter — A mixture of flour, liquid, and sometimes other ingredients of a thin, creamy consistency.

Blend — To mix together thoroughly two or more ingredients.

Coat — To cover food that is to be deep-fried with batter.

Curdle — To separate milk into yogurt and whey by acid or excessive heat.

Deep-fry — Sufficient oil is used to cover the food completely. The pan used must be deep enough to be only half full of oil before the food is added.

Fry — To cook in hot oil.

Garnish — An edible decoration added to a dish to improve its appearance.

Grease — To coat the surface of a dish or tin with fat to prevent food from sticking to it.

Grind — To reduce hard food such as legumes, lentils, spices, and so forth, to a fine or coarse paste in a grinder or blender.

Knead — To work a dough by hand or machine until smooth.

Purée — To press food through a fine sieve or blend it in a blender or food processor to a smooth, thick mixture.

Sauté — To cook in an open pan in hot, shallow fat, tossing the food to prevent it from sticking.

Seasoning — Salt, pepper, spices, herbs, and so forth, added to give depth of flavor.

Shallow-fry — A small quantity of fat is used, in a shallow pan. The food must be turned halfway through to cook both sides.

Simmer — To boil gently on low heat.

Steam — To cook food in steam. Generally food to be steamed is put in a perforated container which is placed above a pan of boiling water. The food should not come in contact with the water.

Stir-fry — To fry rapidly while stirring and tossing.

Stock — Liquid produced when vegetables are simmered in water with herbs and spices for several hours.

Syrup — A concentrated solution of sugar in water.

Temper — To fry spices and flavorings in hot oil or clarified butter, and to pour this over the main preparation.

Whisk — To beat rapidly and introduce air into a light mixture; such as yogurt.

Queen of the Outback Margaret Way and new
Australian talent Michelle Douglas bring you
two tales of brave heroines, gorgeous heroes
and adorable families.

Enjoy our new 2-in-1 editions of stories
by your favourite authors—

for double the romance!

with

CATTLE BARON: NANNY NEEDED
by Margaret Way

BACHELOR DAD ON HER DOORSTEP
by Michelle Douglas

Dear Reader

We hope you like our new look and format!

We want to give you more value for your money—and the same great stories from your favourite authors! Now, each month, we're offering you two Mills & Boon® Romance volumes. Each volume will include two stories. This month:

Sizzling Australian heroes will melt your heart…

CATTLE BARON: NANNY NEEDED
by Margaret Way

&

BACHELOR DAD ON HER DOORSTEP
by Michelle Douglas

* * *

Hot bosses are on the agenda in…

GREEK BOSS, DREAM PROPOSAL
by Barbara McMahon

&

BOARDROOM BABY SURPRISE
by Jackie Braun

For more information on our makeover, and to buy other Romance stories that are exclusive to the website and the Mills & Boon Bookclub, please visit: www.millsandboon.co.uk.

The other titles available this month are: **HIRED: CINDERELLA CHEF** by Myrna Mackenzie and **MISS MAPLE AND THE PLAYBOY** by Cara Colter.

Best wishes

Kimberley Young

Senior Editor, Mills & Boon® Romance

CATTLE BARON: NANNY NEEDED

BY

MARGARET WAY

® MILLS & BOON®

First published in Great Britain 2009
Harlequin Mills & Boon Limited,
Eton House, 18-24 Paradise Road, Richmond, Surrey TW9 1SR

© Margaret Way Pty., Ltd. 2009

ISBN: 978 0 263 86958 3

Set in Times Roman 12½ on 14 pt
02-0809-55098

Harlequin Mills & Boon policy is to use papers that are natural, renewable and recyclable products and made from wood grown in sustainable forests. The logging and manufacturing process conform to the legal environmental regulations of the country of origin.

Printed and bound in Spain
by Litografia Rosés, S.A., Barcelona

Margaret Way, a definite Leo, was born and raised in the sub-tropical River City of Brisbane, capital of the Sunshine State of Queensland. A Conservatorium trained pianist, teacher, accompanist and vocal coach, her musical career came to an unexpected end when she took up writing, initially as a fun thing to do. She currently lives in a harbourside apartment at beautiful Raby Bay, a thirty-minute drive from the state capital, where she loves dining al fresco on her plant-filled balcony. It overlooks a translucent green marina filled with all manner of pleasure craft—from motor cruisers costing millions of dollars and big, graceful yachts with carved masts, standing tall against the cloudless blue sky, to little bay runabouts. No one and nothing is in a mad rush, and she finds the laid-back village atmosphere very conducive to her writing. With well over 100 books to her credit, she still believes her best is yet to come.

Recent books by the same author:

BRIDE AT BRIAR'S RIDGE*
WEDDING AT WANGAREE VALLEY*
CATTLE RANCHER, SECRET SON
PROMOTED: NANNY TO WIFE†
CATTLE RANCHER, CONVENIENT WIFE†

Barons of the Outback duet
†*Outback Marriages* duet

CHAPTER ONE

A SATURDAY afternoon in late spring. October in the Southern Hemisphere.

Glorious sunshine, vibrant blue sky, the sweet warbling of a thousand unseen birds sheltering in the cool density of trees. A white limousine pulled up outside the lovely old Anglican church of St Cecilia's, one in a stately procession bearing guests to the "Wedding of the Year". As a caption, "Wedding of the Year" was more hackneyed than most, but that was how Zara Fraser, society columnist for the *Weekend Mail*, phrased it at the behest of her boss, a golfing pal of Sir Clive Erskine, the bride's grandfather. Be that as it may, it was difficult for Zara to quibble. This was definitely a *big* society wedding.

Nearly everyone on the bride's guest list was mega-rich; on the bridegroom's side the usual sprinkling of savvy young lawyers with their dressed-to-the-teeth partners, a lesser sprinkling of everyday folk struggling with the kids, the mortgage and keeping it all together. As for the bride's soon-to-be in-laws, they had taken off on a round trip to Antarctica and thus couldn't attend. It had been suggested at a mid-week dinner party that they had deliberately planned their trip to coincide with the wedding because their only son hadn't lived up to the rules of behaviour they had endeavoured to instil in him. Doing the right thing was what got one through life. What today's bridegroom was doing wasn't right in anyone's book. The word on the street was that the groom had sunk lower than a worm shuffling under a leaf.

Two hundred people had been invited to the church and two hundred and *one* were in attendance. Almost as many more had been invited along to the grand reception. The setting was idyllic. The magnificent shade trees, the jacarandas, the golden shower trees and the apple-blossom cassias were in radiant bloom all over the city, lifting the heart with their splendour. A particularly lovely jacaranda—the grass ringing the tree with spent lavender-blue blossom—dominated the precinct of the old Gothic-style church with its pointed arches and tall slender columns and much admired medieval-style marble pulpit. To either side of the stone building with its token buttresses lay large circular flower beds that literally teemed with fragrant pink roses. A picture-book setting for a picture-book wedding.

To one person at least—the *uninvited* guest—the whole thing was nothing less than a ghastly nightmare.

That person now emerged so gracefully from the white limousine that she appeared to flow out of it, quite mesmerizing to watch. She accepted a hand from the uniformed chauffeur, who couldn't believe his luck that his boss had given him such a plum assignment. The young woman looked amazing—tall, very slender, a vision of female perfection and glamour. Looking to neither left nor right, she moved off in her sexy stilettos towards the short flight of stone steps that led to the church portals.

The wedding guests who alighted from the luxury limousines behind her, however, were frozen in their tracks. They gawped after her, some panic stricken, some downright intrigued.

"Surely that's…?"

"It couldn't be." Shock and a touch of gleeful anticipation.

"She's right, you know. It is!"

"For God's sake!" A substantial matron, Rosemary Erskine, mother of the bride, wearing an amazing electric-blue hat sprouting peacock feathers, gasped, "Cal, you have to *do* something!" She looked to the tall, commanding young man at her side as though if anyone could save the situation he could.

"What's the problem, Rosemary?" Callum MacFarlane, Outback cattle baron and a cousin to the bride, was busy watching the progress of a walking work of art. He had no idea who the goddess was, though he was aware that all eyes were riveted on her. Why not? She looked pretty darn good to him. In fact she would take a man's breath away. Not *him*, mercifully. He had gained immunity to beautiful women the hard way. But there was no harm in *looking*, surely?

Maybe Rosemary was het up because the latest arrival looked dead set to outshine Georgie, the bride? Or was it something far more problematic? The only thing that could account for such a reaction was the ex-fiancée had turned up. He'd been assured that she was behaving impeccably, so that couldn't be it. So publicly humiliated that she was bound to have taken off for the wilds of New Guinea. This young woman was beautifully dressed in what was obviously a couture two-piece suit of an exquisite shade of pink. A dream of a picture hat shaded her head and face from the hot rays of the sun, one side weighed down by full blown silk roses in pink and cream. Such a hat, while affording protection, offered tantalizing glimpses of her classically beautiful face with a truly exquisite nose. The sort of nose women paid cosmetic surgeons a fortune to try to recreate.

The trouble was that most people, unlike Cal MacFarlane whose Channel Country cattle station Jingala was just about as far off the map as one could get, were familiar with that face. They fixated—in the case of the male viewer salivated—on it every week night on television when she read the six o'clock news with Jack Matthews, the long-time male presenter who behind the scenes gave Ms Wyatt a bad time.

"It's that dreadful Amber Wyatt!" Rosemary hissed, her formidable face working tightly. Not a pleasant sight. This was a woman who was known to make people's hair stand on end.

Well, fancy that! Cal had to wrench himself away from imagining what it would be like to have a woman like the vision in front of him. Despite his multiple defensive shields he felt a lunge of desire; swiftly killed it. Euphoria only lasted the proverbial fifteen minutes anyway.

"Hell, Cal!" A relative standing just behind him came to Rosemary's aid. "*Everyone* knows who she is. She's—"

"Okay, okay, I've got it!"

So this seriously stunning young woman with what had to be the best pair of legs in the country was the woman Sean Sinclair, the bridegroom, had thrown over for Georgette. *Would wonders never cease?* It had fortune-hunting stamped all over it. Ms Amber Wyatt had been *jilted*. One had only to be jilted once, never to get it out of the system, he reflected grimly, his mind going off on a tangent. His ex-fiancée, Brooke Rowlands, had played as dirty as a woman could get. Like some knight of old, he had let her get away with it. The betrayal had happened while he'd been in Japan, part of a trade delegation. Brooke had taken a little holiday at the swank Oriental Hotel in Bangkok with one of his polo buddies. Ex-buddy. Ex-fiancée. He might have shaken off what black thoughts remained over that fiasco, but he had no illusions left about women.

No illusions about Sinclair either. He was a fortune-hunter. As fond as he was of Georgie, for her to believe she had utterly bewitched a man into abandoning a woman as beautiful as Amber Wyatt was as probable as her knocking back a previous proposal from George Clooney.

Cal had heard mentioned at last night's family dinner that Ms Wyatt had won an award for a story about street kids, wringing admissions and follow-up promises from the Government. She should feel good about that. Nevertheless, in coming here today she had flagrantly disregarded the rules of wedding etiquette. How rash was that? And Rosemary had chosen him to be the Enforcer. This totally unexpected appearance was giving quite a few of his relatives a bad case of the jitters. Just when they'd thought the whole thing had been sorted out:

Enter the ex-fiancée.

How could he do this to me? Amber was experiencing a brief moment of wanting to turn tail and run.

The malicious gods up there, the ones who toyed with human lives, would be expecting it, but that wasn't going to happen. She was determined on keeping a lid on her emotions, even if this was possibly the most foolish and, let's face it, the most *unacceptable* thing she'd ever done. Gatecrashing weddings was a serious breach of the rules, even for a fiancée cruelly dumped. She put it down to post traumatic stress. PTS was big these days. Even the courts listened.

Giving no outward sign of her nerves, she kept moving in line up the stone flight of steps. This was the very church where they had planned their own wedding. It was unbelievably callous. Sean couldn't be allowed to get off scot-free. For every crime, one had to expect punishment. The bride had experienced no sense of guilt either at stealing another woman's man. That put her on the hit list as well.

There was a shake in her now ringless hands. Of course she had sent the damned thing back by courier. Probably if she'd had the stone checked out she would have found it was a zircon. To counteract her tremulousness, she clasped the chain of her pink Chanel shoulder bag for support. She needed to be as cool as a cucumber to pull this off. There would be some satisfaction in making him cringe. Plenty of women, so cruelly jilted, had been known to run over their ex in a car, then try it in Reverse. She had an idea of herself that precluded violence.

But, given the despicable behaviour of Sean and his bride, a frisson of fright was well within her parameters of revenge.

Payback time.

She had just the moment picked out. The *symbolic* moment when the Bishop, revelling in a role he was famous for, began to intone…. "I am required to ask anyone present who knows a reason why these persons may not lawfully marry, to declare it now."

That was her cue to rise. At near six feet in her stilettos it would be difficult not to spot her. Then, when all necks were craned and unbelieving eyes were focused on her, she would calmly turn and walk out of the church, leaving the guests either bitterly disappointed that there hadn't been more drama or aghast at such an assault on wedding etiquette.

All she had to do now was get past the ushers and inside the church. Though she kept her eyes trained ahead, she was aware that her presence was causing a stir. Little whispers wafted to her on the rose-scented breeze.

" Oh, goodness, it's Amber Wyatt!"

"Has she got some guts, or hasn't she?" Admiration there from a sister-at-arms.

"If I were her I'd kill myself, poor thing!"

Come on, why should I kill myself? Amber reasoned. *I haven't done a thing wrong. Wrong has been done to me, just when life was going so great.* God, she felt ill. Buck up, Amber. It won't be much longer. She was the sort of person who regularly gave herself pep talks. Hundreds of them of late. She was dressed to kill. Confidence in how one looked always helped. One couldn't pity her and gape open-mouthed in admiration simultaneously. Her suit was the *exact* shade of pink that complemented her hair—neither red nor gold nor copper but a combination of all three.

"We just have to call this little angel Amber!"

That had been her darling dad, holding his brand-new daughter in his adoring arms.

So Amber she was, though her bright, eye-catching hair was all but hidden by her masterpiece of a hat. It offered a modicum of camouflage. Her accessories were colour co-ordinated, perfect. The whole outfit had cost her way too much money, but her pride demanded she look staggeringly glamorous. She wouldn't have been content with anything less. Her friend Jono, gay man about town who lived in the penthouse apartment above her and charged unheard of prices for writing other people's software programs, a man who could be counted on to deliver a totally reliable verdict when it came to fashion, had given her the thumbs up and a spontaneous, "Wow!"

Ironically, it was her friend, the society columnist Zara Fraser, who had first broken the news to her...

* * *

She sat up in bed, bracing herself on one elbow as she made a grab for the phone. She nearly rapped, Who the blazes is this? but stopped just in time. There was a remote possibility it could be her boss. The digital clock on her bedside table read: A.M. 5.35. To make it worse, it was Sunday—her morning to sleep in. It couldn't be Sean, although she hadn't spoken to him for a few days. He wouldn't ring at this time. Sean was safely in London on business, or as safe as one could be in the great cities of the world these scary days. Immediately the thought crossed her mind, she started to panic.

"Hi Amby?"

"Who else do you suppose? Is that you, Zee?"

"Jeez, love, I know it's early. But you have to hear this.'

"If you're ringing to tell me you've found Mr Right again, don't dare put him on. I'm not in the mood."

None of the usual infectious giggles from Zara. "Amby, love, you've got to listen. This is *serious*!"

Amber groaned. "They *all* are. Just remember, men aren't to be trusted."

"Ain't that the truth!" Zara sounded very down-mouthed. "This isn't about me, Amby. It's about *you*. Are you still lying down?"

"No, I'm *not*!" Amber swung her feet to the floor. "Spit it out, Zee. There's a good girl."

"Why should it be *my* destiny to have to tell you?"

Zara moaned. "Okay, there's no easy way to say it, so here I go. Your fiancé, Sean Sinclair—"

Amber was finding it difficult to swallow. "There hasn't been another terrorist attack, Zee, has there? Please God, tell me no!" Disasters could and did come out of the blue.

Zara hastened to reassure her. "Not something as terrible as that, but bad enough on a totally different scale. Trish McGowan, you know Trish, she's in London. She let me know. I didn't get home until after three. I didn't want to wake you then but I couldn't sleep and I couldn't hang on any longer. Wait for it, girl. Sean, *your* fiancé, married Georgette Erskine, Sir Clive Erskine's granddaughter, at a civil ceremony yesterday afternoon London time."

"No kiddin'!" Amber crowed, not for a moment taking her friend seriously. " I know you like your little pranks, but that's pathetic!"

"No joke, Amby. Proof of what a bastard he really is. This will come as a blow to you, but I can't pretend I don't think you haven't had a lucky escape."

Amber fell back on the bed as if she were taking a long backward fall off a cliff. " I suppose there's no question Trish was having a little joke? It has April Fool's Day written all over it."

"No chance, love," Zara said unhappily." It's October. I never had a clue the rat even knew her, did you?"

Recollections were filtering through. "He met her

several times when she came into the office with her granddaddy. Nothing to look at, he told me. All she had going for her was the family fortune."

"*All?*" Zara screeched. "He must have started thinking long and hard about that. Listen, give me twenty minutes and I'll be over. You shouldn't be on your own."

Zara had arrived with freshly baked croissants and genuine Blue Mountain coffee. Zara had been wonderful to her. So had lots of other people, though inevitably there were some—like her co-newsreader— who got a warped pleasure out of seeing her suffer such a public king hit. This follow-up wedding ceremony was being held so the happy couple could seek God's blessing. If they got it, God wouldn't be winning any Brownie points with her. It was even possible Sir Clive Erskine had God onside.

The Erskines purported to be a pious bunch. Sir Clive was a billionaire who owned coal mines, gold mines, luxury beach resorts, shopping centres, a string of prize-winning racehorses, country newspapers, and had been the biggest contributor to the Cathedral restoration fund. The bridegroom, Sean Sinclair, was an associate with the blue chip law firm of Langley, Lynch & Pullman, a high profile practice whose clientele included major mining companies, multinationals and billionaires like Sir Clive Erskine. The bridegroom, smart and ambitious, was very good-looking if one found "boyish" attractive. Most women did. He had thick floppy golden-brown hair, dark blue eyes and an engaging whimsical smile. He wasn't terribly tall but tall enough at five foot ten. The bride wouldn't have struck even her mother as pretty, but she was said to be a very nice person, which counted for a lot.

How could that be? Georgie Erskine had stolen another woman's man right from under her nose. Surely that made her a man-eater? No question it was immeasurably better to be from an immensely wealthy family than to be a working woman, however high on the ratings. One way or the other, Georgette Erskine thoroughly deserved the man who awaited her at the altar.

No one better placed than I am to sit in judgement, Amber thought bleakly. *Why can't I hate him? I want to hate him, but I can't.* Her own nature was betraying her. Was it somehow *her* fault? What had she done wrong? Was she too critical? Too ready to debate the issues of the day, instead of falling into line with Sean's play safe opinions? Sean liked to keep his finger on the politically expedient pulse. But she was an intelligent woman with strong opinions of her own. She had even gained a reputation for defending the underdog, the little guy. There was the story last year that had won her an award. Whatever the problem, Sean should have been honourable enough to tell her. He should have broken off their engagement, then waited at least a few months before asking another woman to be his wife. She couldn't have done to him what he had done so callously to her. Sean had only worn the façade of an honourable man…

Late wedding guests, cutting it fine, were still arriving. Up ahead, Amber could see the ushers, decked out in morning suits. Each wore a white rosebud in their lapel. She had to get past them, though by now she was feeling like a clockwork doll badly in need of a rewind. At least they weren't burly bouncers, just good-looking youngsters probably just out of school or at university. They would have been given a list of guests, although they weren't holding anything in their hands. Maybe they would only check on guests arriving at the reception, which was being held in a leading city hotel.

No matter what, nothing was going to stop her getting into that church.

Even as Amber plotted, a few feet behind her Cal MacFarlane considered ways and means of controlling a potentially inflammable situation. He couldn't carry Ms Wyatt off screaming. He couldn't very well slap her into a pair of handcuffs and make a citizen's arrest, but it should be possible to avert a scene. He wished he could see her face properly. She had a beautiful body. Tall and willowy. She held her head high and kept her back straight. She moved as a dancer would. She looked enormously chic. In fact she was making the women around her look *ordinary*, although they had obviously gone to considerable pains over their wedding finery. The brim of the hat was perhaps a bit too wide. It called to mind the picture hats his beautiful mother had used to wear before she ran off with the man he had affectionately called "Uncle Jeff" for much of his childhood. His eyes glittered with the tide of memory even if he had grown many protective layers of skin.

One of the ushers had stopped her. A challenge, or did he want a close-up of the goddess? Rosemary prodded him so hard in the back, he actually winced. "Callum, I beg of you, see to it."

Rosemary, mercifully not a blood relative, always had that combative look. Had he really travelled a thousand miles and more for this? He'd only met Sinclair the night before and had barely been able to disguise his scorn for the man. Whatever Georgie saw in Sinclair was invisible to him. Of course with Sinclair it was all about money. Money was the fuel that drove everything. Follow the money. Way to go. Money and ambition. Sinclair was a covetous guy.

"We just looked at each other and fell in love!" Georgie had told him, her myopic grey eyes full of stars. The truth was that Georgie was overwhelmed to be loved—and had been given the heaven-sent opportunity to get away from her mother. *"I'm so desper-*

ately sorry we had to hurt Sean's ex-fiancée but once he met me he knew he couldn't go through with it."

"Pity the two of you didn't bother to tell her," he had challenged her squarely but Georgie hadn't been able to come up with a ready answer. Maybe too intellectual a question? It was all he could do not to enquire if being an heiress had anything to do with it. He wondered how long Georgie would go on hiding that fact from herself? Inwardly disgusted, Cal made a swift charge up the few remaining stone steps, lifting a hand in greeting to another young cousin who beamed at him. Nice kid, Tim. He'd always enjoyed having him out to Jingala, the MacFarlane ancestral desert stronghold, for holidays.

"How's it going, Tim?"

"Great, just great, Cal," the young fellow responded, feeling mightily relieved to see his dynamic cousin who so emanated authority. "I was just about to ask this lady…"

Cal turned away from his hero worshipping young cousin to centre his gaze on the "loose cannon".

A voice in his head spoke as loud and clear as any oracle: *This, MacFarlane, is your kind of woman.*

The realisation made his whole body tense. Wouldn't that be one hell of a thing—to get involved with Ms Wyatt, a woman on the rebound? Yet he swore a leap of something extraordinary passed between them—something well outside an eroticized thrill. *Recognition?* Such things happened. Instantaneous connection? The wise man would do well to ignore the phenomenon. The wise woman too. The question remained. How in the world had Sinclair given up this goddess for Georgie, even if Georgie came draped in diamonds, rubies and pearls?

Cal held the goddess's gaze for long measuring seconds, more entranced than he cared to be. Even his cynical old heart seemed to have gone into temporary meltdown. He reined himself in. The sweetest woman could suck the life out of a man, as his bolter mother had sucked the life out of his dad.

"Sorry I'm late. I got held up by a phone call." He took her arm in a light grasp, disturbed to find she was trembling.

Yet she had the wit to reply smoothly, "No problem." If that weren't enough, she reached up and calmly kissed his cheek. "As you can see, I made it on my own."

"You look wonderful!" He didn't have to strain to say that.

"Thank you so much." She gave him a smile that would have taken most men's breath away.

Okay, so that smile affected him! Lucky for him he'd built up an immunity to beautiful women with smiles like the sunrise.

"So do you," she returned the compliment. "I've rarely seen a man wear a morning suit so well." She had no difficulty in acknowledging the simple truth. He was a very handsome man in a style that hitherto hadn't been her cup of tea. She went for a *gentler* look. If Sean's looks were often described as "boyish", this guy was *hard set handsome*, with electricity crackling all around him. Strong cleft chin. Very tall, very lean with a strongly built frame. Not *macho*. Nothing as self-conscious or as swaggering as that. Here was a guy who was strong in every sense of the word. Maybe too aggressively *male* for her taste. And how exactly was he eyeing her?

"Shall we go in?" Cal suggested smoothly. Obviously they couldn't go back down the steps. She had exquisite creamy skin and the nearest thing he'd seen to golden eyes. It was the oddest thing, but he wanted to sweep off that confounded hat so he could see her hair, which appeared to be a wonderful vibrant bright copper…no, amber, which no doubt accounted for her name.

"Just what I was thinking," she agreed in a sweetly accommodating voice.

It didn't fool him one bit. This was one beautiful woman laden with *intent*. She was here for one singular purpose. To create an almighty stir. So far she was doing extremely well. Little whispers were being passed from one wedding guest to another. There was a lot of compulsive head swivelling, short gasps. Some were staring openly, making no bones about their avid interest. Not that he altogether blamed her for doing this. It took a lot of nerve. But it was his job to stop her. It must have been appalling for Amber Wyatt, squarely in the public eye, to be so publicly humiliated. Sinclair must come from a long line of jackals.

"See you later on, Tim," he called to his young cousin, aware that Tim was looking after them in wonderment as he swept this gutsy, downright fool-hardy young woman inside the church.

Who is he? Amber, despite appearances, was only just managing to keep her nerve. She had to admit this guy was something to behold—and chock-a-block with surprises. She had fully expected to be exposed as a woman in the commission of a serious crime, yet he was acting as though they were a couple. Did he feel desperately sorry for her? Or was he someone who would bundle her out of a side door after a few chastening words? It took her roughly ten seconds to hit on the last option. He wouldn't have much difficulty doing it. He was several inches over six feet and looked superbly fit. She could see the ripple of lean muscle beneath the close fit of his jacket. He was enormously self-assured. Probably had every reason to be. The un-shakeable air of male supremacy that generally put her teeth on edge was well in evidence. It warned against any outrageous behaviour on her part. That and a certain glitter in his eyes. They were—well— *lovely*, though he would probably cringe to hear that. Shots of sparkling colour in his bronzed face—

the cool green of one of her favourite gemstones, the peridot. She couldn't help registering that not only was the colour remarkable, so too was the intensity.

One thing was certain. She had never seen him before in her life. She'd remember. She liked the fact that she had to tilt her head to look up at him. Not something she did every day. Sean had been forever asking her to wear low heels or even flatties, when she was a girl for whom high heels were not only a necessity but a passion.

Now that her eyes had adjusted to the cool interior of the church after the brilliant sunshine outside, she could see that it was beautifully decorated. She bit down hard on her lip lest a cry escape her.

Even so, it did. "Aah!"

"You'll get through it," he told her, his expression Byronic.

"How did I ever convince myself I loved him? Why did I choose him of all the men in the world to marry?" she wailed.

"Seemed like a good idea at the time? You couldn't have been short of other offers."

"So what does that say about me? I'm a very poor judge of character?" Zara, unfairly regarded by some as an airhead, had seen through him right from the beginning.

"Maybe love—or what passes f r it—truly is blind."

"It *wasn't* love." She shook her head. More being

in love with love. The constant awareness that her biological clock was ticking away? She was twenty-six. She wanted kids. She loved children and they loved her. She had four godchildren at the last count. She was a real favourite with her friends. A marvellous, trustworthy babysitter.

Time to break off her philosophical meanderings with her new best friend.

Masses and masses of white and soft cream flowers shimmered before her distressed eyes. Roses, lilies, peonies, double cream lisianthus, carnations, gladiolus and the exquisitely delicate ivory-white petals of the Phalaenopsis orchids, all wonderfully and inventively arranged. And oh, the perfume! The rows of dark polished pews were lavishly beribboned in white and cream taffeta.

Amber just stood there, letting it all overwhelm her.

Her rescuer drew her to one side as the wedding guests continued to stream in. Amber watched dazedly as he acknowledged this one and that, giving what appeared to be a reassuring inclination of his head to a stony-faced society matron in a drop-dead ghastly misfit of a hat. If looks could annihilate, Amber was sure she would be gasping her last breath. But of course! It was the bride's mother. As such, didn't she have a right to demand Amber be thrown out? Mrs Rosemary Erskine in the flesh was an awesome sight.

It was all so unreal she might have been having

an out of body experience. And who was this man
who kept a light but *secure* rein on her? Obviously,
he was well known. His thick crow-black hair, swept
back from a high brow, had a decided deep wave that
was clipped to control. The bronze of his skin wasn't
fake. That tan came from a life in the sun. The light
grey morning suit, which a lot of men couldn't successfully carry off, only served to accentuate his
height, width of shoulder and the natural elegance
of his body. A man of action? He wasn't any man
about town. Impossible to remain anonymous when
you looked like that. He certainly wasn't a friend of
Sean's—his friends tended to be much like
himself—so he had to be from the bride's side.

"Ms Wyatt, isn't it?" His voice, as classy as the
rest of him, broke into her speculations.

"Round one to you. I can't for the life of me
figure out who *you* are and I'm really trying."
Though she spoke banteringly, she felt like a butterfly about to be pinned for his private collection.
Indeed her heart was fluttering like a butterfly
trapped in a cage. He had a beautiful mouth. How
odd that she should even notice. Firm, very clean-
cut, the rims slightly raised. He was someone Zee
would describe as *drop dead sexy*. She was almost
on the point of conceding that herself.

She wondered what he would look like when he
smiled. Teeth were important to her. Good teeth.
Even on this humiliating day, a woman publicly

scorned, she couldn't seem to take her eyes off a perfect stranger. But then that was her training, she reassured herself. Her life as a journalist was spent checking people out, remembering faces. She was naturally observant.

"Cal MacFarlane," he introduced himself. "I'm the bride's cousin."

Her heart shook. But she wasn't ready to buckle. Instead, she levelled him with a dubious stare. "Really? You don't look in the least like her." He looked more like that British actor Clive Owen. The same uber-male aura.

"I'm a MacFarlane, but we do share a grandfather, Sir Clive Erskine."

"Ah, yes, Sir Clive." She nibbled on her lower lip as her memory bank opened up. "You're the Cattle Baron, right?" She was tuned in to a degree.

"Exactly." Amusement cut sexy little grooves into the corners of his mouth. "You're awfully audacious coming here, aren't you, Ms Wyatt?"

She decided to wing it. After all, he couldn't be one hundred per cent sure. "How do you know Sean didn't send me an invitation? We were very close up until *very* recently."

"So you intend to go out in a blaze of notoriety?" Her skewed gallantry smote his hard heart.

"Mr MacFarlane, I don't know what you mean." She let some of the sweetness slide. "I'm dedicated to doing the right thing. Or I have been up to date.

And where did it get me? Lighten up. I promise I won't cause any *real* bother."

"You're causing it already," he told her very dryly. "This isn't a joyous occasion, is it? Not for you and not particularly for me. I think, ultimately, my cousin is going to have to pay for marrying Sinclair in more ways than one."

Amber's brows rose. "Sweet Lord!" she said reverently. "You've got Sean's measure already! It took me ages."

"How that must lacerate you."

"It does. I take it you don't like him either?"

He inched her further away from the front doors. "I only met him last night. I fear he may be totally unscrupulous which is one reason why I'm standing here *with* you instead of ushering you out the back."

Her gaze turned appealing. "Come on, you wouldn't do that?"

"Not if we can work something out."

"Actually, I was hoping you wouldn't interfere."

"Haven't I just told you I'm family?" He smiled down into her face.

"Well, I don't need you to feel *sorry* for me." God, what a smile!

"I'm *not* sorry for you. I think you've had a lucky escape. So what are we going to do? Team decision. The bride will be arriving any minute."

"Why, take our seats, of course." She tried to peer around those wide shoulders.

"Tell you what, I'll sit beside you." Humour hovered around his mouth. "How's that?"

"But I wouldn't dream of taking you away from the bosom of your family Mr MacFarlane."

"No problem. On second thoughts, I think we might slip up to the choir loft." He cast a quick glance upwards. "We can't be standing here when Georgie and her entourage arrives. By the sound of the clapping outside, it's about to happen."

"I do love it when they clap," she said bleakly. "Supposing we stand here and goggle. After all, your cousin is the wittiest, prettiest, richest girl in town. And the most underhand. She stole my fiancé—such as he is—right from under my nose."

"And I understand your hurt. But my guess is you'll live to thank her. I suggest the choir loft. *Now*. Move it, Ms Wyatt. I'm quite capable of picking you up."

"What, and fling me over your shoulder?"

"If I have to." He slipped an arm around her waist and steered her towards the curving flight of wooden steps.

"I don't know that I *want* to." She was endeavouring to resist him but not making much headway.

"I don't care what you want. Just *do* it. Sinclair might *deserve* a bloody good fright but he's not worth it."

"Why don't *we* get married?" she turned her head over her shoulder to ask with biting sarcasm.

"Well, you were about to do a hell of a lot worse."

The organist and the well known lyric soprano who had been hired to sing a selection of the bride's favourite hymns looked around, startled, as they made their unexpected appearance in the spacious loft.

"Go ahead. Don't take any notice of us." Amber wiggled her fingers when she really wanted to scream. The cattle baron could ruin everything. "You have a lot to answer for, forcing me up here." She kept it to a mere whisper. His ears were set beautifully against his shapely head. Sean's weren't. That was why he always wore his hair full and floppy.

"You'll thank me in the end. Why don't we find somewhere safe and sit it out? Unless you really do want to see the bride arriving?"

"Don't you?" She was taken aback. "I mean, you're family."

"So I am," he reminded himself. "You look beautiful, by the way." As exquisite as a long-stemmed rose. "All things pass, Ms Wyatt. I'm merely preventing you from making a spectacle of yourself. You could lose your job, do you know that? My grandfather has influence everywhere. I believe he was impressed with the way you've handled yourself up to date. Don't give him cause to damage your career," Cal warned. "My grandfather can be ruthless when opposed or seriously displeased. In coming here today, you've run a big risk."

"Get a lawyer. Sue me." She broke off as the

organist started up with a great ear-splitting fanfare that had her instinctively wrapping her ears with her hands. "God, that's worse than a car alarm," she muttered.

Even the cattle baron, used to stampedes, was looking aghast. "I'm tempted to go over to the balustrade and throw something." The organist, on a roll, belted out the triumphant opening bars of Mendelssohn's *Wedding March*. Why, oh why, did organists have to hit the keys so hard? Pianists didn't hit the keys like that, even at a double forte.

"One can only wonder how the soprano will compete when her time comes," Cal observed sardonically.

"How corny can you get? Mendelssohn!" Tears sprang into Amber's eyes.

"No time to cry," he warned her.

"Mr Tough Guy."

"No, I'm a softie at heart. And no point in taking it out on the composer. Poor old Mendelssohn had to work like everyone else."

"Except your cousin," she reminded him tightly. "She must have fallen through the cracks. So are you going to take a peek at what she looks like? The dress is said to have cost thousands and thousands. I've heard she's carrying a teeny bit of excess weight."

"And who knows how long her pre-wedding diet will last?" He glanced down at the jilted Ms Wyatt, seeing the combination of delicacy, strength and intelligence in her features. He also saw the tremendous upset. She was very lovely. Beauty could sometimes be severe. She was beautiful in a tender way. Not even an old cynic like him could view such a woman with indifference. "Now, don't go worrying about me. I've been to a thousand weddings." He took a firm hold of her hand, just in case she decided to storm the balustrade.

"Is that what made you determined to remain a bachelor? You *are,* aren't you? You don't look tamed at all." In fact he looked as *untamed* as a high coasting eagle.

"I'm comfortable with it," he told her smoothly. "If I didn't want children, I don't think I'd get married at all."

"Same with me. But don't you get lonely, way out there in the Never Never?"

"Don't have time to be lonely," he said.

"I spotted you right off for a hard-working man. Listen, I'm going to take a peek. No one would hear me if I yelled something impolite, with that bloody organ." She stood up and immediately he joined her.

"Promise you'll be good?"

"When *haven't* I been good?" she muttered bitterly.

"Just make sure you don't throw your hat."

"Would you blame me?"

"I prefer you keep it. I love it."

He gave her another one of his smiles. It had the

most peculiar effect on her knees. And his teeth were *perfect*. Beautifully straight and white.

"Keep your chin up, Amber. I may call you Amber? You can't really love a man who crawled out from under a rock."

The bride wore white duchesse satin decorated with crystals, silver beads and thousands of seed pearls, hand-applied. The waist appeared narrow, so she had to be wearing a boned waist-cincher, which made her bosom flare out of the tight-fitting bodice. Her sheer organza veil, complete with long train, was held off her face by a diamond tiara that Amber considered pretentious. The wedding guests didn't. They responded with a spontaneous burst of applause that seemed to go on over-long, even for a billionaire's granddaughter. The bridesmaids—there were four—all taller and slimmer than the bride, wore strapless chiffon gowns in pastel colours with tiny flowers twisted into their faintly messy height-of-fashion hairdos. To add to the spectacle, there was an angelic little flower girl with golden curls carrying a basket brimming with rose petals that she was scattering about the aisle with joyful abandon. The women guests wearing high heels would have to be very careful when the time came for them to step back into the aisle or come a cropper.

"Where did she get the tiara?" Amber whispered. "Borrow it from the Queen?"

"The Queen doesn't give tiaras away, except to her own. Look, why don't you go and sit down? There's nothing here for you but heartache."

Wasn't that the truth?

CHAPTER TWO

THERE was a proud smile on Sean's face. He looked *happy*! Amber had a terrible image of him, cavorting naked on his wedding night, a glass of Bollinger in hand. Sean loved Bollinger. He also loved getting rid of his clothes. Amber forced herself not to make a sound, yet the Cattle Baron took her hand, his grip tight and reassuring. She rather liked the feel of those calluses. What might they be like on a woman's body? In a mystifying way, just having him there was like being wrapped in a security blanket.

Once during the ceremony she felt faint and he put his arm around her. He smelled *wonderful*! And he was being so kind when he didn't look particularly kind. He was a perfect stranger, yet somehow they had made a connection. Either that or he had reasoned that this was the best way to keep her quiet. She couldn't lose sight of the fact that his loyalty lay with his family. Still, he *was* being genuinely kind. Some things you couldn't fake.

* * *

How long was it going to go on? Quite a while more
with the Bishop in the spotlight. A handsome man,
he traded on the fact that he looked a bit like Prince
Philip. She couldn't have borne a long Nuptial
Mass. At least the soprano sang in tune, her high
notes soaring above the hellish din of the organ.
The organist kept moving about on the stool. Why?
Had white ants taken up residence in it? What
should the soprano break into, of all things, but that
old war horse "O Promise Me?"

It was the blackest of black jokes.

When had Sean first started having sex with his
little bride? Amber's mind was seized by that
thought. When had he first realised the Erskine
heiress was his for the taking? Not that Sean was all
that terrific in bed, she found herself suddenly considering, though he had considered himself a real
stud. She, on the other hand, had got around to
thinking that great sex didn't have to mean everything. Well, not absolutely everything. Sean had
been such fun—good company, charming, good-
humoured, though he did tend to laugh a lot at his
own jokes. Then he'd messed up by being miserably
unfaithful. There had been a time when she had
actually considered letting him move in with her. At
least she had been spared that.

When the time came for him to make his vows
he spoke in a calm, strong voice that resonated
around the church. A born actor. The bride's re-

sponses were as soft and gentle as the cooing of doves. Totally dispirited, Amber slumped back against the Cattle Baron. He'd been great. Pity their paths would never, never cross again. The two of them were pressed together like co-conspirators or maybe, to the casual observer, lovers. She just bet if *this* guy committed to a woman he would never betray her.

The moment arrived. The Bishop began to ask that crucial question of the congregation. Surely none had the expectation of hearing a voice yell Stop! Amber felt her heart swell with anger. She had done the best she could all these past weeks. She had behaved impeccably, even when mikes had been thrust under her nose and cameras had gone off in her face, recording her instinctive flinch. She had even gone so far as to wish the couple well. But now? Didn't despicable behaviour count against anyone any more? Had they rewritten all the rules of common decency? It wasn't that long ago that she could have sued him for breach of promise. Surely some degree of payback was in order? Sean was lucky she was an upright citizen and not some member of a notorious crime family who boasted about giving people who offended them "cement shoes".

Cal, who had supported the goddess all this time—no hardship whatever—felt the moment of crisis when the adrenalin started to pump through her blood. Her willowy body stirred from near

swooning into action. Ms Amber Wyatt was about
to cause an upheaval. The question was, what did
she intend to do? Her fiery expression indicated
something spectacular. Something *hugely* embarrassing for all concerned and shockingly inad-
visable for her. She could finish up waiting tables.

Sinclair and Georgie were as good as married.
Nothing could stop that, but at least he could
prevent Ms Wyatt from doing something she would
live to regret.

"Come here." He pulled her urgently to him.

Completely off balance, Amber found herself
doing exactly what she was told. He was that kind
of man. She couldn't push him away. He was much
too strong. She didn't even know if she *wanted* to.
This was the most extraordinary pseudo-embrace
she had experienced in her life.

He literally crushed her to him.

God, a *real* man! She had a crazy notion of being
ravished. Quite possibly she'd let him. If not now,
at the first opportunity. Even as her mind spun out
of control, he propelled her back across the loft,
then, before she could recover, lowered his head
and kissed her in a way that she knew with absolute
certainty would leave a lasting memory. She even re-
gressed to her teens…all those fabulous bodice-
rippers she had devoured.

Her body felt sparkly all over, trembling under
the influence of a battery of energising electric

shocks. The pressure of that firm mouth coming down over hers, the sheer heart stopping eroticism, had her opening her soft lips like a rose opened up its petals to be drenched by the sun. The pleasure was tremendous.

Should she be craving such pleasure *now*? It was bizarre! It made a mockery of her engagement to Sean. This man's tongue was locating erogenous zones inside her mouth that had her seizing his lapels. What in the world had taken possession of her? Maybe she was getting the pain and humiliation out of her system? More likely it was the sheer *power* of this man, the way he handled himself. Even as she clutched him, he moved her closer in.

She was receiving the full impact of his superb male body. A natural scent came off his skin— warm fine leather, sunshine, the great outdoors, just the right touch of aftershave. Both of them were behaving like lovers in the white-hot grip of passion. She had no history of such extravagant behaviour.

Did *he*?

One didn't associate this unbridled behaviour with perfect strangers. It had to be something else. Both of them were playing a role. That was it! Playing it to the hilt! Either that or she had morphed into an entirely different person. Only as recent as five minutes ago, she had thought herself desperately unhappy. Now, heat was spreading through her body, into her stomach, plunging lower…

Oh, Amber, Amber, have a care!

Could shock and unhappiness derange a woman's body as well as her brain? Did being jilted loosen a girl's morals? Or was this a temporary state of dementia?

Whatever it was, the incandescent *glow* behind her eyes remained even when she was able to lift her heavy lids. She had never felt such sexual excitement with Sean. Now this tumultuous reaction with a *kiss*! Had it something to do with the dominant male? Had Sean been a subordinate male? She would have to give that a lot of thought. But it would have to be later on, when she was safely on her own.

"Well, it didn't take us long to make friends," he remarked with breathtaking coolness.

The tricky part was to find her voice. "Is that what it was? I thought it was more a spur of the moment bid to shut me up."

"And there's no doubt it worked! Further, Ms Wyatt, it was an absolute pleasure."

"You could have shown a bit more restraint." She put a trembling hand to her mussed hair.

"Don't be picky. *You* were going for broke. Anyway, don't let's worry about it. Look, your beautiful hat has floated off." It was now wedged in a cool dark corner, the petals of the pink and cream silk roses softly gleaming. He moved in what seemed like slow motion to pick it up, brushing off a speck of dust before restoring it to her. Amber, never short of a word, couldn't even utter *thank you*. Her heart was pounding hard and fast. Her legs were weak. Had there been a smoke alarm in the loft, she was sure it would have gone off. What did it all mean?

Cal found himself stretching out a hand to smooth her glowing hair. It was in disarray and such an indescribable shade! Tone on tone, from golden through to dark copper with glossy strands of apricot and Titian woven through. She wore it pulled back into a lustrous updated chignon—appropriate, he supposed, when wearing a picture hat like that.

"Look, I'm sorry," he said, when he clearly wasn't. "But it seemed like a good idea at the time. I *had* to stop you. Whatever you had in mind, you would only have regretted later."

"Is that an apology?"

"Could be." His laugh was slightly off-key. "Maybe we can discuss it more fully over dinner?"

She drew back, astonished . "Wh-a-a-t?"

"Not a trick question. Let me break it down. Are—you—free—for—dinner?"

"Are you serious?" Her beautiful golden eyes grew huge.

"Of course I am." He smiled at her confusion. "We can relax now. It's all over."

"So it is." Amber exhaled a deep sigh. "So what do we do now?"

"Well, I'm up for anything," he mocked. "We could continue kissing until you can't remember you ever had a fiancé?"

"Who is now married to your cousin. Thank you, but no, Mr MacFarlane. I don't think you could top the first kiss anyway."

"Well, I'd like to give it a shot," he returned smoothly. "You're not *still* looking for a husband, are you?"

She met the sparkling ironic gaze that was fairly centred on her. "I could very well remain married to a career. I may have climbed the ladder in television, but actually I want to be a writer. You know, another Colleen McCullough. *Love* her."

"Another *Thorn Birds*?"

"I wish! But I *can* write."

"You might have to make a start after today," he suggested dryly. He may have prevented Ms Wyatt from causing further disturbance and bringing down the full force of Rosemary's wrath on her beautiful head, but a lot of people had marked her imprudent attendance. Cal had a hollow feeling that there could be unpleasant repercussions for Ms Amber Wyatt. They were a vengeful lot, the Erskines.

"Is that a warning?"

"I'm putting you on your guard." He looked serious.

"I see. Your dear aunt was giving me the evil eye."

"Aunt by marriage," he corrected.

"Well, she does lack your style. I take it one wouldn't want to cross her."

"Believe me, when Rosemary is crossed, heads roll."

"That's the downside of having too much money," Amber murmured caustically. "I can't imagine her getting the better of you."

"Well, I do have the advantage of living well over a thousand miles away. But don't worry, Ms Wyatt, I'm going to put in a good word for you."

"*Why*, exactly?" She stared up at him. It was, she found, a very pleasant sensation. He made her feel almost petite.

"I was engaged once," he remarked, offhandedly. "I didn't exactly catch my fiancée in the arms of her stop-gap lover, but a good friend of mine happened to bump into them when they were taking a little holiday together in Bangkok. That's classified information, by the way."

"My lips are sealed." Amber made a little sealing gesture with her pearl-tipped fingers, astonished by his admission. "How could she possibly have preferred the other guy to *you*?"

His laugh was off-key. "Thanks for that little vote of confidence, Ms Wyatt. You would have to understand my ex-fiancée. Sexual encounters on the side she didn't regard as *meaningful*."

"But it was the end of the engagement for you?"

"Most definitely, though she tells it differently. That, again, is between the two of us, okay?"

She nodded. "Mr MacFarlane, I am to be trusted. Besides, I owe you one. So what now?"

He looked down into the fast emptying church. "You stay here until the church clears. I have to join the family—stick around until the happy couple embark on their wedded bliss."

"They've already done that," Amber said tartly. "Don't be surprised if Sean takes it into his head to run off with one of the bridesmaids." She settled her lovely picture hat back on her head, looking at him to check the angle. "Have I got it right?"

"Perfect! No woman could look more ravishing. Now, you can follow when the coast is clear. Everyone will be focused on getting to the reception. You should be able to make your escape."

"I didn't come here to make a spectacle of myself, you know." Suddenly she wanted to explain herself to him. She didn't want him to think badly of her. "Or disrupt the service, as you seemed to think. Sean really deserved it, but that wasn't my intention. That would have been cruel and I'm not a cruel person. The plan was to calmly walk out when the Bishop called for any objections—you know the bit—but I just felt so *angry* I momentarily lost control."

"You're free of him now."

"So I am." She couldn't conceal the bitterness and the pain.

"So what about dinner?" He repeated the invitation bracingly, as if dinner would be a form of therapy. "Are you up for it? I think it might do you a lot of good to be seen out on the town enjoying yourself. Or making a good show of it."

She felt a moment of turmoil, not knowing if it was a good or a bad thing. Was it possible she was getting into very deep water? Being with Sean, it had only come up to her ankles, she now realised. "Why are you being so kind?"

"I'm not being kind. Not at all." He cast a quick look at the near-empty pews. "I just don't feel ready to say goodbye to you, Ms Wyatt. That's all. I fly home in a few days."

"In your own little Airbus?" She lifted her high arching brows. "It's so nice to be rich."

"I assure you it's quite an effort holding on to it. However, where I come from, having your own plane is a necessity, not a rich man's toy. I have a couple of helicopters as well."

"I'm terrified of those," she said. "I was involved in a scare in the TV station's chopper some months ago. Anyway, aren't you supposed to be attending the reception? It will go on for hours and hours."

"Not for me it won't," he said firmly. "Where do you live?"

She held up her hands. "Please...no. This is madness!" She wasn't at all sure she could handle a man like this. Sean had been one thing. This man was really, *really* something else.

"Maybe that's why I like it." He smiled. "Address, please?" He checked again on the remaining number of guests. Maybe a dozen. The organist was still playing triumphantly, although the soprano, probably with perforated eardrums, had made her escape.

"I don't know if this is a good idea." Amber, who never dithered, dithered. How could a woman feel like jumping off a cliff one minute and be going out to dinner with a handsome stranger the next? But then she realized that it *did* happen.

"Just give me your address," he prompted.

Bemusedly, she did so. She might need him to put in a good word for her with his Godzilla of an aunt by marriage.

"I'll pick you up at nine," he informed her briskly. "I'll be able to make it by then. You'll feel better if you're out and about."

"Just don't alert the paparazzi."

He laughed, lifted a hand in salute, then began moving lithely down the flight of stairs.

His grandfather, accompanied by Rosemary, lost no time in seeking him out. They looked an incongruous duo, propelling their way towards him like two ocean-going liners breasting the high seas. Rosemary was a big woman who had become ever more substantial over the years. She towered over her father-in-law. But whereas Rosemary had reduced her doomed husband, Ian, to a tiny planet in orbit around her, his formidable grandfather radiated power, authority and a kind of physical indestructibility.

It had always been like that. Cal's mother, the bolter, Stephanie, was Sir Clive's only daughter. Her brother, Ian, was Georgie's father, the only son. Their mother, Rochelle, had been killed a week after her fortieth birthday when her high-powered sports car, a birthday present, had slammed into a brick wall, doing one hundred miles per hour. Ian had taken after his father in looks if nothing else; Stephanie had inherited Rochelle's beauty, wit and high octane nature. Stephanie had been idolized by Sir Clive and endlessly indulged, whereas Ian had never been able to cope with a stern and exacting father's expectations and demands.

Georgie, the Erskine heiress, had never worked a day in her life. But then she hadn't lived a life devoted exclusively to the pursuit of pleasure either. Georgie, like her father, lived her life under Rosemary's thumb. How then had a moral lightweight like Sinclair hoodwinked Rosemary, let alone his grandfather, into thinking he would make Georgie a good husband? Cal had believed them more than capable of sniffing out a rat. Well, they would know soon enough. Ms Amber Wyatt had made a very lucky escape. He didn't doubt that for a minute.

His grandfather laid a steely hand on his arm. "I want to thank you, Cal, for getting that outrageous young woman out of harm's way. What was she thinking of, coming to the church? Simply not done!" he huffed. "Especially not to me or my family. She'd behaved herself up until now. I had every intention of offering her a holiday. Anywhere in the world she cared to go. Certainly not now. That's gone by the board." He nodded his large balding head several times, then pulled his right ear lobe.

"Why not forget it?" Cal suggested. "Maybe she shouldn't have turned out for the wedding, but she must have taken the public humiliation hard. A lot of women in her shoes might have been prepared to do a whole lot worse."

"That was bad enough," Sir Clive grunted, still red in the face. "You're not defending her, surely, m'boy?"

"I suppose I am," Cal admitted. He was in no way intimidated by his authoritarian maternal grandfather. Not even as a child.

"I can't believe this!" Rosemary shook with rage. "Seeing that girl arrive was almost the death of me. To think she would try to spoil our Georgie's big day!"

"It could have been a lot worse," Cal said provocatively. "As I understand it, Ms Wyatt has drawn a lot of public sympathy."

"Cheap! She's cheap, cheap, cheap!" Rosemary

glared back, shoulders shuddering. "Of course she's very beautiful."

"Dangerously so," he suavely agreed. "But she didn't intend to do anything too dreadful."

"That's your view, is it?" Sir Clive gave a sudden bark. He stared back at Cal as if he had suddenly gone mad. Worse—disloyal. "This was your cousin's—*my* granddaughter's—big day, might I remind you, Cal? A bloody fortune has gone into it." Even he had been gobsmacked by the cost.

"You know it was well worth it, Grandfather, dear," Rosemary appealed to her father-in-law, who had fronted the monumental bill.

That didn't curb Sir Clive's rage. "That young lady made one very big mistake today. It has turned me against her. The whole thing will be reported in the newspapers. I don't take kindly to being made a fool of. What exactly did she intend to do?"

"Nothing really. She just took it into her head to attend."

"You're covering for her, Callum," Rosemary said with fierce disapproval. "There's only one explanation—she intended to cause a massive scene. You couldn't let her do that."

"No, of course I couldn't," Cal agreed quietly; he had known Ms Amber Wyatt was a bundle of trouble from the moment he had laid eyes on her. "But I'm defending her because she came quietly. Always a good sign. If she were as bad as you seem to think, she could have turned on quite a show. Instead, she let me escort her up to the organ loft."

Rosemary showed her mean eyes. "I think it had more to do with the fact she knew she wasn't any match for you. All through the ceremony my Georgie would have been frantic with worry. Sean too. Which brings me to why he said he had to be free of her."

Cal kept his eyes fixed on Rosemary's face. "Do tell, Rosemary. You're dying to. Why did your son-in-law have to make the break? A physical description of Ms Wyatt would have to be glorious."

"Be careful you're not giving yourself away, Callum," Rosemary retaliated, nostrils flaring. "You always were susceptible to a beautiful woman. Take Brooke now—"

"That will do, Rosemary," Sir Clive sternly intervened. "Kindly remember this is my grandson you're talking to. Brooke Rowlands wasn't anywhere near good enough for Callum. Now, we have to go in to our guests. This is supposed to be a joyous occasion. I have to tell you I'm none too happy about Georgie's new husband, but the deed is done. We would have had to admit her to a psychiatric facility if any of us had tried to stop her. That doesn't excuse Ms Wyatt's part in the day's proceedings, however. She looks such a lady too. I'm disappointed. However, for this outrage she might find herself behind the cameras for a while. Give her time to reflect."

It was as good as done, Cal thought. His grandfather was way too powerful.

CHAPTER THREE

AMBER had only been inside her apartment six or seven minutes when Jono knocked on the door, his mobile face bright with anticipation.

"Well, how did it go?"

Amber stood back, waving him in. "It was very, very sad."

"Really?" Jono spun. "What happened? Remember you can't keep it private, sweetie."

Amber led him into the stylishly decorated living room. "Like a coffee or something?"

"Let me make it. You just sit down and talk to me. You don't *look* sad."

"Oh, how do I look?" She was quite unaware that she looked radiant from head to toe.

"Like you've just met some new guy, hot on the heels of the old?"

"What makes you think I *want* a new guy?"

"You mightn't think so now, dear, but you will," Jono told her with certainty. "When that dirty rotten scoundrel Sean committed to being a love rat he made up his mind to be the best one around. But there *are* good men out there, Amby. Never doubt it. Sometimes I wish I weren't gay."

"Don't tell Jett that." She had to smile. She did a lot of smiling when Jono and his partner, Jett, a fellow computer whiz, were around. "But there *was* a new guy. The bride's cousin, of all things. He was the one who dealt with me."

"Lord sakes! He didn't chuck you out?" Jono paused in what he was doing.

"No. He whisked me off to the organ loft and stayed with me throughout. He's a Cattle Baron by name of Cal MacFarlane."

"A Cattle Baron!" Jono shrieked, throwing up his hands. "Not a redneck, I hope?" He set the coffee to perk. "Rich?"

"Without a doubt. And he's no redneck. He's very cultured. His grandpop is Sir Clive Erskine."

Jono's face fell. "Then he *can't* be good-looking. There's always a downside."

"Oh, I don't know. How does Clive Owen-ish sound?"

Jono's jaw dropped. "You're joking."

"You can meet him if you like," Amber promised. "He's picking me up at nine. We're going out to dinner."

Jono whistled in admiration. "And I thought I was

a fast worker! As I'm very fond of saying, love, life's an adventure. One chapter finishes, another begins."

The Cattle Baron had a limousine waiting. "You look ravishing."

Hugely gratified, she could see that he meant it. She had picked out a short, glittery gold dress that showed off her long limbs and, if she said it herself, a tantalizing décolletage.

"Thank you. Hard to get away?" He was still wearing his formal wedding suit. It was absurd how well it suited him.

"It wasn't *that* easy. But I'm here."

"So, what you promise you deliver?"

"I really do like it that way."

The uniformed chauffeur held the door while Amber slipped gracefully into the back seat. A moment more and the Cattle Baron joined her. She was almost shivery with the intimacy. He was just so *physical*, the quintessential man of action.

"So Jono and Jett are your friends?" he asked when they were underway.

"Jono for years now. He's a very clever, very gentle man. He likes to keep an eye out for me."

"You must feel good about that. He couldn't have approved of you know who."

"I don't have a clue who you're talking about," she said airily, gazing out of the window at the glittering cityscape, above it a starry sky.

"Right. I admire the way you've disposed of *that* problem."

"Where are we going, by the way?"

"The best establishment in town. Where else?"

Where else, indeed? It dawned on her that she was looking forward to spending a few hours with the Cattle Baron. In fact, she was excited. Didn't that underscore her poor judgement about Sean?

The restaurant was seriously good. Wonderful ambience, excellent, discreet service. She had dined there a number of times. Always as a guest, not the one footing the bill. No one in their right mind could say the price was right. But the food—inspirational stuff—was superb, the wine list a long selection of the very best the world's top vintners could offer, the upper end pricey enough to give even the well-off a heart attack.

"Tell me what wine you like?" the Cattle Baron asked, looking across a table set for two. One of the best positions in the room. How had he managed it on a Saturday night?

"And put you at my mercy?" she joked. "You've seen the prices."

"We can forget the prices for tonight," he told her calmly. "What if we start with a nice glass of champagne? Can't go past Krug. You have to celebrate your lucky escape." His cool green eyes glittered.

"Let me make it perfectly clear that I'm still upset."

"Of course you are. But the Krug will help."

It was all *too* tempting.

She had thought she never would again, but she laughed. Really laughed. She hadn't expected him to be so entertaining, but he was a born raconteur. He kept telling her wonderful stories about Outback life—hilarious incidents, interposed with the tragic and poignant realities of life in a harsh, unforgiving land. It was what gave him the heroic image, she suddenly realised. It was emblazoned all over him. *Hero figure.*

From the arrival of the *amuse bouches*, tempting little morsels to tease the palate, the starters, a carpaccio of tuna and swordfish garnished with a delicious little mix of green herbs, the main course of fillet of barramundi with a sweet-and-sour pepper sauce over risotto, the rim of the plate decorated with baby vegetables, he kept her enthralled. So much so she was eating with abandon. It struck her that they liked the same food, because independently they came up with the same choices. Even to the bitter chocolate mousse with coffee granita and gingered cream.

"That was superb," he said, laying down his dessert spoon.

"I know it. Good thing you're paying. There's a poor soul over there choking over the bill."

He laughed. "I daresay it takes a lot to run a three star restaurant and make a nice profit. Coffee?"

"Absolutely. I need to sober up."

"You won't be wanting a liqueur, then?" There was a twinkle in those mesmerizing green eyes.

"I didn't say that."

"So, feel ready to tell me a little about you," he said, settling back to enjoy his coffee.

"I knew there was a catch."

He leaned forward slightly, aware that they had been under scrutiny since they had walked into the restaurant. She was obviously well known. He wasn't. But he *was* wearing wedding gear. A big clue. "I didn't ask if I could sleep at your place."

"Where *are* you staying?' She circled the rim of her coffee cup with a forefinger, not daring to look up and perhaps give her living dangerously self away.

"Why, with Grandpop, of course."

"He *does* have a mausoleum."

"And he insisted I stay over. I know it's not a nice thing to say, but I do my level best to avoid Rosemary."

"Look, I don't blame you. As soon as I got home I had to lie down to recover from her evil eye. So, your uncle and aunt and dear little Georgie—up until her dicey marriage—live with Grandpop?"

"You've got it."

Those distracting little sexy brackets at his mouth again. "So it's more than likely Georgie and Sean will move into the mausoleum when they return from Europe?" She was able to raise a blasé brow.

"I wouldn't be a bit surprised. It's a 'till death us do part' situation with Georgie and her mother."

"Poor thing! Even I can feel sorry for her. But not for Sean. How did he pass muster with your people anyway? Your grandfather is rumoured to have the hardest nut in town. Rosemary could have been a pushover. Sean can be very good at buttering up the women." Even a Brunhilde.

"Forget them," he said. "It's *you* I want to hear about. From the beginning. You must have been an extraordinarily pretty baby."

"My dad thought so." She couldn't stop a tender smile breaking out when tears still ran down the walls of her heart. "It was he who named me Amber. My mother wanted to call me Samantha."

"Then you'd have got Sam for short."

"So you think he made a better choice?"

"Amber suits you." His eyes were very bright. "You're an only child?"

"Yes."

"And your parents?"

She sighed deeply. "I lost my dad when I was fourteen. A teenage driver ran the red light and collected him in a crossing. He could have saved himself but he chose to save a child instead. A little boy and his mother were on the crossing at the same time. There could have been more people hurt.'

"I'm so sorry, Amber." He reached over to grip her hand, divining her sense of loss. "It's brutal losing a much loved parent."

"It is that." Her topaz eyes misted with tears. "My mother remarried the year I finished school. Needless to say, I didn't take to my new stepfather, though he's not a bad guy. Not my dad, though. I lived on campus through my university days. Not much to tell about the rest. I became a cadet journalist. Got a break on television. I guess the way I look has kept me there."

"You're being hard on yourself. Didn't you win a prestigious award for your article about street kids? It couldn't have been easy going into tough places. Exploring the drug scene, the Dead On Arrivals presenting at hospital, the hopelessness and deep depression."

"What do you think?" Unshed tears continued to shimmer in her eyes. "Some are born to sweet delight, some are born to endless night."

He nodded. 'You're still in touch with your mother?"

"Of course. I love my mother. But I don't see her as much as I'd like. They live in Cairns. They love the tropics, close to the Reef. My stepdad has money and a big motor cruiser. They take lots of trips because he's retired. Tell me about you."

"Me?" His mouth faintly twisted.

"Yes, you. You sound like you know all about missing a parent."

"It happens I do. Like you, I lost my dad, a little over four years ago. He ignored a gash in his arm until it was too late. Lots of barbed wire around the station. Died of septicaemia in a very short time."

"How terrible!" Amber felt moved to exclaim. "Couldn't your mother have made him see a doctor? Men can be so careless with their injuries."

"He'd had his shots. We all have them but the effects must have worn off. My mother left us for a guy I called Uncle Jeff for years of my childhood. So, no mother, no guardian angel. I was away at a trade conference when it happened."

"So you know all about having a hard time?"

"I learned. I grew tough."

"Well, you may *appear* tough—"

"Do I?" His look was very direct.

"In a striking sort of way. But you have a heart of gold. You've been very kind to me."

"What's kind about taking a beautiful woman out to dinner?" he asked, then issued a quiet warning. "Don't look up. The people at the table over there haven't taken their eyes off us since we walked in."

"Isn't that our cue to walk out?" she whispered back. They were finished anyway. The hours had rippled by like silk.

"Sure. What I really want to do is get a better look at your apartment."

"You sound hopeful."

His green eyes were amused. "I am."

"And then seduce me?"

He gave her that dizzying smile. "Ms Wyatt, if you knew how I *want* to! But I won't. Scout's honour. I really liked your apartment. You've got great taste. Besides, the night is young." He turned his handsome raven head. "I wonder if they have a back door. I wouldn't be in the least surprised if there were photographers waiting for us out there. Someone is bound to have tipped them off."

Anyone would have thought she was a rock star. Even a TV star, albeit not in the ascendant wasn't safe anywhere. The paparazzi, as he'd predicted, *were* waiting.

"What do we do? Make a run for it?" She pushed herself into the sheltering crook of his arm. It was *so-o* good to have a man around. Especially one so big and strong. The limo wasn't too far off. He had instructed the chauffeur to meet them in the alleyway at the rear of the restaurant, where the more enterprising had gathered.

"Might as well let them get a few shots. But don't say a word," he advised.

"You got it, boss!" He was perfect in the role.

Afterwards, she thought she would be forever astonished by the speed and efficiency with which he shielded her from the mob, successfully steered her past all their shouted questions, then smoothly bundled her into the waiting limo. Even so, they got their shots. No matter! Wasn't that the reason she and the Cattle Baron had decided on a night on the town? She had proven beyond any doubt that she wasn't the girl to run and hide.

True to his word, he was the perfect gentleman. Clearly, he was a man to be trusted. She watched him roam her spacious living room, studying the artwork. Downlighters picked out the colours and brought the paintings to life, especially the large oil of a field of yellow tulips.

"That's good enough to step in and pick a bunch," he commented, thinking she had an excellent eye and a fine sense of style. She would love the paintings at Jingala. "Yellow would be your favourite colour, right?"

"How did you know?"

He took in a sharp breath. He had spent so much time turning his feelings into a fortress it was unnerving to know the whole damned apparatus could crumble into dust. Roaming about, he paused at her prize piece of sculpture, a large gilded bronze horse. As someone who was practically born in the saddle, he found the anatomy of the horse, the sense of movement, spot on.

"It cost me six months' salary and then some but it was worth it," she said.

"If you ever want to sell it, you have a buyer."

She shook her head.

"You ride?" He shot her a quick enquiring look. The downlights were caught in her glorious hair, which was brushed back from her smooth wide forehead and cascading loose.

Amber nodded. "I love horses. I belonged to a pony club as a child. My dad bought me my first pony when I was six."

"I bet he was so proud of you."

She bit her lip. "My dad thought I was a star. His shining star."

"I'm not surprised," he said very gently. "Have you been able to keep your riding up?" He picked up a jade snuff bottle, one of a small collection, examined it, then put it down again. "Nineteenth century?"

"Yes. Bought them in Hong Kong. I don't keep up my riding as much as I'd like. I don't—*didn't*— have a lot of free time. But nothing would stop me getting out now and then."

"Good!" He clipped it off as though he would have held it against her had she not tried.

The lush plants on her balcony too found favour— the luxuriant mass of philodendrons, large succulents and a variety of other plants. Later, he came to sit opposite her on one of her new sofas—soft, supple leather in an inviting shade of vanilla. One long arm shifted two of the silk cushions to one side. She hadn't the slightest desire to send him on his way. Instead, they fell back effortlessly into conversation…

It was all pretty astonishing stuff.

She had fully expected to cry herself to sleep that night. Instead, she found herself confiding to the Cattle Baron things she had never told anyone before.

Ships that pass in the night? That theory had been advanced.

He, in turn, didn't appear to hesitate in filling her in on his own life. Like her, he was an only child. He rarely saw his mother. He said it without visible upset or apology. Clearly, he had never forgiven her for deserting him and his father. More so for his father's sake, she thought. He spoke so glowingly of his father. It must have been a great relationship. That she could well understand. "I want him back," he said.

"Me, too. I want *my* dad back."

He had an uncle Eliot, his father's much younger brother, a mid-life child who lived with him on the MacFarlane cattle station. She made a mental note to learn more about Jingala, a historic station, she seemed to remember.

"Eliot lost his first wife, Caro, to breast cancer. It hit us all very hard. Caro was a lovely person, incredibly brave. And such a fighter. She should have won. We were afraid Eliot might do something…" He hesitated, his expression grim.

"Might harm himself," she gently supplied.

"You read that right. Janis came along almost two years ago. She's a few years older than I am. She's very good-looking in a high-strung sort of way. Jan got pregnant almost at once. They have a baby boy, Marcus, named after my father. My dad and Eliot were very close, more like father and son than brothers. The age difference and the fact that my father was the strong one, the stuff of legend. I love my uncle but he certainly has his problems."

"They weren't straightened out with his new wife and the baby?" she asked. "I would have thought he'd be just so proud and happy."

"Well, of course he is proud and happy," he returned a shade tersely. "None of us thought he would ever remarry."

"What's worrying you?" she asked, studying his frowning face. Gosh, he was a handsome man! The more she looked at him, the more she was coming to develop a taste for the hard-wired dynamic male.

"Do I look worried?"

"It wasn't a match made in heaven?" she suggested soothingly.

His expression turned ironic. "Aren't matches made in heaven said to be like ghosts? One hears about them but never sees them. Jan is having a lot of difficulty bonding with little Marc."

"Well, now, that's *sad*." She was taken aback. "It's possible she's suffering post-natal depression. It's not at all uncommon, but it can't be allowed to go untreated. There *is* help."

He pushed an impatient hand through his thick

dark hair, tousling the crisp waves. He should leave it like that, she thought. It looked great. "You don't think we've had it? The problem is that Jan rejects help. Anyway, I've said enough about that."

"But isn't there someone to persuade her—her own mother, a close friend? Surely they'd want to help?" It seemed very much as if her husband couldn't. Neither could the Cattle Baron, but it was obvious that he didn't want to interfere in his uncle's marriage.

"Jan and her mother aren't close," he said. "I think she stopped talking to her mother years ago. At any rate, she wasn't invited to the wedding. Another problematic family. Jan's mother and father divorced when she was around ten. Marriage break-ups always have repercussions."

She took a deep breath. "And you're not looking for a wife? Don't let—Brooke, wasn't it—sideline you."

"Don't let Sean sideline *you*," he retorted very smartly indeed.

"Well, both of us have jobs to do."

"I can only hope you have yours on Monday," he said. "Offending my grandfather is to encourage disaster."

"If the worse comes to the worst I guess I'll have to live with it," she said.

CHAPTER FOUR

THERE was a great shot of them in the Sunday papers: *Amber Wyatt and her Mystery Man*. They looked like a pair of movie stars. Anything to keep the public on the edge of their seats.

Monday morning came and she found to her horror that the Cattle Baron had been right. She didn't have a job any longer.

"What possessed you, Amber?" Paddy Sweeney, the station manager, asked in dismay. "You've really blown it *this* time, girl. Insulting old man Erskine! How bright is that? I'm worried about you. The public love you. The station would have tolerated just about anything from you, including appearing topless, but I have to tell you no one ticks off Clive Erskine. You did it Big Time. It doesn't make me happy—far from it—"

"Who likes to be the hatchet man?" She gave him a wry smile.

"Don't say that, love. You know how I've always

fostered your career, but the order has come down from on high."

"The Almighty?" Anger was expressed in derision.

Paddy grunted. "Always supposin' the Big Fella exists. Or, to His everlasting credit, He doesn't like to interfere."

"Perish the thought! So, no warnings, no last chances, no last-minute reprieves?"

"I wish!" Paddy groaned. "It's such a shame. We're top of the ratings. But it was a horrendous idea, showing up at the wedding, Amber. Why didn't you speak to me about it?"

"Hello, Paddy? I *did*."

He paled. "But I thought you were joking! You're always joking."

"You're kidding me."

"Amber, I'm sorry. To think I could have stopped you from causing a scandal"

"Oh, yeah?" Amber was getting angrier by the moment. It went with the red hair. "It was Mr and Mrs Sean Sinclair who caused the scandal," she snapped back. "Don't call *my* behaviour brazen, Paddy."

It was barely ten o'clock but Paddy looked as if he'd had a really rough day. "Amber, I know exactly what they put you through." He crunched up a memo and lobbed it at a waste paper basket. Missed. He always did. "Sinclair's a blaggard."

"No argument here. The thing is, he is now Sir Clive Erskine's grandson-in-law."

Paddy responded with a despondent wave of his hand. "You could have got away with most anything. But not this. Not for a good while, anyway. Even your chances of getting in to another channel are zero. No one will dare touch you. You crossed a very powerful man. Woe to the station who tries to pick you up. The old bugger would buy it just to make sure he got his way."

"So he's only posing as a pillar of the church?"

Paddy gave a sardonic laugh. "It's the way things work, Amber. Billionaires don't have to throw their weight around. They just give the order. People like Erskine are too powerful to fight."

"So I'm bounced for a misdemeanour?" Amber was trying hard to adjust to it.

"Erskine considers it a near crime. You got yourself engaged to a cad. He betrayed you. You're better off without him. He was never good enough for you."

"So I clear my desk? I take it I'm off air tonight?"

Paddy's cheeks turned ruddy. "I'm sorry, Amber. Really, really sorry. We all are."

"Not dear old Jack, I bet! Jack will be delighted to have the news slot to himself."

Paddy nodded his assent. "Only redeeming feature, he's a pro. He never stuffs up and he's got a great speaking voice."

"I prefer mine."

She stood up and Paddy stood too, coming around his desk to her. "Take a holiday," he advised.

"I'm thinking space travel."

"Keep that for a future project. Let things cool down. This isn't going to last for ever, love. The public will want to know where you are."

She gave a snort of disgust. "I bet it's all over town as we speak."

"And you can bet your life the whole country will be taking sides. Lie low, that's my advice. You know you've got a champion in me."

She gave him a forgiving smile. Paddy had to obey directives like everyone else. "Thanks for trying. You've been a great boss."

"Lemme work on it." Paddy escorted her to the door, genuinely upset. Taking Amber Wyatt off air just went to prove that no one, however popular, was indispensable. It was a tough game.

Stepping out of the lift as Amber was stepping in was the man himself, Jack Matthews.

"Hi, there, if it isn't the beauteous Ms Wyatt!" He greeted her with his trademark toothy smile. "Getting your sorry little ass out of here?"

No point in losing it. "No sound as sweet as your own voice, Jack."

"Good luck, anyway." He sketched a sardonic salute as the lift doors began to close. "You've no future in the television industry."

"Good to have an unbiased opinion, Jack."

There was something deeply satisfying about getting the last word.

Except that didn't happen.

"I'll miss you," Jack called.

Hang tough!

She was barely back in the apartment when someone pressed her door buzzer hard. Australia Post? Flowers and a sympathy card signed by the entire Channel? Maybe a get-out-of-town type delivery, hopefully not one that exploded. She checked the image that came up on the tiny video screen. Good heavens! The Cattle Baron. Erskine's grandson. Never forget that vital point.

"Didn't we agree you'd stop following me?" she said into the receiver.

"I'm *not* following you.'

Even over the crackle, he sounded good. "Never thought to phone ahead?"

"Took a chance with the visit. I'm here with a plan."

She rubbed her aching forehead. "Few things more unworkable than a plan, Mr MacFarlane. Please go away."

"You don't need help?" It was a challenge.

Common sense came to the rescue. "Lucky for you, I need all the help available. Does this plan involve travel?"

"How did you guess?"

"So long as it's not outer Mongolia." She released

the security door. This guy had mesmerized her. The way he kissed. The way he talked. The way he looked. One hundred different warring sensations were assailing her all at once.

His sheer *physicality* was nigh on overwhelming within the confines of her small entrance hall. He was wearing a crisp blue and white checked shirt in fine cotton, great-fitting jeans, a beige linen bomber jacket over the top. He could have posed for an ad for Calvin Klein. "You've got ten minutes. The clock's ticking. I take it you know I've been shunted?"

"The news was broken to me. Rather roughly, as it happens. I did warn you. Dire consequences usually accompany rash deeds."

"Words to live by."

"At least you know what's coming." He followed her into the living room. The sun was pouring over the balcony, the reflected light setting the tulip painting on the wall ablaze.

She turned to face him with a coolness bordering on hostility. He *was* a member of the Erskine family. "So what are you doing here? Boredom, filling in time before take-off?"

"Take-off is tomorrow first thing. I had an early morning visit from my grandfather."

"Trying to rein you in?"

"He's given up on that. But he wa ted to make it quite clear that he's not pleased wit. me. He's not pleased with *you*. But that we know."

"Fancy that!" she said sarcastically. "Well, you know what they say—No good deed goes unpunished."

"Oscar Wilde."

"Certainly attributed to him. And didn't he get it right! It's also one of the primary rules of physics. Every force begets an equal and opposite force."

"So why don't we listen?" He let his eyes roam over her with pleasure. She hadn't changed out of her city clothes. She was wearing a very smart ensemble—a short black and white jacket cropped at the waist over a white silk blouse with some sort of ruffle down the front. The black skirt was tight and short, showcasing legs most women would die for.

"I was an excellent student," she said, without any fanfare at all. "I did my dad and his memory proud. In being kind to me, Mr MacFarlane, you were bucking the system. The Erskine system, of which you are one of the main players. Surely you expected Grandpop to come back at you?"

"Oh, I was absolutely convinced he would," he said, showing no sign of worry. "Are you going to ask me to sit?"

She waved an expansive hand. "Take your pick."

"Any chance of a cup of coffee? That would be nice. Maybe a sandwich. Better yet, let me take you out for lunch."

"I think you've done enough damage, don't you?" Hang tough or not, she was shaking inside.

"Nonsense and let's cut back to first names. After all, we have been up close and personal. I was kind. Now I've done you damage?"

"I'm sorry. I did it all to myself. I threw caution to the winds. Not the best way to succeed in life. Come into the kitchen," she invited in a resigned tone. "We can discuss your plan there. Tell me how is Grandpop going to get square with *you*?"

"Disinherit me?" he suggested.

"That's wonderful," she crowed, then swiftly showed concern. "I'm only joking! What kind of a monster is he?"

"Put it this way. Hell will get hotter when he arrives."

"*That* bad?" She couldn't help but laugh.

"Some of the things he's done would have taken the Devil aback." He flashed her a smile that held more than a hint of the said devilment. Made a girl think white teeth and a great smile made the man. "Even if he disinherits you, you're rich too, aren't you?"

"Depends on what you call rich. I don't have Grandad's astro bucks but let's hear it for the MacFarlanes. The MacFarlanes don't need the Erskines. We do okay on our own."

"Well, that's great. So you're a race apart?"

"In a way." He glanced appreciatively around the shining kitchen—white with a yellow trim, polished golden timber floor, a couple of bright scatter rugs, big, sunny-face yellow gerberas arranged in a copper kettle. "Grandfather Erskine sees himself as the patriarch of the family. My own dad and my paternal grandfather are gone. I don't kowtow to my grandfather. I actually like him some of the time. I won't say he's a *lovely* man—"

"God forbid!" Amber shuddered, taking a container out of the refrigerator that held freshly ground coffee.

"But he's definitely got his good points."

"Naturally, that's not my view of him," she said in disgust.

"Give it time. He'll cool down."

"Are you saying I don't have to *stay* gone?"

"Not for ever," he said.

"Great! Only here's the tricky bit. In the meantime, he's made it impossible for me to get work."

"That's why I'm here." He pinned her with his crystal gaze. "I want to help."

"Pardon?" She lifted supercilious brows. The cool ease was getting to her. It shouted money. Lots of it. A life of privilege, though she didn't doubt for a moment he worked hard. That showed as well.

"Hear me out." His voice was smooth and reassuring. A voice one listened to.

"How can you help when you've just told me your grandfather is furious at your apparent support of me thus far? He would see it as an additional act of gross disloyalty."

"Let's forget my grandfather. He doesn't figure in this."

"That's all right for you to say! But I have nowhere else to turn. For the time being, anyway. The word has gone out. Wyatt's finished in the business."

"Look, do you want *me* to make the coffee?" he asked as progress on that front had stopped.

"God, you're a piece of work!" she muttered. "You just sit there." She shrugged out of her jacket, placing it carefully over the back of a chair. Had she known in advance she was going to be sacked she would never have bought such an expensive outfit.

"I thought you wanted to be a writer?" he was saying, sliding onto one of the high bar stools along the counter. She suddenly saw him as what he was. The Cattle Baron. A man of the great outdoors. He was superbly fit, every movement full of languid grace and perfect co-ordination. The fact that he looked particularly good in formal clothes was just an added bonus. His body gave class to whatever he wore.

"I hadn't intended to start quite so soon." She spooned coffee into the stainless steel basket. "But hang on. Maybe I can get a grant from the Arts Council? Unless Gramps has influence there too?"

"How do you know your chance doesn't await you right now?" he countered.

She gave him a long considering look. "You're telling me to go for broke?"

"You must have a little money put aside?"

"Hey, I'm not in your league. I'm probably somewhere between broke and doing nicely provided I have a steady income. I lease this apartment. I don't *own* it."

He looked back, a slight frown between his strongly marked brows. "I bet your landlord loves you. I'd say you make the perfect tenant. Only they allow you to hang all the paintings on the wall? Holes in the plaster and so forth?"

She stared back with frosty eyes. "Sure the Body Corporate didn't send you?" She waved the spoon, like a teacher with a cane. "A good friend of mine bought the apartment for an investment—"

"And he's allowed you to rent it." He nodded as though he quite understood.

"Who said it was a *he*?" She came close to throwing the spoon.

"Just a lucky guess."

"You're not improving my temper, MacFarlane," she warned.

"Why so aggressive all of a sudden?" He threw up his hands. "Though I bet you're a real firecracker when you get going. I meant no offence, ma'am. Just a guess."

"I'm not a firecracker. I have a lovely nature." For some reason a tear slid down her cheek.

"Why, Amber!" He stood up immediately, radiating warmth and a comforting male presence.

"Don't you dare touch me!" She dashed at her eyes. "That tear got away from me. It's anger, by the way."

"Sure. Let me finish that off." He walked around

the counter, took the percolator off her, screwed it together tightly, then set it on the hotplate.

She stood for a moment watching him. Everything he did was so precise. "You must really need that cup of coffee."

"I didn't get one for breakfast so I'm suffering withdrawal."

"So what's the plan?" She was desperate to hear it. She busied herself setting out coffee cups and saucers. Fortunately, she had some very fancy chocolate biscuits on hand, though she went easy on biscuits and cakes.

"One I'm sure is going to lift your spirits. At least I hope it does." He turned to face her, his green eyes alight. "How would you like a long vacation on one of the nation's premier cattle stations? You said you wanted to write. Start your saga there. Colleen McCullough used a sheep station for one of her settings in *The Thorn Birds*. Why not a cattle station? Jingala has a lot to offer. Have you ever been Outback?"

She didn't think she could sustain the epic pace. "Well, *have* you?"

"I'm too amazed—nay too *grateful*—to speak."

"So you accept my offer?"

She took a deep breath, her voice unsteady. "I didn't say that at all. I said—"

"You were grateful. Think about it. You'll come as my guest. That means you won't have to find a cent. You didn't answer my question. Have you visited the Red Centre, the Channel Country, the Kimberley?"

She gazed back at him, turning a little pink. "I think I've seen more of Europe than my own country, outside the big cities and tropical North Queensland. Now I'm ashamed to say it."

"As you should be." The censure was unmistakable. "So now's the time to discover the real Australia. I promise you it will be an experience you won't forget."

"I'm sure." She was feeling more agitated than she thought possible. A friend had recently come back from the Alice and had found the trip to the Centre and its great monuments fabulous. "Listen, I'm still stunned." She looked right at him. "I take it there'll be no hanky panky?"

"Absolutely not! Unless *you* want it. Seriously, I was brought up a gentleman, Ms Wyatt. *No* from a woman and I'm gone! Out of there!"

"I bet there've been precious few nos," she said sharply.

"A gentleman doesn't tell. If you can be ready, we can leave in the morning."

She held up a hand. "Whoa, there! I'm still too dumbfounded to give you an answer."

The coffee had begun to perk. "That's okay. I don't want to rush you. Take your time. But I'll need to know before I leave."

The pure utter simplicity of the idea!

CHAPTER FIVE

AMBER'S trips up and down the Eastern Seaboard, to the North Queensland rainforest and the Great Barrier Reef, marvellous wine country in New South Wales, Victoria and South Australia, the great cities of the world—nothing had even given her a glimpse into what was the Great Australian Outback. The sheer dimensions were overwhelming. The isolation frightening. It was like looking out at the world at the time of Creation, with no human habitation. Wilderness fanned out to eternity…

She had been concentrating so much on the journey her head felt tight. The Cattle Baron sat beside her at the controls, splendidly serene. Flying his own plane was a piece of cake to him. Equivalent to her taking a cab. She was very grateful to him. He had offered her salvation. For a time, anyway. An unexpected chance to do what she had always wanted to do since she had been caught up as a child into the wonderful realm of books:

Write one herself.

She'd had ideas mulling around in her head for years. She didn't expect to measure up to her great favourites, but she thought she could turn out something that might rate getting published. In her heart she welcomed and embraced this extraordinary chance. And what a setting! She already had the sense of great *separation*. This was another world from the lush Eastern seaboard. She would be seeing the Interior through fresh, marvelling eyes. She would be seeing it too through *his* eyes. This was Cal MacFarlane's world. He had offered her escape and a chance. Now it was up to her. The shock and unexpectedness of it all had shoved the extremes of being jilted, the public humiliation and the loss of her job right to the back of her mind. Truth be known, she felt downright energised!

They were on the last lap of the journey, flying into the MacFarlanes' desert fortress, Jingala. It must have been a phenomenal slog to have achieved so much in this place that few people to this day had ever seen. Over the long journey she had witnessed the landscape totally changing its character. Now its most striking feature, apart from the empty immensity, was the dry, vibrating colour. And what colour! It was spectacular. The great vault of the sky was a vigorous cobalt-blue. It contrasted wonderfully with the flaming orange-red of an ancient land that pulsed in oven-baked heat. The rolling red sand dunes surrounding it were a source of fascination. They ran in endless parallel waves with the anti-clockwise rhythm of the wind curling them over at the top, mimicking the waves of the legendary sea of pre-history.

Spinifex, burnt gold and shaped like spherical bales, gave the impression of the greatest crop ever sown on earth. The mirage she had heard so much about lay beneath them like silvery quivering bolts of material that seemed to change form and shape as she watched. Trees grew in the arid terrain, gnarled and twisted into living sculptures. She could easily spot the ghost gums with their blazing white boles. This was Dreamtime country. Venerable.

As they descended, she caught the full dazzle of chain after chain of billabongs, some silver, some palest blue like aquamarine, others the cool green of the Cattle Baron's eyes. These lakes, waterholes, billabongs and breakaway gullies were the lifeblood of this riverine desert called the Channel Country that lay deep into the South-West pocket of the giant State of Queensland, bordering the great Simpson Desert. She knew it was second only to the Sahara in area.

Thick belts of trees marked the course of the maze of waterways that snaked across the landscape. From the air, the foliage appeared to be more a light-reflecting gun-metal grey than green. She could see kangaroos in their hundreds bounding their way across the desert sands. Her eyes could pick up camels too. She knew they were not indigenous to Australia. Outback camels, progeny of the camels brought into the country by their Afghan handlers as beasts of burden for the Outback's trackless regions, had thrived and multiplied to some seven hundred thousand. Some said this was a bad thing. Camels were long-lived and they did so much damage to the fragile desert environment. Others went along with a live and let live policy. There was something rather romantic about them, she thought, but she could well see the serious side of the problem.

Acutely alert to everything coming up before her, she had her first sight of Jingala's great herds. She couldn't begin to count the number of head in one area alone. A smallish section of the herd was being watered at a creek. She could see camps alongside. Whole collections of holding camps, cattle packed in, men on the ground, men on horseback, supply vehicles. Not so far off, wild horses were galloping at breakneck speed, a stallion most likely in the lead, the others running four abreast. What a thrilling sight! City born and bred, it was just as well she was at home on a horse. She might not have rated an invitation had she said she was scared of horses, as a lot of people were. Horses were very unpredictable animals. She had taken a few spills in her time, mercifully without major injury.

MacFarlane gestured to her.

The homestead was coming up.

Her first thought as they were coming in to land was that they were arriving at a desert outpost that a small colony of intrepid settlers had made their home. The silver roof of a giant hangar was glittering fiercely in the sun, emblazoned with the legend Jingala. Beyond that, outbuildings painted white to throw off the sun fanned out in a broad circle surrounding a green oasis that had to be the home compound. She could see a huge dark bluish tiled roof, roughly three times the size of any city mansion. But so far no real sighting of the actual house. A line of dark amethyst hills in the distance took her eye. They had eroded into fantastic shapes with the shimmering veil of mirage thrown over them. The brightness of it all was splintering her eyes. The far-off hill country, though of no great height, by comparison with the endless flat plains served as the most spectacular backdrop. It was paradise in its own strange way. Even at this early stage, it was already establishing a grip on her. Hard to believe the continent had once been covered in rainforest. That was one hundred million years ago. But still a blip in geological time.

Never for a moment of the trip had she felt an instant's fear, though she had heard plenty of scary tales about light aircraft crashes in the wilds of the rugged Outback. Something about desert thermals bouncing light aircraft around. She would have to ask the Cattle Baron. As expected, he was a fine pilot. She guessed he was a fine just about everything. And a devilishly handsome man. After her sad experience, she was determined she wasn't going to be swept away by his undoubted charisma. Better to turn the cheek than do the kissing. A whole lot safer too.

After hours in the air, they were ready to land…

The homestead itself was an unforgettable sight. She had expected the sort of colonial architecture she had seen in the big coffee table books, the rather grandiose mansions of the Western Districts of Victoria or South Australia, reminders of Home that almost exclusively had been the British Isles, maybe the classical architecture of New South Wales and Tasmania, but what confronted her was *her* idea of a great country house that wouldn't have been out of place in South East Asia. She had enjoyed several trips to Thailand. The house put her in mind of that part of the world and she said as much to the Cattle Baron.

He gave her a smile that brought her out in the trembles. "You got it in one. A big section of the original homestead was destroyed by fire in the late nineteen-forties. My grandfather razed what remained to the ground, then brought in a friend of his, a Thai prince he had met on his travels, who was also an architect, to design the new homestead. It's a one-off for our neck of the woods."

"And it's wonderful," she said. "Not at all what

I expected. You should have peacocks patrolling the grounds."

"Maybe we can rise to a few emus."

"You can't tame emus, surely?"

"Yes, you can," he said, watching her. He had set her a number of little tests to gauge her reactions when removed from her comfort zone. She had passed all of them with flying colours. He didn't know if he was pleased or the fact bothered him. This astonishingly beautiful woman belonged in the city, surely? That was her future. Jingala was a far cry from anything she was used to. His mother couldn't hack it.

She was staring up into his face, noting the darkening change of expression. "I never know if you're serious or fooling."

"You'll know when I'm serious."

Some note in his voice had her flushing. To hide it, she turned away, resuming her study of this fascinating and totally unexpected house. For all its size, it sat unobtrusively in its oasis of a setting, which she put down to the fact that it was constructed almost entirely of dark-stained timber.

"The pyramid form is exactly right."

"Glad you like it. Five in all, as you can see, with broad overhangs to shelter the upper verandas. The central section is the largest. It acts as a portico."

"So you have a group of separate places."

He nodded. "What we call the Great Room is the common room, our reception room."

"I recognise the Khmer style. I've been to Thailand three or four times. The roof and window treatment, the timber grilles and framework are all recognisably Khmer style."

"Educated eyes, obviously."

She glanced up at him to see if there was mockery involved. Even then she wasn't sure. "The house is perfect for the tropics, yet it appears equally well at home in the desert. Not that everything around us resembles a desert. The grounds are thriving."

"We had a wonderful drenching over the cooler months. But we do have an underground source of water from the Great Artesian Basin. My great-grandmother saw to it that the grounds were heavily planted out with date palms and desert oaks. She was one smart lady, all the way from the Scottish Highlands. The other trees and plants were selected to cope with the hot dry environment."

"You must tell me about this clever great-grandmother of yours," she said. "That's when you have the time."

"Ms Wyatt, I'll make time," he said with considerable aplomb. "We'll go inside. Surely you're feeling the heat of the sun?" Amazingly, she looked as if she wasn't feeling it one bit. In fact, she looked magnolia-cool.

"It *is* hot," she agreed. "But I can tolerate *dry* heat. It's the humidity of the tropics that gets to me. Anyway, being a redhead, I always use sunblock."

"And a good wide brimmed hat would be very helpful. You've packed one, I hope?" He frowned slightly.

"Well, I didn't have time to race out to buy an Akubra, if that's what you mean. But I threw in a couple of decent broad brimmed hats."

"Thank God for that! I can only hope and pray our Outback does nothing to harm that exquisite skin. Tell me, did you *ever* have freckles?"

The way he looked at her caused little sparkles in her blood. Not that there was anything overtly sexual about it. He just happened to be a very sexy man, which wasn't all that easy for even a good-looking man to pull off. "It may be news, but the answer is no," she said lightly. "I don't know that my mother ever let me out of the house without a hat. I was never able to bask beachside, for instance. But I don't crinkle and wrinkle in the sun either. Why, are you disappointed I don't have a few freckles?"

He laughed. "The short answer is no. So come into the house. Chips, one of our groundsmen, will attend to your luggage and bring it to your room."

"I *am* expected?" She tilted her head to look up at him. It was a great feeling.

"Of course you're expected," he said.

"How good is that!"

The housekeeper, Dee, early fifties, dressed uniform style in crisp navy and white checked cotton, showed her to her room. Dee was a small, wry, smiling woman with a pretty cap of salt and pepper curls, velvety dark eyes and a copper skin. Amber guessed she was highly efficient. She gave the impression of being a durable sort of woman. A woman one could depend on. From her colouring and a certain lilt in her speech, Amber thought she might also have aboriginal blood in her. Later, she was to find out that it was through Dee's maternal grandmother.

"I hope you like where I've put you, miss," Dee was saying, turning to gesture to the tall lanky man with a head like a bald tyre who suddenly appeared with Amber's luggage in hand. This had to be Chips. "Just beside the bed, thanks, Chips." Chips nodded, giving Amber lots of curious looks, almost as a child would.

"Leave 'em, dear," Dee continued in a brisk motherly tone. "God bless."

Chips deposited the luggage where told, then reached out to shake Dee's hand. "Bless you, Dee. You're a lovely person."

Dee took his arm and began to walk him to the door. "You're a lovely person too."

"That was Chips," Dee said when she returned from seeing him off. "If you wondered why I didn't introduce you, Chips would have plonked himself down on the bed and told you the story of his life. Not a happy one until he arrived on Jingala. He's a good bloke is Chips. He used to be a stockman, but he took a terrible kick to the head from his horse.

Its name was Lazy May, believe it or not, six and more years ago. Since then he's been a little slow, but talkative if you know what I mean. Once he gets started, it's hard to get him to stop."

"But he's got a good home."

"We *all* have." Dee gave a heartfelt exhalation. "The MacFarlanes have always been revered the length and breadth of the Outback. Cal is the best there is. Now, want me to unpack for you?"

Amber smiled. "Thanks, Dee, but I can manage. I'm sure you've got other things to do. And please do call me Amber."

"Beautiful name for a beautiful woman," Dee announced, giving Amber's face and bright mane of hair a worried glance. "You're gonna have to watch yourself out here, Amber. I'd hate to see you burn. You the redhead an' all with that lovely skin."

"I'll take care," Amber said. "My colouring isn't as fragile as it looks."

Dee laid a hand briefly on Amber's arm. "I'll look around for an Akubra," she said. "Got a whole bunch o' hats for guests and the like. Lunch in a half hour. Mrs MacFarlane not so good today. So you mightn't see her. Had a real bad night with the little fella. I've given up offering to watch him. We don't get on so good and I get on with most people. That's me and the young Mrs MacFarlane, that is. I have to say she's got herself one difficult little soul. Doesn't want to be held. Doesn't even want to eat. Cries all the time, poor little scrap. Mrs MacFarlane is kinda delicate, high-strung, and it's communicating itself to the little fella, in my opinion. Not that I ever had any kids, I'm sorry to say. Me fiancé, Des, was killed in the big stampede nearly thirty years ago. So that was that! Just thought I'd fill you in. Ya have to know."

"And I appreciate it, Dee." From what she had seen of the easy-going Dee, Amber had to wonder just how nerve-ridden Jan MacFarlane was. "Cal did mention about the baby," she said, finding his first name strange on her tongue. This guy was an Outback prince! "Mrs MacFarlane is suffering post-natal depression?" she asked. "Life must be very harrowing for someone going through such a trauma. So many cases reported lately."

Dee nodded. "Celebrities coming forward to tell of their experiences."

"In the hope it might help other young mothers in the same situation. It must ease the burden and anxiety to know you're not alone. Others suffer and come through." She had sensed a certain lack of empathy in the Cattle Baron. She didn't expect it in this nice motherly woman. It could be difficult for a man—especially a man of action blessed with superb health—to properly understand how badly a woman could suffer from PND. But why wasn't Dee more openly sympathetic? "There isn't a nanny to help out?" Obviously there was money to burn.

"Two ex-nurses-cum-nannies came and went.

Experienced, capable women, especially the second, Martha. Unfortunately, Mrs MacFarlane made them feel bad," she confided with a hint of grimness. "She's just come unstuck. Not every woman is a mothering kinda woman. She won't have any of my girls, my house girls, good girls, look after the little fella. Not good enough. It used to be called racial discrimination."

"Surely not?" Amber was appalled.

"Beyond reason!" Dee shrugged. "She wouldn't let me even pick 'im up for a good while until things got too tough and Cal had to step in."

"But what about her husband?" Amber asked, feeling dismay for mother and child.

Dee gave a sad smile. "Mr Eliot is a lovely man. He adored Miss Caroline, but she died of breast cancer. We didn't think anyone would ever come along to measure up. But then he met Mrs MacFarlane at a big fund-raiser in Melbourne. She had some job in finance. Worked for a merchant bank. It was a kinda whirlwind affair. Cal didn't even meet her until the wedding. Small and quiet. I think she thought Mr Eliot would buy a place in Melbourne so they could settle there. They couldn't have discussed it because Mr Eliot's heart is here. He's terribly distressed about it all but he's kinda useless in this type of situation. And Mrs MacFarlane!" Dee lifted her narrow shoulders. "You'll see."

* * *

With Dee gone, Amber looked around her, her mind awhirl. So even in Paradise there was trouble. Her accommodation, however, was everything she could have wished and dreamed. She had been given a beautiful room—it was big, bright and airy, with the characteristic Asian elegance and simplicity. The colour scheme was subtle—brown, beige and white with colour coming from silk cushions and the beautiful rugs on the dark polished floor. She sat on the canopy bed, staring upwards. It was very romantic. She tried a few bounces. Lovely! The bed was made of ebony, draped in mosquito netting with a heavy ivory satin flounce to match the flounce on the canopy. The timber floor simply glowed. There was a long antique Asian chest at the foot of the bed, two teak tub chairs and a big comfortable day bed upholstered in white cotton with brown and white scatter cushions. As a touch of whimsy, near the shuttered doors was a wooden camel, honey-gold in colour, about four feet high with topaz glass eyes. She loved it.

She stayed where she was for a few more minutes, soaking everything in, then she rose from the bed to inspect the workmanlike desk and chair in another corner, exquisite ivory lilliums in a glass vase standing on the desk's surface. She wondered if the desk had been installed especially for her. Directly outside the series of open shutter doors were some densely planted green shrubs of much the same height, she later found out to her astonishment were Camellia sinensis. In other words, tea. She had thought the crop required a tropical environment with high rainfall. The bushes she was looking at appeared to be thriving in a place that rarely saw rain. She wondered if all those soft green shoots were ever plucked. It was all so exotic, so wildly incongruous, she couldn't wait to begin her desert adventure. Her image of the charming, debonair Sean, who had so badly let her down, was fading daily under this battery of change and excitement.

The thought struck her that *she* was good with children. Maybe in some way she could help out? A problem existed. Another thought popped up. Could that have anything to do with the Cattle Baron inviting her to stay? Was she to fill the post of nurse-nanny? Was it too churlish to wonder? Two nannies had come and gone. Was she Nanny Number three?

Don't be ridiculous, girl. She chided herself for the thought. The invitation had nothing whatsoever to do with the current crisis.

Could it? she see-sawed. Why he hadn't even asked her if she was good with kids? A fit person in every sense of the word. She was being plain silly. And cynical. It wasn't the Cattle Baron's crisis anyway. Little Marcus's mother and father had to address their own problems. Help was available. Favourable results were on record.

She headed to the stylish en-suite bathroom,

which was stocked with everything she could possibly want for the foreseeable future, to take a quick shower to freshen up after the long trip. The Cattle Baron had promised to show her around as much as he could of the vast station.

Vive Le Cattle Baron!

She was hardly out of her room in the east wing on her way downstairs to the living area when she heard raised voices much further down the wide corridor. The polished floor was partially covered with a jewel-toned Persian runner which muted her footsteps. Correction: she heard *one* raised voice— a woman's, head-splittingly emotional, and the low rumble of a man's. What to do? Pop back into her room? For the life of her she couldn't move…

"Jan, *please*…" The male voice, closer this time, was full of anguish and pleading.

Better to go forward than backwards. Amber pinched herself and moved on.

"I swear to God I'm going crazy! I don't know what to do. I never thought it would be like this. I wish I'd never married you. I wish you'd never talked me into having a baby. I only did it to please you. I hated being pregnant, big and bulging, my figure ruined, my breasts turned to marshmallow. I don't *want* babies. I don't want this one. It's not normal. All it can do is cry."

A door must have opened because now Amber

could hear a baby screaming. She winced. It had to be filling its little lungs with painful pockets of air. The sound was heartbreaking and, she had to admit, very hard on the nerves.

The low rumble again in response. The next moment a tall, spare man with a gentlemanly elegant air stepped into the corridor. Frozen in place, Amber met his deeply troubled eyes. They were bright blue in his tanned face. Though the colour of the eyes was different, she could see the strong family resemblance between Eliot MacFarlane and his nephew.

It was a bad moment. "I'm so sorry," Amber found herself apologizing. "I'm Amber Wyatt, Mr MacFarlane. Cal invited me to stay. I was just on my way down to lunch." She hastened to move on, not wanting to embarrass him further, but his wife, looking more like his daughter, and holding a screaming baby, made a rush through the open doorway at him, leaving Amber fearing she was going to throw him the distressed little bundle.

"That's right! Go and leave me," she shouted with a kind of withering contempt. "Go on. That's all you're good for, Eliot. Shut me out."

Eliot MacFarlane didn't answer. He looked unbearably embarrassed. It was then that his wife spotted the agonised Amber. "Who the devil are you?" she demanded in a tone of voice one wouldn't use with a masked intruder.

"For goodness' sake, Jan, this is Ms Wyatt, Cal's

house guest," Eliot MacFarlane broke in, sounding seriously horrified.

"Right!" Jan MacFarlane's acknowledging laugh had nothing to do with good humour. "You haven't struck us at a good moment, Ms Wyatt, as you can see. You married?"

"No." Amber shook her head. She had arranged her hair in little side plaits, with a thick plait to hang down her back.

"It's not what it's cracked up to be." Jan MacFarlane spoke bitterly, still studying Amber in detail. "I'm not myself any more."

Amber was trying hard to imagine what "myself" was like. Janis MacFarlane was good-looking, as the Cattle Baron had told her, but devoid of any hint of softness or warmth. She had long dark hair, huge dark brown eyes that dominated a fine-boned face. Thin enough to be anorexic.

"Would you like me to take the baby for a moment, Mrs MacFarlane?" Amber offered. The poor little scrap was scarlet in the face, little arms clawing the air. He was clearly deeply distressed. That really smote Amber's tender heart.

"Sure. Take him. But to where?" That bitter laugh again. "I'd say he comes from hell."

"That's unforgivable, Jan," Eliot MacFarlane protested, looking utterly mortified. He let his hand rest lightly on his little son's head.

Amber reached them in a flash. Janis

MacFarlane was a teenie bit scary, maybe self-obsessed. "Here, give him to me, Mrs MacFarlane. Dee told me you'd had a bad night. You should rest." Gripped by compassion, she took the little bundle that was all but thrust at her. Marcus MacFarlane's tiny face was all bunched up, flushed scarlet with the effects of exertion.

"Hey, little fellow. You're in some distress, aren't you? Hey, little Marcus?" she began to croon, hoping the gentleness in her voice would take effect. She had soothed friends' babies plenty of times but this little fellow's cries had a different ring. She began to walk, putting the baby very gently over her shoulder, holding him firmly and rubbing his tiny back. "You must stop crying now, little man. Everything is going to be just fine. Stop crying now, Marcus." She rubbed and patted as she spoke. "You'll see."

Busy calming the baby with her back to the others, she didn't see Cal MacFarlane stride up the staircase, his body language tense. He was quickly followed up by Dee, kneading an apron.

"Well, I never!" Dee exclaimed, eyeing the spectacle of nurturing woman and child. "The little guy likes you, Amber," she said with relief, studying the pinched little face inclined over Amber's shoulder. They had heard the baby's crying. It had gone on more or less non-stop for months. Now, incredibly, the crying had turned off like a tap and the baby was making a grab for Amber's red-gold and copper plait.

"For two minutes, I'd say!" Incredibly, Jan MacFarlane sounded so furious with Amber's success she might have been jealous.

The Cattle Baron sloughed a heavy sigh. "Lovely! We came to collect you for lunch, Amber."

"And I'll be there. I'm hungry." Amber resettled the baby in her arms, enormously glad the little fellow had settled, if only for the time being. The angry red was leaving his small face, leaving isolated blotches that looked so pathetic that tears sprang into her eyes. Marcus at this stage didn't appear to have inherited his parents' good looks, but he was staring up at Amber as if to say, *This is the way I want to be held.*

"Maybe Marcus can come with us?" she suggested, meeting the Cattle Baron's ultra-cool eyes. She was wary of putting Marcus down, even warier of handing him back to his mother. "He seems to have settled now. He can lie beside us while we eat?" She waited for approval, in the next breath realizing she should have looked to the baby's parents.

"Well, we can give it a try." Cal was as surprised and grateful as Dee. "You're joining us?" He looked to his uncle.

"You go, Eliot." Janis MacFarlane all but spat the words, as though she would be better off without him. "Ms Wyatt is right. I need to rest."

"See you soon," Cal MacFarlane said smoothly, but with a saturnine edge to his voice.

A fearful worry from birth, little Marcus, to all appearances, was thoroughly intrigued by the new woman in his life, especially her warming, glowing red hair. He lay on the floor beside Amber in his bouncinette, which she kept rocking from time to time with a little movement of her foot.

This is nothing short of a miracle, Cal was thinking. It was clear the beautiful Ms Wyatt loved babies and babies loved her. Maybe the gentleness of her manner, the soft crooning voice—she had a lovely voice, which would have worked well for her on television—and the beauty of her person was central to the big turnaround. He could see his uncle was so grateful he had tears in his eyes. Like little Marc, Eliot had taken a shine to their guest. The real tragedy was that Jan wasn't trying an inch. She was tremendously self-involved. In his judgement, it was part of her character. So when did the baby blues end and this post-natal depression begin? As a condition, it was a curse. But did every sufferer set out to be nasty to everyone they came in contact with? Was Jan by nature nasty? Cal didn't think nastiness was specific to the condition they kept going on about. He was no expert on such matters, but he knew Jan had held down a very good job in the world of finance before her marriage—she was highly intelligent—but directly after the civil ceremony she had begun acting as if she had married into royalty. How Eliot had never spotted her social ambitions during their all too brief courtship he didn't know. Not that he was any expert either at spotting the flaws in women. Brooke was trying pretty hard to make a comeback. No chance!

"Just a moment of madness, darling. I was so lonely without you and Chris was there. Love had nothing to do with it. It was just sex, which was pretty damned ordinary. Nothing like you and me."

Talk about an excuse! At least Brooke had her own money, the only daughter of a fellow station owner. Jan had expected that she and Eliot would settle down in Melbourne, where she could swan around enjoying Eliot's not inconsiderable fortune. The honeymoon had lasted six months of luxurious world travel, but he knew how much his uncle had missed Jingala. He was a MacFarlane. It was in his blood.

Lunch consisted of a delicious tomato and goat's cheese tart with wonderful flaky puff pastry, and a beautifully crisp green salad with just the right dressing. It went down well. Baby Marcus remained calm and at peace as though all he ever needed was to be with people, having his bouncinette gently rocked. With coffee Dee, aided by her well-trained, part-aboriginal helper, Mina, a gentle, pretty young girl aged around sixteen, served another delectable tart, nectarine this time, oozing fruit, with a scoop of ice cream. Normally Amber didn't do sweets for lunch but this time she made an exception.

"So what now?" Cal asked, readying himself for just about anything. Ms Wyatt might very well elect to bring the baby on their tour of the station. Talk about a woman who used her own initiative!

Unaware of his wry admiration Amber looked down at the baby in the bouncinette, a considering expression on her face. "I think our little Marcus might sleep. Look, his breathing is giving way to a nice easy rhythm. Isn't that lovely? I wouldn't even take him out of the bouncinette. What do you think, Dee?"

"I'm with you, love," Dee answered with a nod of approval, as though she had known Amber all her life. Eliot looked happy but slightly bemused. Why couldn't Janis get this result?

She had only been on Jingala a matter of hours, yet Ms Wyatt appeared very much at home, Cal thought. She had Dee and his uncle on side. In fact a visitor would assume she was very much part of the family. It had its piquant side.

"I can sit and watch him," Eliot MacFarlane volunteered, even though Cal could see his uncle was uneasy about the outcome. Baby Marcus had screamed non-stop almost from birth.

"See, his eyes are closing," Amber pointed out with a lovely tender smile.

Eliot's breath whistled. If only. If only. "Poor wee

mite hasn't been getting any sleep at all. My wife is a total wreck. It's been *very* hard on her."

"So what is she going to do about it?" Cal tried hard not to show his impatience. He knew all about "baby blues". He was godfather to quite a few kids. But this was something else again. Something he couldn't put his finger on.

So what then was it? The marriage wasn't working out. He already knew that. The age difference? It wasn't all that great. What exactly was causing Jan's nonstop lashing out at anyone within earshot? He suspected she had always been a bit on the emotionally unstable side. Even before she'd fallen pregnant his uncle had told him Jan was given to mood swings. He really wanted to be sympathetic. He didn't enjoy seeing anyone suffering but his own assessment, backed by a top nurse from the Royal Flying Doctor Service, was that Jan was furiously disappointed her life wasn't working out as she had planned.

"Mainly Mrs MacFarlane doesn't want to take on the role of mother. Not everyone is cut out to be a parent, you know."

Like he needed to be told! He had the miserable experience of his own runaway mother.

Amber, her eyes trained on the Cattle Baron's high mettled face, could see the banked-down rage, impatience, frustration, whatever, behind his controlled exterior. Fabulous though he was, he appeared to be lacking in sympathy, which didn't win him a batch of Brownie points from her. Then she felt ashamed. He had been very sympathetic in relation to her; that didn't appear to be the case with his aunt by marriage. A bit weird to think that Jan MacFarlane was only a few years older than he was.

"Why don't we find you a comfortable chair, Eliot?" She swiftly intervened. He had asked her almost immediately to call him by his Christian name. Warmth and friendliness rarely failed.

"Yeah, let's fix you up," said Dee.

They had been dining in a lovely relaxed place, an informal area off the kitchen. Tall, timber framed glass doors were folded concertina fashion to give the spacious seating area the effect of a breezy veranda where the indoors met up with the outdoors. The view across the grounds, liberally dotted with majestic date palms and desert oaks, stretched away to the mirage-shrouded hills that had lightened by the hour to a dusky pink. She had read about this changing of colour of the great rocks of the Interior, especially Uluru and Kata Tjunta that was said to be spectacular. Now she was in this part of the world, she wondered why she had never made the trek to the Centre. Her career and other destinations had kept getting in the way.

They rose from the table as one but it was Cal who gently took hold of little Marcus in his bouncinette and gestured to Amber rather imperiously, she thought, to select her idea of the suitable chair for his uncle to mind baby. It was all she could do not to bob a curtsy.

"I'll have a bottle of formula ready," Dee whispered, placing an encouraging hand on Amber's shoulder.

Marcus made no protest as his bouncinette was lowered to the floor beside the comfortable armchair Amber chose. It was close to an antique Asian chest with quite an accumulation of interesting-looking books piled on top of it. Eliot would have something to read, though he too looked as if he was in desperate need of sleep.

The manoeuvre successful, Cal resisted the temptation to give Ms Wyatt a sardonic salute. At the very least, her coming had brought a breath of sanity. That took some doing. But what next? He hadn't invited her to Jingala to fill the role of nanny. He just hoped she knew that.

CHAPTER SIX

NO SOONER had Amber taken her seat in the four-wheel drive than he took off like a rocket.

"Hey, what is this, lift-off?" she yelped. She had been comfortably settling herself in, enveloped in a warm glow of excitement and anticipation, now she had to scramble to secure her seat belt.

"We've got a lot of ground to cover." He turned his dark head to give her a challenging smile. "Hold still now. We're going to do a lot of winding in, out and over some pretty rough terrain, fording a creek or two. Why, are you terrified already?"

"Gosh, I thought I looked relaxed."

"You don't."

"Darn and I was trying to make a good impression. Might be a stupid question, but are there any crocs in your lagoons?"

"Ms Wyatt, I don't want to have to rope in your level of IQ."

"Nothing wrong with my IQ. A friend of mine

was chased by a croc up at Mount Isa where crocs shouldn't be."

He laughed. "Somebody introduced saltwater crocs into a dam up there when they were babies. They survived in fresh water. There would have been a sign about that your friend obviously ignored."

"He said not. He had multiple lacerations trying to get through the barbed wire."

"Barbed wire, really?" He glanced at her with sparkling eyes. "Barbed wire generally means, *Stay Out*, Ms Wyatt."

"Great! I've got that right," she answered dryly.

"One learns best when under threat."

"Words to live by," she drawled, then broke off in amazement. "Oh, look at the birds!" She stared out of the window at a fantastic V-shaped formation of tiny emerald-and-gold winged bodies. "Budgies," she proclaimed, absolutely delighted with the massed display. "There must be *thousands* of them."

"A common sight around here," he told her, secretly very pleased by her enthusiasm and the radiance of her expression. "You're in the land of parrots, the sulphur-crested cockatoos, the pink and grey galahs, the millions of chats and wrens and finches. The pretty little zebra finches—you'll spot them from the stripes—form the staple diet of the hawks and falcons, sad to say, but that's the wilds. The predators just swoop down very leisurely to collect their prey."

"So, these zebra chats? Black stripes on a white body or white stripes on a black body?"

"Are you serious?" He headed cross country for the glinting chain of lagoons.

"I kid you not."

"Damned if I know," he said. "I've lived here all my life and I've never given it a thought."

"That's okay. I guess you're too busy. I'll check it out."

"Check out our biggest bird while you're at it."

"Wedge-tailed eagle, right?"

He nodded. "Listen, you should have come out here sooner. I can see you're going to make a great student of Outback flora and fauna. You'll see plenty of eagles, especially up in the ridges. I'm thrilled you're so interested in our bird life. A couple of months back when the channels were in flood the nomadic water birds arrived from all over. Countless thousands of them. Jingala is a major breeding ground, as are the other big Channel Country stations. There are huge colonies of ibis. Hundreds of birds in one colony. They nest in the lignum swamps. The pelicans love isolation so they pick the most remote lagoons to make their nests. Then you have spoonbills, shags, herons, water hens, ducks of all kinds. You can see them gathered in great numbers at any waterhole. Water birds are nomads. They have to be. When the water dries up they fly off to better country."

"And I've missed them," she said regretfully, struck anew by the beauty of the mirage. It was pulsing away like a silvery fire amid the green line of trees.

"They haven't *all* gone," he assured her. "So buck up. Jingala will fulfil its promise, Ms Wyatt. You won't be starved for the sight of birds. There's still plenty of water around. We've had more glorious rain than we've had in a very long time. The most prolific display of wildflowers is over. You would have loved it, but there are still areas covered in paper daisies and a lot of beautiful little spider lilies near the banks of the billabongs. The water lilies flower all the time. They're quite magnificent. Oddly enough, some of the most exquisite little flowers bloom in the arid soil and the rocky pockets of the hill country. I'll show you another day. The hardiest plant, virtually indestructible, is the spinifex, which you see growing all around us. The reason the spinifex survives is because the root system is always shaded from the sun. See all the long vertical spikes?"

Amber looked out with interest at the great golden clumps that formed a thick three hundred and sixty degree circle. "Yes."

"They have a waxy coating to prevent moisture loss. Even a scorching sun is thrown off by the pointed tips, while the roots are protected.'

"So the spinifex is perfectly adapted to this incredible environment. What I'm finding so unusual are the endless chains of billabongs. It's the desert but not the desert. It's like magic."

"It's a riverine desert," he corrected. "When the big floods are on and the water is brought down from the monsoonal tropical North through our inland river system, the Diamantina, the Georgina and Cooper's Creek, those same billabongs we're heading for can run fifty miles across."

"Good grief!" She tried to visualize such a scene. "Now that's downright scary. Have you ever been marooned?"

He turned his head to look squarely into the golden lakes of her eyes. "Of course. It's drought or flood, Amber. We have to live with both. Many have died in the struggle. Every one of us, right from the first days of settlement, have had to make huge sacrifices. I love my country—this country around us—with a passion. I love it—I wouldn't want to be anywhere else—but the one thing you couldn't call it is *safe*. There are always huge hazards, danger all around you. So don't go getting too carried away."

"Is that a warning?" she asked, her eyes on a solitary conical shaped rock formation standing like a beacon amid the spinifex.

His eyes glittered. "I'm just putting you straight. How would a woman with apricot hair and exquisite creamy skin stand up to this harsh environment?"

Under his intent scrutiny she flushed. "Obviously,

you don't think it can be done, or not without consequences. What about your mother?"

"What about her?"

A definite snap. "Not a good subject, right?"

"Sorry," he said. "But my mother, a beautiful woman, by the way—she got all the looks in the Erskine family—had to be the world's worst mother. No, hang on," he said as though seriously considering, "maybe Jan."

She turned her head to face his handsome, hard-edged profile, more than ready to take him to task. "Now that's unkind. *Very* unkind."

"I never claimed to be *kind*," he said and gave her a slight smile. A sexy smile, damn him, but he wasn't getting off the hook.

"Yet you've been kind to me," she pointed out crisply. "Amazingly kind."

"Perhaps I have an ulterior motive?"

"Aah!" She let her bright head fall back. "Why didn't you tell me you wanted an unpaid nanny?"

He let his impatience show. "Surely you're getting free board?" He let his challenging tone hang between them for a second or two. "Don't be ridiculous. I invited you here to enjoy yourself, see our Outback, maybe derive inspiration for your forthcoming blockbuster, and don't you forget it."

"I was only joking."

He took another moment to consider. "No, you weren't."

"Heck, Cal, are we going to fall out on our very first day?" she asked wryly.

His deep laugh, like a chuckle, caught her by surprise. "Amber, you're not supposed to say silly things like that. I had no idea little Marcus would take to you like you were his appointed guardian angel. We had two good women with lots of experience to help and advise Jan. Like I told you, she drove them away with her flash bang verbal breakouts. They took it as long as they could, then literally flew off. Jan doesn't have mood-swings, like Eliot once said. She's in a filthy mood *all* the time. She takes no pleasure or interest in anything. She gives my uncle a really bad time."

Amber had seen enough of Jan's behaviour to well believe it. Still, she felt compelled to stick up for a deeply depressed new mother. This could and did happen to the best of women. "But surely these are symptoms of PND?" she challenged more disapprovingly than she intended. "The appearance of being out of control, the inability to cope with her baby. Jan's to be pitied. She's to be helped. The condition can be quite severe."

"And you think I'm blaming Jan for what she can't control?" He threw her a hard, impatient look.

"Yes." Amber nodded emphatically. The first time she'd laid eyes on him she'd thought he was the kind of man who'd have difficulty in getting in touch with his feminine side.

"And that's a snap analysis?" was his sarcastic rejoinder.

"I'm only saying what I believe. I'm a woman, after all."

"And I haven't noticed?" The green eyes whipped over her, increasing her heart rate. "The thing is, Ms Wyatt—"

"Yes, Mr MacFarlane?" She feigned strict attention.

"The thing is, Amber, we've all lived with it for months now. We thought things would gradually get better. Everyone has been kind and supportive, believe it or not. Even tough old me. I can see you've already labelled me a hard-hearted man. No, don't begin to deny it."

"I wasn't going to," she said sweetly. "It's just that you can't know what it's really like."

"So what do you suggest? I rush out and father a child. See how I go?"

"You'll find out eventually," she pointed out calmly. "I didn't say I don't think you'd make a good dad."

"But your preference is for sensitive New Age guys," he mocked. "I won't at this point mention that wimp, Sinclair. It defies logic that a woman as intelligent as you dedicated herself to such a louse. How the hell did that happen?"

She gulped in air. "Hey, might I remind you you're not my keeper? Anyway, you're not the one to talk."

"Of course I'm not," he agreed. "Maybe one

day they'll isolate the hormone that causes physical attraction."

"You're suggesting they find the antidote? Believe me, it won't work."

"Well, we can save that for another time. There's nothing to be gained from mooning about the past."

"Who's mooning?" she sweetly asked.

"You said that as if you meant it."

"I do. What about you?"

"I do the best I can." He gave her a sideways grin. "As for Janis, Eliot has had loads—and I mean *loads*—of her favourite flowers flown in. The most expensive flowers ever packed up by a florist, I guarantee. They cost oodles! The bill put even me into shock. Anyway, why don't we get off the subject of Jan?" He knew he sounded a little harsh.

"Her problems won't go away. I do hope Marcus sleeps for your uncle."

"Poor little scrap is suffering pretty severe sleep deprivation," he said, his tone miraculously becoming gentler.

So it was the mother. Not the child. "I just want to say this."

He gave a knowing smile. "Course you do. The investigative journalist. Prize-winning to boot."

She ignored the taunt. "Mrs MacFarlane could be feeling very guilty. She could be feeling shame she can't handle her own baby. She could even be feeling worthless. Have you taken that into account?"

"Would you like to know?" He swerved to avoid an all but hidden boulder, causing the four-wheel drive to rock.

"Of course I would." She straightened up, slightly dizzy with their close proximity. He was *such* a physical man. "I'm asking."

"*You* have taken into account *I'm* not the husband. I'm not the father. I am what I am. Fed up to the back teeth and, before you take me further to task, a very experienced nursing sister from the Royal Flying Doctor team told me privately on her last visit she very much doubted Jan was suffering genuine PND."

"Go on." She turned to him.

"I intend to. Sister Ryan is very familiar with the condition. She advises many young mothers rearing their babies in our Outback isolation."

Amber blew a stray coppery-red lock off her brow. "Okay, so maybe I'm out of line here."

"Don't let *that* bother you," he said dryly. "That's how we met, remember? You being out of line."

"You know, maybe I shouldn't have come out here. Why don't you just tell me to leave?"

He laughed out loud. It was a great sound. "Asking you to leave wouldn't come easily to me. I *like* you, Amber." His eyes sparkled over her. "You're a woman without inhibitions."

"I wouldn't count on that!" She gave him a very speaking glance, at the same moment she felt the imprint of his kisses on her mouth. "Even I, a woman without inhibitions, dare not ask if your uncle's marriage isn't working out. You may well bite my head off. There is the age difference, but it's not all that great. Your uncle is a handsome, very gentlemanly man."

"He's that." The Cattle Baron sighed deeply. "Sometimes it doesn't work with women."

"And no doubt you're a good judge?" Just being with him was giving her a mad rush of exhilaration. Both of them were dealing with old wounds and, maybe now, a resurgence of hormones, chemicals, whatever. The Cattle Baron was manhandling her poor broken heart, though right now she had to question the depth of what she and Sean actually had *had*.

"No better than you, Amber," he said, throwing her another narrow sidelong glance.

That hit a nerve, as it was meant to. "You mean we've both made serious mistakes in the romance stakes," she retaliated.

"Partners in error, you might say. Hindsight has made me think myself a fool."

"And that wouldn't come easily to you. Never mind. Next time we have to lift our standards," she told him briskly.

"Next time?" His vibrant voice positively rasped.

"No need to yell. You're not going to throw me out, are you? I wouldn't like to have to set out on foot."

"You wouldn't get far," he said, laughing.

"So *you* say. Don't underrate me."

"Never!" As a matter of fact, he was half convinced she'd make it.

"I've been in dangerous spots before. Once in Thailand—" She broke off, stunned by the sight that swam into her line of vision. "What in the blue blazes is that? A komodo dragon?" A gigantic lizard, taller than a tall man, was standing on its hind legs and tail, calmly surveying their progress. Its skin, she saw in near horror, was black, strikingly marked with yellow spots. It looked almost as terrifying as a croc.

"That, Ms Wyatt, is a perentie, second only to the komodo dragon in size."

"Thank you, that's quite big enough." She shuddered. "It must be well over six feet."

"Six and a half. That's Yuku. Actually, you're very lucky to see him. Possibly you deserved such a treat. Spotting him isn't all that common. Especially first time out."

"So I've been blessed?"

"Yep." He smiled and her heart twisted that little bit more. In his own way, the Cattle Baron was dynamite. Not an easy man. Not at all. Not overly sympathetic, either. At least to his uncle's wife. She was troubled by that. Frankly, she was trying to find flaws in the superhero.

"You know, this is quite an experience for a city

born, city bred girl," she confided. "I'm finding it all very intoxicating."

"Me included?"

"Nope," she answered briskly. "I need to keep my wits about me. I wouldn't like to be out for a stroll and run into Yuku. What does the name mean? No, don't tell me. Aboriginal for Godzilla. You may not be around to protect me."

"And you couldn't outrun him," he pointed out. "Stand perfectly still. But don't worry, Amber. I'll keep an eye on you."

And lead me where? "That's good to know. It must be an extraordinary feeling, knowing you're master of all this." With her hand she indicated the infinite open plains. "I never expected the landscape to be so *dramatic*, or so awe-inspiring. I love all the dry ochre colours. The mirage must be an endless source of fascination, the way it dances and throws up such extraordinary effects. I have to thank you, yet again, for inviting me out here. For the first time in my life, I'm filled with the sense I'm in the *authentic* Australia."

His lean hand reached out, fingers drumming a brief tattoo on her shoulder. "And so you are." He could see her interest in everything she saw, everything she said, was totally unfeigned. He had given her an opportunity and it looked as if she was determined to take full advantage of it. That pleased him more than he cared to acknowledge. Ms Amber

Wyatt was rewarding company. "You're in the land of the great explorers," he said. "The overlanders, the incredible brave pioneers, my own ancestors among them, who started up their huge cattle and sheep runs. They built their Outback castles and kept themselves, their families, their employees, stockmen and station hands, and their vast herds and flocks alive."

She could hear the pride in his voice. "And it's a grand achievement to carve out a cattle kingdom in the wilderness."

That afternoon the Cattle Baron showed her life on a great Outback station. They parked on a rocky escarpment that glowed an unbelievable orange with charcoal and sapphire striations. The whole area was littered with curious white stones. Below them a mob of mixed steers, bullocks, cows and calves were being watered at a stream. The trample of so many hooves had churned the water to a rusty red. To Amber's eyes, the cattle looked to be in prime condition. Stockmen on horseback, battered Akubras pulled down low on their foreheads, quietly sat in the saddle, watching on. Moments later, one of the men began to head a number of beasts away from the water. Obviously they had had enough to drink because they went without urging, trotting sedately up the bank, with the stockman harmlessly wielding a whip in the air.

The men were all, so far as she could see, aboriginal or part aboriginal. Outback stations would owe a great vote of thanks to their indigenous workforce, she thought, which led her to believe that Mrs MacFarlane was making a huge mistake in not utilizing the skills of Dee's house girls with baby Marcus. The one who had waited at lunch, young Mina, looked as if she would be very gentle and caring with the little fellow.

As the afternoon wore on the glare became more intense. Once she was shocked into crying out in panic, *"Look!"* Her hand shot out to grasp his shoulder.

"I'm looking," he answered with a casualness that unnerved her.

"We're going to drive right into a lake. Look. Dead ahead." Her anxiety was mounting to the extent she was braking hard and quite uselessly with her feet.

"Give it a minute and it will disappear."

Just as he predicted, in under thirty seconds the lake disappeared.

"So what was that?' she asked in astonishment. "The mirage?"

"Get used to it. You're going to see it a lot. The mirage is what so cruelly tricked the early explorers time and time again. Tricked many a traveller. Tricked you."

"It sure did!" Amber had no trouble admitting. "It looked so cool and inviting, then again so oddly out of place in the middle of the spinifex. Makes me wonder if I'm going to be able to trust my eyes."

"Borrow mine." He slanted her a smile.

Her whole body received it like some wonderful benediction.

Last on the agenda was a drive through the holding camps, men waving, calling out greetings to the boss. The Cattle Baron was popular with his workforce. "We won't stop today. Just for now, I don't want you agitating the men."

"Agitating the men?" she echoed in disbelief.

"I'm sure none of them has seen a woman like you in their entire life," he explained. "Another time you can meet them."

"Am I supposed to wear camouflage?"

He laughed and let it go.

Several times they forded creeks and branch creeks, the larger stretches of water afloat with waterlilies, magnificent blooms, pink in one place, lotus-blue in another, cream and ivory. How marvellous they would look in a vase! They bumped across a rushing, rock-strewn gully to get to one lagoon in particular, a huge open span of clear crystal water dotted with little islands covered in palms to rival the tropics.

"A good place to swim," the Cattle Baron told her casually. "You've brought a swimsuit?"

"Sorry, I didn't think. How could I when the rush was so great?"

"Never mind. You can always dive in au naturel."

Normally self-assured, she found herself blushing. All over. "I wouldn't consider it, even if I were on my own."

"So what would you be hiding?" He had to laugh at her expression—half embarrassment, half outrage. "It's all right. Take it easy." He was, in fact, mentally contemplating what Ms Wyatt would look like unclothed. Divine. He kept veering from powerful attraction to remanning his barricades and possibly saving himself a good deal of grief.

Head things off at the pass, MacFarlane.

When they arrived back at the homestead, the sun was setting in such splendour that Amber was reluctant to go indoors.

"Let's stay outside for a few minutes," she begged. "I want to celebrate such beauty. You may be used to it but I've never seen a sky so awash with those breathtaking colours—fiery reds, gold, pinks, glorious apricots! And look at the long trails of pale green, silvery-blue and amethyst. How beautiful!"

"It is that," he agreed. Her responses were spontaneous. She really was soaking it all in. The remoteness that was so threatening to a lot of people, Ms Wyatt appeared to be quite comfortable with.

"The intensity of colour seems almost unreal," she was saying, her eyes on the glory of the western sky.

"I've witnessed countless beautiful sunsets before, but nothing like this."

"Now that cheers me, Ms Wyatt," he said and he realised he meant it. "But wait until you see the stars tonight. No city pollution. I can guarantee you'll never have seen a clearer Southern Cross."

How could he miss the heat reflected in her cheeks? If a man had sexual radiance it was he! Exposed to it at such close quarters, it was dazzling.

Inside the great house, peace reigned. The Cattle Baron looked at her with a wry grin. "The world needs more women like you, Ms Wyatt."

"Let's see what's happening first." Amber walked briskly into the informal living area where they had left Eliot MacFarlane and his baby son. Eliot had disappeared but, seated in the armchair, a tender smile on her face, one small brown sandal-shod foot rocking the bouncinette, was Mina. Baby Marcus was wide awake, staring up into Mina's gentle face.

As soon as Mina realised that Mr MacFarlane and his visitor—a bright spirit being, Mina thought—were behind her she jumped up, trembling, out of the chair, a look of guilt on her face. "Dee give me permission," she wailed. "I would never hurt the baby. *Never.* I have little brothers and sisters of me own."

The Cattle Baron held up a hand. "Mina, we would never think for a moment you would harm the baby. Whatever gave you that idea?"

Mina shot a look from the Cattle Baron to Amber, who smiled reassuringly at her. "Missus Eliot don't want me anywhere near baby."

"That's because she doesn't understand how good and reliable you are, Mina," Cal said, a vertical frown between his strongly marked brows. "You can go now. And thank you. What happened to Mr Eliot, by the way?"

Mina relaxed into a big smile. "Mr Eliot, he fell fast asleep with baby. Dee told him to go an' have a good lie down."

"Thank you, Mina," Cal said. After Mina had hurried off, he turned his attention back to Amber. "So what now?"

"Looks like we're in charge," she said a little wryly.

"Eliot should never have pegged Janis for a full-time mum. He made a bad decision there."

"Now don't go losing your jolly mood." She bent to free baby Marcus from the bouncinette, swooping him into her arms. "Hello, sweetheart. How's it going?"

"I'm sure he can't talk as yet."

"Do *you* want to hold him?" she asked pointedly.

"This is blackmail, Ms Wyatt."

"You know, you need to get more in touch with your tender side." She gave him a challenging look. "Take a crash course in how to handle babies. This is your little cousin. Say hello, Marcus. This is Cousin Cal, the big-shot Cattle Baron."

"Please do *not* condescend, Ms Wyatt. You're entirely at my mercy."

The man could conjure up body heat at a glance. "I'm only having a joke." She really felt that adrenalin jolt.

"You joke a lot."

"What makes you think it's not a good idea? God forbid I should make you angry. Look, Marcus is smiling." Her tone carried surprise and delight.

"Wind?" he suggested, mock polite.

"Marcus is *smiling*," she repeated.

"So he is!" He came in close, an electric presence, letting the baby take hold of his finger. "You're an angel, Ms Wyatt."

"I'm not an angel." She was thrilled with the way Marcus and his powerful cousin were connecting. The gentleness of the Cattle Baron's smile startled her. Maybe he had a lot of heart, after all.

Then he messed up. "I know you're not," he said crisply. "But you are pretty darn special."

"Well, thanks for that."

"It's the least I can say." He bent nearer to the baby. "He's looking at us like *we're* the proud parents." Marcus was still tightly gripping his finger.

"I've been struck by the same thought. You want kids?"

He gave her a long, cool, slow look. "Did I say I wanted kids?"

"Who then shall inherit your kingdom? Seriously now, who? You must want kids. You *need* kids. You wouldn't want me to think otherwise, would you?"

"What if I confess I'm scared of women?"

"You're not scared of me."

"I swear to God I am."

At the devilry in his eyes, every pulse in Amber's body ignited. It was as if she had swallowed a fire-cracker. "See how contented he is." She lowered her head quickly. "I wonder when he had his last bottle. He's not breastfed?"

"Hell, what a question!' He gave her a look that was positively unnerved for a superhero. "Not my place to go into the details."

"Just thought I'd run it by you."

"Well, I have no idea. I keep right out of the way with that stuff. Anyway, he loves your hair."

"The bright colour." She bent and kissed the top of the baby's head. "At which point do we find out?"

"About what?" Myriad expressions flitted across his dynamic face.

"Don't snap. There *are* limits to my tolerance. And, just to get the record straight, I don't intend to free up time for an affair."

"You wish!" he said witheringly.

Her golden eyes sparkled. "Such arrogance!"

"You'd do well to remember. Anyway, don't let's upset the baby." He turned his dark head as footsteps sounded on the marble floor, which was inlaid with a grid of rosewood, in the central hall. "Here's Dee," he said. "I'm sure she can answer all your questions."

"Got it! But I don't have to like it."

"Meaning what?" He shot her a glance. "No, don't bother. You're finding it too easy to push my buttons. Now I have to go. I have a hundred and one things I need to attend to."

"Well, you're halfway to your office." She gave him a sweet smile. "And thank you once again for your time."

"My pleasure." He gave an exaggerated suave bow.

CHAPTER SEVEN

THEY all came together for dinner. In the interim, with Dee looking on, offering helpful suggestions, Amber had managed to bathe Marcus and give him his bottle—no, he wasn't breastfed, Mrs MacFarlane hadn't considered it an option. Next, she'd settled him once again in his bouncinette, where he'd immediately returned quite happily to napping.

"The poor little soul is catching up on a whole lot of lost sleep," said Dee. "He's had the roughest time of the lot."

"Let's hope he's coming out of it." Amber was grateful that she and Dee were getting on so well. "It could be time. Some little ones don't settle for a few months, then overnight they're okay."

"You hope! Ya know Mrs MacFarlane is her own worst enemy," Dee half covered her mouth as she said it, as though Janis might be right behind her. "I suppose the poor girl can't help her nature."

"It's sad if she feels inadequate for the task."

Amber was still not persuaded that Janis MacFarlane wasn't a victim of PND.

But Dee harrumphed. "She's confident enough to tell everyone off."

"Maybe it's the isolation," Amber suggested. "No support and no contact from another woman from her own family. Her mother."

"I think she has a very poor relationship with her mother," Dee said, folding and refolding a clean bib. "Don't tell her I sent young Mina to mind the child. That'll set her off."

"Surely Eliot would tell her?" Amber's eyes widened. "Why can't he make her see she needs all the help she can get? Mina is only too willing to mind the baby."

"Little thing wouldn't hurt a fly and she's utterly trustworthy," Dee said, very loyal to her staff. "All my girls are. I train them. They pay close attention. They were all born on the station. Went to the station school. They're happiest here. This is *their* country. But it's like I told you, Mrs MacFarlane has… issues."

"Now that *is* sad," Amber said, her voice quiet. "Maybe she needs a little time to adjust to Outback life."

"Maybe." Dee's sceptical response hung in the air. "Might help if she tried to put on a happy face now and again. Not that I'd recognise it if I saw it. The lady has never wasted her charm on me. Unlike others," she added cryptically. "I've seen a lot of people come and go, Amber. You either love the Outback—take to it like a whistling duck to a lagoon—or you never adapt. Cal's mum didn't, though a fair amount of time went by before she lit out. She loved her husband. Not that Jeff Rankin. Never married him anyway. She *adored* her son. I know he won't have it, but she *did*. Big mess up there. Cal's mum couldn't cope with the life. Got to feel like a prisoner. City girl, ya see!"

"Like me," Amber had to point out.

"*Not* like you." Dee gave a quick shake of the head. "You came in from your trip with your eyes shinin'"

"That's a good sign?"

"The best sign there is!" Dee pronounced, patting Amber's arm.

What to wear? The homestead was so splendid, the MacFarlanes so clearly used to the best, she picked out a dress she thought appropriate—a silk maxi. She could have worn it to a garden party. It had lovely full-blown roses, apricot, pink and yellow, printed on a white ground. She'd loved the fabric the minute she'd seen it. It swished delightfully around her ankles. She hoped Janis MacFarlane would join them. She wanted to get her own take on what was so badly troubling the woman. Restored to well-being, Janis MacFarlane could be beautiful. She had to take into account that trained professionals

had ruled out PND as the cause of Janis
MacFarlane's distress. She wanted her own view.
Offer support if permitted. Janis hadn't come
forward to object to her bathing and feeding baby
Marcus, at any rate.

They dined in yet another area on the east side of
the house—a stone colonnaded terrace with a series
of arches extending the full length of the rear
exterior. The floor was tiled in mosaic form, tur-
quoise, white and orange lifting the deep terracotta.
A monumental hewn timber table was beautifully
set, the table surrounded by the traditional heavy
wicker chairs of South East Asia. It was a wonderfully inviting setting, very cool, lit by many hanging
brass lanterns. Amber was able to look out and enjoy
a section of the garden which was densely planted
with bougainvilleas that thrived in the dry. They
spilled and climbed everywhere—pink, orange,
bronze and a lovely deep violet. The long flower-
ing bracts simply blazed in the lights.

Rolling the stem of her crystal wineglass between
her two fingers, Amber watched the interaction of
the family. The Cattle Baron looked marvelous, she
thought, realising she was now admiring his style
of looks—the strong distinctive features, the taut
toughness and his great body. The man fitted his
setting. He was simply dressed but high quality all
the way—white cotton shirt very up to the moment,

safari style, buttoned down pockets, open-necked, over perfectly fitted khaki-coloured trousers. In the middle of the desert he didn't need anyone to give him any style tips. His uncle was his elegant self in a cotton striped shirt and charcoal trousers to match one of the stripes. Janis MacFarlane looked a great deal better than the first time Amber had seen her. She wore a scarlet dress of surprisingly bold cut. The neckline dipped precariously low. Amber supposed it was because of weight loss. She wasn't wearing a bra. Her long dark hair was arranged in an elegant knot, large dark eyes shining. Or was that more a feverish glint? Amber could see when she was well and happy how Janis would have dazzled her husband. Her long nails were painted the same colour as her dress. No housework to break them. No catching of nails in baby's nappy. She wore no jewellery around her delicate neck, but the central diamond in her engagement ring was so big it was a wonder she could lift her fork.

And she was inexcusably rude. After the initial head to toe inspection of Amber's person, she rarely looked at her again. She looked—not at her husband—but, for God's sake at the *Cattle Baron*. In fact Amber realised with some surprise that she talked almost exclusively to him. Once her finger reached out and touched his hand where it lay on the linen and lace table mat.

Dear God!

Amber was shocked into giving a gasp, which she hurriedly turned into a cough. With utter dismay, she perceived the truth as if it were all spelt out for her in neon letters ten feet high.

Janis MacFarlane is in love with The Cattle Baron.

How was that for a scenario? It smacked of madness. Worse, danger. No wonder the woman wasn't functioning properly.

Did Cal know? Did his uncle know? Did Dee know? Surely Dee had dropped a hint to fuel her perceptions?

A hard lump lodged in Amber's chest. She thought it would take ages before the shock waves wore off. Janis MacFarlane's high levels of anger and bitter resentment directed towards her husband and baby were symptoms not of PND but of being caught in a taboo situation. She had flipped the switch herself. Loving the wrong man would be akin to desolation. Eliot MacFarlane was a fine-looking man, gentle, cultured, but, seen side by side with his nephew, with his youth and blazing aura, his immense sexual radiance, Eliot's attractions all but faded away.

Was that disaster?

Was it ever!

Cal turned his dark head to give her an odd look. "You okay?"

With her head full of horror, she fetched up a smile. "Never better!" She was uncertain now whether her compassion for Janis MacFarlane was lessening or growing. What a penance, falling in love with your husband's nephew!

"So what's your opinion of Jingala beef?" he asked, unaware of Amber's train of thought.

Dee, who was revealing herself as a great cook, had roasted a prime fillet of beef served with a red wine sauce and cooked-to-perfection buttered vegetables.

"Mouth-watering," she said. She'd been hungry when the meal had arrived but the latest revelation had killed her appetite stone dead.

"You can have another glass of shiraz for that." He smiled.

"I hear you lost your job, Ms Wyatt." Janis suddenly spoke up. Her words seemed to carry an odd sting. Amber had the bizarre thought that Janis MacFarlane was jealous of her very presence. Or was she a naturally nasty person? You couldn't just fake PND. One might have to look elsewhere for a cause.

And now Amber knew *where*.

"Give us a break, Jan," Cal groaned. "Amber asked you to use her first name as soon as she walked in."

"Amber, of course." Janis MacFarlane's scarlet mouth pouted. "So sorry. If you were after seclusion…Amber, you couldn't do better than here."

"Then I have to say I love seclusion." Amber caught the Cattle Baron's glittering eyes.

"What?" Janis exclaimed. "You love the vast

empty spaces—well, of course you love the home-stead—" this delivered very dryly "—or is it the diplomatic thing to say?"

"You don't believe me?" Amber smiled, though it took quite an effort. "But tell me. How did you know I'd lost my job?" Had Cal told her? What *else* had he told her? She hoped she looked cool. She didn't feel cool. In fact, she was beginning to steam up.

"Janis didn't get it from me," the Cattle Baron intervened as though he'd read Amber's mind.

Janis MacFarlane threw back the rest of her wine. She had eaten very, very sparingly but the beautiful wines on offer were quite a different matter. "You're not a complete unknown... Amber," she said, making an unsuccessful attempt at sounding friendly. "Even in the wilds, with the satellite, it's very easy to trace faces and names."

A moment of stunned silence. "You *traced* her?" Cal asked before Amber had a chance to.

"Why, yes! I recognised Amber's face right off. Naturally, I was interested in her story. And does she *have* one!"

"Run it by us," Cal invited, again beating a simmering Amber to a retort. Unless she was growing super-sensitive, Janis MacFarlane's tone wasn't far from open contempt. *Calm down, dammit. Don't let this very odd woman get under your skin.*

"I swear I would have done the same thing in your place, Amber," Janis now assured her. "In fact, I would have been lying in wait for him somewhere."

"Not with a gun, I hope?" This time Amber beat the Cattle Baron off. She was beginning to think Janis MacFarlane well capable of pulling a trigger.

Janis shrugged a thin ivory shoulder. "He deserved punishment for what he did to you. I suppose you still love him?"

Once more the Cattle Baron opened his mouth to reply, presumably on Amber's behalf, but she turned to him sweetly.

"May I speak, please?"

His mouth twitched. "Go right ahead."

"Without interruption?"

His eyes sparkled. "Be my guest."

"Thank you." Amber shifted her gaze to Janis MacFarlane's face. It was openly hostile at this quick exchange between Cal and his guest. More signs of jealousy here? Amber would have been pleased to know that she, on the other hand, looked completely unperturbed. "I really don't know if I ever did love him, Janis," she said. "That's the truest answer I can give. At any rate, I'm not having any vulnerable moments. I'm not spending any time thinking about him. He's married. I doubt I'll speak to him again."

"And I don't blame you." Janis spoke darkly, as though she abandoned men every day. "It's a miracle you've survived so much public humiliation. But you, Cal—" she turned eyes huge with concern on him "—you've risked a lot, haven't you, upsetting your grandfather?"

The Cattle Baron let his irritation show. It caused his uncle to take belated action. It obviously took time for Eliot to marshal his thoughts, Amber mused, not without sympathy. After a blissful first marriage that had ended in tragedy, Eliot appeared to have no real idea what this young woman he had married in such a hurry was on about. Either way, it was up to him to put a stop to her treating him like dirt.

Eliot pressed down on his wife's fingers. "Why are you talking about this, Jan, and at dinner? All of us want a pleasant evening. Cal is his own man. He has never kowtowed to his grandfather. No MacFarlane would. The very last thing we want to do is upset Amber, our guest, never mind Clive Erskine."

"May I have my fingers back?" Janis MacFarlane snapped. "You're hurting me." She snatched her hand away, looking martyred. "I was just worried about Cal. That's all."

Somehow they got through coffee. At any rate, Janis didn't speak to Amber again. Afterwards, Cal suggested Amber might like a stroll around the home compound before bed.

With that, Janis gave her husband the sharp order. "On your feet, Eliot. I too would like some fresh air."

Eliot's answer was surprisingly tranquil. He looked around the outdoor setting. "I would have thought we were getting plenty. I think we'd do a whole lot better looking in on our son."

Right on!

Outside, under the gloriously blossoming stars, Amber started to unwind. "Gosh, does Janis ever have a good day?"

"She could well do," Cal replied after a moment's consideration. "It's just I haven't seen it. Eliot isn't terribly good at pulling her into line either."

"How *does* one pull a woman into line?" Amber asked, wondering how the Cattle Baron would go about it.

"You sound like you'd expect me to break teeth?"

"Is that an answer?" she said, laughing.

"You're not getting a rise out of me, Amber," he told her dryly.

"Okay, let's regroup. Tell me about the stars. You're absolutely right. I've never seen anything to equal the numbers, the size and the brilliance. The Southern Cross has never looked so bright or so close, or the Milky Way so luminous." She lifted her head in a gesture of worship to the great dazzling vault of the sky, spanned by millions of twinkling, sparkling stars. "The aboriginal people have all sorts of myths and legends about the stars, don't they?"

"Sun, moon and stars. Every living thing, every mystery explained. The Milky Way is the home of the great beings. It's also our home if we've lived a good life. Of course the myths vary from region to region. One of the most interesting facets of mythology is ritual. The two complement each other. I'll speak to one of our tribal elders, Jimmy Possum, about organising a corroboree for you, one that's not sacred—"

"Before I go?" She was unwilling to explore her burgeoning feelings about the Cattle Baron, but she had to admit that he had gained powerful entry into her life.

"Do you *want* to go?" He looked down on her from his superior height.

"Not for ages! This is the most exciting adventure I've had in my life."

"And you're barely into it," he answered suavely.

"Listen, I *meant* it." The challenge in his manner kept her on a knife edge. "You have major trust issues with women, don't you?" she ventured. "What do you actually *need* from a woman to trust her?" She allowed him to take her arm to draw her away from an overhanging frond. If she had been carrying something she would have dropped it, so nerveless did he render her limbs.

"You think that's my problem?" He released her, taking his time.

"Like me, your fiancée betrayed you. That's got to hurt!" She shook her head with real feeling, the movement making the deep sinuous waves of her hair bounce.

"Hurt at the time, but betrayal is part of a man's education," he returned in a clipped voice.

"Don't forget us girls."

"I doubt if I could forget *you*, Ms Wyatt." He gave a mocking sigh of admiration.

"You ticked Janis off for calling me Ms Wyatt."

"The problem with Janis is that, unlike me, she wasn't doing it in fun."

"So it's fun, is it?"

"We both know it is."

She did know. Had it been another two people, she would have said they were flirting. Silly word. The Cattle Baron was above and beyond flirting. So was she, for that matter. "So what about a few legends?" Here, in the perfumed semi-dark, excitement was picking up at an alarming rate. The man's aura of sexuality had a tremendous edge.

"I'm weighing up which ones to tell you," he said. "Some of them are pretty damned erotic."

"Like the tales of the Arabian Nights?"

"Are you telling me you've read them?" he asked with a catch of laughter in his voice.

"Actually, when I was a kid I got hold of an old copy. I used to read everything and anything I could get my hands on. I remember it was in a trunk with lots of other old books. I couldn't make head or tail of it, but it sure beat a comic book."

"I should hope you couldn't understand it, not if you were a child. Anyway, I'm sure you've caught up over the years. Did you and Sinclair live together?"

"No, we didn't!" she said crossly. "I guess I had that much sense. Anyway, I've warned you. Let's forget about him unless you want us to have a heart to heart about your ex."

"Brooke is history."

"So *you* say. You never run into her?"

He extended a long arm to hold up another frond overhanging the pathway. "Not often when so many miles separate us."

"So where does she live? As the crow flies?"

"You can go on the Internet and find out all about her family," he said. "Her father is Peter Rowlands. They're an old pastoral family. It would seem the Internet is Jan's only form of relaxation. The Rowlands' flagship station, Goorack, is about one hundred and fifty miles north-east of here."

"Impressive?"

"Well, it's not right up there with Jingala, Kinjarra, Daramba and the like, but impressive enough," he said.

"Did you ever give her a chance to say she was sorry?" She felt compelled to know.

"Ms Wyatt, as far as I'm concerned, being unfaithful wraps the whole thing up."

"So that's a no, then?"

"Well, I won't screw up and appear at her wedding."

"Couldn't resist it, could you?" she said in disgust. "Your ex is getting married?"

"Not as far as I know." The reply was bland.

"Oh, that is so like you!" Her tone was laced with irritation.

"But you don't have any real idea what I'm like, Amber Wyatt. For instance, did you know I'm dying to kiss you?"

She had to brace herself against the shock. The man had sex appeal on tap. "One way of shutting me up?"

"You know what they say. The only way to get rid of temptation is to yield to it."

"Oscar Wilde." She sucked in a breath as his hands dropped to her waist. "What's going on here, Cal?"

"Just a kiss in the dark," he said smoothly. "All part of your Outback adventure. We can revert to our normal selves the minute we go back inside."

His handsome face was very close, his male charisma scattering her defences to the desert winds. "Look, the last thing I should do is encourage you." She braced her hands against his hard muscled chest.

"Sure about that?"

"Spare me the arrogance, Cal MacFarlane."

"Not arrogance. Think of it as therapy. For both of us and our wounded hearts. Neither of us is looking for a long-term involvement right now, are we? Our lifestyles are totally incompatible and so forth. Going on our past experience, a shared kiss would be a very pleasant way to round off the evening."

"I don't know if pleasant is the right word. A bit tame in comparison to our last encounter. But then both of us were het up at the time. Right now, I think it best if I pull away."

"Why don't you?"

"You may well ask. It's not easy." She laughed. She was still laughing when he covered her mouth with a low murmur that sounded very much like yearning.

Whatever, she lost it.

Entirely.

How could her body be responding, *rejoicing,* in this way? She had never believed herself to be fickle. And yet she was opening her mouth to him, feeling the warm pressure of his lips, his tongue sliding over her teeth, bringing up her arms to clasp behind his neck, closing her eyes tight with the brilliant stars shining down on her heavy lids.

How long did it last?

She didn't know. The only thing she *did* know was that she hadn't pushed him away. The mouth that covered hers with so much passion and mastery might well have encircled her heart. It was tremendous. It was dizzying. It was also very bewildering. She would have to re-evaluate her whole adult life. It wasn't all that long ago she'd believed her heart to have been slashed to ribbons.

What a turnaround that was! She had sloughed off the old Amber and become a new woman. Maybe a touch demented.

When he finally lifted his head she leaned heavily against him, revelling in his height and his strength. Temporarily she felt unable and unwilling to stand free.

He kissed the top of her head. "I thought when I kissed you at the wedding that no woman could have responded better. Now you've thrown in a little extra."

"That I have! Take it as glorious lunacy. Don't expect *all* my self-control to disappear."

"God knows I'll have to get a handle on my own." There was a mixture of laughter and self-mockery in his tone. "But on no account need you fear I'll overstep the boundaries," he assured her. "Are you able to walk on?"

Her response was a little tart in the face of his mockery. "How many other women have you kissed that swoon?"

"None more thrilling than you," he replied.

"As if I believe you!"

Even so, she seemed to be floating in the perfumed darkness. She had never been more conscious of her own body, of her skin, its largest, most sensitive organ. She might not have been wearing any clothes at all, she felt so exposed to his every glance, let alone the touch of his hand.

"You should."

He sounded serious. "All the more reason to keep the brakes on, surely?" she warned. "Both of us have had our trust smashed."

"More like dented."

She lifted her head. "I thought you loved your ex-fiancée?"

"At one time, so did I. It seems obvious now that I didn't search far enough for the woman I want. Neither did you for the right man."

"When you get right down to it, no," she admitted with a sigh. "But don't let's spoil a beautiful night mulling over our past mistakes. What about a legend or two? As a child I loved stories. My father used to read to me at bedtime. I loved him so much."

"And he would have loved you, his little princess." Again, he surprised her by dropping another kiss on the top of her head. His empathy was genuine. It filled her with warmth and a surprising measure of comfort. "Maybe you don't have your father, Amber, but you have a lot of happy memories."

"He has never really died for me." Her voice broke a little.

"My dad either," he said, so much the man he wasn't afraid to show his feelings. "I still see him around the station." He lifted his dark head, pointing with one hand. "He's up there among the countless millions of stars in the Milky Way. That's where heroes go. There's a story about the Milky Way's creation. What to hear it?"

"I told you. I love legends."

"Well, then…" He took her arm. "Once, during the

Dreamtime, there was a giant Being called Ngurunderi who resolved to brighten the night sky…"

Going to sleep was out of the question. She was too wound up. To be honest, too erotically charged. Amber moved around her bedroom in her night-dress, touching this, studying that, unable to relax. Not to put too fine a point on it, she had never felt more stirred up in her life. That was just how good the Cattle Baron was. Out of nowhere an irresistible force had blasted his way into her life. She barely knew him, yet she felt as though he had always been somewhere at the back of her mind. She could still feel the warmth of his skin, the strength of his hands, the male scent of him, the slight rasp of his beard, the wondrous pressure of his mouth on hers. She felt weak even thinking about it. How in the world had his ex-fiancée ever let him go? She had to be mad. Or she had so missed the excitement of the man, the marvellous sex, when he was away, that she had surrendered to a one-night stand for simple relief? Such things happened.

Not apparently to the Cattle Baron. One strike and you're out! Not that she would have taken Sean back, even if he hadn't married his Georgie. She didn't even waste time wondering if they were enjoying their honeymoon.

The other thing that was really worrying her was Janis MacFarlane. Eliot should pack up his wife and child and never come back. Not until his nephew was safely married to someone who wouldn't let another woman in the world steal her man. It must be utter agony for Janis, living under the same roof with an impossible dream. It didn't excuse her lashing out but it did explain a good deal. The biggest victim here was little Marcus. Surely Janis realized that love for her little son could save her? So many women were desperate to have a child—undergoing protracted procedures—yet Janis couldn't see her baby as her most precious possession.

Amber had no answer for that.

Just as she was contemplating turning in, a thundering came on the heavy mahogany door. Those were some tough knuckles! Could the Cattle Baron be so blatant? Not possible. Even if he were, that didn't lower her level of desire.

Swiftly she belted her satin robe tightly around her, thrust her long hair over her shoulder and went to answer before the door was broken down.

"Cal!" Her heart leapt. She couldn't bank it down. "What is this—a very noisy seduction scene first night off?"

"Is that what it looks like?" His green eyes, normally so cool, were ablaze.

"Well…" She hesitated, not sure she could handle this veritable powerhouse of passion, let alone herself.

"Oh, for God's sake, do I look nakedly desirous?" he asked jaggedly.

"I can't pronounce on that with any degree of confidence. Are you?"

"More than you'll ever know," he groaned. Here was this glorious woman, her hair springing back from her radiant creamy face, her slender body just barely hidden by a filmy pink nightdress and a slinky satin robe right there in front of him. Maybe even his for the taking. She would have turned on a monk. She was turning him on right now. But there was an embarrassing crisis to hand. "Janis is having the mother of all tantrums," he explained. "It's the baby I'm worried about. He's screaming. The seduction scene will have to keep for another night. I promise I'll make it worth the wait. For now, we desperately need your calming hands."

She could handle that. "And leave the rest of me behind?" she joked, to bring down the tension.

"Bring the lot."

Her gaze swept over him. He wore a red T-shirt and a pair of jeans he must have hastily pulled on, crow-black curls tousled. She was experiencing a heaviness in the lower part of her body. God, she wanted him…wanted him… An overpowering sexual urge. No need to feel guilty. "Should I dress?"

"I've never seen a woman look better in my life. Come now. Just as you are. Babies shouldn't be allowed to cry like that. Janis just gives in to her moods. I'd say histrionics."

He could well be right. But either way the woman was in pain. Amber couldn't find it in her heart to entirely blame her.

Following in his tempestuous wake, Amber all but flew down the corridor as Cal strode towards the suite of rooms his uncle and Janis occupied, the adjoining sitting room turned temporarily into a nursery. Eliot, white beneath his tan, must have heard Cal's heavy footsteps—he was making no attempt to walk quietly or to keep to the muffling Persian runner—because Eliot opened the bedroom door, dressed in pyjamas covered by a navy silk robe.

"This is not my finest hour," he said.

Amber fancied he was right. Why *did* he let things get so out of hand?

Inside, Janis was standing in the middle of the huge opulent room, yanking at her long hair, her dark eyes the size of saucers. "Who asked her?" she screeched. It was so loud it almost pinned Amber to the door. "I don't want her. What's she doing here?"

No one answered her. Cal strode through to the adjoining room where the baby was screaming his tiny head off, as well he might. He was back within seconds, making for Amber and handing her the baby. "Boy, I bet he's glad to see you again," he muttered.

"Amber, I'm so sorry," Eliot MacFarlane said. "Much to our relief, Marcus had been sleeping. Then he woke up."

"Screaming his head off as usual, just as I had fallen asleep," Janis MacFarlane complained bitterly, her delicate features drawn tight. "Doesn't *anyone* sympathize with me? It's always the *baby*. What about *me*? Don't I matter?"

Again no one answered. Janis MacFarlane's main concern seemed to be herself. Even then, Amber was reluctant to lay blame. Was she using anger as an antidote to thwarted passion?

"Eliot, doesn't Janis have a tranquilliser?" Cal turned to his uncle, trying very hard to curb his impatience. "She sounds like she's in need of one."

"She's already downed a couple of pills," Eliot told his nephew unhappily.

"Here, let me help you, Janis." Amber settled the baby over her shoulder, swaying gently. "I'll take him outside until he settles down again. I might go down to my bedroom, if that's okay." Exhausted, little Marcus snuggled in to Amber's warm receptive body, the piteous cries banking down to shuddery whimpers and hiccups.

"What *are* you?" Janis was fuelled by an overriding jealousy that had nothing to do with the baby. "A bloody earth mother? I wonder how good you'd be if you had a little monster like this one."

"Ever wonder if it's because you're rejecting

him," Cal retorted curtly, unable to help himself. He turned to join Amber. "I'll stay with Marcus if I have to, Eliot. You look terrible. I'm worried about you. Both of you go back to bed. We have to find a solution to this. It's gone on far too long. The best professional help has been made available to you, Janis, but you've driven everyone away. You have no choice now. I won't abide it."

"God, what a mess!" Cal followed Amber, baby over her shoulder, into her bedroom. "I shouldn't have brought you out here. I apologise a million times. You've been the best!"

"Hush!" she whispered.

Very quietly he approached. The baby's tiny body was rising and falling very gently. His little hand was caught into the glittering mass of Amber's hair. Her robe had fallen open—the satin sash had come loose, dangling in its loops. He could see the exquisite curves of her naked breasts. Never had the sight of a woman and baby moved him so profoundly. No wonder the great artists of the Renaissance had produced masterpiece after masterpiece of Madonna and child. He couldn't help himself. He imagined her nursing *their* child. The thought shocked him, not only with its element of eroticism. It was all he could do not to pull the three of them into bed.

"So what now?" he whispered. "Do you want me

to take him?" He was fully prepared to. It struck him how much sympathy he had for this poor little unloved scrap. Unloved by his mother. At least at this point. Would it ever change? Eliot loved his son but it seemed that he had come to fatherhood too late. He certainly couldn't control his wife.

"I think he needs to be close to me for a while," Amber said. "I felt very sorry for Janis and your uncle but Janis does need help. I couldn't help noticing at dinner she hardly ate a bite, as if food was irrelevant. She could be missing out on essential vitamins and minerals."

"All this has been pointed out to her, Amber," he said testily.

"I guess. Why don't you advise them to go away for a while until she's feeling more able to cope? Take a trip."

"And leave Marcus behind?" His black eyebrows shot up.

"Yes," she answered, matching whisper for whisper. "We can get things organised."

"We? God, Amber, there aren't enough hours in the day for me. I have a big station to run. Outstations to visit."

"Don't think I don't admire the level of your dedication."

"So you surely don't expect me to babysit the little chap?"

"Who's asking you to?" She stared into his face,

his handsome features drawn tight. There was a pulse throbbing away in his temple. She realised that, one way and another, he had put up with a good deal. This wasn't *his* problem. "Though you might be expected to babysit at some time in the future. Modern dads have to pull their weight."

"Whoa!" He held up his hands. "I take it you mean if and when *I* become a dad?"

She gave him a smile full of unconscious allure. "Come on, you know you want to."

Of course he would! With *her* as his child's mother. The thought just surfaced. "No wonder you're a journalist," he said. "Winkling information out of people."

"I'm taking your measure, Cal MacFarlane."

"And I'm taking yours."

"Don't think I haven't noticed." They were indeed evaluating one another. To what purpose? Forming an intimate bond? Crazy as it was, she was more than willing to give it a go. "If your uncle and Janis are agreeable, Dee and I and young Mina will get baby Marcus into a routine. Janis's unhappiness has been contagious. For the time being, Marcus might settle better without her."

"Have you any idea what you're taking on?" He cast an eye on the child. Marcus had fallen off to sleep again. How had *that* happened? It had to be woman magic. *This* woman's magic. What a God-given asset!

"Of course I do, silly man."

"Silly man?" He gave her a look of pure disbelief. "Excuse me, Ms Wyatt."

"You're a big boy. You can take it. Why don't you go back to bed? Marcus can stay with me for the night."

"Maybe it would be a good idea if I slept on the other side?" There was a sudden sparkle in his green eyes.

"You're joking, of course?"

"Actually, I wouldn't mind." He pinned her with a beautiful wry smile. "I wouldn't mind at all. The bed is big enough to make us all comfortable."

"I'm not going to let you tempt me." And he definitely was. "There's no need to stay. Go now. We'll be fine."

"Why don't I sit down and wait until you're both in bed?" he suggested, not happy at the thought of leaving her alone to cope.

"No, I'm kicking you out now. You're too much of a distraction. See, Marcus is breathing quietly. I'm quiet. He's quiet. I can manage. I'm a babysitter from way back."

"Okay," he agreed reluctantly. "You know I'm building up a big debt to you?"

"Don't worry. I'll see to it you pay up."

"The sooner the better," he said.

It sounded lovely. "Night, night, Cal," she softly called. "Pleasant dreams."

He walked to the door—tall, dark, terrific. "I have a sneaking feeling they'll be about *you*. You're a rare woman, Amber Wyatt."

"Hardly!"

"You're too modest. I, for one, am ready to elevate you to that status."

CHAPTER EIGHT

CAL thought he wouldn't sleep a wink, body and mind so aroused, but he didn't stir until dawn.

One glance at the bedside clock and he leapt out of bed, raced into the shower, afterwards throwing on his everyday gear, all the while his mind filled with the sight of a beautiful copper-haired woman cradling a baby to her breast. What had he been thinking of, inviting her out here with things being what they were? Janis running off the rails, little Marcus crying and wailing non-stop, although *he* didn't have to listen to the crying all day, his uncle rendered near impotent in the face of his wife's total inability to cope—worse, her rejection of all help. Good, caring women had been driven away with Jan screaming after them that she just wanted to be left alone. Yet Amber Wyatt with her beauty, her humour, her grace and compassion had reached out to little Marcus and miraculously found a connection.

But it was only a temporary solution to a big

problem. Not all women were nurturers. His own mother had cleared off, but at least she had seen him through a lot of years of his childhood. This post-natal depression thing was a mystery to him. In the beginning everyone had shown the greatest tolerance to the baby's crying and Jan's displays of anger and bitter resentment, but she had rejected all help. It was more like she felt *trapped*. Trapped by motherhood? Trapped by her marriage? He would have said Jan wanted *out* of the whole caboodle. He knew Amber was watching him closely, gauging his reactions, concerned he wasn't showing enough sympathy. Maybe he wasn't. His sympathy lay with Marcus and his uncle. Jan's behaviour was just plain bizarre.

No sound from either wing of the house. Peace reigned. He walked very softly down the corridor, making sure he kept to the Persian runner. He would take the little fellow down to Dee, who was always up early. He would feed the baby himself if he had to. Hell, it couldn't be that hard. And, as Amber had reminded him, he had better get in some practice. Of course he wanted kids. He had planned to have his own happy family for most of his life. Brooke had failed him. He shunned the idea of infidelity. Why wouldn't he? His mother had betrayed him and his father. Were his veins clogged up with mistrust? They had been up to date.

Amber too had had a painful lesson. But she was one gutsy lady. And she was his guest. Not the new nanny. He was seriously embarrassed. Very gently, he tapped on the door, waited. No sound from within. His hand on the brass knob, his body tense, he turned it slowly, opening back the door a fraction, listening all the while.

Dawn was casting a soft pearl-grey light over the room. A single bedside lamp was still burning. Amber lay sleeping with the baby cradled in her arms. Just as in his vision, Marcus lay cuddled up contentedly against her breast, his light cap of dark hair contrasting with this vision in pink, copper, cream and vanilla.

The image was so powerful, so beautiful, he stood transfixed. She hadn't made it into bed. The day bed had made a comfortable resting place for both of them, a light rug serving as a blanket. He had a tremendous urge to kiss Amber's sleeping mouth. It was gently parted on the lightest exhalations.

"Amber?" Unable to stop himself, he bent low over her, brushing her mouth with his own. Even that light pressure made his head swim. Despite his every reservation, he had connected with this woman. He had from the moment he'd laid eyes on her. Something had happened. He knew she felt it too. Something that had confounded them both. Could he allow himself to believe she was the woman to bring him lasting happiness? For that matter, could she believe it of him? Both of them had been hurt by infidelity. Since Amber had moved into his life, he had come to see that Brooke's defection hadn't left lasting scars. They had all but healed up.

She must have been dreaming because she thought Cal had kissed her. A butterfly kiss that nevertheless flew deep inside her. "Oh, my goodness, it's morning," she said, blinking.

"Dawn." He was unsettled by the rush of emotions he was fighting. A mere leaf in a storm. "Let me take him. I can put him down on the bed. Bolster him with pillows."

"I was afraid I'd fall off to sleep and maybe roll on him." She was speaking so softly he barely heard her. "He's so *tiny*."

Very gently, Cal took the sleeping child from her, holding him a while. He was a dear little fellow really. He could see a family resemblance. The eyes were blue, not Jan's dark brown. Why should there be such trauma in life?

Amber stretched her arms first, next her legs. Then she wiggled her toes, trying to get the circulation back into her body. Truth be told, she felt quite groggy. Even on her feet she swayed.

"You okay?" Cal wanted to go to her. The effect she was having on him was gaining an awesome momentum. He had already started to fantasize about her. So what was he going to do about it? Was he ready for another serious commitment? Was she? There were big barriers in the way. He couldn't give up his heritage. It was the woman who would have to come to him. Could Amber turn her back on a glamorous city lifestyle?

The higher a man flies, the bigger the crash, said the voice in his head.

He had built a lot of defensive strategies. She was making rubble of them.

Amber began to plait her hair. "I'm fine. Don't worry. The day bed was quite comfortable. What are you going to do with Marc? I'd like to take a shower to wake myself up."

"Go ahead." God, if only there were no restraints! He'd give anything to join her. Soap his trembling hands. Run them over that beautiful woman's body. Instead, he lay the sleeping baby on the canopied bed. "I'll wait here with him. When you're ready we can go downstairs."

She gave him another one of those smiles that wrapped him like a cloud. With this woman he was going some place he had never been before.

"I'm sure he'll be ready for a bottle by then." Amber grabbed up a few clothes, making for the en-suite bathroom.

"Well, for cryin' out loud!" Dee exclaimed when she caught sight of them. "This is borderin' on a miracle."

"And good morning to you too, Dee," Cal said. "Any chance of breakfast?"

"Don't I always get you breakfast?" She gave

him an indulgent smile before glancing quickly at Amber, carrying the baby. "How are *you*, love?"

"Fine, Dee." Amber returned the smile. "Our little man had a good night. As you can see, he's awake now and I'm guessing he wants his bottle."

"Breakfast and a bottle comin' up!" Dee bustled away.

Breakfast over, the Cattle Baron was on his feet to go. "The vet will be flying in around eleven," he informed Dee, throwing his linen napkin down on the table. "We'll give him lunch, Dee, as usual."

"No problem," Dee said, busy stacking plates.

He turned quickly to Amber, who was giving the baby a bottle. Miracle of miracles, Marcus was feeding contentedly. How different was one human being from another? Cal marvelled. "When I've got a minute I'll take you around to the stables and let you pick out a horse," he told her. "I didn't bring you here to—"

"Forget it," she broke in, knowing he was embarrassed by his family situation. "I'm enjoying this. Maybe baby Marcus is getting over his problem. It does happen."

Eliot came down not long after, anxious to give his nephew a hand. Cal was handling far more than could be asked of one man and he had been for some time. Eliot knew it and felt bad. "Fitz" Fitzgerald, the vet, was flying in to make a spot check of the herd. He and Fitz went back a long way. He wanted to be on hand. He and Fitz could make their tour while Cal got on with more pressing matters. The big muster was on before Christmas. Back-breaking, often dangerous work.

Janis didn't appear until around ten and what a world of difference there was between husband and wife! Eliot MacFarlane couldn't have been more courteous, courtly, Amber thought, but Janis freaked out when she saw who was sitting happily minding a wide awake, tranquil baby.

"Get up. Get out of here." Janis zoomed in on the hapless Mina, waving her arms as one might wave at a wallaby that had invaded the home gardens.

"Miss Amber…Miss Amber…" Mina stood cross-legged, looking as if she was about to wet her pants with fright.

"Miss Amber is *no one* around here," Janis exploded furiously. "Is that understood? Haven't I told you never to go near the baby?"

"Yes, Missus." Mina was now in floods of tears.

"Yet you've disobeyed me. I'll see to it you lose your place in the house."

Mina, deeply distressed and frightened, hit herself in the head with both hands.

Amber and Dee, a room away, heard the uproar. "Oh, my God, I'll have to get in there," Amber cried.

"My fault again." Dee hung her head.

"Don't be silly." Amber rushed away, desperate

to ease the situation. Janis had no hesitation in taking all the help that was offered while still reserving the right to abuse whomever she liked. Everyone wanted to help her. Didn't she know that? Or was she too self-involved to care?

Mina looked as though she was about to break into a run. The lovely peace had been shattered. Marcus had passed from contentment to distress, his wails gathering strength.

"Is this your doing?" Janis swung on Amber, her cheeks red with rage. "Exactly *who* declared you in charge? How dare you override my orders?"

The articulate Amber swallowed the retort that came to mind. For the moment she had to placate this ill-tempered woman. "Mina, I'd like you to go into the kitchen," she said to the shaking girl. "You've done nothing wrong. Dee will have a cup of tea for you."

"May I ask if you're crazy?" Janis stared at Amber as if she'd taken leave of her senses.

"You may *ask* certainly." Amber recovered her equilibrium fast. She waited calmly for Mina to disappear.

"You come in here, a visitor, and defy me?" Janis was shuddering all over with outrage.

Amber kept her tone low. "Spare me, Mrs MacFarlane. Have you noticed your baby? Are you going to pick up your little son or shall I? Didn't you see when you came in he was quite content. Now he's screaming his head off. Look at him. Really *look*. He's every bit as distressed as you are."

Janis didn't even glance down. "You interfering bitch," she said with great venom. "Wait until I tell Cal about this."

"Why tell Cal anything?" Amber gave the other woman a straight look. "You have your *husband*. Now, are you going to try to settle your little son? Please look at him. He's yours. You brought him into the world."

"And a sorry mistake that was." Janis turned on her heel. "I'm going to find Cal."

Poor deluded woman! "I don't think you'll get a good reception," Amber warned. "You heard him last night. The household is at the end of its tether. Please make an effort to calm down, Mrs MacFarlane. I know it's easier said than done, but *please* try. I'll take Marcus, shall I?" Amber didn't wait for a reply, though none appeared to be forthcoming. She settled the baby over her shoulder, patting his heaving little back, while he sicked up on her cotton shirt. Well, she could change it. "Wait here, will you, Mrs MacFarlane?" she begged. "I'll take Marcus through to Dee. She'll take care of him. I'm sure you don't want his crying to continue."

"And I'm supposed to be *grateful* to you?" Janis's dark eyes flashed.

Definitely, Amber thought. "Mrs MacFarlane, I don't need or expect gratitude but you might learn from me about calming a distressed baby. I'll go now, but I'll be back. Please stay. I want to help you, in case you haven't noticed."

"You think you could?" Janis gave a dry smile.

"I'd like to try."

Although Amber fully expected to find the room empty, Janis MacFarlane was standing rigid, as though cemented in place.

"Why don't we sit down?" Amber suggested as pleasantly as she could. This was one difficult woman. She wondered what a happy Janis would look like. *Was* there a happy Janis? She appeared to be highly strung by nature. Had pregnancy and giving birth exacerbated an underlying psychological problem? Eating might help. Thinking that, she said, "You haven't had anything to eat. What would you like for breakfast? It won't take me a minute to tell Dee."

"Don't bother. I'm not hungry." Janis flopped into an armchair.

"You mightn't feel hungry but it's difficult to function without food. What about fruit juice and cereal or maybe scrambled eggs?"

"Do shut up," Janis said rudely. "When I need your help I'll ask for it. And I *don't* need it. I pegged you for an opportunist the moment I laid eyes on you. What's your connection to Cal?"

Amber wasn't in the least surprised this particular question had surfaced. "None of your business, Mrs MacFarlane."

"Are you sleeping together?" Janis's dark eyes

ran all over Amber's body. She looked as though she would have liked to use a cattle prod instead.

"Again, none of your business. You might consider I was fully occupied looking after your baby son, though I didn't catch a thank you. Why do you treat him as though he's not yours? I know a little about post-natal depression. I have great sympathy for women who have to confront and deal with it. It would be extremely difficult to handle without help and support. Why did you send those two nannies away? Had you allowed them to help you, you might be feeling a whole lot better by now."

'That's your half baked opinion, is it?" Janis mocked. "No one can fix me." She said it as if it were the end of the world.

"What's so unfixable?" Amber asked with real sympathy, though she could darn near taste the answer. "You have a child—a son, a priceless gift. You have a husband, a lovely man. Perhaps you'd be happier in your own home?"

Janis snorted. "Trying to get rid of me?"

Leave the coast free? Amber shook her head. "I just thought you might be finding the isolation tough going. A lot of women would. Especially one who has had a successful city career. I had the idea that you and Eliot intended living in Melbourne."

"Here's the problem," Janis said savagely. "Eliot brought me back *here*."

"Are you saying he reneged on his word?" Amber

was shocked. Had Eliot deliberately put his wife into a situation she couldn't handle?

"We had a very short courtship." Janis presented a bitter face. "I never met Cal until the day of the wedding."

Here it was. Cause and effect. Janis meets Cal. Janis is instantly infatuated with Cal. Husband and baby bear the brunt of wife and mother's unrequited love.

Janis stood up abruptly, angry she might have given an insight into her real problem. "I've endured your company as long as I can, Ms Wyatt. You're nothing more than an ambitious hustler, even if you are beautiful in a way I don't admire. If you're hoping to land Cal, you'd better think again. He and Brooke Rowlands have a *long* history. Brooke may have stuffed up but she's looking for an opening to get back into his good graces. Very persistent lady is Brooke. Once she finds out *you're* here, she'll come calling. Mark my words."

"Sorry, is that supposed to affect me?" Amber sat back, a model of calm outside, upset within. "It doesn't. I understood from Cal that Ms Rowlands isn't all that welcome." How she was succeeding in maintaining a level tone, Amber didn't know. She put it down to her training and withstanding the likes of Jack Matthews.

"That's what he *says*!" Janis pronounced bitterly, as though no man on earth was to be trusted. "The last time she stayed—which wasn't all that long ago—she managed to share his bed. There, shocked you, didn't I?"

"You look more shocked than I do," Amber pointed out quietly, even though the woman was right. She *was* shocked. "If I were you, Mrs MacFarlane, I'd start counting my blessings. The closest man in the world to you is your *husband*. Your most precious possession is your baby son. If you keep that in mind, you might start to feel better. By the way, unless you intend to take over the management of Marcus, you'll allow me, Dee and young Mina, who is the gentlest little soul in the world, to give you a hand. I can see Cal's opinion is important to you. You must realise Cal has had enough of your issues with the staff."

"Oh, how splendid!" Janis clapped her hands. "A crusader for staff rights!"

"Unlike you," Amber returned quietly.

Janis MacFarlane gave her a furious stare. "And you can go to hell, Ms Wyatt. I begin to see why your fiancé dropped you for the Erskine girl. This conversation is over. It bores me. I'm going to get a little air." She headed towards the front door, mistress to servant.

"Doesn't that leave us holding the baby?" Amber called ironically. The woman's failure to assume responsibility was incomprehensible. Janis Mac-Farlane appeared to have written her baby off, as though he didn't exist.

Now she swung back with such a strange smile that Amber's heart sank. "You can have him if you want him," she said.

Could there be anything worse than that?

Cal and Eliot came back at lunchtime with their regular vet, an amiable man with a mop of sandy hair that might at one stage have been ginger, the countless freckles his skin had thrown up for protection forming a pseudo tan. Pleasant though he was, he nevertheless managed to stir the cauldron by asking Janis, albeit very kindly, if she was getting on any better with her baby.

Janis let her face show her extreme resentment. "I'm beginning to think he should be taken into care until he settles," she said as though she had just come up with the solution to her problems. "That's if he *ever* does."

"But of course he will, poor little fella!" Fitz Fitzgerald, grandfather of eight, protested, staring from Eliot to his young wife in astonishment. "Where is he now?"

"Ask Ms Wyatt," Janis suggested tightly. "She seems to have taken over the running of the household."

Beneath the starched white tablecloth Amber clamped her hand down hard on the Cattle Baron's knee. She knew he was longing to intervene. But she could fight her own battles. She offered the vet a smile. "Marcus is coming along just fine. Mina is watching him at the moment. She's good with children. She has little brothers and sisters."

Janis's cheeks flushed as she spluttered, "This is not *my* idea, Mr Fitzgerald. Next thing we know, Ms Wyatt will have the girl taking Marcus walkabout."

"I think we'll take it more gradually than that, Janis," Cal said, feeling yet another uncontrollable wave of dislike for his uncle's wife. Was there ever a time her manner with people wasn't freezing? Oddly enough, he seemed to get the lion's share of her better moments. "Mina is a sweet, respectful, responsible girl. You should be grateful to her for the help."

"Grateful is the *last* thing I am," Janis huffed.

Somehow they got through lunch, with Janis throwing Amber malevolent looks across the table. Obviously she had moved up to the top of Janis's hit list. She had to keep telling herself that Janis had problems. But it seemed that at least some of her problems were by choice. Afterwards, Eliot took his wife by the elbow, moving her away with a polite, "Excuse us." It looked very much like Janis was digging in her heels, refusing to go. Women had been strangled for less.

Amber found herself asking Cal quietly if Janis had found him earlier on.

He eyed her with nagging worry. "I know this sounds weird, but I swear Janis could find me anywhere!"

To him it obviously presented a great mystery. Amber moved closer in, to whisper low, "And why is that, do you suppose?"

"How the hell should I know?"

Later Fitz offered a comment. "Poor lady! It's the PND then, is it?"

"I thought the condition was more civil than that." Cal was so mortified by Janis's behaviour that he skipped any excuses. He put his hand on the vet's shoulder, deliberately changing the subject. "By the way, I forgot to ask you, Is Charlie Morrissey recovering okay?"

Fitz shook his head. "No, he's still pretty crook."

"Crook in the head as well." Cal tapped his forehead. "That was a fool thing he did, trying to pick up a taipan by the tail."

Fitz gave a snort of laughter. "Drunk at the time. Drink always fuels stupidity." He turned to Amber, who was standing quietly. "I must say it's been a great treat to meet you, Amber. I don't need to tell you to watch that skin of yours in the sun."

Amber had to ask herself, why hadn't he?

"We'll look after her, Fitz," Cal assured him. "There's a ton of sun block on tap. I tell you that every time I see you."

"Too late, m'boy!"

"Wrong attitude, Fitzy," Cal pointed out, half turning his shoulder. "Ah, here's Eliot back again. You two can go off. I'll meet you a little later on. I want to fix Amber up with a horse to ride. She tells me she's good."

"Which means she is." Fitz gave Amber another warm, approving smile. This was a young lady who mightily impressed him. He had never known what to make of Eliot's second wife. The first one had been an angel, gone to God. This one might have strayed from the other place. Even before the little fellow had arrived no one could have called Janis MacFarlane pleasant. It wasn't a marriage that had been planned in heaven.

Almost immediately, Amber settled on her choice. She picked out a handsome coal-black gelding called Horatio, a seven-year-old ex-racehorse that had won handsomely for Cal's grandfather, Clive Erskine, only to be told that the gelding was too strong for her. Too mercurial by temperament.

"You haven't seen me ride yet," she said, affronted. The big gelding stood some seventeen hands high, but she was convinced she could ride him.

"We'll fix you up with something else." He ignored her tone. "What about this one now?" They moved down the line of stalls. "Star Belle. Isn't she beautiful? A bright chestnut almost the colour of your hair. Star Belle is another ex-racehorse. She's a little bit skittish with a new rider, but if you can handle her she'll settle down nicely."

"Sure you can trust me to have a go?" she challenged dryly, showing the mare her hand.

"I'd like nothing better than to trust you, Amber." He smiled, but the expression in his eyes was oceans deep.

"We've got issues, haven't we? They pop up all the time."

"It takes time to build back eroded confidence and trust."

"Loss of trust is a fact of life, Cal." She shrugged, still petting the responsive mare. "It's hard at first, but I don't think we really have an option but to reach out again. If we do everything in our power to avoid getting hurt, we'll never get to know what real love means."

"And you *really* loved him?" he mocked, when he was hurting with the desire to touch her. Pull her into his arms. Cover the beautiful creamy skin of her face with kisses, before settling ecstatically on her mouth—full, luscious, made to be kissed. If he had to describe his picture of the perfect woman it would be Amber Wyatt.

"I might ask, did you really love Brooke?" Amber countered, unnerved by the quality of his glance. It was like a mirror giving back her own desire. Stupid to allow a flash of jealousy for his ex-fiancée to mar it. But human enough, she supposed.

"I must have been in love with her at some stage. That's all you need to know."

"Ditto with Sean. I don't hate him. Maybe that's a telling thing. I despise him. That's entirely different. At any rate, his marriage to your cousin is no longer causing me grief."

"I'm glad to hear it." In fact it was a big relief. "But doesn't it prove you never really loved him?"

She gave him a defeated look. "I'm afraid you could be right. It's a little hard getting used to the idea I was such a rotten judge."

"Maybe we only have an *idea* of the people we love," he mused.

"Very likely. But what you see is what you get with me, MacFarlane. Now, why don't I show you how good a rider I am?"

He laughed. How could he not? She entertained him. "I'm telling you I can't wait. You look great in tight jodhpurs at any rate."

Despite herself she blushed. "They're not too tight, are they?" She didn't think she had put on weight.

"On the contrary, they're *perfect*! They need to be tight. If I were a better adjusted man I could really fancy you, Ms Wyatt."

"I think the fancying got out of hand at the wedding, don't you?"

"One of those instant inexplicable bondings," he suggested very dryly.

"Or a pretty powerful chemical reaction."

"Either way, it was great." He rested a hand lightly on her silk-covered shoulder. Just a gesture but it sent a series of shock waves through her very receptive body. She couldn't recall a touch like it.

In the end, he made her parade round and round the exercise yard before he was satisfied, making her finish with a working gallop.

"You'll do!" Afterwards he lifted his arms so she had to slip down between him and the chestnut mare.

Her breasts were grazing his chest. She pulled back before she went to pieces. Behind her the mare whinnied. "I knew I would!" She tried for a cheeky smile, not easy when she was beset by desires she mightn't get the chance to fulfil.

He had to be feeling the same because he muttered, "I want to kiss you."

"Okay." She took a deep preparatory breath. The two of them were taking big risks, but the temptation was too powerful to resist.

His mouth came over hers as though he knew just what she wanted. At first it was soft and easy, a sort of learning experience, then she heard the groan in his throat before he pulled her in closer. The kiss deepened, changed character. His hand sought and found her breast, moving over it in an exquisite caress. Their lower bodies were pressed together, as if yearning to fuse as nature intended. This was what it meant to play with fire.

"Cal…" Her voice sounded unnaturally shaky. "This is so…"

"I know." He lifted his head, his hands dropping to her hips. "Just reaching out. Don't move. Not for a minute."

"I don't think I can." It was the solemn truth.

He continued to hold her. "Do you want this to come to anything, Amber?" He lifted her chin so he could stare into her eyes.

"I don't know what you're offering," she said. "I didn't see this coming."

"And you think I did?"

"So is it a good feeling or a scary feeling?"

For answer he bent his dark head and kissed her again. "Both. But let's say you make me feel more than I've ever felt before."

It was some admission coming from him.

Weeks sped by in a dazzle of excitement. Janis had been more or less forced into accepting the new regime that, thankfully, was getting encouraging results. Amber had taken to giving little Marcus a soothing massage after his nightly bath—something she had once seen demonstrated by a close friend, a mother of two, and to her delight he loved it. Marcus was getting much more sleep, as were his sleep-deprived parents. The entire household was hoping and praying that Janis's tensions would ease. But, if they did, she didn't show it. Truth be told,

Janis seemed to get meaner, even if she was less vocal about it. That had to be a plus.

She did, however, do everything in her power to avoid Amber, who was getting a little tired of it. When it came right down to it, Amber had effected the changes. But no thanks there. Amber might have been a highly paid mother's helper. Disturbingly, she had the feeling that Janis hated her. Or maybe it wasn't her personally. Janis would hate any woman who took Cal MacFarlane's eye. Both Cal and his uncle appeared to be misreading the situation. Much as she wanted to give Janis the benefit of the doubt, Amber couldn't help thinking that Janis was simply hiding behind the label of PND and, in doing so, missing out on one of the greatest gifts in life—the bottomless well of love a mother had for her child.

Wasn't she then to be pitied? A miracle was in order here. But sadly miracles didn't occur all that often in life.

Janis badly needed a fresh start in her own home. Amber knew she would have wanted a home of her own. Eliot couldn't have it both ways. His wife and child were his top priorities. Back in the city, Janis might try a lot harder. There was plenty of help readily to hand. Surely she had made female friends over the years, even if she was estranged from her mother?

She wanted to toss up a few ideas with Cal, though she knew she was winging close to danger.

She couldn't, for instance, try him out on, *Janis seems overly attached to you*. She would have to pack her bags, when she had never been happier in her life. Still, she made it her business to stop him one morning when he was almost out of the door. The man seemed to be getting up earlier and earlier and working later. He put in a full day's hard work and then some.

"Cal, could I have a word with you?" She hurried down the timber staircase.

He swung back, looking so damned glamorous she gulped. "If you make it quick," he clipped.

She tried to find her voice. He was the very picture of Action Man, a red bandana sweatband style around his head, raven locks curling over the top. The temperatures were climbing as they moved into high summer. The bandana would keep the sweat out of his eyes. It made him look so dashing, so unbelievably sexy, that she was hit by a dizzy spasm and had to rest against the balustrade. Little tremors were running up, down, all over her body. Day by day she was leaving all sense of caution behind. What else could she do? Cal MacFarlane was a revelation!

"Hey, are you okay?" Cal couldn't suppress the note of worry. This beautiful, never complaining woman, was his guest, yet she was handling everything like a highly paid employee. He was so much in her debt it was beginning to really bother him.

Right from the beginning he had seen her in a number of stressful situations. She always acted in a manner he understood and approved. It was getting harder and harder to fault her. He had all but given up trying. What would he do if she vanished from his life? He wasn't playing any game. He was certain she wasn't playing a game, either. The truth was he wanted her to be *always* there, an integral part of his life. Damn it, the *centre* of his life. He was a man living with a secret.

What he hadn't thought could happen *had* happened.

Too late now, MacFarlane.

She continued on down the stairs, unaware of his thoughts, but hugging close that note of concern. "Sure,' she answered happily. She knew he and some of the men had already started to bring in the clean skins from the desert fringe in preparation for the big muster. She had heard with horror from Dee of the death of a station hand a few years back. The man had taken a fall from his spooked horse and was crushed to death. Since then Amber had been trying hard to block the image. Trying hard not to think of Cal in some life-threatening situation, even though she knew he confronted them on a daily basis. His well-being was vitally important to her.

"You'd tell me if you weren't?" Cal's brows knotted as he stared down at her.

Of a sudden she was feeling strong and ready, as

though her energy had fed off his. "Don't worry, I'm not about to burn out."

"I *am* worried," he said. "I want you to get out more. Enjoy yourself. The plan wasn't to have you stuck in the house."

"Look, it's all happening. I have a really good feeling about Marcus. From now on he should start to thrive."

"You really like him, don't you?" He smiled, his beautiful eyes full of a mesmerizing glitter.

"Like him? I love him. He's a dear little fellow. He just had a rough start. Look, I won't hold you up now, Cal. You're obviously in a hurry."

"I'll give you ten minutes. How will that be?"

"Let's walk outside." She started to move to the door.

"Get your hat," he said in a no-nonsense voice.

"You got it, boss." She hurried away. When she returned she was wearing a wide-brimmed straw hat atop her hair and tied it at the nape with an inky-blue ribbon to match her tank top.

The need to *head things off at the pass*, so pressing at the beginning, had lost focus. No bigger risk than giving your heart away. He knew that. Even so, Cal surrendered to the magic of having Ms Wyatt around. He reached out a lazy hand and pulled the ribbon from her hair. As expected, it set her magnificent mane free, every conceivable shade of red, copper and gold. "A little bit of provocation, is it?" he asked, pocketing the ribbon, then flipping down the brim she had deliberately turned up all the way round to get his reaction.

"Who said you could pinch my ribbon?"

"Why, do you want it back?"

Oh, that glitter in his eyes! "Keep it. Put it under your pillow. Dream of me."

"What else can I do, since it seems too darned hard to get you into my bed?"

She looked up sharply, then smiled. "Haven't we agreed to get to know one another better, Cal? Sleeping with you could be as dangerous as jumping off a cliff."

"I'm game if you are."

The sensuality in his voice reeled her in. "Maybe I've got more to lose?" she suggested very seriously. "It can be worse for women."

"Nonsense!" His answer was blunt. "Okay, Amber. For you, I can wait. Maybe you'll start to want me as much as I want you."

She stood there with sensation nearly sweeping her off her feet. "Oh, I *want* you all right, but things are moving very fast, don't you agree?"

"Maybe they *have* to when our time is limited. What happens when they want you back? And they will."

"Don't talk about it," she begged. "I want to stay here for a long, long time."

"*I* won't be sending you away," he said. "Count on it. And don't dare turn that brim back again."

She laughed. "I've never had a man outside my dear father pay so much attention to protecting my skin."

He ran a finger down her cheek. "It's called meaning well. Your skin's great. Let's keep it that way." He was back to the bantering style he adopted when things got intense. Inside, Cal's nerves were stretched taut. "My mother used to wear big-brimmed straw hats like that," he said in a faintly melancholy voice. "She was beautiful, too."

"So when did you first decide you wanted nothing more to do with her?" Amber asked as gently as she could. There was a lot of unresolved feeling here. A mother was forever part of one's identity.

Instantly his body language radiated warning. "It's too long ago to remember."

"Is it?" She stared up at him, suddenly seeing him as a proud and handsome young boy.

"Don't *do* this, Amber," he warned, his green eyes aglitter.

She looked away across the garden, the air wavery in the heat. "Thought I'd give it a shot. Deep down I think you feel badly about the whole sorry situation. The trouble is, Cal, if you let your grievances go on too long, they become part of you like a second skin."

He took a minute to answer. "You know, you were wasted in television. You should have given psychoanalysis a shot."

"Hey, there's still time," she said, trying for

breeziness. "All I'm saying is, where there's a will, there's a way. I'm like you. I mean well."

His firm mouth twitched. "Then could I remind you that a couple of wasted minutes have gone past. What's on your mind?"

She wasn't such a fool that she didn't know she had put a serious dent in his armour. "We're friends, aren't we, Cal?" she asked, fixing her gaze on his brooding face. "You're happy we're friends? Friendship is important. Maybe more important than sex."

He laughed, beginning to unwind. "Hell, Amber, I liked you right off. Of course we're friends. It's not the *perfect* relationship. Don't knock sex, but I guess it will have to do."

"Want to tell me what the perfect relationship *is*?" she asked.

"I'd love to. I will. But it would take time. I don't have it at the moment. The men will be waiting on me for their orders. I think I can guess your question in one—When are you going to tell Eliot to take a break away with his wife?"

She nodded. "I'm not sure Jingala is the best place for them long-term. Janis might be a whole lot happier if she had a home of her own."

"Gets my vote," he answered tautly. "It's Janis who won't move away."

"But she told me otherwise." She stared at him, puzzled. "She understood they were to live in Melbourne but Eliot brought her here."

The severity was back. "So when did you have this little chat?"

"Hey, listen, don't get cranky with me." She placed a calming hand on his arm.

He stared down at the sight of her creamy skin, a stark contrast to his dark tan. "Amber, the last thing I'd do is vent my wrath on you. You're a godsend. This has turned into a dilemma in more ways than one. I'd like to put as much distance as I can between Janis and myself, but then I lose the uncle I've lived with all my life and love. Plus the fact I also lose out on seeing Marcus grow up."

"Well, I understand that," she said with characteristic empathy. "But you'll have children of your own. Eliot and family would always be welcome. Who knows, they might add to it."

"For God's sake!" He reacted with extreme impatience. "I couldn't tell you how many times I've heard Jan yelling she hated being pregnant. She swore she'd never allow herself to get pregnant again. I, for one, believe her. And you're wrong. I don't care what Jan told you. It was *Jan* who convinced Eliot she wanted to come out to Jingala. You've had time to get to know Eliot. You must see he would have done whatever she asked. They were to live in Melbourne, but at some point Jan had a change of heart."

She fell in love. A huge mistake on every count. *The wrong kind of love could be a sickness.*

"Jan's spirits might lift if you convinced Eliot to take her away for a holiday," she bravely soldiered on.

"And I haven't tried? What the hell keeps her here?" he asked. "She has never shown the slightest interest in the station and station life. She's not in the least like you. She sees no beauty—gets no pleasure—from her environment. She doesn't ride and she doesn't intend to learn. Horses are another one of her hates. So what's the attraction?"

To her absolute horror, Amber muttered a thoughtful, "Um…"

"You have an answer?' He fired up.

He really was a high-voltage man. "I do, but I'm not sure I should go with it."

"Now's as good a time as any," he told her with a darkening frown. "Spit it out, Amber."

"You can't guess?"

He retorted by putting his hand beneath her chin. Just the barest hint of force. "I'd like you to tell me. You're the oracle around here."

"And you don't like it?' Just looking up at him made her heart pound.

"On the contrary, I'm obliged to you." He relented with a smile.

"That's a relief! But I'm beginning to think telling you might be more than my life's worth."

"Can you prove what you think?" The challenge was back.

"Not one hundred and ten per cent, no."

"Then I'll take a pass on it until you can. For now, I'm off. Don't think I'm not grateful to you for all you've done, Amber. When I have the time I'm going to buy you the biggest present you've ever seen. I will speak to Eliot again. I'll do it tonight."

"Insist!" Amber transmitted her own seriousness. "Your uncle will take notice."

CHAPTER NINE

MID-MORNING a very unexpected thing happened. Brooke Rowlands arrived on Jingala, piloting her own Cessa 310.

How cool was that!

Was it a chance occurrence? Or had she come on a specific mission? Had she despaired of getting an invitation and taken matters into her own hands? One might well wonder. All except Janis. Janis, unbeknown to anyone, had sent Brooke an email telling her, in effect, if she still wanted to land her man she had better get over to Jingala chop-chop.

Even Janis herself didn't know why she'd done it. She was ill with her own tortured feelings for Cal. Horrified that such a thing had happened to her. She had thought she had her life under control. She had been reasonably content. She never expected to be happy. Happiness was for simpler souls. She regarded herself as a highly intelligent, complex woman, wound tight, much like the heroines of fiction. She had met and married a distinguished man. Rich, of course. She wouldn't have looked sideways at anyone with less than fifty million dollars. Hardly worth the effort. But the MacFarlane family wealth combined came in at over a billion. She had checked it out. The old man, Cal's grandfather Clive Erskine, had at least six billion, not that she had any chance of getting her hands on that. The MacFarlanes had a fine family name. Another big plus. They were one of the biggest landowners in the country, with a massive four million hectares spread over a dozen properties right across the State of Queensland. So marriage had come at a time when she'd doubted she would give herself to anyone at all. After all, she had the brains to make her own way in life.

Never for a moment had she anticipated what would happen to her. It had come like a lightning bolt, flattening her in the process. A monumental strike!

She didn't love her husband. Love hadn't come into it. It had seemed like a great career move at the time. She wanted to be pampered. She wanted to be rich. She wanted to establish herself in society. It wasn't as though she could actually say that she had ever loved anyone. She had thought herself incapable of it and wasn't by any means desperate about it. Some people were natural born loners.

Until she'd laid eyes on Cal MacFarlane.

Cal, her husband's nephew, with his enormous charisma and those glittering green eyes!

It was lunacy. But for a while it was glorious! To *feel* as she did! It was so extravagant, so real that she didn't have a single moment of remorse, or shame, much less guilt. She was always on the verge of telling him. Later she would spend endless time thanking God she hadn't. The humiliation would have crushed her. But back then! Finally, at the age of thirty-four, she had fallen in love. She was human after all. She would never think of herself as a loner ever again. Only it was her cruel fate to learn the hard way that it was all a terrible mistake—a mistake made all the more bitter because, from the very day of her wedding, Cal had kept his distance. Restraint she had expected, the situation being what it was. But the searing truth, impossible at first to grasp, was that he didn't *like* her, much less desire her. She had divined that once the haze had started to clear. It had come as a tremendous shock.

How could such a thing happen? She had thought the powerful attraction just *had* to be mutual. But Cal gave her a wide berth. He loved his uncle. They had a great relationship, when she had never had a significant relationship in her life. Her top businesswoman mother, by and large, had ignored her most of the time she was growing up. Having a child didn't sit comfortably with her career-oriented mother.

These days, burdened with her own extremely difficult, demanding child, she had more empathy for her mother. Having Marcus didn't sit comfortably with her, either. Neither woman was the nurturing kind. So mother and daughter shared a trait. Where was this mystical, magical bond she was supposed to experience with her child? Maybe she might have felt it had she and *Cal* created Marcus together. But Cal had no sexual interest in her. She could taste the steely humiliation in her mouth.

It was that interfering, sickeningly capable firehead, Amber Wyatt, who had somehow established a strong connection with Marcus, who had definitely taken Cal's fancy. So desperately in love with him herself—how did one go about killing love?—she could easily read the signs. It disturbed her terribly that Amber Wyatt might succeed where she had failed. By necessity, she had to let Ms Wyatt organise the baby's needs, but no way was she going to stand by and allow such a woman to convince Cal she was just the kind of woman—the kind of *wife*—he needed. For some reason she didn't fully understand, she didn't feel threatened by the idea of Brooke Rowlands coming back into Cal's life. If Brooke could hang in there and Cal eventually married her she would know his heart wasn't in it. It would be an arrangement like hers with Eliot.

She could live with that.

* * *

Amber was on her way back from the stables after her routine morning ride when Dee appeared on the pathway. She had her arms extended frantically, as if trying to block a runaway horse.

"Everything okay?" Instantly Amber was beset by panic. When she had left the house Marcus was perfectly fine. Had something happened?

"The baby's fine," Dee cried, knowing how important little Marcus's well-being had become to Amber. "It's somethin' else. Did ya happen to notice a plane comin' in?"

"Sure." She hadn't taken a lot of notice. Even during her short stay, light aircraft had been flying in and out of the station. Freight, supplies, the vet et cetera.

Dee reached her, grasping her arm. "Listen, love," she panted, "you'll have to go back and warn Cal. He won't be at all happy about this."

"About what, Dee?" Amber was confused.

"About Brooke showin' up." Dee looked less than delighted. "She's on her way up to the house."

That earned Amber's full attention. Cal's ex-fiancée had come calling? The woman he had most certainly slept with. It was highly unlikely they hadn't consummated their relationship. "What does she want?" She could hear the anxious note in her voice, but Dee didn't appear to notice.

"Why, to try again, girl," she said, heaving a deep breath. "She'll *never* give up, on the principle that Cal won't be able to hold out. 'Course she always comes with an excuse. An invitation to some 'do' or other. Some books or CDs she thinks the family might like. Random check on Janis and the baby. Any excuse will do. We can't talk now. You'll have to find Cal. He's at the Four Mile. Well, get goin', love!" Dee urged Amber on with a stout tap on the shoulder.

This time she took a fresh horse, the handsome coal-black gelding, Horatio, her first choice. Cal had convinced her to get her bearings first, as well as ride her way back into form before she took on the big gelding. Today she was ready. The morning's ride, always in the company of winged formations of birds, had been delightful. Star Belle was the smoothest mover. Now that she had got used to Amber up on her back they made a fine pair, horse and rider. She had promised Cal she would stick to a certain radius and, mindful of possible dangers, she had obeyed him implicitly. Eagerly she waited for the time when he would join her for a long ride. He had promised her he would, but she knew how things were revving up on the station.

Up on Horatio's back, she felt a tiny twinge of nerves. This was another animal altogether, much bigger, with longer, stronger legs. She bent low over the gelding's ebony neck, keeping her voice down to a calm, low pitch to reassure the animal of her presence. "All's well, boy. All's well. Just do your best for me."

Out in the grasslands without mishap, she soon

discovered this was a horse that was all fluid power. No wonder Horatio had dazzled in his heyday. Obviously the horse was demonstrating his willingness to trust her. She felt over time they could build up quite a rapport. If she kept heading north-west, following the line of coolibah over-hung billabongs, she would come on the Four Mile where the cows and calves were being herded. It was even possible she might be invited to join in damper and billy tea. She had met most of the men by now. Most of them were very shy around women, which didn't stop them ogling Amber, but very discreetly. What was she going to say to Cal? *Boy, are you in trouble or not! Your girlfriend's here.*

What if he answered, *Great!*

This had been a time of intense excitement but also great uncertainty for her. A testing time. She thought of it as going on a journey. She thought Cal was going along with her. Could she be proved wrong? She'd have to make a point of asking Dee just how often in recent times Brooke Rowlands had come calling. Although Janis had made it her business to tell her that Cal and Brooke had slept together on her last stay, she wasn't at all persuaded. Maybe she couldn't *bear* to be persuaded. There was a good deal more to learn about Cal. He was one complex man and his mistrust of women was ingrained. His mother leaving at a critical stage of his development had kick-started that condition.

His fiancée betraying him with, of all people, a friend had entrenched it. Women weren't to be trusted. Or forgiven. Men weren't to be trusted either. Not a woman alive would dispute that.

Amber reviewed the developing situation with some trepidation. Brooke could still pose a threat. Life could be astonishingly uncertain. Cal had become engaged hoping for happiness, after all. But no one could take happiness as an absolute certainty. There were always risks. Always unanswered questions. Maybe Brooke's visit would clear up all those vital points?

Approaching the Four Mile she reined the big gelding in. "We've made it, my friend!" There was elation in that.

She rode quietly into camp. There was a whole lot of ribaldry passing to and fro among the stockmen but, when they sighted her, silence fell like a blanket.

"The boss here?" she called to the seemingly stunned group. She might well have been an apparition.

Instantly there was rectitude. The head stockman was the first to respond. He touched a respectful hand to his battered hat. "Go get him, miss." He strode off in one direction, but Cal confounded them all by appearing from another, cool eyes flashing.

"Say it isn't so!" He indicated for her to take her

feet out of the stirrups before sweeping her out of the saddle. "That's not Horatio?"

They were standing so close. His arm had slid around her waist, bringing their hips together. His polished skin gleamed gold with sweat. She could feel beads of moisture start trickling between her breasts. Their relationship was more than ripe for sex. But, once they took that step, both of them would be altering their worlds. Fate had led her on this fantastic journey. In the process it had showed her her true nature. She was a passionate woman—passionately in love. It had never been remotely like this with Sean. Sean's betrayal had actually done her an enormous favour. It had opened a new door on life. A life she was rapidly coming to hope was full of promise.

"Horatio it is!" She spoke breezily when her blood was sizzling. "I thought I'd give it a shot. Actually, we went very well together."

"You know what they say? Pride comes before a fall." He looked back over his shoulder. "Take Horatio, would you, Toby."

"Sure, boss." Toby came on the double to collect the gelding.

Cal led her into the shade. "Did you expect me to be impressed?" There wasn't the most approving note in his voice.

"No need to get testy." She glanced up at his handsome high-cheekboned face, shadowed by the brim of his hat. His light eyes were such a shock. "I took my usual ride on Star Belle in accordance with your wishes, Mr MacFarlane, but returning to the house I met up with Dee with a message to pass on. I needed a fresh horse, okay? No worries, anyway. Horatio and I are pals."

"You could have had trouble controlling him," he said, wanting to grab hold of her and keep her safe. "Horatio doesn't take to everybody." That was the sorry truth.

"Is that so? Well, I have to tell you it was love at first sight. Ever happen to you?" She stared challengingly into his cool green eyes.

"It has, up until recently, been a point of pride with me to keep a level head, Ms Wyatt. But, if such a thing happens, you'll be the first to know."

"Can I count on it?" There was a betraying wobble in her voice.

"I've said so, haven't I?"

"Right." She dipped her head before her rioting feelings became too obvious. "Do you want to hear the message or not?"

He gave a laugh, half maddened, half amused. "Amber, that was the Rowlands Cessna that flew in. Do you really think I don't know what's happening over my own land? Who is it—Peter and Brooke, or Brooke on her own?"

She mustered a smile. "I'm delighted to tell you it's Brooke on her own. It's a wonder you didn't *feel* it." She lightly tapped her breast. "You know, here in the heart."

"That's it, fire away." He brought up his hand, passing it over his eyes. "Could you do yet another thing for me? Go back to the homestead and tell Brooke I'll be away for a few days."

"You speak in jest, sir?" His face was so perfectly straight.

"Hell, I half mean it," he groaned.

"So where would you be if you decided to chicken out?"

"Fair question." He reached out and yanked her thick copper plait.

"Gone bush?" she suggested. "I suppose, if you wanted, you'd have a chance of pulling that off. Unless you really want to see her. Do you?" She spoke lightly but her expression was alert.

"You're kidding. I'm *dying* to see her."

Her heart lunged. "I thought you'd moved on?"

"Me?" He leaned in very close. "For such a beautiful, intelligent, perceptive woman you're mighty unsure of yourself."

"Put it another way. My emotions are fragile. So just don't go treading on them."

"As if I would!" He stared into her eyes. "We've got to trust one another, Amber. Or learn how." He broke into a quotation, his voice deepening with some emotion that caused a delicious shiver to run down her back. "'I have spread my dreams under your feet. Tread softly because you tread on my dreams.'" That said, he reverted to his normal crisp tone. "Isn't that a poem?"

"Yeats. At least I think it's Yeats. You have a great voice, Cal. It's a bit like Russell Crowe's. Or even Mel Gibson's. Anyway, I've delivered my message. Now it's up to you. And to think I rode all this way for nothing. You already knew."

He laughed quietly. "Would a cup of billy tea make it up to you?"

"I thought you'd never ask."

Brooke Rowlands couldn't have been nicer. A young woman of style. Well, she had to have something for the Cattle Baron to have fallen in love with her in the first place, Amber reasoned. She wasn't proud of the fact that she felt more than a few flashes of some unwelcome emotion that had to be jealousy. She wasn't a jealous woman by nature. She had never felt jealous of Georgie Erskine, which was odd. But she found she really cared about Cal and Brooke's relationship. Was it firmly in the past or not? It would be too, too *awful* if Cal were to decide somewhere along the line he wanted Brooke, the countrywoman, back. Confounding things happened every day of the week. Human behaviour was beyond rational explanation.

On Jingala Amber was showing remarkable resilience. She never gave Sean a thought now. He was history. She wasn't sure what that said about her. All she knew was that meeting Cal MacFarlane had proved a life-altering experience. It had nothing whatever to do with warding off the pain and humiliation of her broken engagement. Something absolutely unique had happened. She was certain enough of own powers of attraction, backed up by Cal's words and actions, to recognize that Cal had been plunged into a similar situation. But he wasn't a *trusting* guy. The thing was, attraction took on its own dimensions. What *she* felt was *powerful*. Brooke, who had been desirable enough to land Cal in the first place, obviously wanted a second chance. Who could blame her?

What exactly did Cal, the object of all their longings, feel? With the arrival of Brooke on the scene, Amber came to the full realisation that she wanted him all to herself. The world could offer her no more than Cal MacFarlane.

As soon as she strode through the front door, a strikingly attractive brunette with a glossy chin-length bob, a deep fringe to show off her lovely big brown eyes, a great figure in designer jeans and a red tank top that tightly hugged her pert breasts surged from the Great Room.

"Amber Wyatt! I may call you Amber? You're even more beautiful in person than you are on our TV screens. I'm one of your fans." Appearing slightly breathless, the young woman held out her hand. Amber took it, feeling silky, pampered skin. There was something underlying the cordial manner but Amber put it down to understandable concern. Women could spot possible rivals in a nanosecond.

"It's Brooke, isn't it?" Amber smiled back. It was hard not to. Brooke sounded so sincere, earnest even. She had to be aware that during her stint in front of the cameras she had won over a lot of viewers.

"Of course it's Brooke," Janis's voice rang out from behind them. "Where's Cal?"

"Patience, patience. I only saw him briefly. He's right in the thick of it."

"I bet you went looking for him," Janis countered.

Brooke Rowlands pre-empted any retort by linking her arm through Amber's and turning her towards the Great Room. "You'd like coffee?"

"Love some," Amber said. "First I'd like to freshen up after my morning ride."

"You enjoy riding?"

Why the note of surprise? "Sure do."

"So what horse did Cal let you take?"

You'd swear it was a test. "Belle Star is my usual mount. She's lovely. Very sweet-tempered when you get to know her. I have taken Horatio out. A different horse altogether."

"Then you must ride very well." Brooke didn't sound all that pleased to hear it.

"My dad put me on my first pony at age six," Amber explained. "I love horses."

"Dreadful, unpredictable animals!" Janis shuddered as though life was hard enough without having to contend with horses.

Amber and Brooke, both fine horsewomen, ignored her. "Give me ten minutes," Amber begged, turning towards the staircase.

"How did you know Brooke was here?" Janis called after her, like some detective.

Amber's heart skipped a beat but she turned back casually. "Just as Brooke knows my face, I know hers. You're often in the society pages, aren't you, Brooke?" For one awful moment she thought Brooke was going to deny it. She hadn't, in fact, ever laid eyes on Brooke Rowlands before. There were certainly no silver-framed photographs of her in Cal's study.

But Brooke gave a gratified smile. "I do love to get away to the city from time to time. You can't imagine how relieved I am the paparazzi don't follow me around."

As promised, Amber was downstairs ten minutes later, having dashed under the shower and re-dressed in a short loose kaftan that wafted around her body. First she checked in with Dee in the kitchen.

"Find the boss?" Dee asked in a conspiratorial whisper, though no one could have heard her even if they were hiding behind the door.

"My horse could have found Cal on his own." Amber smiled. "He said he'll be out of town for a few days."

"I bet he'd like to be!" Dee muttered, never having forgiven Brooke for betraying Cal.

"I thought he might like having her around?" Amber ventured uncertainly.

Dee gave a grunt. "Been chattin' to Mrs MacFarlane?"

"Anyway, how's our little sweetheart?" Amber broke off a couple of seedless white grapes, popping them in her mouth.

"He's fast asleep." Dee gave a satisfied smile. "I've set Mina to watching over the dear little soul. I tell you, Marcus is a totally different baby. All your doin', my girl!"

"Modesty prevents me from taking the credit, Dee." Amber smiled.

"Don't interrupt me. We're all indebted to you." Dee spoke with feeling. "And you can count Mrs MacFarlane in, though she'd die before she'd ever admit it."

"Let's give her a chance, Dee." Amber gently touched Dee's shoulder. "I don't like to be *too* judgemental."

"Me, either." Dee sighed. "At the same time, I can't condone her behaviour. Best go back to them, love. Brooke will be acting like you're her new best friend, but be on your guard. She's pleasant enough,

I'll grant ya that. She might have thought she could get away with playin' around, but Cal will never forgive her or have her back.'

"Surely she can gauge that?" Amber asked. Could it be true that Brooke had recently received a measure of encouragement? "What about when she stayed before? Janis was insistent they were still… *close*."

Dee snorted. "Cal would have put bars on his doors and windows if he could. There was no hanky-panky, love. Set your mind at rest. No sneaking up and down the corridors. Now, I'll have coffee and some nice little cup cakes ready in a few minutes. Someone has to spare Brooke Mrs MacFarlane's endless railing against life. If you ask me, she acts more like a woman in the throes of a mad passion than a new mother with a medical problem."

Amber had already formed that opinion but it still gave her a shock to hear it more or less confirmed by Dee—someone more in a position to know.

They all came together again at dinner. Brooke had ridden out that afternoon in search of Cal, coming back to the homestead an hour later to lament, "I couldn't find him anywhere." Amber didn't feel able to offer a comment. Cal must have led the muster into the depths of the lignum swamps before making his return to the homestead alone.

Brooke regrouped with seduction clearly on her

mind. She looked lovely in a short silk dress in a gorgeous shade of blue. Her make-up was impeccable and her glossy fringe drew attention to her big brown eyes.

Amber, for all her qualms, enjoyed looking at her. The Cattle Baron would hardly be human if he didn't appreciate what a sight for sore eyes she was. Brooke Rowlands was a glamour girl and very flirtatious by nature. She was certainly giving Cal the treatment, by no means throwing in the towel.

And she was a lot of fun. A most welcome change from Janis, who sat looking exhausted, pushing the delicious food around her plate as though it deserved to be thrown out. Not that Brooke left Janis out of the conversation. She constantly made efforts to draw Janis in but she wasn't terribly successful if monosyllabic replies were anything to go on.

"Janis and I are planning a short trip away," Eliot, looking a good deal happier, at one point announced.

"Excuse me?" Janis turned on him so sharply that Amber winced.

Eliot didn't back down. "You need the break, my dear," he said with just the right amount of command. "We both do. Our darling boy has given you a hard time—not his fault, of course—but miraculously he appears to have settled."

"No miracle," Cal drawled, savouring another mouthful of a very fine Shiraz. "I'm sure Jan is happy to give Amber credit for bringing about a few changes."

"Amber, of course." Eliot saluted Amber with his wineglass. He had thanked Amber over and over privately but he knew that thanking her on an occasion like this was like waving a red flag in front of his wife's nose.

"Well, that's grand then, isn't it?" Brooke exclaimed. "You'll be staying on to look after little Marcus, Amber?'

"Amber isn't a minder, Brooke," Cal broke in. "She's a miracle worker. Eliot and Jan can go away, happy in the knowledge that we're *all* here to look after Marcus."

"Excuse me, but I don't think I *want* to go away!" Janis threw up a hand, thus sending her wineglass—mercifully empty—over.

"Doctor's orders." Eliot attended swiftly to the wineglass.

"You're raving!" Janis drew back in her chair. "I haven't seen a doctor for ages. I don't need a doctor. I don't like doctors."

"You want to look after your own baby, is that it, Jan?" Brooke intervened with real kindness. She had tried to like Eliot's second wife but Janis MacFarlane was incredibly difficult to like. However had Eliot married her? Sex couldn't be the answer. Janis looked as if she'd scream the place down if ever a man came near her. Yet she had produced a child, as difficult a little soul as his mother from all accounts.

"My figure's gone." Janis made a very revealing answer. "I don't know my own body any more."

"It will come right again," Brooke assured her in a soothing tone. "You're way too thin. A short break seems just the thing, wouldn't you say?" She looked to the others to back her up.

"I have mentioned the Great Barrier Reef," Eliot said. "Sun and surf."

"What, with all the concern about skin cancer?" Janis's brows shot up. "You're raving! The sun will *kill* you, so you'd better watch out, Ms Wyatt."

"Ms Wyatt?" Brooke pulled a droll face, catching Amber's eye.

"I hate this trend of calling people by their first names right off," Janis explained loftily.

Cal gave a sardonic laugh. "Just as well you didn't go into public relations, Jan. You'd have had no future whatever."

Over coffee, Brooke asked if Amber would like to visit the Rowlands' station, Goorack. Brooke was Outback born and bred, which made her a hospitable young woman.

"I'd love to!" Amber replied with genuine warmth. She liked Brooke, for all her fall from grace. Most people would. Brooke was bright and friendly. She didn't blame her at all for trying to get Cal back. She understood it completely. She even understood Janis's sad fixation and her refusal to go away with her husband for a short break. How the marriage was going to work out, Amber didn't know. Divorce looked like the best option at this point, except—and a *huge* except—they shared a lasting bond. They had a small child desperately in need of tender loving care, not from well-meaning people around him, but from his mother.

Amber prayed that would happen. And happen soon. Janis MacFarlane might have a passion, but sadly it wasn't for motherhood.

Amber had been lying sleepless for about an hour, staring up at a moonlit ceiling. The ceiling stared back, offering no answers. She realized she had been straining to hear a baby's cry. Janis had been in such an odd mood, even for an odd woman. Eliot would have a job on his hands getting her to go away. Seeing Cal on a daily basis was something Janis clearly had to have. No future in that!

She was giving her pillows a hearty punch when an unmistakable summons came on her door. Hadn't she been half expecting it? Janis MacFarlane was too much under a hypnotic spell to go quietly. She threw on her robe, padding to the door.

Cal stood there, his arms holding on to the door frame, wide shoulders hunched.

"Another raid?" She tried for a joke, seeing the strain in his face. "Janis again?" She didn't want to go to Janis. She wanted to pull Cal inside. Sweep every scrap of caution under the Persian rug. Her body was aching for him. She was even ready to rope him in. Deep down she was sorry for Brooke. But she had to remind herself: all's fair in love and war.

"'Fraid so," he said, sounding as sexually deprived as she felt.

"Just when I was getting my hopes up," she felt emboldened to say, a splash of colour in her cheeks.

"I didn't say I won't be back."

"I didn't say I won't let you in."

"That's good. You're so darn beautiful I can't keep it a secret. I want to kiss every inch, every fold, every crevice of your sweet creamy body. That's for starters. Then I want to work around it with my tongue. I want to do *everything* you want." He broke off with a huge sigh. "Hell, I can't take this!"

"You mean we have to put the ravishing on hold." Statement not a question.

"I couldn't be unhappier about it, but the idea of a holiday has really got Janis going. You'd think she'd been sentenced to a stint in jail. You have to come. Eliot and I are stalled. She was trying to shake Marcus quiet."

Amber was stunned. This was a warning sign, impossible to ignore. "She didn't. She *couldn't*."

Cal ran a frustrated hand through his hair. "No one could call her a gentle soul. Not even with her own child. Are you coming?"

"Of course I'm coming. You didn't wake Brooke? You did consider her at one time for mother of your children."

"And I guess she'd make a good mother," he answered tersely. "Just not for *my* children."

"Maybe you'd better make sure she knows that. She's still in love with you."

"God forbid she should *stay* that way."

He sounded absolutely on the level. It should have allayed her fears, yet she said with a touch of disapproval, "Oh, you're cruel!"

"Tell me something I don't know." He grasped her arm, lucid green eyes sharpening over her body. "Isn't that a new robe?"

"You're paying me so many after hours visits I thought I'd better shake a new one out. It's a genuine Japanese silk kimono. Bought it on a trip to see the cherry blossoms. They don't come cheap. Not this quality. Glad you noticed."

"I've got used to noticing everything about you, Amber. Janis's behaviour would chill out the hottest-blooded male, but that's not happening here. What's *wrong* with the blessed woman? She's so utterly dissatisfied with her life—it's a total mess."

He'd hit it on the head. "Eliot has to assert himself. They need that break. Get life back into perspective. Janis is a married woman with a child. It's called responsibility. Commitment."

"If you ask me, she wants to put as much distance

between herself and Eliot and the baby as she can."
Cal spoke with a world of regret.

Brooke asked over breakfast, "Did I hear a lot of
noise last night, or was I dreaming? I have to say I
had one glass of wine too many."

"Just the baby," Amber explained the incident
away. No matter how much she had wanted Cal to
join her, little Marcus had got the vote.

"What the heck is wrong with Janis?" Brooke
asked, lightly buttering a piece of toast. "A friend of
mine suffered post-natal depression after her second
baby. She was quite okay with the first. She said it
was pretty bad but she got lots of love and support.
From the very first time I met Janis... maybe I
shouldn't say this—" she swept on "—Janis struck
me as overwound. You know, the neurotic sort, with
the main focus on themselves, what *they* need and
want out of life. I guess having a baby might have
worsened the condition. I can see how worried
everyone is. Can I hold the little fellow before I go?
I need to be back home by mid-afternoon."

"Of course you can!" Amber agreed straight
away, pleased that Brooke had asked.

"I know this seems absolutely crazy—" Brooke
was back to muttering behind her hand "—but Janis
seems to have the hots for Cal. Tell me it isn't so?"
She pinned Amber with her big brown eyes.

"Janis is fragile at the moment," Amber offered

quietly. She didn't mention the huge fight that had broken out after Eliot and Janis had retired, an argument initiated by Janis and her aversion to leaving the homestead. Marcus had settled into his routine of sleeping quietly, only to be woken by his mother's high-pitched rant. It had been more than enough to set him off. It had taken Amber ages to quieten him after taking him down to her room.

"So have *you* got the hots for him?" Brooke asked. "Don't be offended. I have to ask. You're so beautiful...but I've never stopped loving him."

"Brooke, I don't know what's in Cal's mind." She hoped Brooke wouldn't press her further.

"So how long *have* you known him?" Brooke asked, intent on finding out.

"Only a matter of weeks."

"Long enough." Brooke fetched up a huge sigh. "He's terrific, isn't he?"

Amber poured them both a fresh cup of coffee. "Sure is," she said.

Cal returned to the house to see Brooke off. He had long since made the decision not to forgive her but it appeared he was undergoing some sort of sea change of late. And he knew since when. Since the arrival of Amber Wyatt into his life. She was making him over. Maybe making him a better man. He wouldn't be in the least surprised if she talked him into seeing his mother again. The perennial globetrotter, his mother spent some time in her own country. Would he ever forgive her? Could Amber persuade him to? He could only wait and see.

Brooke was trying hard for composure, but in the end she pulled Cal's head down to her. "I'm so sorry we didn't make it, Cal." Real tears stood in her eyes. "I'll always love you." She stood on tiptoe, pressing her mouth against his so passionately she would have left him in no doubt.

Amber, about to make her entrance to say her goodbyes and tee up a visit to Goorack, diplomatically stepped back a few paces, sheltering behind a luxuriant golden cane. She could hear the distressed note in Brooke's voice as though she had somehow divined that any further attempt to get him back would fail. Amber of the tender heart felt like offering condolences. At the same time she had to ask herself—if Cal and Brooke had still been engaged would he have asked her to Jingala?

The answer had to be a resounding *no*! So, at the end of the day, Brooke's loss was her gain. That was if she knew how to convince Cal of the depth and steadiness of her feelings. He in turn had to do the same thing for her. No greater risk than giving one's heart away. No spontaneous recovery. Healing took time.

To Brooke's great credit, her manner with Amber remained warm and friendly, so much so that Amber went along for the ride while Cal drove Brooke to Jingala's giant hangar where her Cessna was parked.

"It must be wonderful to be able to fly," Amber said dreamily as the Cessa lifted off the runway and climbed into the wild blue yonder.

"I'll teach you." Though his answer was abrupt, his hand was resting on her shoulder, his thumb absentmindedly caressing the bone.

"You think we will have that amount of time together?" She tipped her head so it lay along his hand.

"That's up to you, Amber." His caressing hand moved to her cheek. "I know this has had the elation of an adventure for you. I know you genuinely love the Outback. You see its wild beauty. Feel its mystique. But what of your career? You might suddenly go off and never return. Jingala will be something to look back on. God, you're beautiful enough to get into movies."

"There's a price to be paid for all that fame," she pointed out. "There's even a price to be paid for being on national television. I haven't told you about a few stalkers who caused me some grief. There is always some nutcase out there. Anyway, I've never had the slightest ambition to become a movie star, even supposing I got a break." She didn't mention that she had been approached some time back by a top agent for a lead part in a new television series. She had turned the role down.

"Okay." His handsome features were taut. "But loneliness is very threatening and it's a lonely life out here. The absence of so many things you're used to. I'll go further and say you don't really know what you'd be getting yourself into."

"So you *are* taking me seriously?" Her heart lifted in hope.

"You know damned well I'm taking you seriously." Intensity blazed out of his eyes. To prove it, he lowered his head to catch her mouth, kissing her so deeply that she found herself clutching him for support. "I want *you* in my bed," he groaned. 'No one else but you."

"But you fear I'll put a dent in your heart, then go away?" She pulled back a little so she could look into his eyes.

"Maybe that fear is chronic." He gave a harsh laugh. "I couldn't bear to have you, then lose you. Surely you can understand that?"

"It works both ways, Cal," she told him gently. "You have me, then you drive me away with your fears. I think you always carry the image of your mother in your mind, a beautiful woman who was unfaithful to her husband. Probably driven into an affair through sheer boredom or loneliness. Please don't cast me in that role."

"Did I say I have?" he asked with a note of anguish. "You've never known the pain of loneliness and isolation, Amber. *Have* you?"

"I think you're just trying to find reasons to reject me."

A faraway look came into his beautiful green eyes. "Hard to reject you when I'm hooked."

Elation filled every nerve, every fibre of her body. "You'd give up your freedom?"

"Would you?" He held her gaze.

"Gracious me, yes. Total commitment is a very serious business. That's why we're in this holding pattern. The other problem isn't going away."

"You mean Janis?" he asked impatiently. "What are we going to do about Janis? God, it ought to be the title for a psychological thriller. Except it's not funny. Eliot can't cope. He and Caro were so much in harmony, he doesn't know what's struck him with Jan. I know some people might deem his lack of action as gutless but he's far from that. I've seen him being incredibly brave. It's just he's a fish out of water in this situation, even if he *has* done his best. Jan has resisted all offers of help. So what next?"

"You ask, so I'll say. Eliot has to act. He's not *engaging* as much as he should."

"I know." Cal shook his dark head. "My fear is Janis wants to abandon Marcus."

"Mothers don't abandon their babies." The thought shocked her.

"Of course they do," he answered bluntly. "And this one *will*."

"She can't remain at Jingala."

"Why is it I feel you're trying to tell me something?" he asked sharply.

Amber looked away to where a flock of corellas had covered the branches of a river gum like fantastic white blossom. "It's not pretty," she warned.

He gritted his fine teeth. "For God's sake, Amber, let's hear it."

"Okay. You asked." She drew in a quivering breath. "Janis is in love with you."

His darkly tanned face visibly lost colour. "No, no, no, *no*!"

The tension was so palpable she could feel it on her skin. "I'm sorry, Cal, but I say it as I see it. Janis is infatuated with you. That's the reason she's so unhappy. It's not PND. The Flying Doctor people were right. It's not a mood disorder, something mood enhancers and good counselling can counteract. Her feelings are all tied up with *you*. You had your own experience with Brooke. I had mine with Sean. We can't love to order."

"Bloody hell, *no*!" he repeated, looking supremely outraged.

"Think about it."

"This is wrong!" He spoke roughly, green eyes flashing. "She's my uncle's wife. She's the mother of his child. I don't even *like* the woman and God knows I've tried. How could she be so disloyal?"

Amber gave him the only answer she knew. "It

happens, Cal. Brooke still loves you. I suppose she'll regret her indiscretion to her dying day."

"Indiscretion! What a lightweight label. I didn't know about Janis." He looked and sounded extraordinarily tense.

"I know you didn't."

"Does Eliot know?"

"He may not have grasped the *depth* of her feelings," Amber said. "Doomed love can be awful. Both of us got a taste of that."

"Because we weren't really in love in the first place," he decided tautly. "They were *there*. That's all there is to it. Seeing Brooke beside you confirmed that for me."

At his admission her heart gave a great leap of joy, but she didn't follow up that revealing piece of information when his energy was focused on something else entirely.

"If what you say is even halfway true, I can see no happiness ahead for my uncle." Cal gave vent to a bitter sigh. "The situation is far more worrying for Marcus."

She shared his distress. "First step is to get Janis some help. Eliot can call in a doctor."

They swept through the massive gates that lay open to the homestead. There was fresh urgency in Cal's manner. "We need a nanny back for Marcus. You've been wonderful, but that's not your job. I have no option but to get back to the men. We're coming into our busiest time and I have outstations to check on yet. God, what a mess!" His tone was a mixture of grief and contempt.

CHAPTER TEN

As soon as Amber walked into the house she veered off to make her routine check on Marcus.

"He's outside, love," Dee told her. Dee was busy punching down dough to get a good even texture for her bread. In the time Amber had been on the station she had enjoyed all sorts of Dee's delicious, freshly baked breads and rolls. The woman never stopped but she obviously thrived on and took a great deal of pride and pleasure in running the household.

"Asleep?" Amber asked.

"Sleepin' his head off," Dee confirmed. "I guess he would after such a helluva night."

"And Janis?"

"Madam hasn't stirred as yet," Dee told her dryly. "I reckon she'd feel a whole lot better if she got some decent tucker into her."

"And Eliot?"

"He's with the baby." Dee had taken to whispering. "If this keeps up he could be a good candidate for a heart attack."

"Don't say that!" Amber shuddered. "I'll go out to them."

"I'll make coffee. I'll just shape this into loaves and set it aside for a while."

"Lovely!"

"You got on pretty good with Brooke?" Dee called.

Amber turned back. "I liked her, Dee. I think she took the message that she had no future with Cal on the chin."

"Seems like it." Dee shrugged. "Big surprise there or she had the sense to recognise she was outclassed. But what about Mrs MacFarlane?"

"Oh, Dee!" For a moment they just stared at each other.

"Okay, love." Dee relented. "Pity you got drawn into this. On the other hand…" She left the rest unsaid. Their whole relationship had taken a conspiratorial direction.

The long covered porch to the rear of the kitchen area had been turned, of late, into a day nursery for Marcus. It was beautifully cool and a great deal of care had gone into achieving an atmosphere of simplicity and balance. A seated stone Buddha sat high on a tall decorative stone plinth. Today Buddha was holding a basket of freshly picked bougainvillea flowers. Clumping bamboos provided foliage, mixed with golden canes and kentia palms. Little Marcus was benefiting from the peace and serenity.

Eliot stood up. "Brooke got safely away?"

Amber smiled. "I do so admire her ability to fly a plane."

"You could learn if you wanted to. To be honest, I've never met a young woman so capable."

"Well, thank you. But how much are we born with, Eliot?" she asked wryly. "It's the luck of the draw."

"So far as I'm concerned, you've been very lucky," he said. "Shall we sit down?" He pulled out a wicker chair for her.

"I'll just take a peep at Marcus. Dee is making coffee."

"I'm so sorry for last night," Eliot said when Amber returned. "I don't believe I've ever felt so terribly ineffective. I can't seem to say the right thing or offer the comfort my wife needs."

"Get the doctor back," Amber suggested gently. "Forgive me if I'm overstepping the mark."

"How could you be overstepping the mark?" Eliot's expression was bleak. "You've been an enormous help. Jan and I had no right to ask it of you. You're here as Cal's guest."

Amber thought she had rarely seen a more tormented face. "Today would be a good time, if it could be managed. The right medication will help Mrs MacFarlane. Get her through a bad patch."

"Doctors have been here before, Amber," Eliot

reminded her. "My wife has drained an enormous well of sympathy with her behaviour."

"Make the call," Amber urged.

"I will, my dear," Eliot promised, his face eerily calm.

When Cal saw the Super King Air fly over he knew the RFDS was coming in to land. He threw himself into the Jeep, determined to be back at the house in case of any trouble. How had he never picked up on Jan's feelings? How *could* she have developed such feelings when he had never given her the remotest encouragement? For God's sake, she was his uncle's *wife*. The whole thing was sickening. He couldn't think about it and do his job. The only thing that seemed to hold him in place was returning to the homestead to find Amber there. She had touched his life in every possible way. He could feel her all around him, in the very air he breathed. He'd never imagined he *could* feel about a woman like he felt for her. He had thought himself in love with Brooke. He had come very close to marrying her. Outback born and bred, Brooke knew and understood exactly what their life would be. Amber was right. The whole torment of the breakdown of his parents' marriage had never left his mind.

It was crucial for his own happiness to find a woman with the strength to face life on the land squarely. A brave woman he could love and trust.

His life's partner. Wasn't she right under his nose? Could he possibly be that lucky? He had been allowing himself to dream of winning Amber's heart. But was it unwinnable? Even if he *could* win it, would the marriage survive the early days of high romance that had made his parents commit to each other in the first place? Or would the full force of *remoteness*, the epic struggles with drought and flood, give rise to feelings of being trapped in a world that took more than it gave?

Amber was a city girl. A beautiful, accomplished woman. Wouldn't it be madness to expect a woman like that to settle for a life on the desert fringe? So she wanted to write? She'd have plenty of peace and quiet, he thought ironically. That was if Eliot and Jan could save their marriage and move away. In all probability Amber would soon be getting offers to return to television. Come back, all is forgiven. The very idea of her going away shook him to the bone.

Romantic love was an agony, so elemental one was powerless to fight it.

He knew in his heart that his uncle's hasty marriage wasn't going to last. Where then did that leave an innocent child? The greatest blessing of all to most women had turned out to be a real calamity for Janis. Not all women were born to be nurturers. He had learned that the hard way.

* * *

Cal made the home compound in record time, parking the Jeep in the shade. His stomach muscles were knotted with tension. He wanted to turn away from all this; he had no option but to go forward. He was master of Jingala.

Dee met him in the entrance hall. Not Amber. Only the sight of her could ease his tension.

"How's it going?" He fixed Dee with a questioning stare.

"Doc Trowbridge has persuaded Mrs MacFarlane she needs a while being looked after in a clinic." Dee spoke without expression.

"Okay. That's good, is it?"

"Better than any of us thought. We expected resistance."

"So she's agreed, then?" There was no reason to doubt what Dee was saying, yet he felt enormously on edge. "Where's Amber?"

"She's upstairs," Dee assured him with a backward jerk of the head. "Eliot wanted her along. Poor man is right out of his depth. He'll travel back with Mrs MacFarlane, of course. By the sound of it, they're coming now."

Both of them looked up as a small group of people moved into view at the top of the timber staircase. Dr Tim Trowbridge—well known to them—and a nurse brought up the rear. Amber was a little in front of Eliot, who was gently leading his wife by the arm, an expression of great unhappiness on his face. Janis, on the other hand, looked mute and sullen, eyes dark in their sockets. What shocked Cal most of all was the fact that Janis had cut her long dark hair. No, not cut, she'd *hacked* it so it fell in jagged layers.

Cal moved very fast to the bottom of the stairs, his senses finely honed to all sorts of dangers, on full alert.

At the sight of him Janis suddenly erupted, shaking off her husband's hand with a single violent motion. "*She* did this," she shouted. "We were all right until *she* came."

While the others stood transfixed by this unexpected burst of rage, Janis swooped on Amber. Though thin, Janis was now possessed of a manic strength.

"Bitch! You won't have him." She locked her arms around Amber, thrusting her forwards to the very top of the stairs.

"Janis!"

"Mrs. MacFarlane!" Behind them startled cries rang out in horror and protest.

Only Cal had read Janis's mind. Off balance with jealousy and her perception of Amber as the enemy, Janis had been driven to act. He tore up the stairs as Janis, with unnatural strength, was attempting to push her intended victim down them. It was all happening too fast...

Amber had begun to resist strongly but, in the shocked interim, Janis had gained the upper hand. Janis pushed out with all her might, her expression so triumphant she might have been disposing of the one person who stood between her and all future happiness.

"There!" she shouted in triumph.

With sick terror Amber could feel herself go. She was falling…toppling… Even as it was happening, her brain flashed a picture of her prone body at the foot of the stairs. A tragedy, with Janis MacFarlane to blame. What a blot that would be on the proud MacFarlane name.

Feeling utterly disconnected, beyond help, Amber braced herself for the worst. A broken hand, a broken shoulder, a broken wrist, a broken neck? Only, instead of her fall continuing, it was interrupted on the way by a hard male body thudding into hers.

Cal.

He crossed strong arms around her, knowing he couldn't stop the momentum but fully prepared to take the worst of the fall. He had taken plenty of falls before. There was a trick to the rolling and he had long since learned it. Even so, something could always go wrong. He wasn't just saving himself, he was endeavouring to save the woman he loved. It only made things that much harder.

"Go with me, Amber!" he muttered urgently, not even sure if she heard him.

She did, allowing her body to go pliant. She was

putting all her trust in Cal's ability to cushion their inevitable stunning descent.

Even Janis was momentarily silenced, taken in hand now by both her husband and Trowbridge, who was appalled and not bothering to hide it.

Cal hit the floor first, deadening the impact for Amber, who came to rest half slumped over his back. Her breath was rattling through her body with shock, but she knew with enormous relief that she had come out of it unharmed. Both of them just lay there, Cal winded. Amber was frantic that he might have taken a hard knock to the head. She tried to sit up to make sure he was all right, with Janis all the while at the top of the stairs shouting down at her, "I wish I'd killed you! I wish you were dead."

Truthfully, Amber was so grateful to be unharmed she called with black humour, "I'm doing my best!" If it hadn't been for Cal, Janis might have got her wish. Surely Janis hadn't planned it? Amber had to reject that. It had been an unpremeditated act. Janis needed a scapegoat for her perceived failure in life. Amber had been elected.

Cal, however, saw no humour whatever in the situation. He brought himself into sitting position, getting his breath and ignoring the stabbing aches and pains through his upper body and a worse one at the back of his head.

"Are you okay?" Amber begged him, her heart in her eyes. Incredibly, Janis, at the top of the stairs, was demanding to be released, as if she had done nothing wrong.

"I wouldn't have had you within a thousand miles of harm," he told her bleakly. "Now this. That performance was enough to last me my lifetime."

He rose to his feet a shade gingerly, bringing Amber with him but keeping her within the shelter of his arm. "I hope you find health and peace, Janis," he said. "I truly do. But you'll never set foot in this house again."

A sombre pall fell over the household for the rest of the day. Even the two house girls went about their chores hushed. No merry giggles resounded around the big open rooms. All was quiet. Even little Marcus didn't break the silence with a single cry for attention. It seemed that in the absence of his mother Marcus was turning into a model child.

How sad was that?

Even though Janis had intended her real harm, Amber couldn't find it in her heart to condemn the woman. Some part of her would always pity Janis MacFarlane, who was later to abandon the child she had given birth to without a backward glance. It was as though it had never happened.

Cal returned to work, a sombreness on him like a dark veil. He was devastated that real harm could have been done to Amber, and in his own home. He had accepted that Janis needed help, but never until those very last minutes had he come to the realisation she was an actual *danger* to the one woman she saw as a threat. In a way, it was all *his* fault. There must have been clues along the way but, all unknowing, he had missed them like a fool. Why hadn't Eliot hinted at the bizarre situation—probably paralysed with embarrassment—or at least taken Janis away whether she wanted it or not? Why had Eliot allowed Janis to call the shots? Was he trying to save his marriage? Eliot was only staving off the inevitable. This was a marriage that should never have taken place.

It shocked and humiliated him that Tim Trowbridge and his nurse had witnessed what had happened. It could easily have been a tragedy. A police investigation. Cal knew not a word of the incident would go any further, but that didn't stop him from agonizing over the whole terrible business. After that, Amber would surely be determined on going back home.

And who could blame her? She had come as close to serious assault as she was ever likely to in her life. He could see how it had shaken her, even though she had gazed quietly at him with tears glistening in her beautiful golden eyes. "Thank you, Cal. You saved me."

She might have been part of the family already, prepared to close ranks. That she had come so close to real danger while under his roof and his protection he found shattering. For the first time he confronted head on what he had been trying to keep within manageable limits.

If he lost Amber, he lost *everything*.

Dee was busy, ladling three teaspoons of sugar into Amber's teacup, her preferred antidote to shock. "She coulda killed ya!"

"Well, she didn't." Amber took a sip, face screwed up at the excessive sweetness. "Let that be an end to it."

"Good thing you feel like that. You're so forgiving!" Dee shook her head in wonderment.

"Cal can't forgive himself," Amber lamented.

Dee nodded. "He's taken it to heart. You were brought here as his guest, yet Janis and her troubles wrecked all that."

"No, Dee, I've loved being here. I love this place. I love the wilderness, this extraordinary desert environment. I love the way I can go riding any time I please. A dozen scenarios for a book having been filling my head. *We* get along so well." She reached out to take Dee's hand. "I love little Marcus—I pray things will work out for him. Eliot loves him. There could be light at the end of the tunnel for Janis."

Dee clicked her tongue in dissent. "You mark my words. When a bit of therapy gets her back on her feet, she'll file for divorce. Eliot will have to part with a few million. That should keep her going. It's a no-brainer who gets Marcus. Janis won't want him. I have an idea that's what the beef was with her mother. Her mother probably didn't want Janis, either. What Janis convinced herself she felt for Cal wasn't love. It was a *sickness*."

Amber set down her cup so quickly it rattled in the saucer. "And you knew all about it, Dee?"

Dee looked ashamed. "I had a struggle with it at first. Couldn't believe it. But it was in everything she said, the look in her eyes. She fell for him, hook, line and sinker. I reckon it was the first real bond of her life. No one was attractive to her but Cal. Not even her own baby. That's how bad it was. Fatal attraction."

"Oh, dear me, yes." Sadly Amber shook her head. "Cal hates the very idea of it. I think he's blaming himself."

"Well, then, you'd better talk to him," Dee said. "You care about him, don't ya?" She fixed Amber with her shrewd black eyes.

"What does it look like, Dee?" Amber gave this knowing woman a wry smile.

"Ask me, ya perfect for each other," Dee grunted, to cover a little sob.

Amber got away for her ride late afternoon. She could feel the kinks and twinges in her body from the fall. She wondered how Cal, who had taken the brunt of it, was faring. In all likelihood he had experienced far worse. A good gallop might straighten her out. Her whole being was too restless to remain at the homestead.

She took Horatio in preference to the mare. Horatio would test her. She felt like being tested. Janis MacFarlane's lesson in loving—or lusting— had been a harsh one. It had crushed love for her husband and, even more sadly, love for her baby out of existence. Amber couldn't shake off a sense of pity, not knowing then what she would learn in the future. She had no need to spend any time pitying Janis MacFarlane. Janis was destined to fall on her feet.

In the afternoon light the landscape was glowing with colour, all the brilliant dry ochres—burnt umber, cinnabar, chrome-yellow, black, white and charcoal—to complement the intense opal-blue of the sky. The Hill Country was washed with colours from another spectrum—the mauves, the soft purples, the grape-blues. High above them an eagle coasted, sometimes appearing to hover motionless. She knew the great wedge-tailed eagles made their eyries in the far-off hills with their prehistoric rock galleries she had yet to see. Once she spotted, to her delight, a group of kangaroos in company with almost as many emus, the emus stalking around majestically, as befitting giants of the bird world. The grace and freedom of these animals. She thought she could watch them all day. The great plains that at first seemed so empty were actually swarming with life. The bird life alone was beyond belief.

This was the real Australia. The Outback. The home of the cattle kings. She was hoping to get to ride that exotic beast, the camel. Hundreds of them were roaming the station. A camel could go anywhere and everywhere in the desert, comfortably travelling twice the distance even a big thorough-bred horse like Horatio could travel. Jingala had drawn her in to the point she felt she would have difficulty in letting go. She had thought she would be visiting one of the world's harshest environments, an immensity of *brown*. What a surprise she'd been in for! She hadn't been privileged to see the miracle of the wild flowers, although swathes of paper daisies still lingered across certain sections of the station. Jingala wasn't the desert proper. It bordered the real desert, the Simpson, fifty-six thousand square miles of rolling red sand dunes. In her receptive frame of mind she felt a close affinity with this ancient land. She would have no difficulty in making it her home.

Returning to the homestead, the beauty of the sunset once more held her spellbound. No wonder the aborigines worshipped the land. It had such power—power to ease the mind. She felt immeasurably better after her ride. Jingala homestead was extraordinary, set down as it was in an oasis of green, with no sign of human habitation to all points of the compass. She could understand the desolation Cal's mother must have felt. Outback life had proved unliveable in the end to a woman who had been at war with her environment. She understood too how Cal, suffering the experience of his mother's abandonment, had settled, whether consciously or unconsciously, on Brooke Rowlands for a wife. His main priority would have been to choose a woman he could hold onto. A woman who had been reared to Outback life. Sexual desire would have been necessary, but Brooke was very attractive with a charming way to her. She had been very good with little Marcus, too. Holding him in a way he'd responded to and liked. She didn't think Brooke was actually promiscuous. She had probably been having fun, had too much to drink and fell into bed with a young man she knew well. Brooke would have realized her dreadful mistake the instant she'd woken up.

Alas, too late!

Cal demanded total emotional commitment. Asking another woman to marry him would involve considerable practical and emotional risks. Was he ready to take the chance? In the time she had been on Jingala they had discovered they had a lot in common. Not just the powerful sexual attraction that gathered strength with every passing day. The question of when they would come together was like a constant crackle in the atmosphere.

It had been Janis MacFarlane's unstable behaviour that had piled on the pressure. It hadn't been a normal holiday; or a normal getting to know one another. Far from it. She was happy with the way she had gained Cal's respect. Her fear now was that recent events would cause him to retreat, at least for a period of time before he took any final step. He had to see her not just as a desirable woman. He had to see her as the *right* woman. She had to live up to what he wanted in his life's partner.

Her own feelings had settled into absolute certainty. She loved him. Her search for her soulmate had come to an end. Cal MacFarlane was a man she was ready to love, honour and obey. She was comfortable with all three.

From habit, she entered the office to check whether she had any emails. She had received quite a few from Zara that made her smile. Zara was one of the few people who knew where she was. They'd had great times together. Only one message came up. She eased herself into the leather desk chair to read it.

Greetings, Amber!
Your friend Zara parted with your email address. The price—she wants a job—could find her a spot. As for you, I'm delighted to

hear you're having such a great time. Might be an idea if you got an interview out of the MacFarlane Cattle King. I remember the shot of the two of you coming out of that restaurant. You looked like a couple of movie stars. You'll be heartened to hear scores of angry viewers have been inundating the station with emails demanding to know when we're going to put you back on air. You're loved, kiddo! Erskine is a decent enough guy after all. Word has come down from on high, you're free to come home. We've all missed you. Even Jack. He and Liv Sutton aren't making it as the dream team. He thinks she's a lightweight. She thinks he's a pain in the ass. So Jack is ready for your return. Please let me know when that great day will be. Make it real soon but give me time to arrange a welcome home party.

All my best,

Paddy

When she was done reading it, Amber printed it off, then read it once more, all the while quietly muttering to herself. Instead of being thrilled, as she would have been under normal circumstances, she felt hugely unsettled. She couldn't ignore Paddy. She would have to answer him. What would she say? She'd take the next plane?

How unexpected was life! Today, of all days,

yet another emergency had been forced on her. What was she supposed to do? Hand Cal the email? Let him read it, digest the contents, then make a telling comment?

What would she do if he handed back the email with the casual enquiry, *So when are you thinking of leaving?*

Depending on the way he said it and the accompanying look in those enigmatic green eyes, she might have to answer, *On the first flight available.*

She had no idea what she would do if he took her imminent departure in his stride. Probably tear her hair out. But surely tearing her hair out would come close to Janis's hacking off *her* locks? Was it a female thing? One of the ultimate expressions of grief?

For the first time Dee insisted Marcus spend the night with her. "The nanny will be flying in tomorra and you need a break," she told Amber in a no-argument voice.

"My TV station wants me back, Dee," Amber confessed.

"Wh-a-t?" Dee fell back as if she'd been shot.

"There was an email waiting for me. The viewers miss me."

"We'll be missin' you too." Dee started to pull frantically on an ear lobe. "What are you gonna do? Sorry, it's none of my business, love."

"I think it is." Amber moved to hug her. "I'll tell Cal over dinner, but I'm worried how he'll react. He

mightn't care as much about me as I'd like to think."
It came out *so* forlornly.

"Tell him all the same," Dee advised.

Towards the end of dinner Cal suddenly grasped
Amber's narrow wrist. "What's on your mind?" His
tone was sharp and alert.

"You think there's something on my mind?"
Madness to deny it.

"Amber, don't let's get into that question for
question stuff," he warned. "Are you sure you're
feeling okay?" His eyes swept over her. She was
wearing a short dress with little ruffles in a shade
almost the colour of her hair. She looked beautiful, if sad.

"I told you, Cal, just a few twinges here and there.
You're the one who took the brunt of it."

"It's my job to look after you." His mouth
faintly twisted.

She had to glance away to cover her emotional
agitation. Another beautiful desert night, a dazzling
canopy of stars. All her nerves bunched. Unsure
what to tell him. Terrified he would take her news
calmly, thus crushing her hopes.

"*Tell* me," he said in that clipped tone he used to
express displeasure. "You want to go home. You
want to go back where you belong."

"And you're going to let me go?"

His light eyes darkened. "I know, apart from Janis

and the whole situation, you've been enjoying yourself here. But you have the whole world at your feet. You're as much out of your element as a yellow rose springing from a desert rock."

She leapt to her own defence, temper flaring. "Aren't you the one who told me about all the exquisite little wild flowers that manage to survive growing out of rocks? I'm no hothouse flower."

"No, you're a species of your own."

"A hardy one, I'd like you to know. Does this mean I should start packing?" Without meaning to, she found herself standing, more overwrought than she knew. "That's enough to send me home."

He stood as well, his expression intense. "I thought you said you wanted to go?"

"I said no such thing. Here, read this." She turned about to snatch up the email she had left folded on the carved console.

"I don't need to read it." He took it all the same. "You've told me all I need to know. They want you back. I knew they would. You're obviously very valuable to them."

"It was your wicked old grandfather who gave the okay," she said, conscious there was too much heat in her voice. "Does he know I'm here?"

"Who cares what he knows," Cal responded bluntly. "Seems like the trip is over and the crying begins."

"I don't see *you* crying," she accused, furious to feel the sting of tears at the back of her eyes.

"Not now, anyhow," he said with heavy humour. "Are you going to sit down again? We haven't finished dinner. Dee will be upset."

"You should have waited until *after* dinner," she said, lowering herself back into the rattan armchair.

"I wish I had," he said wryly, taking the chair opposite her. "What do you want from me, Amber?"

"What do you want from *me*? Let's get it on the table." She reached for her half empty wineglass, tossing the contents back. She must have learned that from Janis.

"Well, I'm mad to make love to you," he announced in a don't-push-me-too-far voice. "I'm not going to pretend about that. It's chronic by this stage. I don't think I can last another day without having you. Are you taking me seriously? You should."

"Okay, then. You've cited desire." She ticked off a finger. "Kindly explain what else, if anything, makes me attractive to you."

"Don't start this, Amber," he begged, like a man fast reaching his limits. "Don't, don't, *don't*."

"Annoying you, am I?' Her golden eyes flashed.

"Inciting me, more like it. As if you didn't know. Maybe we can sleep together tonight, then pretend it never happened?"

She tried to breathe steadily. Couldn't manage it. "Apologise for that."

"No." His answer was blunt. "You might like to

calm down, though. Dee's coming with the coffee. She told me she's taking care of Marcus tonight."

Sure enough she fired. "Does that mean we're free to give in to our desire?"

"Well, I've been considering it if you haven't," he returned sardonically. "In some ways I regret my inability to withstand you."

"Of course you do," she said. "You much prefer to maintain a distance."

"That's what's kept me from knocking your door down."

He looked as if he meant it. "Ah, so you're a caveman? You've been keeping that from me. Anyway, here's Dee," she warned as Dee wheeled the trolley into the room. "She's within earshot. I don't want her to see us fighting."

"Is that what we're doing?" he asked with a lift of the brow. "You know I pictured something quite different for tonight. But nothing is certain in life."

"You can say that again!"

They called it a night before the two of them worked up a *real* argument.

"I'd really appreciate it if you'd let me stay until Eliot comes home and Marcus is responding well to the new nanny" was Amber's parting shot. Extremely unfair because he hadn't said a thing about her leaving. Over-emotional with the events of the day, she was in a perverse mood, deliberately provoking him.

"*Former* nanny," he corrected shortly. He stood in the entrance hall, watching her flounce up the stairs with those long beautiful legs. "She was here when Jan was ringing the changes. She's a very nice woman—widow, early forties, ex-nursing sister, Martha Fenton. She was handling Marcus just fine only Janis swore an oath to get rid of her, just like her predecessor."

"And me!" Amber reminded him. "Never a kind word. Goodnight, Cal." She clipped the words off in a tone she had perfected from him.

"You're not going to your martyrdom, are you?" he called after her in a dark, sardonic voice.

"I'm trying not to charge down the stairs and hit you." Every electrical circuit in her blood was hot-wired.

Cal gave a short laugh. "And what do you think would happen if you did?" Desire was shooting through his body like a flaming arrow, but he tried to bank it down. She could flounce off tonight. It had been a terrible day for her. But he knew, beyond all denial, he would never let her go. Lock her up if he had to. The sun shone more brightly with Amber around.

She paused to look down at him. His green eyes glittered brilliantly, but his handsome features looked unusually drawn. Her breath caught. "I thought you were trying to put the brakes on, not play with fire?" She hesitated uncertainly.

"I've never stopped playing with fire with you round." He gave that twisted smile. "Go to bed, Amber. Try to get a good night's sleep. It's been one hell of a day. I'm sure you'll agree."

"Oh, I do!" To her absolute horror she found herself close to tears. Once more her life was running off the rails. And serve her right! There was always something to cause fresh pain. Sean had hurt her pride. This was the kind of pain that went on for ever.

"We'll talk again," he promised.

She spun in a passion, a single tear sliding her cheek. "Thanks a lot."

"Well, it's a good thing, isn't it, our talking?" he appealed to her.

"Oh, talk, talk, talk!" she burst out over the lump in her throat. "Why can't you embrace life, Cal? There are worse things than trusting a woman. Even one with red hair. The trouble with you is you're *frightened* to reach out."

"Am I?" he asked crisply.

She ignored the hard challenge. "Of course you are."

"We'll see about that."

To her shock, he started to come after her. There was only one thing to do. *Run!* Though exactly why he was running perplexed her. Maybe it was another weird insight into female behaviour. Her heart pounding, tremors running up and down her arms and legs, she reached her bedroom door. She

had left it open when she had gone down to dinner
so she was able to fly through the door, slamming
it after her.

The speed with which he arrived at her door
was like a jolt to the heart. "Open the door
Amber," he commanded.

That got to her. No plea. An *order*. "I'm locking
it," she cried. Even to her own ears her voice
sounded wild. Lock the man out of his own house?

"Like who owns this house—*you*?"

"You seem to have forgotten I'm your guest."

"Guests don't usually start lecturing their hosts,"
he called back. "Open up, before I break it down."

"Suit yourself." He wouldn't break down his own
beautiful timber door. That would be a crying shame.

Silence. Oh, Lord! He must have gone away. She
had to be a basket case because she was terribly
terribly disappointed. Dispiritedly, she collapsed on
the side of her bed, trying to calm down. Her heart
had been racing in delicious terror; now she waited
for it to slow. She could have handled this differently. Why hadn't she? Didn't he know how much
she loved this life? He damned well *did*. She had no
fears of the remoteness. What the heck was her job
anyway? Reading the news. What was the enormous
satisfaction in that? She wanted a *life*. She wanted
kids. She wanted to write. She wanted *him*. Surely
he could see the sort of woman she was?

There were footsteps along the outside veranda. Heavy, purposeful footsteps. How the heck had he got up there? She leapt up from the bed, ready for anything.

"So you want to play. Is that it?" He was framed by the open French windows. He looked extraordinarily masterful, all strength and dominant sexuality.

"How did you do that?" she asked with some wonder. He had a few green leaves caught in his thick crow-black hair.

"Good question."

"You climbed a tree?" Her voice was shaking with excitement.

"How else would I do it?" His brilliant eyes ranged over her. Her lovely face was surrounded by her bright cascading hair. It swirled over and around her shoulders. There was a high flush in her cheeks from excited blood. "I thought I was right," he said. "You're crying."

"So what?" She dashed the sparkle of tears away. "I'm good at it too when I get started. Sometimes tears are outside a woman's control, didn't you know?"

"And sometimes a man can hurt a woman when he doesn't intend to." Emotion deepened his voice. "Look at me, Amber."

Look at him! She was desperate to *run* to him but uncertainty continued to pin her in place.

"All right, if Mahomet won't come to the mountain, the mountain must come to Mahomet."

"Oh, Cal what are we doing?" Even as she said it, her body was up and swaying towards him. She was in a high state of arousal. Her sensitive nipples had already tightened into buds that desperately needed the touch of Cal's forefinger and callused thumb.

"Nothing as yet," he gritted, hauling her into his arms. "Just let yourself go. All you have to do is hold onto me."

His dark head blocked out the overhead light. She breathed in his warm breath. "But Cal, I need to know—"

He cut her off. "Ask me afterwards. I know what you want. I know what *I* want. Let our bodies do the talking for us." He brought up his right hand, weaving his long fingers into the loose mass of her hair. "Open your mouth."

Her mind went clear of everything but *want*. She could feel her limbs dissolving. Her body was as alight as if a fire blazed inside. She could have wept from the conflagration. She did in fact make a little sound that could have been interpreted as dissent, only Cal was having none of it. He lowered his mouth over her cushiony lips, kissing her so deeply, so voluptuously that her arms came around him, tightening, pulling him in to her as if she would never let him go.

Surely that settled everything, he thought, moving into a high state of elation. She tasted wonderful. Like peaches and sunshine. Their tongues were meeting, mating, in a sinuous love dance. He could feel her supple fingers begin to knead his back. She seemed desperate to touch not fabric but *skin*. He understood perfectly. He had only to release a zipper to have her satiny dress slip from her body and pool at their feet. His hands moved compulsively to the undercurves of her beautiful breasts, taking their weight, his fingertips centring on the rose-coloured nipples. He could see the agitated flutter of her eyelids. He already knew she wasn't wearing a bra, so it would be naked flesh he would find beneath his hand.

Once he fell to kissing and caressing her he couldn't stop. But neither was she stopping him. She was giving him everything he so desperately desired. It was all out in the open. The passion they shared for one another couldn't be denied. Something this powerful demanded trust. He was ready to embrace it. There was wisdom in listening to her…

Gradually their lovemaking escalated to a pitch where it was hard to tell what was teasing and what torture. Still holding her, he stripped back the quilted silk coverlet of the bed, urged on by the soft little mewing sounds she was making.

"I love you," she cried frantically. She couldn't hold it in. Her whole body was vibrating with it.

He all but tossed her onto the bed in his urgency. "Yes, I know." He began to strip his splendid body naked, the lamplight gilding his skin.

"You *know*?" She half rose up from the bed, then fell back again, transfigured by his words.

"Of course I know," he said in a voice pent-up with emotion. "I think we've pretty well cleared that small point up."

"Then I'm waiting to hear you tell me you love me." Ecstatically she threw her arms back over her head, inviting the adoration that was emblazoned on his dynamic face.

"I plan to." He half loomed over her, all strength and sinew and rippling muscle. "But it's going to take hours—" long kisses "—and hours…"

Rapture shone from her face, resounded in her soul. "So you don't want me to go away?"

His green eyes were impossibly brilliant. "There's one thing I haven't told you yet, my beautiful Amber. You want me to say it, right?"

She pulled him down bedside her, spooning her body into his, welcoming his powerful arousal. "I'm listening."

"I want to tell you something I haven't told another soul." He gathered her even closer, binding her to him as if by invisible chains.

"Yes?" she whispered, shaking with excitement, her thighs already moving apart.

"I'm ready to reach out. It was you who worked that miracle. I see a woman so beautiful, so strong, so full of character, I worship at her feet. I see a woman I will love for as long as I live. I see a woman I can trust. I love you, Amber. I adore you. I'm not letting you get away. I'm going to keep you for ever and ever."

Saying it, he reached down to capture her yearning mouth.

And so it turned out. A lifetime of sharing, fiery little clashes, passionate making up, the maintaining of a dynasty. Three children in total. A boy and girl of their own. Steven first, then Stephanie named in honour of their grandmother, who often came to visit. Their cousin, Marcus, more a big brother than a cousin, was raised as part of this loving brood. Janis MacFarlane never remarried but she did reach dizzy heights in the world of finance. She became CEO of a merchant bank, which gave her absolute fulfilment. Eliot MacFarlane eventually found true love. He married his son's former nanny, Martha Fenton, a woman as gentle and loving as his first wife, Caro. Amber wrote her books to critical acclaim.

It was a great life. A total life. A life to shout about!

BACHELOR DAD
ON HER DOORSTEP

BY
MICHELLE DOUGLAS

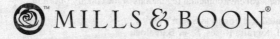

MILLS & BOON®

All the characters in this book have no existence outside the imagination of the author, and have no relation whatsoever to anyone bearing the same name or names. They are not even distantly inspired by any individual known or unknown to the author, and all the incidents are pure invention.

First published in Great Britain 2009
Harlequin Mills & Boon Limited,
Eton House, 18-24 Paradise Road, Richmond, Surrey TW9 1SR

© Michelle Douglas 2009

ISBN: 978 0 263 86958 3

Set in Times Roman 12½ on 14 pt
02-0809-54084

Harlequin Mills & Boon policy is to use papers that are natural, renewable and recyclable products and made from wood grown in sustainable forests. The logging and manufacturing process conform to the legal environmental regulations of the country of origin.

Printed and bound in Spain
by Litografia Rosés, S.A., Barcelona

At the age of eight **Michelle Douglas** was asked what she wanted to be when she grew up. She answered, 'A writer.' Years later she read an article about romance-writing and thought, *Ooh, that'll be fun.* She was right. When she's not writing she can usually be found with her nose buried in a book. She is currently enrolled in an English Masters programme, for the sole purpose of indulging her reading and writing habits further. She lives in a leafy suburb of Newcastle, on Australia's east coast, with her own romantic hero—husband Greg, who is the inspiration behind all her happy endings. Michelle would love you to visit her at her website: www.michelledouglas.com

Recent books by the same author:

THE ARISTOCRAT AND THE SINGLE MUM
THE LONER'S GUARDED HEART
HIS CHRISTMAS ANGEL

To Varuna, The Writers' House, with thanks.

PROLOGUE

JAZ hadn't meant her first return to Clara Falls in eight years to occur under the cover of darkness, but she hadn't been able to get away from work as early as she'd hoped and then the traffic between Sydney and the Blue Mountains had been horrendous.

She was late.

At least a fortnight too late.

A horrible laugh clawed out of her throat, a sound she'd never heard herself utter before. She tried to drag it back before it swallowed her whole.

Not the time. Not the place.

Definitely not the place.

She didn't drive up Clara Falls' main street. She turned into the lane that led to the residential parking behind the shops. Given the darkness—and the length of time she'd stayed away—would she even recognise the back of the bookshop?

She did. Immediately.

And a weight slammed down so heavily on her

chest she sagged. She had to close her eyes and go through the relaxation technique Mac had taught her. The weight didn't lift, but somehow she found a way to breathe through it.

When she could, she opened her eyes and parked her hatchback beside a sleek Honda and stared up at the light burning in the window.

Oh, Mum!

Sorry would not be good enough. It would never be good enough.

Don't think about it.

Not the time. Not the place.

She glanced at the Honda. Was it Richard's car?

Richard—her mother's solicitor.

Richard—Connor Reed's best friend.

The thought came out of nowhere, shooting tension into every muscle, twisting both of her calves into excruciating cramps.

Ha! Not out of nowhere. Whenever she thought of Clara Falls, she thought of Connor Reed. End of story.

She rested her forehead on the steering wheel and welcomed the bite of pain in her legs, but it didn't wipe out the memories from her mind. Connor Reed was the reason she'd left Clara Falls. Connor Reed was the reason she'd never returned.

The cramps didn't ease.

She lifted her gaze back to the bookshop, then higher still to stare at the flat above, where her mother had spent the last two years of her life.

I'm sorry, Mum.

The pain in her chest and legs intensified. Points of light darted at the outer corners of her eyes. She closed them and forced herself to focus on Mac's relaxation technique again—deliberately tensing, then relaxing every muscle in her body, one by one. The pain eased.

She would not see Connor Reed tonight. And, once she'd signed the papers to sell the bookshop to its prospective buyer, she'd never have to set foot in Clara Falls again.

She pushed open the car door and made her way up the back steps. Richard opened the door before she could knock.

'Jaz!' He folded her in a hug. 'It's great to see you.'

He meant it, she could tell. 'I… It's great to see you too.' Strangely enough, she meant it too. A tiny bit of warmth burrowed under her skin.

His smile slipped. 'I just wish it was under different circumstances.'

The warmth shot back out of her. Richard, as her mother's solicitor, had been the one to contact her, to tell her that Frieda had taken an overdose of sleeping pills. To tell her that her mother had died. He hadn't told Jaz that it was all her fault. He hadn't had to.

Don't think about it. Not the time. Not the place.

'Me too,' she managed. She meant *that* with all her heart.

He ushered her inside—into a kitchenette. Jaz

knew that this room led through to the stockroom and
then into the bookshop proper. Or, at least, it used to.

'Why don't we have a cup of coffee? Gordon
should be along any moment and then we can get
down to signing all the paperwork.'

'Sure.' She wondered why Richard had asked her
to meet him here rather than at his offices. She
wondered who this Mr Gordon was who wanted to
buy her mother's bookshop.

Asking questions required energy—energy Jaz
didn't have.

Richard motioned to the door of the stockroom.
'You want to go take a wander through?'

'No, thank you.'

The last thing she needed was a trip down memory
lane. She might've found refuge in this bookshop
from the first moment she'd entered it as a ten-year-
old. Once upon a time she might've loved it. But she
didn't need a refuge now. She was an adult. She'd
learned to stand on her own two feet. She'd had to.

'No, thank you,' she repeated.

Her mother had bought the bookshop two years
ago in the hope it would lure Jaz back to Clara Falls.
She had no desire to see it now, to confront all she'd
lost due to her stupid pride and her fear.

Regret crawled across her scalp and down the
nape of her neck to settle over her shoulders. She
wanted to sell the bookshop. She wanted to leave.
That was why she was here now.

Richard opened his mouth but, before he could say anything, a knock sounded on the back door. He turned to answer it, ushered a second person into the kitchenette. 'You remember Gordon Sears, don't you, Jaz?'

'Sure I do.'

'It's Mr Sears who wants to buy the bookshop.'

A ball formed in Jaz's stomach. Mr Sears owned the 'baked-fresh-daily' country bakery directly across the road. He hadn't approved of Jaz when she was a child. And he certainly hadn't approved of Frieda.

Mr Sears's eyes widened when they rested on Jaz now, though. It almost made her smile. She sympathised wholeheartedly with his surprise. The last time he'd seen her she'd been a rebellious eighteen-year-old Goth—dressed in top-to-toe black with stark white make-up, spiked hair and a nose ring. Her chocolate-brown woolen trousers and cream knit top would make quite a contrast now.

'How do you do, Mr Sears?' She took a step forward and held out her hand. 'It's nice to see you again.'

He stared at her hand and then his lip curled. 'This is business. It's not a social call.'

He didn't shake her hand.

Memories crashed down on Jaz then. The ball in her stomach hardened, solidified. Mr Sears had never actually refused to serve Jaz and her mother in his 'baked-fresh-daily' country bakery, but he'd let them know by his icy politeness, his curled lip, the placing of change on the counter instead of directly into their hands, what he'd thought of them.

Despite Jaz's pleas, her mother had insisted on shopping there. 'Best bread in town,' she'd say cheerfully.

It had always tasted like sawdust to Jaz.

Frieda Harper's voice sounded through Jaz's mind now. *It doesn't matter what people think. Don't let it bother you.*

Jaz had done her best to follow that advice, but…

Do unto others…

She'd fallen down on that one too.

Frieda Harper, Jaz's wild and wonderful mother. If Frieda had wanted a drink, she'd have a drink. If Frieda had wanted to dance, she'd get up and dance. If Frieda had wanted a man, she'd take a man. It had made the more conservative members of the town tighten their lips in disapproval.

People like Mr Sears. People like Connor Reed's mum and dad.

Jaz wheeled away, blindly groped her way through the all-too-familiar doorways. Light suddenly flooded the darkness, making her blink. She stood in the bookshop…and all her thought processes slammed to a halt.

She turned a slow circle, her eyes wide to take in the enormity of it all. Nothing had changed. Everything was exactly the same as she remembered it.

Nothing had changed.

Oh, Mum…

'I'm sorry, Mr Sears.' It took a moment before she realised it was her voice that broke the silence. 'But it seems I can't sell the bookshop after all.'

'What?'

'Good.'

She heard distinct satisfaction in Richard's voice, but she didn't understand it. She was only aware of the weight lifting from her chest, letting her breathe more freely than she had once during the last two weeks.

CHAPTER ONE

JAZ made the move back to Clara Falls in bright, clear sunlight two weeks later. And this time she had to drive down Clara Falls' main street because an enormous skip blocked the lane leading to the residential parking behind the bookshop.

She slammed on the brakes and stared at it. Unless she turned her car around to flee back to Sydney, she'd have to drive down the main street and find a place to park.

Her mouth went dry.

Turn the car around…?

The temptation stretched through her. Her hands clenched on the steering wheel. She'd sworn never to return. She didn't want to live here. She didn't want to deal with the memories that would pound at her day after day.

And she sure as hell didn't want to see Connor Reed again.

Not that she expected to run into him too often.

He'd avoid her the way the righteous spurned the wicked, the way a reformed alcoholic shunned whisky…the way mice baulked at cats.

Good.

Turn the car around…?

She relaxed her hands and pushed her shoulders back. No. Returning to Clara Falls, saving her mother's bookshop—it was the right thing to do. She'd honour her mother's memory; she'd haul the bookshop back from the brink of bankruptcy. She'd do Frieda Harper proud.

Pity you didn't do that a month ago, a year ago, two years ago, when it might have made a difference.

Guilt crawled across her skin. Regret swelled in her stomach until she could taste bile on her tongue. Regret that she hadn't returned when her mother was still alive. Regret that she'd never said all the things she should've said.

Regret that her mother was dead.

Did she honestly think that saving a bookshop and praying for forgiveness would make any difference at all?

Don't think about it! Wrong time. Wrong place.

She backed the car out of the lane and turned in the direction of the main street.

She had to pause at the pedestrian crossing and, as she stared up the length of the main street, her breath caught. Oh, good Lord. She'd forgotten just how pretty this place was.

Clara Falls was one of the main tourist hubs in Australia's breathtaking Blue Mountains. Jaz hadn't forgotten the majesty of Echo Point and The Three Sisters. She hadn't forgotten the grandeur of the Jamison Valley, but Clara Falls…

The artist in her paid silent homage. Maybe she'd taken it for granted all those years ago.

She eased the car up the street and the first stirrings of excitement started replacing her dread. The butcher's shop and mini-mart had both received a facelift. Teddy bears now picnicked in a shop window once crowded with tarot cards and crystals. The wide traffic island down the centre of the road—once grey cement—now sported close-cropped grass, flower-beds and park benches. But the numerous cafés and restaurants still did a bustling trade. This was still the same wide street. Clara Falls was still the same tourist hotspot.

The town had made an art form out of catering to out-of-towners. It had a reputation for quirky arts-and-craft shops, bohemian-style cafés and cosmopolitan restaurants, and…and…darn it, but it was pretty!

A smile tugged at the corners of her mouth. She cruised the length of the street—she couldn't park directly out the front of the bookshop as a tradesman's van had parked in such a way that it took up two spaces. So, when she reached the end of the street, she turned the car around and cruised back down the other side, gobbling up every familiar landmark along the way.

Finally, she parked the car and sagged back in her seat. She'd spent so long trying to forget Connor Reed that she'd forgotten…stuff she shouldn't have.

Yeah, like how to be a halfway decent human being.

The sunlight abruptly went out of her day. The taste of bile stretched through her mouth again. Her mother had always told Jaz that she needed to return and face her demons, only then could she lay them to rest. Perhaps Frieda had been right—what had happened here in Clara Falls had overshadowed Jaz's entire adult life.

She wanted peace.

Eight years away hadn't given her that.

Not that she deserved it now.

She pushed out of the car. She waited for a break in the traffic, then crossed the road to the island. An elderly man in front of her stumbled up the first step and she grabbed his arm to steady him. She'd crossed at this particular spot more times than she could remember as a child and teenager, almost always heading for the sanctuary of the bookshop. Three steps up, five paces across, and three steps back down the other side. The man muttered his thanks without even looking at her and hurried off.

'Spoilsport,' someone hissed at Jaz. Then to the man, 'And one of these days you'll actually sit down and pass the time of day with me, Boyd Longbottom!'

The elderly woman turned back to Jaz. 'The only entertainment I get these days is watching old Boyd trip up that same step day in, day out.' Dark eyes twinkled. 'Though now you're back in town, Jazmin Harper, I have great hopes that things will liven up around here again.'

'Mrs Lavender!' Jaz grinned. She couldn't help it. Mrs Lavender had once owned the bookshop. Mrs Lavender had been a friend. 'In as fine form as ever, I see. It's nice to see you.'

Mrs Lavender patted the seat beside her and Jaz sat. She'd expected to feel out of place. She didn't. She nodded towards the bookshop although she couldn't quite bring herself to look at it yet. She had a feeling that its familiarity might break her heart afresh. 'Do you miss it?'

'Every single day. But I'm afraid the old bones aren't what they used to be. Doctor's orders and whatnot. I'm glad you've come back, Jaz.'

This all uttered in a rush. It made Jaz's smile widen. 'Thank you.'

A short pause, then, 'I was sorry about what happened to your mother.'

Jaz's smile evaporated. 'Thank you.'

'I heard you held a memorial service in Sydney.'

'I did.'

'I was sick in hospital at the time or I would have been there.'

Jaz shook her head. 'It doesn't matter.'

'Of course it does! Frieda and I were friends.'

Jaz found she could smile again, after a fashion. According to the more uptight members of the town, Frieda might've lacked a certain respectability, but she certainly hadn't lacked friends. The memorial had been well attended.

'This place was never the same after you left.'

Mrs Lavender's voice hauled Jaz back. She gave a short laugh. 'I can believe that.'

Those dark eyes, shrewd with age, surveyed her closely. 'You did the right thing, you know. Leaving.'

No, she hadn't. What she'd done had led directly to her mother's death. She'd left and she'd sworn to never come back. It had broken her mother's heart. She'd hold herself responsible for that till the day she died. And she'd hold Connor responsible too. If he'd believed in Jaz, like he'd always sworn he would, Jaz would never have had to leave.

She would never have had to stay away.

Stop it!

She shook herself. She hadn't returned to Clara Falls for vengeance. Do unto others…that had been Frieda's creed. She would do Frieda Harper proud. She'd save the bookshop, then she'd sell it to someone other than Gordon Sears, then she'd leave, and this time she would never come back.

'You always were a good girl, Jaz. And smart.'

It hadn't been smart to believe Connor's promises. She shook off the thought and pulled her mind back, to find Mrs Lavender smiling at her broadly. 'How long are you staying?'

'Twelve months.' She'd had to give herself a time limit—it was the only thing that would keep her sane. She figured it'd take a full twelve months to see the bookshop safe again.

'Well, I think it's time you took yourself off and got to work, dear.' Mrs Lavender pointed across the road. 'I think you'll find there's a lot to do.'

Jaz followed the direction of Mrs Lavender's hand, and that was when she saw and understood the reason behind the tradesman's van parked out the front of the bookshop. The muscles in her shoulders, her back, her stomach, all tightened. The minor repairs on the building were supposed to have been finished last week. The receptionist for the building firm Richard had hired had promised faithfully.

A pulse pounded behind her eyes. 'Frieda's Fiction Fair'—the sign on the bookshop's awning—was being replaced. With…

'Jaz's Joint'!

She shot to her feet. Her lip curled. Her nose curled. Inside her boots, even her toes curled. She'd requested that the sign be freshened up. Not… Not… She fought the instinct to bolt across the road and topple the sign-writer and his ladder to the ground.

'I'll be seeing you then, shall I, Jazmin?'

With an effort, she unclenched her teeth. 'Absolutely, Mrs Lavender.'

She forced herself to take three deep breaths, and only then did she step off the kerb of the island. She would sort this out like the adult she was, not the teenager she had been.

She made her way across the road and tried not to notice how firm her offending tradesman's butt looked in form-fitting jeans or how the power of those long, long legs were barely disguised by soft worn denim. In fact, in some places the denim was so worn…

The teenager she'd once been wouldn't have noticed. That girl had only had eyes for Connor. But the woman she was now…

Stop ogling!

She stopped by the ladder and glanced up. Then took an involuntary step backwards at the sudden clench of familiarity. The sign-writer's blond-tipped hair…

It fell in the exact same waves as—

Her heart lodged in her throat, leaving an abyss in her chest. *Get a grip. Don't lose it now.* The familiarity had to be a trick of the light.

Ha! More like a trick of the mind. Planted there by memories she'd done her best to bury.

She swallowed and her heart settled—sort of—in her chest again. 'Excuse me,' she managed to force out of an uncooperative throat, 'but I'd like to know who gave you the authority to change that sign.'

The sign-writer stilled, laid his brush down on the top of the ladder and wiped his hands across that denim-encased butt with agonising slowness. Jaz couldn't help wondering how it would feel to follow that action with her own hands. Gooseflesh broke out on her arms.

Slowly, oh-so-slowly, the sign-writer turned around…and Jaz froze.

'Hello, Jaz.'

The familiarity, the sudden sense of rightness at seeing him here like this, reached right inside her chest to twist her heart until she couldn't breathe.

No!

He took one step down the ladder. 'You're looking…well.'

He didn't smile. His gaze travelled over her face, down the long line of her body and back again and, although half of his face was in shadow, she could see that she left him unmoved.

Connor Reed!

She sucked in a breath, took another involuntary step back. It took every ounce of strength she could marshal to not turn around and run.

Do something. Say something, she ordered.

Her heart pounded in her throat. Sharp breaths stung her lungs. Connor Reed. She'd known they'd run into each other eventually, but not here. Not at the bookshop.

Not on her first day.

Stop staring. Don't you dare run!

'I…um…' She had to clear her throat. She didn't

run. 'I'd appreciate it if you'd stop working on that.' She pointed to the sign and, by some freak or miracle or because some deity was smiling down on her, her hand didn't shake. It gave her the confidence to lift her chin and throw her shoulders back again.

He glanced at the sign, then back at her, a frown in his eyes. 'You don't like it?'

'I loathe it. But I'd prefer not to discuss it on the street.'

Oh, dear Lord. She had to set some ground rules. Fast. Ground rule number one was that Connor Reed stay as far away from her as humanly possible.

Ground rule number two—don't look him directly in the eye.

She swung away, meaning to find refuge in the one place in this town she could safely call home… and found the bookshop closed.

The sign on the door read 'Closed' in big black letters. The darkened interior mocked her. She reached out and tested the door. It didn't budge.

Somebody nearby sniggered. 'That's taken the wind out of your sails, nicely. Good!'

Jaz glanced around to find a middle-aged woman glaring at her. She kept her voice cool. 'Excuse me, but do I know you?'

The woman ignored Jaz's words and pushed her face in close. 'We don't need your kind in a nice place like this.'

A disturbance in the air, some super-sense on her

personal radar, told her Connor had descended the ladder to stand directly behind her. He still smelt like the mountains in autumn.

She pulled a packet of gum from her pocket and shoved a long spearmint-flavoured stick into her mouth. It immediately overpowered all other scents in her near vicinity.

'My kind?' she enquired as pleasantly as she could.

If these people couldn't get past the memory of her as a teenage Goth with attitude, if they couldn't see that she'd grown up, then…then they needed to open their eyes wider.

Something told her it was their minds that needed opening up and not their eyes.

'A tattoo artist!' the woman spat. 'What do we want with one of those? You're probably a member of a bike gang and…and do drugs!'

Jaz almost laughed at the absurdity. Almost. She lifted her arms, looked down at herself, then back at the other woman. For a moment the other woman looked discomfited.

'That's enough, Dianne.'

That was from Connor. Jaz almost turned around but common sense kicked in—*don't look him directly in the eye*.

'Don't you go letting her get her hooks into you again, Connor. She did what she could to lead you astray when you were teenagers and don't you forget it!'

Jaz snorted. She couldn't help herself. The woman—Dianne—swung back to her. 'You probably think this is going to be a nice little money spinner.' She nodded to the bookshop.

Not at the moment. Not after reviewing the sales figures Richard had sent her.

'You didn't come near your mother for years and now, when her body is barely cold in the ground, you descend on her shop like a vulture. Like a greedy, grasping—'

'That's enough, Dianne!'

Connor again. Jaz didn't want him fighting her battles—she wanted him to stay as far from her as possible. He wasn't getting a second chance to break her heart. Not in this lifetime! But she could barely breathe, let alone talk.

Didn't come near your mother for years...barely cold in the ground...

The weight pressed down so hard on Jaz's chest that she wanted nothing more than to lie down on the ground and let it crush her.

'You have the gall to say that after the number of weekends Frieda spent in Sydney with Jaz, living the high life? Jaz didn't need to come home and you bloody well know it!'

Home.

Jaz started. She couldn't lie down on the ground. Not out the front of her mother's bookshop.

'Now clear off, Dianne Keith. You're nothing but

a troublemaking busybody with a streak of spite in you a mile wide.'

With the loudest intake of breath Jaz had ever heard anyone huff, Dianne stormed off.

Didn't come near your mother for years...barely cold in the ground...

A touch on her arm brought her back. The touch of work-roughened fingers on the bare flesh of her arm.

'Are you okay?'

His voice was low, a cooling autumn breeze. Jaz inched away, out of reach of those work-roughened fingers, away from the heat of his body.

'Yes, I'm fine.'

But, as the spearmint of her gum faded, all she could smell was the mountains in autumn. She remembered how it had once been her favourite smell in the world. When she'd been a girl...and gullible.

She *would* be fine. In just a moment. If she could stop breathing so deeply, his scent would fade.

She cleared her throat. 'It's not that I expected a fatted calf, but I didn't expect that.' She nodded to where Dianne had stood.

She hadn't expected a welcome, but she hadn't expected outright hostility either. Except, perhaps, from Connor Reed.

She'd have welcomed it from him.

'Dianne Keith has been not-so-secretly in love with Gordon Sears for years now.'

She blinked. He was telling her this because...

'Oh! I didn't sell him the bookshop, so his nose is out of joint…making her nose out of joint too?'

'You better believe it.'

She couldn't believe she was standing in Clara Falls' main street talking to Connor Reed like…like nothing had ever happened between them. As if this were a normal, everyday event.

She made the mistake then of glancing full into his face, of meeting his amazing brown eyes head-on.

They sparkled gold. And every exquisite moment she'd ever spent with him came crashing back.

If she could've stepped away she would've, but the bookshop window already pressed hard against her shoulder blades.

If she could've glanced away she would've, but her foolish eyes refused to obey the dictates of her brain. They feasted on his golden beauty as if starved for the sight of him. It made something inside her lift.

The sparks in his eyes flashed and burned. As if he couldn't help it, his gaze lowered and travelled down the length of her body with excruciating slowness. When his gaze returned to hers, his eyes had darkened to a smoky, molten lava that she remembered too well.

Her pulse gave a funny little leap. Blood pounded in her ears. She had to grip her hands together. After all these years and everything that had passed between them, how could there be anything but bitterness?

Her heart burned acid. No way! She had no intention of travelling down that particular path to hell ever again.

Eight years ago she'd believed in him—in them—completely, but Connor had accused her of cheating on him. His lack of faith in her had broken her heart…destroyed her.

She hadn't broken his heart, though, because nine months after Jaz had fled town he'd had a child with Faye. A daughter. A little girl.

She folded her arms. Belatedly, she realised, it made even more of her…assets. She couldn't unfold them again without revealing to him that his continued assessment bothered her. She kept said arms stoically folded, but her heart twisted and turned and ached.

'I don't need you to fight my battles for me, Connor.' She needed him to stay away.

'*I*—' he stressed the word '—always do what I consider is right. You needn't think your coming back to town is going to change that.'

'Do what's right?' She snorted. 'Like jumping to conclusions? Do you still do that, Connor?'

The words shot out of her—a challenge—and she couldn't believe she'd uttered them. The air suddenly grew so thick with their history she wondered how on earth either one of them could breathe through it.

She'd always known things between them could never be normal. Not after the intensity of what they'd shared. It was why she'd stayed away. It was why she needed him to stay away from her now.

'Do what's right?' She snorted a second time. She'd keep up this front if it killed her. 'Like that sign?' She pointed to the shop awning. 'What is that…your idea of a sick joke?'

That frown returned to his eyes again. 'Look, Jaz, I—'

Richard chose that moment to come bustling up between them, his breathing loud and laboured. 'Sorry, Jaz. I saw you cruising up the street, but I couldn't get away immediately. I had a client with me.'

Connor clapped him on the back. 'You need to exercise more, my man, if a sprint up the street makes you breathe this hard.'

Richard grinned. 'It is uphill.'

His grin faded. He hitched his head in the direction of the bookshop. 'Sorry, Jaz. It's a bit of a farce, isn't it?'

'It's not what I was expecting,' she allowed.

Connor and Richard said nothing. She cleared her throat. 'Where are my staff?'

Richard glanced at Connor as if for help. Connor shoved his hands in his pockets and glowered at the pavement.

'Richard?'

'That's just the thing, you see, Jaz. The last of your staff resigned yesterday.'

Resigned? Her staff? So… 'I have no staff?' She

stared at Richard. For some reason she turned to stare at Connor too.

Both men nodded.

'But…' She would not lie down on the ground and admit defeat. She wouldn't. 'Why?'

'How about we go inside?' Connor suggested with a glance over his shoulder.

That was when Jaz became aware of the faces pressed against the inside of the plate glass of Mr Sears's 'baked-fresh-daily' country bakery, watching her avidly. In an act of pure bravado, she lifted her hand and sent the shop across the road a cheery wave. Then she turned and stalked through the door Richard had just unlocked.

Connor caught the door before it closed but he didn't step inside. 'I'll get back to work.'

On that sign? 'No, you won't,' she snapped out tartly. 'I want to talk to you.'

Richard stared at her as if…as if…

She reached up to smooth her hair. 'What?'

'Gee, Jaz. You used to dress mean but you always talked sweet.'

'Yeah, well…' She shrugged. 'I found out that I achieved a whole lot more if I did things the other way around.'

Nobody said anything for a moment. Richard rubbed the back of his neck. Connor stared morosely at some point in the middle distance.

'Okay, tell me what happened to my staff.'

'You could probably tell from the sales figures I sent you that the bookshop isn't doing particularly well.'

He could say that again.

'So, over the last few months, your mother let most of the staff go.'

'Most,' she pointed out, 'not all.'

'There was only Anita and Dianne left. Mr Sears poached Anita for the bakery…'

'Which left Dianne.' She swung back to Connor. 'Not the same Dianne who…?'

'The one and the same.'

Oh, that was just great. 'She made her feelings… clear,' she said to Richard.

Richard gave his watch an agonised glance.

'You don't have time for this at the moment, do you?' she said.

'I'm sorry, but I have appointments booked for the next couple of hours and—'

'Then go before you're late.' She shooed him to the door. 'I'll be fine.' She would be.

'I'll be back later,' he promised.

Then he left. Which left her and Connor alone in the dim space of the bookshop.

'So…' Connor said, breaking the silence that had wrapped around them. His voice wasn't so much a cooling autumn breeze as a winter chill. 'You're still not interested in selling the bookshop to Mr Sears?'

Sell? Not in this lifetime.

'I'm not selling the bookshop. At least not yet.'

Connor rested his hands on his hips and continued to survey her. She couldn't read his face or his body language, but she wished he didn't look so darn…male!

'So you're staying here in Clara Falls, then?'

'No.' She poured as much incredulity and disdain into her voice as she could. 'Not long-term. I have a life in the city. This is just a…'

'Just a…' he prompted when she faltered.

'A momentary glitch,' she snapped. 'I'll get the bookshop back on its feet and running at a profit— which I figure will take twelve months tops—and then I mean to return to my real life.'

'I see.'

Perhaps he did. But she doubted it.

CHAPTER TWO

CONNOR met the steeliness in Jaz's eyes and wished he could just turn around and walk away. His over-riding instinct was to reach out and offer her comfort. Despite that veneer of toughness she'd cultivated, he knew this return couldn't be easy for her.

Her mother had committed suicide only four weeks ago!

That had to be eating her up alive.

She didn't look as if she'd welcome his comfort. She kept eyeing him as if he were something slimy and wet that had just oozed from the drain.

The muscles in his neck, his jaw, bunched. What was her problem? She'd been the one to lay waste to all his plans, all his dreams, eight years ago. Not the other way around. She could at least have the grace to…

To what? an inner voice mocked. Spare you a smile? Get over yourself, Reed. You don't want her smiles.

But, as he gazed down into her face, noted the fragile luminosity of her skin, the long dark lashes framing her eyes and the sweet peach lipstick staining her lips, something primitive fired his blood. He wanted to haul her into his arms, slant his mouth over hers and taste her, brand himself on her senses.

Every cell in his body tightened and burned at the thought. The intensity of it took him off guard. Had his heart thudding against his ribcage. After eight years...

After eight years he hadn't expected to feel anything. He sure as hell hadn't expected this.

He rolled his shoulders and tried to banish the images from his mind. Every stupid mistake he'd made with his life had happened in the weeks after Jaz had left town. He couldn't blame her for the way he'd reacted to her betrayal—that would be childish—but he would never give her that kind of power over him again.

Never.

She stuck out her chin, hands on hips—combative, aggressive and so unlike the Jaz of old it took him off guard. 'Why did you change the sign? Who gave you permission?'

She moved behind the sales counter, stowed her handbag beneath it, then turned back and raised an eyebrow. 'Well?' She tapped her foot.

Her boot—a pretty little feminine number in brown suede and as unlike her old black Doc

Martens as anything could be—echoed smartly against the bare floorboards. Or maybe that was due to the silence that had descended around them again. He hooked his thumbs through the belt loops of his jeans and told himself to stay on task. It was just…that lipstick.

He'd once thought that nothing could look as good as the mulberry dark matt lipstick she'd once worn. He stared at the peach shine on her lips now. He'd been wrong.

'Connor!'

He snapped to and bit back something succinct and rude. *The sign, idiot!*

'I'm simply following the instructions you left with my receptionist.'

She stared at him for a long moment. Then, 'Can you seriously imagine that I'd want to call this place Jaz's Joint?' Her lip curled. 'That sounds like a den of iniquity, not a bookshop.'

She looked vivid fired up like that—alive. It suddenly occurred to him that he hadn't felt alive in a very long time.

He shifted his weight, allowed his gaze to travel over her again, noticed the way she turned away and bit her lip. *That* was familiar. She wasn't feeling anywhere near as sure of herself as she'd have him believe.

'I'm not paid to imagine.' At the time, though, her request had sent his eyebrows shooting up towards his hairline. 'Eight years is a long time. People change.'

'You better believe it!'

He ignored her vehemence. 'You told my receptionist you wanted "Jaz's Joint" painted on the awning. I was just following your instructions.' But as he said the words his stomach dipped. Her eyes had widened. He remembered how they could look blue or green, depending on the light. They glittered blue now in the hushed light of the bookshop.

'Those weren't my instructions.'

His stomach dropped a notch lower. Not her directions... Then...

'I just requested that the sign be freshened up.'

He swore. Once. Hard.

Jaz blinked. 'I beg your pardon?'

Her tone almost made him grin. As a teenager she'd done all she could to look hard as nails, but she'd rarely used bad language and she hadn't tolerated it in others.

He sobered. 'Obviously, somewhere along the line a wire's got crossed.' If his receptionist had played any part in the *Jaz's Joint* prank he'd fire her on the spot.

Jaz followed his gaze across the road to Mr Sears's bakery. 'Ahh...' Her lips twisted. 'I see.'

Did she? For reasons Connor couldn't fathom, Gordon Sears wanted the bookshop, and he wanted it bad.

She sprang out from behind the counter as if the life force coursing through her body would no longer allow her to coop it up in such a small space. She stalked down the aisles, with their rows upon rows of bookcases. Connor followed.

The Clara Falls bookshop had been designed with one purpose in mind—to charm. And it achieved its aim with remarkable ease. The gleaming oak bookcases contrasted neatly with wood-panelled walls painted a pale clean green. Alcoves and nooks invited browsers to explore. Gingerbread fretwork lent an air of fairy-tale enchantment. Jaz had always loved the bookshop, and Frieda hadn't changed a thing.

Therein lay most of its problems.

'I'll change the sign back. It'll be finished by the close of business today.'

She glanced back at him, a frown in her eyes. 'Why you?'

She turned around fully, folded her arms and leant against the nearest bookcase. To the right of her left hip a book in vivid blues and greens faced outwards—*Natural Wonders of the World*—it seemed apt. He dragged his gaze from her hips and the long, lean length of her legs. Way too apt.

But…

He'd never seen her wear such pretty, soft-looking trousers before. Mel would love those trousers. The thought flitted into his head unbidden and his heart clenched at the thought of his daughter.

He gritted his teeth and pushed the thought back out again. He would not think of Mel and Jaz in the same sentence.

But…

Eight years ago he'd grown used to seeing Jaz in long black skirts…or naked.

And then she'd removed herself from his world and he hadn't seen her at all.

'Is that what you're doing these days—sign-writing?'

Her words hauled him back and he steeled himself not to flinch at her incredulity. 'Among other things.' He shoved his hands in his pockets. 'After graduation I took up a carpentry apprenticeship.' He'd relinquished his dream of art school. 'I run a building contractor's business now here in Clara Falls.'

Her jaw dropped. 'What about your art?'

Just for a moment, bitterness seeped out from beneath the lid he normally kept tightly sealed around it. 'I gave it up.'

Her head snapped back. 'You what?'

The madness had started the night he'd discovered Jaz in Sam Hancock's arms. When he'd found out the next day that Jaz had left town—left him—for good, Connor had gone off the rails. He'd drunk too much…he'd slept with Faye. Faye, who'd revealed Jaz's infidelity, her lies. Faye, who'd done all she could to console him when Jaz had gone.

Faye whose heart he'd broken. When Faye had told him she was pregnant, he'd had no choice—he'd traded in his dream of art school to become a husband and father…and an apprentice carpenter.

He hadn't picked up a stick of charcoal since.

'Is that somehow supposed to be my fault?'

Jaz's snapped-out words hauled him back. 'Did I say that?'

He and Faye had lasted two years before they'd finally divorced—Jaz always a silent shadow between them. They'd been two of the longest years of his life.

It was childish to blame Jaz for any of that. He had Melanie. He could never regret his daughter.

Jaz's eyes turned so frosty they could freeze a man's soul. Connor's lips twisted. They couldn't touch him. His soul had frozen eight years ago.

And yet she was here. From all accounts a world-class tattoo artist, if Frieda's boasts could be believed.

Dianne was right. Clara Falls had no need for tattoo artists—world-class or otherwise.

And neither did he.

Silence descended around them. Finally, Jaz cleared her throat. 'I take it then that you're the builder Richard hired to do the work on this place?' She lifted a hand to indicate the interior of the shop, and then pointed to the ceiling to indicate the flat upstairs.

'That's right.'

She pushed away from the bookcase, glanced

around. 'Considering the amount of work Richard told me needed doing, the place looks exactly as I remember it.'

Her eyes narrowed. He watched her gaze travel over every fixture and furnishing within her line of sight. '*Exactly* the same.' She turned accusing eyes on him.

'That's because I've barely started work in here yet.'

Her jaw dropped. 'But…but your receptionist assured me all the work would be finished by Thursday last week.'

The muscles in his jaw bunched. 'You're sure about that?'

'Positive.'

He didn't blame her for her gritted teeth response. 'I'm sorry, Jaz, but you were given the wrong information.' And he'd be getting himself a new receptionist—this afternoon, if he could arrange it.

She pressed her lips so tightly together it made his jaw ache in sympathy. Then she stiffened. 'What about the OH and S stuff? Hell, if that hasn't been sorted, then—'

'That's the part I've taken care of.'

Several weeks ago, someone had filed an Occupation Health and Safety complaint. It had resulted in an OH and S officer coming out to inspect the premises…and to close the shop down when it had been discovered that two floor to ceiling bookcases, which should've been screwed fast to battens on the wall behind, had started to come away, threatening to topple and crush anyone who might happen to be below. Connor had put all his other jobs on hold to take care of that. The bookshop had only been closed for a day and a half.

'Why?'

'Why?' What the hell… 'Because it was dangerous, that's why.'

'Not that.' She waved an imperious hand in the air. 'Why is it your company that is doing the work?'

Because Richard had asked him to.

Because he'd wanted to prove that the past had no hold over him any more.

She folded her arms. 'I should imagine the last thing you wanted was to clap eyes on me again.'

She was right about that.

She stuck out a defiant hip. 'In fact, I'd guess that the last thing you want is me living in Clara Falls again.'

It took a moment for the import of her words to hit him. When they did, he clenched a fist so tight it started to shake. She glanced at his fist, then back into his face. She cocked an eyebrow. She didn't unsay her words.

'Are you insinuating that I'd use my position as a builder to sabotage your shop?' He tried to remember the last time he'd wanted to throttle someone.

'Would you? Have you? I mean… There's that

travesty of a sign, for a start. Now the delay. What would you think? You and Gordon Sears could be like that—' she waved two crossed fingers under his nose '—for all I know.'

'God, Jaz! I know it's been eight years, but can you seriously think I would stoop to that?'

She raked him from the top of his head to his boot laces with her hot gaze—blue on the way down, green when she met his eyes again on the way up—and it felt as if she actually placed her hands on his body and stroked him. His heart started to thump. She moistened her lips. It wasn't a nervous gesture, more…an assessing one. But it left a shine on her lips that had him clenching back a groan.

'Business is business,' he ground out. 'I don't have to like who I'm working for.'

Was it his imagination or did she pale at his words?

Her chin didn't drop. 'So you're saying this is just another job to you?'

He hesitated a moment too long.

Jaz snorted and pushed past him, charged back down to the sales counter and stood squarely behind it, as if she wanted to place herself out of his reach. 'Thank you for the work you've done so far, Connor, but your services are no longer required.'

He stalked down to the counter, reached across and gripped her chin in his fingers, forced her gaze to his. 'Fine! You want the truth? This isn't just another job. What happened to your mother… It made me sick to my stomach. We…someone in town…we should've paid more attention, we should've sensed that—'

He released her and swung away. She smelt like a wattle tree in full bloom—sweet and elusive. It was too much.

When he glanced back at her, her eyes had filled with tears. She touched her fingers to her jaw where he'd held her. Bile rose up through him. 'I'm sorry. I shouldn't have—' He gestured futilely with his hand. 'Did I hurt you?'

'No.'

She shook her head, her voice low, and he watched her push the tears down with the sheer force of her will…way down deep inside her like she used to do. Suddenly he felt older than his twenty-six years. He felt a hundred.

'I'm sorry I doubted your integrity.'

She issued her apology with characteristic sincerity and speed. He dragged a hand down his face. The Jaz of old might've been incapable of fidelity, but she'd been equally incapable of malice.

If she'd asked him to forgive her eight years ago, he would have. In an instant.

He shoved his hands in his pockets. 'Am I rehired?'

She straightened, moistened her lips and nodded. He didn't know how he could tell, but this time the gesture was nervous.

'You won't find it hard coping with my presence

around the place for the next fortnight?' Some devil prompted him to ask.

'Of course not!'

He could tell that she was lying.

'We're both adults, aren't we? What's in the past is in the past.'

He wanted to agree. He opened his mouth to do precisely that, but the words refused to come.

Jaz glanced at him, moistened her lips again. 'It's going to take a fortnight? So long?'

'Give or take a couple of days. And that's working as fast as I can.'

'I see.'

He shoved his hands deeper into his pockets. 'I'll get back to work on that sign then, shall I?'

The door clanged shut behind Connor with a finality that made Jaz want to burst into tears.

Crazy. Ridiculous.

Her knees shook so badly she thought she might fall. Very carefully, she lowered herself to the stool behind the counter. Being found slumped on the floor was not the look she was aiming for, not on her first day.

Not on any day.

She closed her eyes, dragged in a deep breath and tried to slow her pulse, quieten the blood pounding in her ears. She could do this. She *could* do this. She'd known her first meeting with Connor would be hard. She hadn't expected to deal with him on her first day though.

Hard? Ha! Try gruelling. Exhausting. Fraught.

She hadn't known she would still feel his pain as if it were her own. She hadn't known her body would remember…everything. Or that it would sing and thrum just because he was near.

She hadn't known she'd yearn for it all again—their love, the rightness of being with him.

Connor had shown her the magic of love, but he'd shown her the other side of love too—the blackness, the ugliness…the despair. It had turned her into another kind of person—an angry, destructive person. It had taken her a long time to conquer that darkness. She would never allow herself to become that person again. Never. And the only way she could guarantee that was by keeping Connor at arm's length. Further, if possible.

But it didn't stop her watching him through the shop window as he worked on her sign.

She opened the shop, she served customers, but that didn't stop her noticing how efficiently he worked either, the complete lack of fuss that accompanied his every movement. It reminded her of how he used to draw, of the times they'd take their charcoals and sketch pads to one of the lookouts.

She'd sit on a rock hunched over her pad, intent on capturing every single detail of the view spread out before her, concentrating fiercely on all she saw.

Connor would lean back against a tree, his sketch pad propped against one knee, charcoal lightly clasped, eyes half-closed, and his fingers would play across the page with seemingly no effort at all.

Their high school art teacher had given them identical marks, but Jaz had known from the very first that Connor had more talent in his little finger than she possessed in her whole body. She merely drew what was there, copied what was in front of her eyes. Connor's drawings had captured something deeper, something truer. They'd captured an essence, the hidden potential of the thing. Connor had drawn the optimistic future.

His hair glittered gold in the sun as he stepped down the ladder to retrieve something from his van.

And what was he doing now? Painting shop signs? His work should hang in galleries!

He turned and his gaze met hers. Just like that. With no fuss. No hesitation. She didn't step back into the shadows of the shop or drop her gaze and pretend she hadn't been watching. He would know. He pointed to the sign, then sent her a thumbs up.

All that potential wasted.

Jaz couldn't lift her arm in an answering wave. She couldn't even twitch the corners of her mouth upwards in acknowledgement of his silent communication. She had to turn away.

When she'd challenged him—thrown out there in the silences that throbbed between them that she must be the last person he'd ever want to see, he hadn't denied it.

Her stomach burned acid. Coming back to Clara Falls, she'd expected to experience loss and grief. But for her mother. Not Connor. She'd spent the last eight years doing all she could to get over him. These feelings should not be resurfacing now.

If you'd got over him you'd have come home like your mother begged you to.

The accusation rang through her mind. Her hands shook. She hugged herself tightly. She'd refused to come home, still too full of pride and anger and bitterness. It had distorted everything. It had closed her mind to her mother's despair.

If she'd come home...but she hadn't.

For the second time that day, she ground back the tears. She didn't deserve the relief they would bring. She would make a success of the bookshop. She would make this final dream of her mother's a reality. She would leave a lasting memorial of Frieda Harper in Clara Falls. Once she'd done that, perhaps she might find a little peace... Perhaps she'd have earned it.

She glanced back out of the window. Connor hadn't left yet. He stood in a shaft of sunlight, haloed in gold, leaning against his van, talking to Richard. For one glorious moment the years fell away. How many times had she seen Connor and Richard talking like that—at school, on the cricket

field, while they'd waited for her outside this very
bookshop? Things should've been different. Things
should've been very different.

He'd given up his art. It was too high a price to
pay. Grief for the boy he'd once been welled up
inside her.

It would take her a long, long time to find peace.

She hadn't cheated on him with Sam Hancock.
She hadn't cheated on him with anyone, but Connor
no longer deserved her bitterness. He had a little
daughter now, responsibilities. He'd paid for his
mistakes, just like she'd paid for hers. If what her
mother had told her was true, Faye had left Connor
literally holding the baby six years ago. Jaz would
not make his life more difficult.

Something inside her lifted. It eased the tightness
in her chest and allowed her to breathe more freely
for a moment.

Connor turned and his eyes met hers through the
plate glass of the shop window. The weight crashed
back down on her with renewed force. She gripped
the edges of the stool to keep herself upright.
Connor might not deserve her bitterness, but she still
had to find a way of making him keep his distance,
because something in him still sang to something in
her—a siren song that had the power to destroy her
all over again if she let it.

Richard turned then too, saw her and waved. She
lifted a numb arm in response. He said something

to Connor and both men frowned. As one, they pushed away from Connor's van and headed for the bookshop door.

A shiver rippled through her. She shot to her feet. She had to deal with more Connor on her first day? Heaven, give her strength.

The moment he walked through the door all strength seeped from her limbs, leaving them boneless, useless, and plonking her back down on the stool.

'Hello, again,' Richard said.

'Hi.' From somewhere she found a smile.

She glanced sideways at Connor. He pursed his lips and frowned at the ornate pressed-tin work on the ceiling. She found her gaze drawn upwards, searching for signs of damp and peeling paint, searching for what made him frown. She didn't find anything. It all looked fine to her.

Richard cleared his throat and she turned her attention back to him with an apologetic shrug.

'These are the keys for the shop.' He placed a set of keys onto the counter in front of her. 'And this is the key to the flat upstairs.' He held it up for her to see, but he didn't place it on the counter with the other keys.

Connor reached over and plucked the key from Richard's fingers. 'What did my receptionist tell you about the upstairs flat?'

Her stomach started to churn. 'That you'd given

it a final coat of paint last week and that it was ready to move into.'

Connor and Richard exchanged glances.

'Um…but then you're a builder, not a painter, right?'

He'd painted the sign for the shop, so maybe…

She shook her head. 'Painting the flat isn't your department, is it?'

'No, but I can organise that for you, if you want.'

'You didn't think to check with me?' Richard asked.

The thought hadn't occurred to her. Though, in hindsight… 'She said she was contacting me on your behalf. I didn't think to question that. When she asked me if there was anything else I needed done, I mentioned the sign.' She'd wanted it bright and sparkling. She wanted her mother's name loud and proud above the shop.

'I'm sorry, Jaz,' Connor started heavily, 'but—'

'But I've been given the wrong information,' she finished for him. Again. From the expression on his face, though, she wouldn't want to be his receptionist when he finally made it back to the office. Shame pierced her. She should've known better than to lump Connor with the meaner elements in the town.

She swallowed. 'That's okay, I can take care of the painting myself.' She wanted to drop her head onto her folded arms and rest for a moment. 'What kind of state is the flat in?'

'We only started tearing out the kitchen cupboards and the rotting floorboards yesterday. It's a mess.'

Once upon a time he'd have couched that more tactfully, but she appreciated his candour now. 'Habitable?'

He grimaced.

'Okay then…' She thought hard for a moment. 'All my stuff is arriving tomorrow.'

'What stuff?' Connor asked.

'Everything. Necessary white goods, for a start—refrigerator, washing machine, microwave. Then there's the furniture—dining table, bed, bookcase. Not to mention the—'

'You brought a bookcase?' Connor glanced around the shop. 'When you have all these?'

For a brief moment his eyes sparkled. Her breathing went all silly. 'I'll need a bookcase in the flat too.'

'Why?'

The teasing glint in his eyes chased her weariness away. 'For the books that happen to be arriving tomorrow too.'

Connor and Richard groaned in unison. 'Has your book addiction lessened as the years have gone by?' Richard demanded.

They used to tease her about this eight years ago. It made her feel younger for a moment, freer. 'Oh, no.' She rubbed her hands together with relish. 'If anything, it's grown.'

The two men groaned again and she laughed. She'd actually laughed on her first day back in Clara Falls? Perhaps miracles could happen.

She glanced at Connor and pulled herself up. Not *those* kinds of miracles.

'Relax, guys. I've rented out my apartment in Sydney. Some of my stuff is to come here, but a lot has gone into storage, including most of my books. Is there room up there to store my things?' She pointed at the ceiling. 'Could you and your men work around it?'

'We'll work quicker if it's stored elsewhere.'

It took her all of two seconds to make the decision. 'Where's the nearest storage facility around here? Katoomba?' She'd organise for her things to go there until the flat was ready.

Connor planted his feet. 'We'll store it at my place.'

She blinked. 'I beg your pardon?'

He stuck his jaw out and folded his arms. 'It's my fault you thought the flat was ready. So it's my responsibility to take care of storing your things.'

'Garbage!' She folded her arms too. 'You had no idea what I was told.' He was as much a victim in this as her. 'I should've had the smarts to double-check it all with Richard anyway.'

'You shouldn't have had to double-check anything and—'

'Guys, guys.' Richard made a time out sign.

Jaz and Connor broke off to glare at each other.

'He does have the room, Jaz. He has a huge workshop with a four car garage for a start.'

She transferred her glare to Richard.

Connor shifted his weight to the balls of his feet. 'This is the last thing you should've had to come back to. You shouldn't be out of pocket because of someone's idea of a…prank.'

It was more than that. They all knew it.

'I'd like to make amends,' he said softly.

She found it hard to hold his gaze and she didn't know why. 'Okay.' She said the word slowly. 'I'll accept your very kind offer—' and it was a kind offer '—on one condition.'

Wariness crept into his eyes. Tiredness invaded every atom of her being. Once upon a time he'd looked at her with absolute trust.

And then he hadn't.

'What's the condition?'

'That you go easy on your receptionist.'

'What?' He leant across the counter as if he hadn't heard her right.

She held his gaze then and she didn't find it hard—not in the slightest. 'She sounded young.'

'She's nineteen. Old enough to know better.'

'Give her a chance to explain.'

He reared back from her then and the tan leached from his face, leaving him pale. Her words had shaken him, she could see that, but she hadn't meant for them to hurt him. From somewhere she dredged up a smile. 'We all make mistakes when we're young. I did. You did.'

'I did,' Richard piped in too.

'Find out why she did it before you storm in and fire her. That's all I'm asking. My arrival has already generated enough hostility as it is.'

Inch by inch, the colour returned to Connor's face. 'If I don't like her explanation, she's still history.'

'But you'll give her an opportunity to explain herself first?'

He glared at her. 'Yes.'

'Thank you.' She couldn't ask for any fairer than that.

They continued to stare at each other. Connor opened his mouth, a strange light in his eyes that she couldn't decipher, and every molecule of her being strained towards him. No words emerged from the firm, lean lips, but for a fraction of a second time stood still.

Richard broke the spell. 'Where were you planning on staying till your stuff arrives, Jaz?'

She dragged her gaze from Connor, tried to still the sudden pounding of her heart. 'I've booked a couple of nights at the Cascade's Rest.'

Richard let the air whistle out between his teeth. 'Nice! Treating yourself?'

'I have a thing for deep spa-baths.' She had a bigger thing for the anonymity that five-star luxury could bring. She couldn't justify staying there for more than a couple of nights, though. 'How long before the flat will be ready?'

'A week to ten days,' Connor said flatly.

She turned back to Richard. 'Is there a bed and breakfast you'd recommend?'

'Gwen Harwood's on Candlebark Street,' he said without hesitation.

Unbidden, a smile broke out from her. 'Gwen?' They'd been friends at school. The five of them—Connor, Richard, Gwen, Faye and herself. They'd all hung out together.

'Look, Jaz.' Connor raked a hand back through the sandy thickness of his hair. 'I can't help feeling responsible for this, and…'

And what? Did he mean to offer her a room too? Not in this lifetime!

She strove for casual. 'And you have plenty of room, right?' Given all that had passed between them, given all that he thought of her, would he really offer her a room, a bed, a place to stay? The idea disturbed her and anger started to burn low down in the pit of her stomach. If only he hadn't jumped to conclusions eight years ago. If only he'd given her a chance to explain. If only he'd been this nice then!

It's eight years. Let it go.

She wanted to let it go. With all her heart she wished she could stop feeling like this, but the anger, the pain, had curved their claws into her so fiercely she didn't know how to tear them free without doing more damage.

She needed him to stay away. 'I don't think so!'

The pulse at the base of Connor's jaw worked. 'I wasn't going to offer you a room,' he ground out. 'You'll be happier at Gwen's, believe me. But I will deduct the cost of your accommodation from my final bill.'

Heat invaded her face, her cheeks. She wished she could climb under the counter and stay there. Of course he hadn't meant to offer her a place to stay. Why would he offer her of all people—*her*—a place to stay? Idiot!

'You'll do no such thing!' Pride made her voice tart. 'I had every intention of arriving in Clara Falls today and staying, whether the flat was ready or not.' She'd just have given different instructions to the removal company and found a different place to stay.

No staff. Now no flat. Plummeting profits. What a mess! Where on earth was she supposed to start?

'Jaz?'

She suddenly realised the two men were staring at her in concern. She planted her mask of indifference, of detachment, back to her face in double-quick time. Before either one of them could say anything, she rounded on Connor. 'I want your word of honour that you will bill me as usual, without a discount for my accommodation. Without a discount for anything.'

'But—'

'If you don't I will hire someone else to do the work. Which, obviously, with the delays that would involve, will cost me even more.'

He glared at her. 'Were you this stubborn eight years ago?'

No, she'd been as malleable as a marshmallow.

'Do we have an understanding?'

'Yes,' he ground out, his glare not abating in the slightest.

'Excellent.' She pasted on a smile and made a show of studying her watch. 'Goodness, is that the time? If you'll excuse me, gentlemen, it's time to close the shop. There's a spa-bath with my name on it waiting for me at the Cascade's Rest.'

As she led them to the door, she refused to glance into Connor's autumn-tinted eyes for even a microsecond.

When Jaz finally made it to the shelter of her room at the Cascade's Rest, she didn't head for the bathroom with its Italian marble, fragrant bath oils and jet-powered spa-bath. She didn't turn on a single light. She shed her clothes, leaving them where they fell, to slide between the cold cotton sheets of the queen-sized bed. She started to shake. 'Mum,' she whispered, 'I miss you.' She rolled to her side, pulled her knees to her chest and wrapped her arms around them. 'Mum, I need you.'

She prayed for the relief of tears, but she'd forced them back too well earlier in the day and they refused to come now. All she could do was press her face to the pillow and count the minutes as the clock ticked the night away.

CHAPTER THREE

JAZ let herself into the bookshop at eight-thirty sharp on Monday morning. She could hear Connor… She cocked her head to one side. She could hear Connor *and* his men hammering away upstairs already.

She locked the front door and headed out the back to the kitchenette. After a moment's hesitation, she cranked open the back door to peer outside. Connor's van—in fact, two vans—had reversed into the residential parking spaces behind the shop, their rear doors propped wide open. Someone clattered down the wooden stairs above and Jaz ducked back inside.

Through the window above the sink, she stared at the sign-writing on the side of the nearest van as she filled the jug—'Clara Falls Carpentry'. A cheery cartoon character wearing a tool belt grinned and waved.

A carpenter. Connor?

Had he painted those signs on the vans?

He was obviously very successful, but did it make up for turning his back on his art, his talent for drawing and painting?

There's nothing wrong with being a carpenter.

Of course not.

And Connor had always been good with his hands. A blush stole through her when she remembered exactly how good.

She jumped when she realised that water overflowed from the now full jug. She turned off the tap and set about making coffee.

Upstairs the banging continued.

Ignore it. Get on with your work.

She had to familiarise herself with the day-to-day running of the bookshop. Managing a small business wasn't new to her—she and her good friend Mac ran their own very exclusive tattoo parlour in Sydney. But she'd been relying on the fact that she'd have staff who could run her through the bookshop's suppliers, explain the accounting and banking procedures… who knew the day-to-day routine of the bookshop.

A mini-office—computer, printer and filing cabinet—had been set up in one corner of the stockroom. The computer looked positively ancient. Biting back a sigh, she switched it on and held her breath. She let it out in a whoosh when the computer booted up. So far, so good.

A glance at her watch told her she had fifteen minutes until she had to open the shop. She slid into the chair, clicked through the files listed on the computer's hard drive and discovered…

Nothing.

Nothing on this old computer seemed to make any sense whatsoever.

She dragged her hands back through her hair and stared at the screen. Maybe all that insomnia was catching up with her. Maybe something here made sense and she just couldn't see it.

Maybe returning to Clara Falls was a seriously bad idea.

'No!' She leapt out of her chair, smoothed down her hair and gulped down her coffee. She'd open the shop, she'd ring the local employment agency…and she'd sort the computer out later.

Without giving herself time for any further negative thoughts, she charged through the shop, unlocked the front door and turned the sign to 'Open'. She flicked through the *Yellow Pages*, found the page she needed, dialled the number and explained to the very efficient-sounding woman at the other end of the line what she needed.

'I'm afraid we don't have too many people on our books at the moment,' the woman explained.

Jaz stared at the receiver in disbelief. 'You have to have more than me,' she said with blunt honesty.

'Yes, well, I'll see what I can do.' The woman

took Jaz's details. 'Hopefully we'll have found you something by the end of the week.'

End of the week!

'Uh…thank you,' Jaz managed.

The woman hung up. Jaz kept staring at the receiver. She needed staff now. Today. Not perhaps maybe in a week.

'What's up?'

The words, barked into the silence, made her start. Connor!

She slammed the phone back to its cradle, smoothed down her hair. 'Sorry, I didn't hear the bell above the door.'

The lines of his face were grim, his mouth hard and unsmiling. She fancied she could see him wishing himself away from here. Away from her.

Which was fine. Excellent, actually.

'I asked, what's up?'

No way. She wasn't confiding in him. Not in this lifetime. He wasn't her knight. He wasn't even her friend. He was her builder. End of story.

Derisive laughter sounded through her head. She ignored it.

He was hot.

She tried to can that thought as soon as she could.

'Nothing's up.'

He wouldn't challenge her. She could tell he wanted out of here asap. Only a friend would challenge her—someone who cared.

'Liar.' He said the word softly. The specks of gold in his eyes sparkled.

She blinked. She swallowed. 'Is this a social call or is there something I can help you with?' The words shot out of her, sounding harder than she'd meant them to.

The golden highlights were abruptly cut off. 'I just wanted to let you know that your things arrived safely yesterday.'

'I…um… Thank you.' She moistened her lips, something she found herself doing a lot whenever Connor was around. She couldn't help it. She only had to look at him for her mouth to go dry. He started to turn away.

'Connor?'

He turned back, reluctance etched in the line of his shoulders, his neck, his back. Her heart slipped below the level of her belly button. Did he loathe her so much?

She moistened her lips again. His gaze narrowed in on the action and she kicked herself. If he thought she was being deliberately provocative he'd loathe her all the more.

She told herself she didn't care what he thought.

'I'm going to need some of my things. I only brought enough to tide me over for the weekend.' She shrugged, apologetic.

Why on earth should *she* feel apologetic?

His gaze travelled over her. She wore yesterday's

trousers and Saturday's blouse. She'd shaken them out and smoothed them the best she could, but it really hadn't helped freshen them up any.

Pride forced her chin up. 'There's just one suitcase I need.' It contained enough of the essentials to get her through. 'I'd be grateful if I could come around this evening and collect it.'

'What's it look like?'

'It's a sturdy red leather number. Big.'

'The one with stickers from all around the world plastered over it?'

'That's the one.' She had no idea how she managed to keep her voice so determinedly cheerful. She waited for him to ask about her travels. They'd meant to travel together after art school—to marry and to travel. They'd planned to paint the world.

He didn't ask. She reminded herself that he'd given all that up. Just like he'd given up on her.

Travel? With his responsibilities?

He'd made his choices.

It didn't stop her heart from aching for him.

She gripped her hands behind her so she wouldn't have to acknowledge their shaking. 'When would it be convenient for me to call around and collect it?'

His eyes gave nothing away. 'Have you booked into Gwen's B&B?'

She nodded.

'Then I'll have it sent around.'

She read the subtext. He didn't need to say the words out loud. It would never be convenient for her to call around. She swallowed. 'Thank you.'

With a nod, he turned and stalked to the door. He reached out, seized the door handle…

'Connor, one final thing…'

He swung back, impatience etched in every line of his body. A different person might've found it funny. 'You and your men are welcome to use the bookshop's kitchenette and bathroom.' She gestured to the back of the shop. The facilities upstairs sounded basic at best at the moment—as in non-existent. 'I'll leave the back door unlocked.'

He strode back and jammed a finger down on the counter between them. 'You'll do no such thing!'

'I beg your pardon?'

'People don't leave their back doors unlocked in Clara Falls any more, Jaz.'

They didn't? She stared back at him and wondered why that felt such a loss.

'And you, I think, have enough trouble without inviting more. Especially of that kind.'

She wanted to tell him she wasn't having any trouble at all, only her mouth refused to form the lie.

'Fine, take the key, then.' She pulled the keys from her pocket and rifled though them. She hadn't worked out what most of them were for yet.

'Here, this one looks a likely candidate.' She held one aloft, sidled out from behind the counter and strode all the way through the shop to the back door again. She fitted the key in the lock. It turned. She wound it off the key ring and shoved it into Connor's hand. 'There.'

'I—'

'Don't let your dislike of me disadvantage your men. They're working hard.'

She refused to meet his gaze, hated the way the golden lights in his eyes were shuttered against her.

'I wasn't going to refuse your offer, Jaz.'

That voice—measured and rhythmic, like a breeze moving through a stand of radiata pine.

'We'll all welcome the chance of a hot drink and the use of that microwave, believe me.'

Amazingly, he smiled. It was a small one admittedly, wiped off his face almost as soon as it appeared, but Jaz's pulse did a little victory dance all the same.

'Do you have a spare? You might need it.'

He held the key between fingers callused by hard work, but Jaz would've recognised those hands anywhere. Once upon a time she'd watched them for hours, had studied them, fascinated by the ease with which they'd moved over his sketch pad. Fascinated by the ease with which they'd moved across her body, evoking a response she'd been powerless to hide.

A response she'd never considered hiding from him.

She gulped. A spare key—he was asking her about a spare key. She rifled through the keys on the key ring. Twice, because she didn't really see them the first time.

'No spare,' she finally said.

'I'll have one cut. I'll get the original back to you by the close of business today.'

'Thank you. Now, I'd better get back to the shop.' But before she left some imp made her add, 'And don't forget to lock the door on your way out. I wouldn't want to invite any trouble, you know.'

She almost swore he chuckled as she left the room.

At ten-thirty a.m., a busload of tourists descended on the bookshop demanding guidebooks and maps, and depleting her supply of panoramic postcards.

At midday, Jaz raced out to the stockroom to scour the shelves for reserves that would replenish the alarming gaps that were starting to open up in her *Local Information* section. She came away empty-handed.

She walked back to stare at the computer, then shook her head. Later. She'd tackle it later.

At three-thirty a blonde scrap of a thing sidled through the door, barely jangling the bell. She glanced at Jaz with autumn-tinted eyes and Jaz's heart practically fell out of her chest.

Was this Connor's daughter?

It had to be. She had his eyes; she had his hair.

She had Faye's heart-shaped face and delicate porcelain skin.

Melanie—such a pretty name. Such a pretty little girl.

An ache grew so big and round in Jaz's chest that it didn't leave room for anything else.

'Hello,' she managed when the little girl continued to stare at her. It wasn't the cheery greeting she'd practised all day, more a hoarse whisper. She was glad Connor wasn't here to hear it.

'Hello,' the little girl returned, edging away towards the children's section.

Jaz let her go, too stunned to ask her if she needed help with anything. Too stunned to ask her if she was looking for her father. Too stunned for anything.

She'd known Connor had a daughter. She'd known she would eventually meet that daughter.

Her hands clenched. She'd known diddly-squat!

Physically, Melanie Reed might be all Connor and Faye, but the slope of her shoulders, the way she hung her head, reminded Jaz of…

Oh, dear Lord. Melanie Reed reminded Jaz of herself at the same age—friendless, rootless. As a young girl, she'd crept into the bookshop in the exact same fashion Melanie just had.

Her head hurt. Her neck hurt. Pain pounded at her temples. She waited for someone to come in behind Melanie—Connor, his mother perhaps.

Nothing.

She bit her lip. She stared at the door, then glanced towards the children's section. Surely a seven-year-old shouldn't be left unsupervised?

If she craned her neck she could just make out Melanie's blonde curls, could see the way that fair head bent over a book. Something in the child's posture told Jaz she wasn't reading at all, only pretending to.

She glanced at the ceiling. Had Connor asked Melanie to wait for him in here?

She discounted that notion almost immediately. No way.

She glanced back at Melanie. She remembered how she'd felt as a ten-year-old, newly arrived in Clara Falls. She took in the defeated lines of those shoulders and found herself marching towards the children's section. She pretended to tidy the nearby shelves.

'Hello again,' she started brightly. 'I believe I know who you are—Melanie Reed. Am I right?'

The little face screwed up in suspicion and Jaz wondered if she'd overdone the brightness. Lots of her friends in Sydney had children, but they were all small—babies and toddlers.

Seven was small too, she reminded herself.

'I'm not supposed to talk to strangers.'

Excellent advice, but… 'I'm not really a stranger, you know. I used to live here a long time ago and I knew both your mum and your dad.'

That captured Melanie's interest. 'Were you friends?'

The ache inside her grew. 'Yes.' She made herself smile. 'We were friends.' They'd all been the best of friends once upon a time.

'I can't remember my mum, but I have a picture of her.'

Jaz gulped. According to Frieda, Melanie had only been two years old when Faye had left. 'I... uh...well... It was a long time ago when I knew them. Back before you were born. My name is Jazmin Harper, but everyone calls me Jaz. You can call me Jaz too, if you like.'

'Do you own the bookshop now?'

'I do.'

Melanie gave a tentative smile. 'Everyone calls me Melanie or Mel.' The smile faded. 'I wish they'd call me Melly. I think that sounds nicer, don't you?'

Jaz found herself in total agreement. 'I think Melly is the prettiest name in the world.'

Melanie giggled and Jaz sat herself down on one of the leatherette cubes dotted throughout the bookshop for the relief of foot-weary browsers. 'Now, Melly, I believe your dad is going to be at least another half an hour.'

Melanie immediately shot to her feet, glanced around with wild eyes. 'I'm not supposed to be here. You can't tell him!'

Yikes. 'Why not?'

'Because I'm supposed to go to Mrs Benedict's after school but I hate it there.'

Double yikes. 'Why?'

'Because her breath smells funny…and sometimes she smacks me.'

She smacked her! Jaz's blood instantly went on the boil. 'Have you told your daddy about this?'

Melly shook her head.

'But Melly, why not?'

Melly shook her head again, her bottom lip wobbled. 'Are you going to tell on me?'

Jaz knew she couldn't let this situation go on, but… 'How about I make a deal with you?'

The child's face twisted up in suspicion again. 'What?'

'If you promise to come here after school each afternoon this week, then I won't say anything to anyone.' At least Melly would be safe here.

Melanie's shoulders relaxed. 'Okay.' She shot another small smile at Jaz. 'It's what I always do anyway.'

'There, that's settled then.' Jaz smiled back at her. She figured it would only take her a day or two, till Thursday at the latest, to convince Melanie to confide in Connor.

And she wouldn't like to be in Mrs Benedict's shoes once he found out she'd been smacking his little girl.

'Who picks you up from Mrs Benedict's? Daddy?'

'Yes, at five o'clock on the dot at Mrs Benedict's front gate,' Melly recited.

Jaz glanced at her watch. 'That's nearly an hour away. You know what, Melly? In celebration of making my very first new friend in Clara Falls, I'm going to close the shop early today and walk with you to Mrs Benedict's.'

Melly's eyes grew round. 'I'm your friend?'

'You bet.'

Then Melly beamed at her, really smiled, and the ache pressed so hard against the walls of Jaz's chest that she thought it'd split her open then and there.

Jaz found Connor leaning against the shop front when she arrived at eight-fifteen on Tuesday morning. He held out the key she'd given him yesterday. 'I had a spare one cut. Sorry I didn't get it back to you yesterday.'

She reached out, closed her fingers around it. It still held warmth from his hand. 'Thank you.'

He looked exactly as the radio weatherman had described the weather that morning—cold and clear with a chill in the air, blue skies hinting at the warmth to come later in the day. She didn't know about the warmth to come.

'You closed the shop early yesterday.'

No judgement, just an observation. He looked tired. Something inside her softened to the consistency of water or air…marshmallow.

Not marshmallow! She didn't do marshmallow any more.

But that weariness…it caught at her.

He and Faye had only lasted two years.

Had Connor married Faye on the rebound?

The thought had never occurred to her before. But that marriage… It had happened so fast…

Her knees locked. No! She would not get involved in this man's life again. She would not give him the power to destroy her a second time.

But that weariness…

She hadn't noticed it yesterday or on Saturday. All she'd noticed then was his goldenness. The goldenness might've dimmed, but that didn't make him any less appealing. With his hair damp from a recent shower, the scent of his shampoo enhanced rather than masked the scent of autumn that clung to him.

She tried to pinpoint the individual elements that brought that scent to life, hoping to rob it of its power. A hint of eucalyptus, recently tilled earth… and fresh-cut pumpkin. Those things together shouldn't be alluring. It didn't stop Jaz from wanting to press her face against his neck and gulp in great, greedy breaths.

Good Lord. Stop it!

'I closed fifteen minutes early. I had things to do.'

She wondered if she should tell him about Melanie.

She recalled the way Melly's face had lit up when Jaz had declared them friends and knew she couldn't.

Not yet. If Melly hadn't confided in Connor by the end of the week, though, she would have to.

'Have you found new staff yet?' Connor all but growled the words.

Jaz unlocked the door, proud that her hand didn't shake, not even a little. 'I'm working on it.'

'Will someone be in to help today?'

'Perhaps.'

He followed her into the bookshop. 'Perhaps! Do you think that's good enough?'

'I don't think it's any of your concern.'

He followed her all the way through to the kitchenette.

'Coffee?'

Idiot. Mentally she kicked herself. Coffee was way too chummy.

Relief didn't flood her, though, when he shook his head. Work boots thumped overhead and an electric saw rent the air. 'Sorry. I hope we're not disturbing you too much.'

'Not at all.' That didn't bother her in the slightest. Seeing Connor every day…now that was tougher.

Don't go there.

'What time do you start work?' she asked, because it suddenly seemed wise to say something, and fast.

'Seven-thirty.'

She swung around from making coffee. 'Yet you didn't knock off yesterday till just before five?'

One corner of his mouth kinked up as if he'd read

the word *slave-driver* in big letters across her forehead. 'My apprentices knocked off at three-thirty.'

But he'd hung around at least an hour longer?

'Look, Connor, you don't need to bust a gut getting the work done in double-quick time, you know. If it takes an extra week or two...' She trailed off with a shrug, hoping she looked as nonchalant as she sounded. He really should be at home spending time with Melly.

His jaw tightened. 'I said it would be completed asap and I meant it. I at least have employees to help me.'

He planted his legs, hands on hips, and Jaz's saliva glands suddenly remembered how to work. Heavens, Connor Reed was still seriously drool-worthy.

'What do you mean to do about it?' he demanded.

She stepped back. Stared. Then she shook herself. He meant her staffing problem.

Of course that was what he meant.

'Get straight to work. That's what I mean to do. I have oodles to get through today.' She wanted to spend between now and nine o'clock trying to coax the secrets out of that ancient computer, particularly the ones that would point her in the direction of her suppliers.

After she'd walked Melly to Mrs Benedict's front gate this afternoon, she'd return and see what else she could coax from it.

Just for a moment, gold sparked from the brown depths of Connor's eyes. 'Have you settled in at Gwen's? Are you comfortable there?'

'Very comfortable, thank you.'

Not true. Oh, her room and en-suite bathroom, the feather bed, were all remarkably comfortable. Gwen's reception, though, hadn't been all Jaz had hoped for.

She made herself smile, saluted Connor with her mug of coffee. 'Now, if you'll excuse me, I have work to do.' Then she fled to the stockroom before those autumn-tinted eyes saw the lies in her own.

The computer did not divulge her suppliers' identities. It didn't divulge much of anything at all. Who on earth was she supposed to phone, fax or email to order in new books? She started clicking indiscriminately on word documents but none of them seemed to hold a clue. Before she had a chance to start rifling through the filing cabinet, it was time to open the shop.

Business wasn't as brisk as it had been the previous day, but she still had a steady stream of customers—all tourists. As she'd had to do the previous day, whenever she went to the bathroom she hung a 'Back in five minutes' sign on the door.

She breathed a sigh when it was time to close the shop and walk Melly the five blocks to Mrs Benedict's front gate.

'Melly, why don't you want to tell your dad that you're unhappy at Mrs Benedict's?'

Melly stopped skipping to survey Jaz soberly. 'Because Daddy has lots of worries and Mrs Benedict is his last hope.' She leaned in close to confide, 'I know because I heard him say so to Grandma. There's no one else who can look after me and I'm too little to stay at home alone.'

'I think your happiness is more important than anything else in the world to your Daddy.' She waited and watched while Melly digested that piece of information. 'Besides,' she added cheerfully, 'there's always me. You're more than welcome to hang out at the bookshop.'

Melly didn't smile. 'Grandad's picking me up today. I stay with him and Grandma on Tuesday nights.'

'That'll be nice.'

Melly didn't say anything for a moment, then, 'Grandma thinks little girls should wear dresses and skirts and not jeans. I don't have any jeans that fit me any more. Yvonne Walker thinks skirts are prissy.'

'Yvonne is in your class at school?' Jaz hazarded.

'She's the prettiest girl in the whole school! And she has the best parties.' Melly's mouth turned down. 'She didn't invite me to her last party.'

Jaz's heart throbbed in sympathy.

'But if she could see my hair like this!'

Melly touched a hand to her hair. Jaz had pulled it up into a ponytail bun. It made Melly look sweet and winsome. 'I'll do it like that for you any time you like,' she promised.

Melly's eyes grew wide.

'And you know what else? I think if you asked your daddy to take you shopping for jeans, he would.'

Jaz waited on the next corner, out of sight, until Melly's grandfather had collected her, then walked back to the shop and installed herself in front of the computer.

She turned it on and stroked the top of the monitor, murmured 'Pretty please,' under her breath.

Above her a set of work boots sounded against bare floorboards, the scrape and squeal of some tool against wood. She glanced up at the ceiling. Why wasn't Connor at home with Melly? Why was he here, working on her flat, when he could be at home with his daughter?

She glanced back at the computer screen and shot forward in her seat when she realised the text on the screen was starting to break up. 'No, no,' she pleaded, placing a hand on either side of the monitor, as if that could help steady it.

Bang! She jumped as a sound like a cap gun rent the air. Smoke belched out of the computer. The screen went black.

'No!'

No staff and now no computer?

She shook the monitor, slapped a fist down hard on top.

Nothing.

She sagged in her chair. This couldn't be happening. Not now. *Not now.*

Don't panic.

She leapt to her feet and started to pace. *I won't let you down, Mum.*

The filing cabinet!

With a cry, she dropped to her knees and tried to open the top drawer. Locked. She fumbled in her pockets for the keys. Tried one—didn't fit. Tried a second—wouldn't turn. Tried a third…

The drawer shot open so fast it almost knocked her flat on her back. She rifled through the files avidly. She stopped. She rifled through them again…slowly…and her exultation died. Oh, there were files all right, lots of files. But they were all empty.

She yanked open the second drawer. More files, very neatly arranged, but they didn't contain a damn thing, not even scrap paper. Jaz pulled out each and every one of them anyway, just to check, throwing them with growing ferocity to the floor.

Finally, there were no more to throw. She sat back and stared at the rack and ruin that surrounded her. Maybe Richard had taken the files for safekeeping?

She smoothed down her hair, pulled in a breath and tried to beat back her tiredness.

No, Richard wouldn't have the files. He'd have given them back to her by now if he had.

Maybe her mother hadn't kept any files?

That hardly seemed likely. Frieda Harper had kept meticulous records even for the weekend stall she'd kept at the markets when Jaz was a teenager.

Jaz rested her head on her arm. Which meant Dianne or Anita—or both of them together—had sabotaged the existing files.

'What the bloody hell is going on in here?'

Jaz jumped so high she swore her head almost hit the ceiling. She swung around to find Connor's lean, rangy bulk blocking the doorway to the kitchenette. Her heart rate didn't slow. In fact, her pulse gave a funny little jump.

'Don't sneak up on a person like that!' Hollering helped ease the pulse-jumping. 'You nearly gave me a heart attack!'

'Sorry.' He shoved his hands in his pockets. 'I thought I was making plenty of noise.' His gaze narrowed as it travelled around the room, took in the untidy stack of files on the floor. 'What are you doing?'

'Having a clean out.' She thrust her chin up, practically daring him to contradict her.

For a moment she thought the lines around his mouth softened, but then she realised the light was dim in here and she was tired. She was probably only seeing what she wanted to see.

His nose wrinkled. 'What's that smell?'

'I was burning some incense in here earlier,' she lied.

He stared at her. She resisted the urge to moisten her

lips. 'I have a question about a wall,' she said abruptly, gesturing for him to follow her through to the bookshop and away from eau de burning computer.

She was lying through her teeth.

Man, he had to give her ten out of ten for grit.

Keeping one eye on her retreating back, Connor bent to retrieve a file. Empty. Like its counterparts, he guessed, air whistling between his teeth as he flung the file back on the top of the pile.

He glanced at the computer. He knew the smell of a burning motherboard. He'd told Frieda months ago she needed to upgrade that computer. He dragged a hand through his hair, then followed Jaz out into the bookshop.

'This wall here…' She pointed to the wall that divided the kitchenette from the bookshop.

He had to admire her pluck. But that was all he'd admire. He refused to notice the way her hair gleamed rich and dark in the overhead light—the exact same colour as the icing on Gordon Sears's chocolate éclairs. He refused to notice how thick and full it was either or how the style she'd gathered it up into left the back of her neck vulnerable and exposed.

He realised she was staring at him, waiting. He cleared his throat. 'I wouldn't advise building bookshelves on that wall, Jaz.' He rapped his knuckles against it. 'Hear how flimsy it is?'

She stared at him as if she had no idea what he

was talking about. 'I can strengthen the wall if you like.' But it'd cost and it'd take time…time she wouldn't want to waste waiting for work to be done if he had her pegged right. 'I could write you up a quote if you want.' What the hell. He'd do the job for cost.

'I don't want bookshelves there. I just want to know if you're doing anything to this wall when you start work down here?'

'No.' One section of floorboards needed replacing and a couple of bookcases needed strengthening, but not the walls.

'So I'm free to paint it?'

'Sure.' He frowned. 'But surely it'd be wiser to wait until all the work is finished, then paint it as a job lot.'

She stared at him. Her eyes were pools of navy a man could drown in if he forgot himself. She moistened her lips—lush, soft lips—and Connor tried not to forget himself.

'I don't mean that kind of painting, Connor.'

It took a moment for her words to make sense. His head snapped back when they did.

She stared at the wall and he knew it wasn't pale green paint she saw.

'I mean to paint a portrait of my mother here.' She turned, a hint of defiance in her eyes, but her whole face had come alive. So alive it made him ache.

A memorial to Frieda? He wanted to applaud

her. He wanted to kiss her. He needed his head read. 'Do you mean to start it tonight?'

'No, but I might prime the wall tomorrow.'

For Pete's sake, did she mean to work herself into the ground? 'I thought you'd be back at Gwen's by now.'

'Hmm, no.'

Something in her tone made his eyes narrow. 'Why not?' Jaz and Gwen had been great pals.

She didn't look at him. She cocked her head and continued to survey the wall.

He resisted the urge to shake her. 'Jaz?'

'I think the less Gwen has to see of me, the happier she will be.'

He'd considered Richard's suggestion that Jaz stay at Gwen's an excellent one at the time. He'd thought it'd give Jaz a friend, an ally. He'd obviously got that wrong…and he should've known better. 'Sorry.' The apology dropped stiff from his lips. 'My fault.'

She glanced over her shoulder. 'I hardly think so.'

'I should've thought it through. Gwen…she was pretty cut up when you left. She wouldn't speak to me for months. She kept expecting to hear from you.'

Jaz stiffened, then she swung around, closed the gap between them and gripped his forearms. 'What did you just say?'

Her scent assaulted him and for a moment he found it impossible to speak. Her face had paled, lines of strain fanned out from her eyes. He couldn't remember a time when she'd looked more beautiful. The pressure of her hands on his arms increased, her grip would leave marks, but he welcomed the bite of her nails on his skin.

'She thought you were friends, Jaz. She cared about you.' After him and Faye, Gwen and Richard had been Jaz's closest friends. 'Then you left and she never heard from you again. You can guess how she took that.'

Air hissed out between her teeth. She dropped his arms and stepped back, her eyes wide, stricken—an animal caught in the headlights of an oncoming truck; something wild and injured trying to flee. Without a thought, he reached for her. But she pulled herself up and away, drew in a breath, and he watched, amazed, as she settled a mask of cool composure over her features. As if her distress had never been there at all.

Hell! That couldn't be healthy. He dragged a hand back through his hair, surprised to find that it shook. His heart hammered against his ribcage and he cursed himself for being a hundred different kinds of fool where this woman was concerned.

'Well—' she smiled brightly '—that's me done for the day.' The knuckles on her hands, folded innocuously at her waist, gleamed white. 'So, if you'll excuse me…'

'No!' He cleared his throat, tried to moderate his tone. 'I mean…' Ice prickled across his scalp and the back of his neck. Was it something like this that had tipped Frieda over the edge? 'I mean, where are you going?'

Her eyes had gone wide again. This time with surprise rather than… He didn't know what name to give the expression he'd just witnessed—shock, pain, grief?

'Why, to Gwen's, of course. I have an apology to make.' Sorrow stretched through the navy blue of her eyes. 'I can't believe how shabbily I've treated her. It—'

She waved a hand in front of her face, as if to dispel some image that disturbed her, and he suddenly realised what it was he'd seen in her eyes—self-loathing. She'd never considered herself worthy of his love, or of Faye, Gwen and Richard's friendship, had she?

Why was he only seeing that now?

She glanced at her watch. 'Where's the best place to buy a bottle of wine at this time of night? And chocolate. I'll need chocolate.'

'The tavern's bottle shop will still be open.'

'Thank you.'

She smiled at him and he could see that concern for herself, for the bookshop, had been ousted by her concern for Gwen. He didn't know why that should touch him so deeply. 'Can I give you a lift?'

She snorted. 'Connor, it's a two-minute walk. Thanks all the same, but I'll be fine.'

She stared up at him. He stared back. The silence grew and she moistened her lips. 'I'll see you later then.'

He nodded, dragged in a breath of her scent as she edged past him, then watched as she let herself out of the shop and disappeared into the evening.

He turned to stare at the wall she meant to paint.

With a muffled oath, he strode into the storeroom, disconnected the computer and tucked it under his arm.

He told himself he'd do the same for anyone.

CHAPTER FOUR

AT LUNCHTIME on Wednesday a group of teenagers sauntered through the bookshop's door and it immediately transported Jaz back in time ten years.

Oh, dear Lord. Had she ever looked that…confrontational? She bit back a grin. All of them, boys included, wore tip-to-toe black, the girls in stark white make-up and dark matt lipstick. Between the five of them they had more body piercing than the latest art-house installation on display at the Power House Museum. Their Doc Marten boots clomped heavily against the bare floorboards.

Jaz stopped trying to hold back her grin. She shouldn't smile. They were probably skiving off from afternoon sport at Clara Falls High. But then…Jaz had skived off Wednesday afternoon sport whenever she could get away with it too.

'If there's anything I can help you with, just let me know,' she called out.

'Cool,' said one of the girls.

'Sweet,' said one of the boys.

Jaz went back to studying the book she'd found in the business section half an hour ago— *Everything You Need To Know About Managing a Bookshop*. So far she'd found out that she needed a new computer and an Internet connection.

One of the girls—the one who'd already spoken—seized a book and came up to the counter. 'Every week, I come in here to drool over this book. I can't afford it.'

It was a coffee table art book—*Urban Art*. Exactly the same kind of book Jaz herself had pored over at that age.

'Look, we know the people who used to work here quit.' The girl ran her hands over the cover, longing stretched across her face. 'If I worked here, how many hours would it take me to earn this book?'

Jaz told her.

'Will you hire me? My name is Carmen, by the way. And I'm still at school so I could only work weekends, but… I'll work hard.'

Jaz wanted to reach out and hug her. 'I'm Jaz,' she said instead. They probably knew that already but it seemed churlish not to introduce herself too. 'And yes, I am looking for staff—permanent, part-time and casual.' At the moment she'd take what she could get. 'How old are you, Carmen?'

'Sixteen.'

'I would love to hire you, but before I could do that I would need either your mum or dad's permission.' No way was she going to cause *that* kind of trouble.

Five sets of shoulders slumped. Jaz's grew heavy in sympathy.

'I hate this town,' one of them muttered.

'There's never anything to do!'

'If you look the least bit different you're labelled a troublemaker.'

Jaz remembered resenting this town at their age too for pretty much the same reasons. 'You're always welcome to come and browse in here.' She motioned to the book on urban art.

'Thanks,' Carmen murmured, but the brightness had left her eyes. She glanced up from placing the book back on its shelf. 'Is it true you're a tattoo artist?'

'Yes, I am.' And she wasn't ashamed of it.

'And are you running drugs through here?'

What? Jaz blinked. 'I could probably rustle you up an aspirin if you needed one, but anything stronger is beyond me, I'm afraid.'

'I told you that was a lie!' Carmen hissed to the others.

'Yeah, well, fat chance that my mum'll let me work here once she catches wind of that rumour,' one of the others grumbled.

The teenagers drifted back outside.

Drugs? Drugs! Jaz started to shake. Her hands

curved into claws. Just because she was a tattoo
artist that made her a junkie, or a drug baron?

She wished Mac could hear this.

The whole town would boycott her shop if those
kinds of rumours took hold. Very carefully, she unclenched her hands. She drummed her fingers
against the countertop for a moment, a grim smile
touching her lips. Very carefully, she smoothed
down her hair. Her smile grew. So did the grimness.

She hooked the 'Back in five minutes' sign to the
window, locked the door and set off across the
street. 'You'll enjoy this,' she said, without stopping,
to Mrs Lavender, who sat on her usual park bench
on the traffic island. She reminded herself to walk
tall. She reminded herself she was as good as
anyone else in this town. Without pausing, she
breezed into Mr Sears's shop with her largest smile
in place and called out, 'Howdy, Mr Sears! How are
you today? Aren't we having the most glorious
weather? Good for business, isn't it?'

Mr Sears jerked around from the far end of the
shop and his eyes darkened with fury, lines brack-
eting his mouth, distorting it.

'I'll take a piece of your scrumptious carrot cake
to go, thanks.'

The rest of the bakery went deathly quiet. Jaz
pretended to peruse the baked goodies on display in
their glass-fronted counters until she was level with
Mr Sears. 'If you refuse to serve me,' she told him,

quietly so no one else heard her, 'I will create the biggest scene Clara Falls has ever seen. And, believe me, you *will* regret it.' Her smile didn't slip an inch.

Mr Sears seized a paper bag. He continued to glare, but he very carefully placed a piece of carrot cake inside it. It was a trait Jaz remembered, and it brought previous visits rushing back. He'd always treated his goods as if they were fine porcelain. For some reason that made her throat thicken.

She swallowed the thickness away. 'Best bread for twenty miles, my mother always used to say,' she continued in her bright, breezy, you're-my-long-lost-best-friend voice. A voice that probably carried all the way outside and across to where Mrs Lavender sat grinning on her park bench.

Carmen emerged from the back of the bakery. 'Hey, Dad, can I…' She stopped dead to stare from her father to Jaz and back again. She swallowed, then offered Jaz a half-hearted smile. 'Hey, Jaz.'

'Hey, Carmen.' Carmen was Gordon Sears's daughter? Whew! His glare grew even more ferocious. She grinned back. *That* was too delicious for words. 'And I'll take a loaf of your famous sour-dough too, Mr S.'

He looked as if he'd like to throw the loaf at her head. He didn't. He placed it in a bag and set it down beside her carrot cake. His fingers lingered on the bag, as if in apology to it for where it was going.

Jaz grinned and winked as she paid him. 'It's

great to be back in town, Mr S. You have a good day now, you hear?'

He slammed her change on the counter.

'And keep the change.'

She breezed back outside.

To slam smack-bang into Connor. His hands shot out to steady her. His eyes danced with a wicked delight that she feared mirrored her own. 'Lunchtime, huh?'

'That's right. You too?'

'Yep.'

His grin widened. It made her miss…everything.

No, it didn't! She stepped away so he was forced to drop his hands. 'I'd…er…recommend the carrot cake.'

'The carrot cake, huh?'

'That's right.' She swallowed. 'Well… I'll catch ya.' Oh, good Lord. Had she just descended into her former teenage vernacular? With as much nonchalance as she could muster, she stalked off.

His laughter and his hearty, 'Howdy, Mr S,' as he entered the bakery, followed her up the street, across the road and burrowed a path into her stomach to warm her very toes.

She unlocked the bookshop door, plonked herself down on her stool behind the sales counter and devoured her piece of carrot cake. For the first time in her life, Mr Sears's baked goods didn't choke her. The carrot cake didn't taste like sawdust. It tasted divine.

When she closed her eyes to lick the frosting from her fingers all she saw was Connor's laughing autumn eyes, making her feel alive again. In the privacy of the bookshop, she let herself grin back.

An hour after she'd last seen him, Connor stormed into the bookshop with a computer tucked under one arm and the diminutive Mrs Lavender tucked under the other.

Jaz blinked. She tried to slow her heart rate, did what she could to moderate the exhilaration pulsing through her veins. Just because she was back in Clara Falls didn't mean she and Connor were… anything. In fact, it meant the total opposite. They were…nothing. Null and void. History. But…

No man had any right whatsoever to look so darn sexy in jeans and work boots. Thank heavens he wasn't wearing a tool belt. That would draw the eye to…

No, no, no. Jaz tried to shoo that image right out of her head.

Connor set the computer on the counter. Jaz glanced at it, then back at him. She moistened her lips, realised his gaze had narrowed in on that action and her mouth went even drier. 'I know the question is obvious, but…what is that?'

'This is a computer I'm not using at the moment and is yours on loan until you get a chance to upgrade the shop's computer. This—' he pulled a computer disk from his pocket '—is the information my receptionist—the receptionist that I didn't fire and who is a whiz at all things computer—managed to save from your old hard drive. Including several recently deleted files.' He set the disk on top of the computer. 'She's hoping it will go some way to making amends for any previous inconvenience she's caused you.'

Jaz stared at him, speechless.

'And this—' he placed his hands on Mrs Lavender's shoulders '—is Mrs Lavender who, if you remember, owned the bookshop before your mother. A veritable fount of information who is finding herself at a bit of a loose end these days, and who would love to help out for a couple of hours a day, if you're agreeable.'

Agreeable? Jaz wanted to jump over the counter and hug him!

'Gives me a front row seat for watching all the drama. I'll enjoy seeing Gordon Sears brought down a peg or two.' Mrs Lavender's dark eyes twinkled.

Jaz slid out from behind the counter and wrapped her arms around the older woman. Over the top of Mrs Lavender's head, she met Connor's eyes. 'I don't know how to—'

'How's Gwen?'

She straightened and smiled, smoothed down her hair. 'Great.' The word emerged a tad breathy, but Connor was looking at her with such warmth that for a moment she didn't know which way was up.

'Gwen is great.' Gwen had accepted her apology. They'd shared the bottle of wine, they'd eaten the chocolate and they'd forged the beginnings of a new friendship.

He reached out, touched her cheek with the back of one finger. 'Good.' Then he stepped back and shoved his hands into his pockets. 'Time for me to get back to work. I'll see you ladies later.'

He turned, left the shop and disappeared. Only then did Jaz realise he hadn't given her time to thank him. He hadn't given her time to refuse his kindness either. She reached up to touch the spot on her cheek where his finger had lingered for the briefest, loveliest moment.

'Come along, Jaz. We've no time for mooning.'

Mooning? Who was mooning? 'I'm not mooning!'

She gulped. Mrs Lavender was right. She had no time for mooning. Absolutely no time at all.

But that afternoon, before it was time to close the shop and walk Melly home, Jaz's painting supplies were delivered to the bookshop. Connor must've searched through her boxes until he'd found everything she'd need to paint her portrait of Frieda.

She carried the box through to the stockroom, rested her cheek against it for a moment, before setting it to the floor and walking away. It didn't mean anything.

* * *

'Have you thought any more about telling your daddy about Mrs Benedict?' Jaz asked Melanie as she walked her to Mrs Benedict's front gate that afternoon.

The child drew herself up as if reciting a lesson. 'I'm not to worry Daddy about domestic matters. He has enough to worry about.'

'Domestic matters?'

'It means household stuff, money and babysitters,' Melly said, rattling each item off as if she'd learned them by heart. 'I checked,' she confided. 'So I'd get it right.'

'Did Daddy tell you not to worry him about domestic matters?' No matter how hard she tried, Jaz could not hear those words emerging from Connor's mouth.

'Grandma did.'

Jaz wondered if she'd go to hell for pumping a child so shamelessly for information. It wasn't for her own benefit, she reminded herself. It was for Melanie's. She wanted the child safe and happy. She couldn't even explain why, except she saw her younger self in Melanie.

That and the fact that Melanie was Connor's child. The kind of child she'd once dreamed of having with Connor.

Which made her sound like some kind of sick stalker! She wasn't. She just wanted to do something…good.

'I think your daddy would be very sad to hear you say that.'

'Why?'

'I think he'd be very interested in everything you do and think, even the domestic ones.'

'Nuh-uh.' The child stuck her chin out and glared at the footpath. 'He was supposed to take me out on the skyway on Saturday, but he didn't coz he had to work.'

Connor had broken a date with his daughter to work on the sign for Jaz's shop!

'Grandma made me promise not to nag him to take me Sunday because she said he'd be tired from working so hard and would need to rest.'

'That was very thoughtful of you.'

Melly glanced up, spearing Jaz with a gaze that touched her to the quick. 'I don't think he needs to work so hard, do you?'

Jaz thought it wiser not to answer that question. 'Perhaps you should tell him you think he's working too hard.'

Melanie shook her head and glanced away. Jaz wondered what else Grandma had made Melanie promise.

'Order, everyone. Order!'

Connor winced. Gordon Sears had a voice that could cut through rock when he was calling a meeting to order. Connor shifted on his seat.

Beside him, Richard half-grinned, half-grimaced in sympathy.

'Now, are we all agreed on the winter plantings for the nature strip?'

There were some mutterings, but a show of hands decided the matter. Connor marvelled that it could take so long to decide in favour of hyacinths over daffodils. Personally, he'd have chosen the daffodils, but he didn't much care. It certainly hadn't warranted half an hour's heated debate.

He glanced at his watch. It was almost Mel's bedtime. He hoped his father was coping okay. He tapped his foot against the floor. He didn't like leaving Mel with his parents two nights running. With his mother mostly confined to a wheelchair these days, he considered it too much work for his father. But Russell Reed adored his granddaughter. Mel put a bounce in the older man's step. Connor couldn't deny him that.

When they'd heard Connor was thinking of attending this evening's town meeting, they'd insisted Mel spend the night with them. He bit back a sigh. It was probably for the best. He'd miss reading Mel her bedtime story, but it had started to become all too apparent that Mel hungered for a female influence in her life—a female role model. He'd seen the way she watched the girls at school with their mothers and his heart ached for her.

He was hoping his own mother's presence would

help plug that particular hole. At least it gave Mel a woman to confide in.

She needs a younger woman. He pushed that thought away. Two women had left him without backwards glances. He wasn't going through that again, and he sure as hell wasn't risking his daughter's heart and happiness to some fly-by-night. He and Mel, they'd keep muddling along.

'Now, to the last item on the agenda.'

That rock-cracking voice had Connor wincing again. Richard rolled his eyes at Mr Sears's self-importance. Connor nodded in silent agreement.

'Now, I believe most of you will agree with me when I say we most certainly do not want a tattoo parlour polluting the streets of Clara Falls. Those of you who are in favour of such an abomination, please put forward your arguments now.'

Mr Sears glared around the room. Connor shifted forward on his seat, rested his arms on his knees. This was the reason he'd come tonight.

Nobody put forward an argument for a tattoo parlour in Clara Falls, and Connor listened with growing anger to the plan outlined by Gordon Sears to halt the likelihood of any such development occurring in the future.

Finally, he could stand it no longer. 'I don't know if this has escaped everyone's notice or not,' he said, climbing to his feet, 'but you can't block a non-existent development.'

Mr Sears puffed up. 'That's just semantics!'

'No,' Connor drawled. 'It's law.'

'This town has every right to make its feelings known on the subject.'

Connor planted his feet. 'If you approach Jaz Harper with this viciousness—'

'No names have been mentioned!' Mr Sears bluffed.

'No names have been mentioned, but everyone in this room knows exactly who you're talking about. Jaz Harper has made no move whatsoever to set up a tattoo parlour in Clara Falls. She's come back to run her mother's bookshop. End of story.'

He glanced around the room. Some people nodded their encouragement. Others shifted uneasily on their seats as their gazes slid away. Bloody hell! If Jaz were susceptible to the same kind of depression that had afflicted Frieda then… then she wouldn't need the likes of Gordon Sears banging on her door and shoving a petition under her nose.

'Connor is right.' Richard stood too. 'Last time I checked, this country was still a democracy. If you approach *my client*,' he stressed those two words, 'with a petition or with any other kind of associated viciousness—' he borrowed the term from Connor, but Connor didn't mind '—I will take out a harassment suit on her behalf. And, what's more, I'll enjoy doing it. She's a local businesswoman who is contributing to the economy of this town and we should all be supporting her.'

'I'll second that!' Connor clapped Richard on the back. Richard clapped him back. They both sat down. He watched with grim satisfaction as Gordon Sears brought the meeting to a close in double-quick time.

Mr Sears approached him as he and Richard stood talking by their cars. Connor could sense the anger in the older man, even though he hid it well. 'If any such proposal does go forward to the local council, I want you both to know that I will use every means in my power to block it.'

'I hope you're talking about legal means,' Richard said smoothly.

'Naturally.' Mr Sears lifted his chin and glared at Connor. 'I should've known you'd take her side.'

Connor planted his feet. 'This isn't about sides. It's about keeping Clara Falls as the kind of place where I'm happy to raise my daughter. A place not blinded by small-minded bigotry.'

'Ah, your daughter…yes.'

His smirk made the muscles of Connor's stomach contract.

'I take it that you are aware Melanie has been seen leaving the bookshop with Jaz Harper every afternoon this week?'

She what?

Mr Sears laughed at whatever he saw in Connor's

face. 'But, then again, perhaps not.' He strolled off, evidently pleased with the bombshell he'd landed.

'There'll be a perfectly reasonable explanation,' Richard said quietly.

'There'd better be. And I mean to find out what it is.' Now. 'Night, Richard.'

'Night, Connor.'

Connor climbed into his car and turned it in the direction of Frieda's Fiction Fair.

He eased the car past the bookshop at a crawl. A light burned inside, towards the rear of the shop. His lips tightened. She was there. He swung his car left at the roundabout and headed for the parking space behind her shop.

He let himself in with the key Jaz had given him. 'Hello?' He made his voice loud, made sure it'd carry all the way through to the front of the shop. He rattled the door and made plenty of noise. He had no intention of startling her like he had last night.

'Through here,' Jaz called.

He followed the sound of her voice. Then came to a dead halt.

She'd started her picture of Frieda.

She was drawing!

He reached out and clamped a hand around the hard shelf of a bookcase as the breath punched out of him. *She looked so familiar.* A thousand different memories pounded at him.

She'd sketched in the top half of Frieda's face

with a fine pencil and the detail stole his breath. He inched forward to get a better view. Beneath her fingers, her mother's eyes and brow came alive—so familiar and so…vibrant.

Jaz had honed her skill, her talent, until it sang. The potential he'd recognised in her work eight years ago—the potential anyone who'd seen her work couldn't have failed to recognise—had come of age. An ache started up deep down inside him, settled beneath his ribcage like a stitch.

He wanted to drag his gaze away, but he couldn't.

He found his anger again instead. What the hell was Jaz doing with his little girl? Why had Mel been seen with her every afternoon this week? And why hadn't Mrs Benedict informed him about it?

His hands clenched. He'd protect Mel with every breath in his body. Mel was seven—just a little girl—and vulnerable… And in need of a mother.

He ignored that last thought. Jaz Harper sure as hell didn't fit that bill.

Jaz exhaled, stepped back to survey her work more fully, then she growled. She threw her pencil down on a card table she'd set up nearby—it held a photograph of Frieda—then swung around to him, her eyes blazing. 'I'm grateful for what you did earlier in the day—the loan of the computer, Mrs Lavender et cetera. You left before I could thank you. So…thank you. But you obviously have something on your mind now and you might as well spit it out.'

'I mean to.' He planted his feet, hands on hips. 'I want to know what the hell you've been doing with my daughter every afternoon this week?'

The words shot out of him like nails from a nail gun, startling him with their ferocity, but he refused to moderate his glare. If she'd so much as harmed one hair on Mel's head, he'd make sure she regretted it for the rest of her life.

'Did you hear this from Melanie?'

'Gordon Sears,' he growled.

Jaz's lips twisted at whatever she saw in his face. Lush, full lips. Lips he—

No. He would not fall under her spell again. He wouldn't expose Mel to another woman who'd run at the first hint of trouble.

'Still jumping to conclusions, Connor?'

Her words punched the air out of his body.

'What on earth do you think I've been doing with her?' She planted her hands on her hips—a mirror image of him—and matched his glare. 'What kind of nasty notions have been running through your mind?'

Nothing specific, he realised. But he remembered the gaping hole Jaz had left in his life when she'd fled Clara Falls eight years ago. He wouldn't let her hurt Mel like that.

'One more day,' she whispered. 'That's all I needed with her—one more day.' She said the words almost to herself, as if she'd forgotten he was even there.

'One more day to do what?' he exploded.

She folded her arms, but he saw that her hands shook. 'You haven't changed much at all, have you, Connor? It seems you're still more than willing to believe the worst of me.'

Bile burned his throat.

'I needed one more day to convince her to confide in you, that's what.'

To confide in him… Her words left him floundering. 'To confide what?'

'If you spent a little more time with your daughter, then perhaps you'd know!'

'If I…' His shoulders grew so tight they hurt. 'What do you know about bringing a child up on your own?' About how hard it was. About how the doubts crowded in, making him wonder if he was doing a good job or making a hash of things. About how he'd always be a dad and never a mum and that, no matter how nurturing and gentle he tried to be, he knew it wasn't the same.

'I…nothing.' Jaz took a step back. 'I'm sorry.'

The sadness that stretched across her face had his anger draining away, against his will and against his better judgement. She turned away as if to hide her sadness from him.

'Are you going to tell me what's been going on?' To his relief, his voice had returned to normal.

She started gathering up her pencils and placing them back in their box. 'I don't suppose you'd trust me for just one more day?'

'No, I wouldn't.' He tried to make the words gentle. He had to bite back an oath when she flinched. 'I won't take any risks where Mel's concerned. I can't.'

She smiled then and he saw the same concern she'd shown for Gwen last night reflected in her eyes now. His chest started to burn as if he'd run a marathon. If Jaz had gleaned even the tiniest piece of information that would help him with Mel...Mel, who'd gone from laughing and bright-eyed to sober and withdrawn in what seemed to him a twinkling of an eye.

Mel, who'd once chattered away to him about everything and nothing, and who these days would only shake her head when he asked her if anything was wrong.

'Mel has been coming to the bookshop after school instead of Mrs Benedict's.'

'Do you know why?'

'I...yes, I do.' She hesitated. 'May I ask you a question first?'

His hand clenched. He wanted his bright, bubbly daughter back—the girl whose smile would practically split her face in two whenever she saw him. He'd do anything to achieve that, pay any price. Even if that meant answering Jaz's questions first. He gave a short, hard nod.

'Why is Melly going to Mrs Benedict's after school? Please don't get angry again, but...if you start work at seven-thirty most mornings, surely you should be able to knock off in time to collect Melly from school at three-thirty? Obviously I don't know your personal situation, but it looks as if you're doing well financially. Do you really need to work such long hours?'

No, he didn't.

She frowned. 'And who looks after Melly in the mornings before school?'

'The school provides a care service, before and after school.'

She didn't ask, but he could see the question in her eyes—why didn't he use that service instead of sending Mel to Mrs Benedict's?

'You don't want to tell me, do you?'

What the hell…? That mixture of sadness and understanding in her voice tugged at him. It wouldn't hurt to tell her. It might even go some way to making amends for bursting in here and all but accusing her of hurting Mel.

He raked a hand back through his hair. 'We had a huge storm on this side of the mountain two and a half months ago. It did a lot of damage—roofs blown off, trees down on houses, that kind of thing. The state emergency services were run off their feet and we jumped in to help. We're still getting through that work now. At the time it seemed important to secure people's homes against further damage, to make them safe again…liveable. But it did and does mean working long hours.' He hated to see people homeless, especially families with small children.

'And you feel responsible for making things right?'

He didn't know if that was a statement or a question. He shrugged. 'I just want to do my bit to help.'

'Yes, but don't you think you need to draw the line somewhere? There are more important things in life than work, you know.'

A scowl built up inside him. Did she think work counted two hoots when it came to Mel? Mel was his life.

Jaz thrust her chin out. 'You worked on my sign last Saturday instead of taking Melanie on the skyway. You broke a date with your daughter to work on my stupid sign.'

'You didn't think that sign so unimportant at the time!'

Guilt inched through him. He had cancelled that outing with Mel, but he'd promised to take her to the skyway the next day instead. She'd seemed happy enough with that, as happy as she seemed with anything these days. Except…

He frowned. When Sunday had rolled around Mel had said she didn't want to go anywhere. She'd spent the day colouring in on the living room floor instead.

He should've taken her on the Saturday—he should've kept his promise—but when he'd found out Jaz was expected to arrive in Clara Falls that day, he hadn't been able to stay away. At the time he'd told himself it was to get their initial meeting out of the way, and any associated unpleasantness. As he stared down into Jaz's face now, though, he wondered if he'd lied.

He pulled his mind back. 'It's not just the work. Mel needs a woman in her life. She's—'

He broke off to drag a hand down his face. 'I see the way she watches the girls at school with their mothers.' It broke his heart that he couldn't fill that gap for her. 'She hungers for that…maternal touch.'

Jaz frowned. Then her face suddenly cleared. 'That's what Mrs Benedict's about. She's your maternal touch!'

He nodded. 'She came highly recommended. She's raised five children of her own. She's a big, buxom lady with a booming laugh. A sort of…earth mother figure.'

'I see.'

'I thought that, between her and my mother, they might help fill that need in Mel.'

Scepticism rippled across Jaz's face before she could school it. 'What?' he demanded. From memory, Jaz had never liked his mother.

'Melanie doesn't like going to Mrs Benedict's.'

'She hasn't said anything to me!'

Jaz twisted her hands together again. 'Apparently Mrs Benedict has been smacking her.'

CHAPTER FIVE

'SHE'S what?' Connor reached out and gripped Jaz's shoulders. 'Did you say *smacking her*? Are you telling me Mrs Benedict is *hitting* my daughter?'

'You're hurting me, Connor.'

He released her immediately. And started to pace.

'Relax, Connor, Melly is—'

'Relax? Relax!' How the hell could she say that when—

'Melanie is safe. That's all that matters, right? You can tackle Mrs Benedict tomorrow. Flying off the handle now won't solve anything.'

She had a point. He dragged in a breath. But when he got hold of Mrs Benedict he'd—

'Working out what's best for Melanie is what's important now, isn't it?'

'She's not going back to that woman's place!'

'Good.'

He dragged in another breath. 'So that's why she's been coming here?'

'Yes.'

'And you've been walking her to Mrs Benedict's front gate each afternoon?'

'Yes.'

'And trying to talk her into confiding in me?'

'Yes.'

He ground his teeth together. 'Thank you.'

'It was nothing.'

She tried to shrug his words off, but her eyes were wide and blue. It wasn't nothing and they both knew it.

He unclenched his jaw. 'Do you have any idea why Mel didn't want to confide in me?'

Jaz hesitated again. 'I…'

She did! She knew more about what was going through his daughter's head than he did.

She eyed him warily. 'Will you promise not to shout any more?'

Did she think he'd lash out at her in his anger? He recalled the way he'd stormed in here, and dragged a hand down his face. 'I'll do my best,' he ground out.

'It seems that because you're working so hard, your mother is concerned about your…welfare.'

He frowned. 'I don't get what you're driving at.'

She moistened her lips. He tried to ignore their shine, their fullness…and the hunger that suddenly seized him.

'It seems your mother has been lecturing Melly

not to bother you with her troubles when you're so obviously busy with work.'

He gaped at her. No! He snapped his jaw shut. 'You never did like my mother, did you?'

'No, Connor, that's not true, but she never liked me. And in hindsight I can't really blame her. She could hardly have been thrilled that the rebellious Goth girl was going out with her son now, could she?'

His mother had always been…overprotective.

'Look, I'm not making this up.'

He didn't want to believe her…but he did.

She grimaced. 'And, for what it's worth, I think your mother is well-intentioned. She is your mother, after all. It's natural for her to have your best inter-ests at heart.'

'She should have Mel's best interests at heart.' He collapsed onto one of the leatherette cubes. Mel needed a woman in her life, but the two he'd chosen had let her down badly.

And so she'd latched onto Jaz?

What a mess.

This wasn't his mother's fault. It wasn't even Mrs Benedict's fault, though he'd still have some choice words for her when he saw her tomorrow. This was his fault. He hadn't wanted to acknowledge it before and he didn't want to acknowledge it now, but Mel needed a younger woman in her life. Not two women who were at least fifty years older than her.

But Jaz?

'Don't look like that,' Jaz chided. 'This isn't the end of the world. So you knock off from here in time to collect Melly from school for the rest of the week. That's no big deal.'

'It'll put work on the flat back by a day.'

She shrugged again. 'Like I said—no big deal.'

'She didn't confide in me!' The words burst from him, but he couldn't hold them back. Mel had refused to confide in him, but she'd confided in Jaz? Jaz!

'So you work on winning back her trust. On Saturday you take her out on the skyway. Tell her she looks so pretty you're going to call her Princess Melly for the day and that her every wish is your command.'

He stared at her and he couldn't help it—a grin built up inside him at the image she'd planted in his mind…and at how alive her face had become as she described it. Who called Jaz Princess Jaz? Who tried to make her dreams come true?

He wondered if she'd like to come out on the skyway with him and Mel on Saturday? He wondered if—

Whoa! He pulled back. No way. He was grateful for the insights she'd given him, but not that grateful. Mel might need a younger woman in her life, but Jaz Harper wasn't that woman.

Jaz's smile faltered. 'You want me to butt out now, don't you?'

'Yes.' There was no sense in trying to soften his intentions.

'I see.'

He felt like a heel. He didn't want to hurt her feelings, but he would not—could not—let her hurt Mel. He hardened his heart. 'I don't want you involved in my daughter's life.'

'Good!' Her eyes flashed. 'Because I don't want to be involved in any part of your life either.'

He didn't want what had happened to Frieda happening to Jaz either, though. The thought had him breaking out in a cold sweat. 'I didn't mean that to sound as rotten as it did. It's just…you tell me you're only here for twelve months.'

She folded her arms. 'That's right.'

He swore he glimpsed tears in her eyes. 'Bloody hell, Jaz. If you're only here for twelve months, I don't want Mel getting attached to you. She'll only be hurt when you leave. She won't understand.'

'I hear you, all right!'

Yep, definitely tears. 'Look, I didn't understand when you left eight years ago and I was eighteen. What hope does a seven-year-old have?'

Her jaw dropped and that old anger, the old pain, reared up through him. 'Hell, Jaz! You left and you didn't even tell me why!'

She'd hurt him. Eight years ago, she'd hurt him. She could tell by his pallor, in the way his eyes glittered. In the way the tiredness had invaded the skin around his mouth.

But he'd married Faye so quickly that she'd thought…

She gulped. 'Darn it all, Connor, I was only going to be gone for three months.'

'Three months!' His jaw went slack. His Adam's apple worked. 'Three months?' he repeated before he tensed up again. 'Where the hell did you go? And why didn't you tell me?'

His pain wrapped around her with tentacles that tried to squeeze the air out of her body. She had to drag in a breath before she could speak. 'You have to understand, I was seriously cut up that you thought I could ever cheat on you.'

He hadn't given her a chance to explain at the time. He'd hurled his accusations with all the ferocity of a cornered, injured animal—even then she'd known it was his shock and pain talking, the unexpectedness of finding her at the Hancocks' house, because she had lied about that.

'Stop playing games, Jaz.' He spoke quietly. 'I *know* you were cheating on me with Sam Hancock.'

A spurt of anger rippled through her, followed closely by grim satisfaction. She wanted—no, *needed*—him to keep his distance. If he thought she was the kind of woman who'd cheat on him and still lie about it eight years later, he'd definitely keep his distance.

She was not travelling to hell again with Connor Reed. It had taken too long to get over the last time. He hadn't trusted her then and he didn't trust her now. He'd jumped to conclusions back then and, on this evening's evidence, he still jumped to conclusions now. So much for older and wiser!

'Does it even matter now?' she managed in as frigid a tone as she could muster.

'Not in the slightest. I understand why people cheat. That's not the issue.'

She didn't bother calling him a liar. There didn't seem to be any point. Perhaps it didn't make an ounce of difference to him now anyway.

'What I don't understand is why people run.' He stabbed a finger at her. 'What I don't get is why you left the way you did.'

The flesh on her arms grew cold. If Faye had deserted him too without an explanation…

Was an overdue explanation better than no explanation at all? One glance into his face told her the answer. She pulled in a breath and did what she could to ignore the sudden tiredness that made her limbs heavy. 'Let's just take it as a given that I was in a right state by the time I got home that night, okay?' It made her sick to the stomach just remembering it.

'Fine.' The word emerged clipped and short.

'My mother calmed me down.' Eventually. 'And, bit by bit, got the story out of me.'

'And?' he said when she stopped.

'Did you know that my mother didn't approve of our relationship?'

He blinked and she laughed. Not a mirthful laugh. Definitely not a joyful one. 'I know—funny, isn't it? The rest of the town thought it was me—the rebel Goth girl—leading clean-cut Connor Reed astray.'

'I thought she liked me!'

'She did. But she thought we were too young for such an intense relationship. She was worried I'd put all my dreams on hold for you.'

She could see now that Frieda Harper had had every reason to be concerned. Jaz had been awed by Connor's love—grateful to him for it, unable to believe he could truly love a girl like her. And she'd hidden behind his popularity, his ease with people, instead of standing on her own two feet. Frieda had understood that.

'She asked me to go away from Clara Falls for three months. She begged me to.'

Connor's face had gone white. Jaz swallowed. 'She told me that you and I needed time out from each other, to gain perspective.' And Jaz had been so hurt and so…angry. She'd wanted Connor to pay for the things he'd said. 'She told me that if you really loved me, you'd wait for me.' And Jaz had believed her. 'I went to my aunt's house in Newcastle for three months.' And she'd counted down every single day.

She lifted her head and met his gaze. 'But you didn't wait for me.'

His eyes flashed dark in the pallor of his face. 'Are you trying to put the blame back on me?'

'No.' She shook her head, a black heaviness pressing down on her. 'I'm simply saying you didn't wait.'

He flung an arm in the air. 'I thought you were gone for ever! I didn't think you were ever coming back.'

He'd jumped to conclusions. Again. 'You didn't bother looking for me!'

He took several paces away from her, then swung back. 'Three months?' He stabbed an accusing finger at her. 'You didn't come back!'

The space between them sparked with unspoken resentments and hurts.

Jaz moistened her lips and got her voice back under control. 'The day before I was due to come home, my mother rang. She told me Faye was pregnant and that you were the father. And that you were engaged.'

Connor dragged both hands back through his hair. He collapsed to the leatherette cube as if he'd lost all strength in his legs. Jaz leant heavily against the wall by the unfinished portrait of her mother.

She reached up to touch it, then pulled her hand away at the last moment. She glanced back at Connor. 'You have to see that I couldn't come back once I'd heard that.'

'Why not?'

'There'd be no chance for you and Faye to sort things out if I'd done that.'

She didn't mean to sound arrogant, but it was the truth. For good or ill, she and Connor would've picked straight up where they'd left off—in each other's arms.

He shot to his feet. 'Am I supposed to take that as some kind of noble gesture on your part?'

That tone would've shrivelled her eight years ago. It didn't shrivel her now.

'Noble? Ha!' She glared at him. 'I can't see there's much of anything noble in this entire situation.' She pushed away from the wall. 'But a baby was going to be involved and…and I wasn't going to interfere with that.'

His glare subsided. He bent at the waist, rested his hands on his knees and didn't say anything.

'But how could you?' Her voice shook. 'How could you sleep with my best friend? Faye, of all people!' The pain of that still ran deep. 'Why Faye?'

Very slowly, he straightened. The emptiness in his eyes shocked her. 'Because she reminded me of you. I was searching for a substitute and she was the nearest I could find.'

The breath left her body. She fell back against the wall. She couldn't think of a single thing to say.

What was there to say? It was all history now. It was too late for her and Connor.

The silence stretched—eloquent of the rift that had grown between them in the intervening years. Connor finally nodded. 'Goodnight, Jaz.' And he made for the door.

For a moment she still couldn't speak. Then, 'If you tell Melly I broke her confidence…it will hurt her.'

He stopped, but he didn't turn around.

'I don't think she deserves that.'

He seemed to think about that and then he nodded. 'You're right.' He took one further step away, stopped again…and then he turned. 'Do you seriously think that, given more time, she would've confided in me?'

'I'm convinced of it.' She tried to find a smile. 'Wait and see. She still might yet.'

She thought he might say something more, but he didn't.

'By the way, did you know that Carmen Sears is looking for an after school job?'

He frowned. 'Why are you telling me this?'

'She'd make a great babysitter for Melanie.'

'But she's—'

He broke off and Jaz couldn't stop her lips from twisting. 'Yes, she's a rebel Goth girl. *And* she seems like a nice kid. Just thought you might be interested, that's all.'

He stared at her for a long moment. 'Why did it take you so long to come back?'

The tone of his voice gave nothing away, and for a brief moment a sense of loss gaped through her. She shrugged and strove for casual. 'Pride, I guess, and resentment at the way things turned out. I was angry with you and Faye. I was angry with my mother. I wanted to forget.'

She shrugged again. She had a feeling she might be overdoing the shrug thing but she couldn't seem to help it. 'In the end it became a habit.' A habit that had broken her mother's heart.

She lifted her chin. 'Goodnight, Connor.'

First thing Thursday morning, Mrs Lavender put Jaz to work changing the book display in the front window. Jaz had a feeling it was a ploy to stop her from fretting about their lack of customers.

'It hasn't been changed in nearly two months. Look, we've all these lovely new bestsellers…and it'll be Mother's Day in a couple of weeks. It needs sprucing up!'

A shaft of pain speared straight into Jaz's heart at the mention of Mother's Day. She kept her chin high, but Mrs Lavender must've seen the strain in her face because she stilled, then reached out and touched Jaz's hand. 'I'm sorry, Jazmin, that was thoughtless of me.'

'Not at all.' She gulped. She would not let her chin drop. 'I'm the one who didn't come back for the past eight Mother's Days. I have no right to self-pity now.' Oh, she'd sent flowers, had phoned, but it wasn't the same.

'You have a right to your grief.'

Jaz managed a weak smile, but she didn't answer. She deserved to spend this coming Mother's Day burning with guilt.

She made Mrs Lavender a cup of tea, noticed Connor's truck parked out the back, and the burning in her chest increased ten-fold.

'Have you looked these over, Jaz?'

Jaz had just climbed out of the window, pleased with her brand new display. She glanced over Mrs Lavender's shoulder. 'Oh, those.' A printout of the sales figures for the last three months. A weight dropped to her shoulders and crashed and banged and did what it could to hammer her through the floor. 'Appalling, aren't they?'

'You have to turn these around, and fast.' There was no mistaking Mrs Lavender's concern. 'Jaz, this is serious.'

'I…' She was doing all she could.

Mrs Lavender tapped her pen against the counter, ummed and ahhed under her breath. Then her face suddenly lit up. 'We'll have a book fair, that's what we'll do! It'll stir up some interest in this place again.'

'A book fair?'

'We'll get in entertainment for the kiddies, we'll have readings by local authors… We'll have a ten per cent sale on all our books. We'll get people excited. We'll get people to come. And, by golly, we'll save this bookshop!'

Jaz clutched her hands together. 'Do you think it could work?'

'My dear Jazmin, we're going to have to make

it work. Either that or make the decision to sell up to Mr Sears.'

'No!' She cast a glance towards the back wall and the unfinished portrait of Frieda. 'I'm not selling to him.' She hitched up her chin. 'We'll have a book fair.'

She and Mrs Lavender spent the rest of the morning planning a full-page advertisement in the local newspaper. They discussed children's entertainment. Jaz started to design posters and flyers. They settled on the day—the Saturday of the Mother's Day weekend.

If the book fair didn't work…

Jaz shook her head. She refused to think about that.

At midday Mrs Lavender excused herself to go and sit on her usual park bench to torment Boyd Longbottom.

'What's the story with you and Boyd Longbottom, anyway?' Jaz asked.

'He was a beau of mine, a long time ago.'

Jaz set her pen down. 'Really?'

'But when I chose my Arthur over him, he swore he'd never speak to me again. He's kept his word to this very day.'

'But that's awful.'

'He never left Clara Falls. He never married. And he's not spoken to me again, not once.'

'That's…sad.'

'Yes, Jaz, it is.' Mrs Lavender opened her mouth as if she meant to say more, but she shut it again. 'I'll see you tomorrow.'

At quarter past twelve Connor jogged across the street to Mr Sears's bakery. On his way back he stopped right outside the bookshop window to survey the new display.

Jaz stood behind one of the bookcases she was tidying and watched him. Her heart squeezed so tight the blood rushed in her ears.

Turn your back. Walk away.

Her body refused to obey the dictates of her brain.

At least close your eyes.

She didn't obey that order either. She remembered how she and Connor had once shared their drawings with each other, offering praise or criticism, suggestions for improvements. She searched his face. Did he like her display?

She couldn't tell.

He didn't lift his eyes and search for her inside the shop.

Eventually he turned and strode away. The tightness around Jaz's heart eased, but nothing could expand to fill the gap that yawned through her.

At a touch after three-thirty the phone rang. Jaz pounced on it, eager to take her mind off the fact that Melly wasn't here. She'd known Melly wouldn't show up here today. Just as she knew Melly wouldn't show up here tomorrow…or any other day from now on.

She didn't know why it should make her feel lonely, only that it did.

'Hey, mate!' Her business partner's voice boomed down the line at her. 'How're you doing?'

'Mac!' She grinned. 'Better now that I'm talking to you. How are Bonnie and the kids?'

'They send their love. Now, tell me, has the town welcomed you back with open arms?'

'Yes and no. Business could be a lot better, though. I'm not getting any local trade.'

'Are they giving you a hard time?'

'Well, there is a rumour that I'm the local drug baron.'

His laughter roared down the line, lifting her spirits. 'What? Little Ms Clean-as-a-Whistle Jaz Harper?' He sobered. 'I bet that's doing wonders for business.'

'Ooh, yeah.'

'Listen, mate, I have a job for you, and I have a plan.'

Her smile widened as she listened to his plan.

CHAPTER SIX

'OKAY, Princess Melly—' Connor held the door to Mr Sears's bakery open '—what is your pleasure?'

Mel's eyes danced. It gladdened Connor's heart.

'Princess Melly wants a picnic!'

'Where…at the park? Or perhaps at one of the lookouts?' He cocked his head to one side. 'On the skyway?' They'd already been back and across on the skyway twice this morning.

Over the course of the morning Mel had laughed with her whole self, and it made things inside him grateful and light. She'd retreated into her shell a couple of times, but so far she'd come peeping back out again.

Jaz had been right. The Princess Melly thing was working a treat. It had disarmed his daughter almost immediately—that and the skyway rides. Not to mention the jeans-buying expedition. Mel had only requested one pair of jeans, but it had suddenly occurred to Connor that she didn't have any—at least, none that fitted her any more. They'd bought three pairs. Mel had near burst with excitement over that one. She wore a pair now.

'A picnic in the botanic gardens,' Princess Melly announced.

'Excellent.' Connor rubbed his hands together, walked her up and down the length of the counter to eye all of Mr Sears's goodies. It was only a touch after eleven o'clock but, given the amount of energy they'd expended already, coupled with the plans he could see racing through Mel's mind, he figured she might need refuelling. 'What should we take on our picnic?'

She stared up at him with big liquid eyes—identical to his, so he was told. He didn't believe it. His eyes couldn't melt a body like that.

'Princess Melly would like a sausage roll now—' she slipped her hand inside his, as if he might need some extra persuasion '—which will spoil her lunch, you know?'

'It will?' He tried to figure out where she was going with this.

'Which means we can just have apple turnovers and lemonade for lunch.'

Connor grinned. Mel's smile slipped. 'Excellent idea,' he assured her. 'Apple turnovers for lunch it is.'

Once in the proverbial blue moon wouldn't hurt, would it?

Her smile beamed out at him again.

Heck, no, it couldn't hurt anything. Still…responsible adult instincts kicked in. 'I am afraid, though, that your humble servant—' he touched his chest '—has a voracious appetite. Would it be permissible for him to order egg-and-lettuce sandwiches to take on the picnic, do you think?'

She nodded solemnly, but her eyes danced. Connor placed their order and they sat at a table in the front window to munch their sausage rolls and sip hot chocolates.

The roar of motorbikes interrupted them midbite. They both swung to stare out of the window. Motorbikes—big, black, gleaming Harley-Davidsons—trawled up the street, chrome and leather gleaming in the sun. There had to be at least a dozen bikes, most with pillion passengers…and all the riders wore black leather. Connor blinked, and then he started to laugh, deep and low, and with undeniable satisfaction. The roar and thunder abated as the bikes found parking spaces down either side of the street. All of the leather-clad visitors made a beeline for Jaz's bookshop.

His gut clenched when Jaz danced out to meet them. He thought a blood vessel in his brain might burst when the biggest and burliest of the visitors swung her around as if she didn't weigh any more than a kitten, rather than five feet ten inches of warm, curvaceous woman. When the burly visitor placed her back on the ground, he kissed her on the cheek.

Kissed her! Something dark and ugly pulsed through him.

Jaz hadn't mentioned being involved with anyone in Sydney, but then they hadn't really discussed what she'd been doing since she'd left.

'Daddy?'

He glanced down to find Mel staring at his mangled sausage roll.

He tried to loosen his grip around it, tried to grin. 'Oops, I obviously don't know my own strength.'

Melly giggled.

Connor wiped his hand on a paper serviette and glanced back out of the window. He couldn't stop a replay of all the kisses he and Jaz had shared eight years ago from playing through his mind now—all of them, in all of their endless variety.

He couldn't remember kissing her on the cheek too often.

On the cheek!

That hadn't been the kiss of some lover impatient to see his girlfriend after a week of enforced separation. Connor couldn't explain the rush of relief that poured into him. Actually, he could explain it, but he wouldn't. Not to himself. Not to anyone.

Some of Jaz's friends followed her into the bookshop. Others broke into groups of twos and threes to stroll down whichever side of the street seemed to take their fancy, for all the world like idle tourists. Which was probably what they were. They didn't wear bike gang insignias on their leather jackets. They were probably a bunch of people who shared a passion for bikes. He'd bet they were carpenters and bookshop owners and bakers like him and Jaz and Mr Sears.

He cast a glance around the bakery. He wasn't the only one transfixed. The arrival of over a dozen bikes in town had brought the conversation in the bakery to a screaming halt. Mr Sears's face had turned the same colour as the icing on his Chelsea buns—pink. Bright pink.

Connor grinned. After the way Mr Sears had treated her this past week, Jaz deserved her revenge. He enjoyed the beauty of her payback. Not that it would boost her popularity rating as far as the rest of the town was concerned. Already an assortment of tourists and locals were surreptitiously returning to their cars and driving away—intimidated by the combination of loud motorbikes and leather.

Then suddenly Jaz was standing outside the Sears's bakery without any of her friends in tow and Connor cursed himself for the distraction that had cost him the treat of watching her stride across the road, head held high and shoulders thrown back. Her eyes met his through the plate glass and that thing arced between them—a combination of heat and history.

The bell above the door tinkled as she entered. 'Hello, Connor.'

'Hello, Jaz.'

She swung away from him abruptly to smile at Mel—an uncomplicated display of pleasure that kicked him in the guts. 'Melly! How are you?'

Melly leaned towards her. 'I'm Princess Melly today.'

Jaz let loose a low whistle. 'Hardly surprising. You do look as pretty as a princess today, you know?'

'Daddy says I look as pretty as a princess every day.' But she said the words uncertainly.

Jaz bent down. 'Princess Melly, I think your daddy is right.' Then she winked. 'By the way, I love the jeans.'

Mel beamed. Connor's gut clenched in consternation. As if she sensed that, Jaz straightened. 'I'd love to stay and chat, but I have visitors to get back to. You have fun today, okay?'

Mel nodded vigorously. 'We will.'

'Hey, Carmen. Howdy, Mr S.' Jaz boomed this last.

Mr Sears raced down to the end of the counter where Jaz stood, the end nearest Connor and Mel. 'What are you doing?' he demanded in an undertone. 'Trying to chase all of Clara Falls' business out of town?'

'I have nearly twenty people for morning tea.' She didn't lower her voice. 'Which, at least for your bakery, Mr S, is going to be *very* good business. I'll take one of your large carrot cakes, a strawberry sponge and…what would you suggest? A chocolate mud cake or a bee sting?'

Connor couldn't resist. 'Go with the orange and poppy seed, Jaz. It can't be beat.'

She swung around to stare at him. That warmth arced between them again. The colour in her cheeks deepened. Connor's groin kicked to life. She swung back to Mr Sears. 'The orange poppy seed it is.'

Every single one of Mr Sears's muscles—at least those from the waist up that Connor could see—bunched. If steam could've come out of his ears, Connor was guessing it would've. And yet he placed each of the three cakes in a separate cardboard box with the same care and reverence mothers showed to newborn babies.

But when he placed them on the counter for Jaz to collect, he leaned across and grabbed her wrist. Connor pushed his chair back and started to rise.

'If the tone of this town is brought down any further,' Mr Sears hissed, 'you'll ruin the lot of us. And it'll be all your doing.'

'No, it'll be yours,' she returned, as cool as the water in the Clara Falls themselves.

With one twist, she freed her wrist. Connor sat back down. She didn't need his help.

'I run a bookshop, Mr S, and I need to attract customers from somewhere. Until my bookshop starts securing its usual level of trade, and the rumours about drugs trafficking start dying down, I'm afraid you'll have to get used to my weekend visitors. They have bikes and will travel. They believe supporting independent bookshops is a good cause.' She hitched her head in the direction of the door. 'Believe me, this lot is only the tip of the iceberg.'

Mr Sears drew back as if stung.

She sent him what Connor could only call a salacious wink. 'Your call, Mr S.' She lifted the cakes and all but saluted him with them. 'Mighty grateful to you. Have a great day now, you hear? I'll be back later to grab afternoon tea for the hordes. Who knows how many extra bodies could show up between now and then? And those Danish pastries look too good to resist.' With that she swept out of the shop.

A buzz of conversation broke out around the tables the moment the door closed behind her. Connor watched every step of her progress with greedy delight as she returned to the bookshop. She walked as if she owned the whole world. It was sexy as hell. You had to hand it to her. The lady had style.

'Jaz is my friend,' Mel said, hauling his attention back.

He sobered at that. He didn't want his daughter getting too attached to Jaz Harper. It wouldn't do her any good. Just like it hadn't done him any good.

'Stop!'

Luckily Connor had already slowed the car to a crawl in expectation of the approaching pedestrian crossing when Mel shouted, because he planted his foot on the brake immediately.

'What?' He glanced from the left to the right to try and discover what it was that had made Melly shout. Katoomba's main street was crowded with shoppers and tourists alike—a typical Saturday. He couldn't see anything amiss. She couldn't want more food, surely? They'd not long finished their sausage rolls and hot chocolates.

'Jaz just went in there with two of her friends.'

He followed the direction of Mel's finger to Katoomba's one and only tattoo parlour.

Mel lifted her chin. 'I want to go in there too.'

He hesitated. He played for time. He edged the car up to the pedestrian crossing, where he had to wait for pedestrians…and more pedestrians. 'What about the botanic gardens and our picnic?'

'Something is wrong.' Melly's bottom lip wobbled and his gut twisted. 'She looked sad and she's my friend and she made me feel better when I was sad.'

Her bottom lip wobbled some more. He gulped. 'When were you sad?'

'Last week.'

'Why were you sad?'

Would she tell him? He held his breath. The pedestrian crossing cleared and he pushed the car into gear and started moving again.

'Because Mrs Benedict smacked me.'

Connor slid the van into a free parking space and tried to unclench his hands from around the steering wheel. That still had the power to make his blood boil…

But Mel had confided in him!

'You won't ever have to go back to Mrs Benedict's again, okay, sweetheart?'

Mel's eyes went wide, then opaque. Connor couldn't read her face at all. He didn't know if she was about to throw a temper tantrum or burst into tears. 'You said I was Princess Melly today.'

The whispered words speared straight into him. 'You are, sweetheart.'

'And that my every wish was your command.'

'Yep, that's right.' If she didn't want to talk about this, then he wouldn't force her.

'Then I want to see Jaz!'

He was hers to command. But how could he explain that neither one of them had the right to command Jaz?

Why was Jaz sad?

The thought distracted him. Perhaps that was why Mel's escape plan succeeded because, before he realised what she meant to do, she'd slipped off her seat belt, slid out of the car and raced back down the street towards the tattoo parlour.

'Bloody hell!'

Connor shot out of the car after her. He fell through the front door of the tattoo parlour in time to see Mel throw her arms around Jaz's waist as Jaz emerged from the back of the shop.

'What's this?' Jaz hugged Mel back but she glanced up at Connor with a question in her eyes.

'I'm sorry.' He shrugged and grimaced. Mel clung to Jaz like a limpet and an ache burned deep down inside him. 'She got away from me. She saw you and thought you looked sad.' He didn't know what else to say because it suddenly hit him that Mel was right—something was wrong. Jaz was sad. He didn't know how he could tell. Nothing in her bearing gave it away.

Two men emerged from the back of the shop—one of them the man who'd kissed Jaz on the cheek earlier. She smiled at them weakly and shrugged, much the same way he just had to her. 'This is my friend, Melly...and her father Connor. This is Mac and Jeff.'

They all nodded to each other, murmured hellos.

'Melly saw me and wanted to say hello.' She knelt down to Mel's level. 'I am a bit sad, but I promise I'm going to be all right, okay?'

Mel nodded. 'Okay.'

'Now, if you'll excuse me—' Jaz rose '—I have some work to do.'

Connor saw the question forming in Mel's eyes and wanted to clamp a hand over her mouth before she could ask it.

'Are you going to tattoo someone?'

Jaz glanced briefly at him, then back to Mel. 'Yes.'

He wondered why she sounded so reluctant to admit it. One thing was clear—she did not want them here.

Her sadness beat at him like a living thing. He remembered what had happened to Frieda. *She has her friends.*

'Can I watch?'

Jaz crouched back down to Mel's level. 'I don't think that's a good idea, Melly, and—'

'I don't mind.' The man called Jeff spoke quietly, but somehow his words filled the entire room.

'Are you getting the tattoo?' Mel breathed, awe audible in every word.

'I'm getting a picture of my little girl tattooed here.' Jeff touched a hand to the top of his left arm.

'Where is she? Can we play?'

He shook his head. 'She's a long way away.'

Melly bit her lip. 'Is it going to hurt?'

'Yes.'

'Will it help if I hold your hand?'

'Yes, it will.' With a glance at Connor, Jeff picked Melly up in his great burly arms. Connor sensed that with just one word or look from him, Jeff would release Mel in an instant, but something in the man's face and manner, something in the way Jaz regarded him, held Connor still.

Then they all moved to the back of the shop.

The tattoo took nearly two hours. Connor had never seen anything like it in his life. Beneath Jaz's fingers, a young girl's face came alive.

This wasn't just any simple tattoo. It was an indelible photograph captured on this man's arm for ever.

It was a work of art.

Mel watched Jaz's movements quietly, solemnly. She held Jeff's hand, stroked it every now and again. Finally she moved to where Connor sat, slid onto his lap and rested her head against his shoulder. He held her tight, though for the life of him he couldn't explain why. Her relaxed posture and even breathing eventually told him she'd fallen asleep.

At last, Jaz set aside her tools and stretched her arms back above her head. She held up a mirror for Jeff to view the finished tattoo. 'Thank you,' he said simply.

Jaz leant across then and placed a kiss in the centre of Jeff's forehead. 'May she live in your heart for ever,' she whispered.

That was when Connor realised why he held Melly so tight.

That tattoo wasn't a work of art. It was a memorial.

'Cherish her,' Jeff said with a nod at the sleeping child.

'I will,' he promised.

Then Jeff left the room, closely followed by Mac, and Connor expelled one long breath. He reached out and touched Jaz's hand. 'That was the most amazing thing I've ever seen.' He didn't smile. He couldn't. But he wanted her to know how much he admired her skill and generosity.

When she turned, he could see the strain the last two hours had put on her—the overwhelming responsibility to do her absolute best work, not to make a mistake. It showed in her pallor, the lines around her eyes and mouth.

He adjusted the child in his arms, rose and put one arm around Jaz's shoulders. 'Let me take you home.'

For a moment he thought she would lean into him, but then she stiffened and edged away. 'Mac will take me home, thanks all the same. Enjoy the rest of your day, Connor.'

Before she could move fully away, Melly stirred, unwrapped an arm from around her father's neck and wound it around Jaz's. It brought Jaz in close to Connor again—her arm touching his arm, his scent clogging her senses. The more of him she breathed in, the more it chased her weariness away.

'That was way wicked!' Melly said.

A spurt of laughter sprang from Jaz's lips at the sheer unexpectedness of Melly's words. She tried to draw back a little to stare into Melly's face. Melly wouldn't let her draw back any further than that. 'Where did you pick up that expression?'

'Carmen Sears. She looked after me for a couple of hours yesterday and I think she's way wicked too.'

Jaz grinned. She couldn't help it. Although she kept her gaze on Melly's face, from the corner of her eye she could see Connor's lips kick up too. Her heart pounded against the walls of her chest as if her ribcage had shrunk.

'Can we go on our picnic now, Daddy?'

'Your wish is my command.'

'I want Jaz to come on our picnic too.'

Jaz stiffened. She tried to draw away but Melly tightened her hold and wouldn't let her go. Oh, heck! Connor had told her he didn't want her as part of Melly's life. She should imagine that included attending picnics with her.

'Princess, your wish is *my* every command,' Connor started.

'You're going to say no.'

Melly's bottom lip wobbled. It wouldn't have had such a profound effect on Jaz if she hadn't sensed Melly's valiant effort to hide it. Connor's Adam's apple bobbed.

'Sweetheart, Jaz isn't anyone's to command. She's her own princess. We don't have the right to tell her what to do.'

Mel leaned in close to her father and whispered, 'But Jaz might like to come.'

He hesitated. He nodded. Then he smiled. 'I guess you'd better ask her, then.'

'Princess Jaz, would you like to come on a picnic with us?' She turned pleading eyes on Jaz. 'Please?'

Thank you, Connor Reed! So she had to play bad guy, huh? She wondered if she could lie convincingly enough not to hurt Melly's feelings. The hope in the child's face turned Jaz's insides to... marshmallow.

'I would love to come on a picnic with you, Princess Melly...' That wasn't a lie. 'But I'm very tired.' That wasn't a lie either. 'And I really should get back to the bookshop.' That was only half a lie.

'But you're still sad!'

Melly's grip eased, but she didn't let go. Her bottom lip wobbled again, making Jaz gulp. If Melly cried...

'Please come along with us, Jaz.'

Connor's voice, warm and golden, slid through to her very core. Her decidedly marshmallow core.

'I'd like you to come along too.'

She had to meet his gaze. Those words, that tone, demanded it. Her breath hitched. His autumn-tinted eyes tempted her...in every way possible.

She shouldn't go.

He couldn't really want her to tag along.

'Bonnie and Gail have the shop under control,' Mac said from the doorway. 'Go on the picnic, Jaz, it'll do you good.'

Three sets of eyes watched her expectantly. 'I...' Exhilaration raced through her veins. 'I think a picnic sounds perfect.'

'Good.'

If anything, Connor's eyes grew warmer.

Oh, dear Lord. What had she just agreed to?

Melly struggled out of her father's arms to throw her arms around Jaz's middle. 'Yay! Thank you.'

She smoothed Melly's hair back behind her ears. 'No, sweetheart, *thank you* for inviting me along. It'll be a real treat.'

She glanced up at Connor and for some reason her tongue tried to stick fast to the roof of her mouth. 'I'll…umm…just go grab my things.'

In the end, Melly decided it was too far to go to the botanic gardens and chose a picnic spot near Katoomba Cascades instead. Jaz couldn't remember a time when egg-and-lettuce sandwiches or apple turnovers had tasted so good.

After they'd eaten, they walked down to the cascades. The day was still and clear and cool. Jaz drank in the scenery like a starving woman. She hadn't forgotten how beautiful the mountains were, but her recollections had been overshadowed by… other memories.

Melly's chatter subsided abruptly when they returned to the picnic area. She stared at the children playing in the playground—two swings, a tiny fort with a climbing frame and a slippery dip—and the hunger in her face made Jaz's heart twist.

Melly swung around, her gaze spearing straight to Jaz's, a question in her eyes that brought Jaz's childhood crashing back—the crippling shyness… the crippling loneliness.

She made herself smile, nodded towards the playground. 'Why don't you go over and make friends?'

Then she remembered Connor. Not that she'd ever forgotten him. 'We don't have to go home yet, do we?'

'This is Princess Melly day.' He spread his arms as if that said it all.

Jaz wished he hadn't spread his arms quite so wide or in that particular fashion. If she took just one step towards him she'd find herself encompassed by those arms.

A small hand slipped inside Jaz's, hauling her back. Melly stared up at her with such trust in her autumn-tinted eyes—eyes the spitting image of Connor's—that it stole her breath.

'But what do I say?' Melly whispered.

Jaz dropped her duffel bag to the grass and knelt down beside Melly. She took a second look at the children playing in the playground. Tourists. 'I think you should go over and say: Hello, I'm Melly and I live near here. Where do you live? And then…' Jaz racked her brain. She remembered her own childhood. She could sense Connor watching them intently, but she did what she could to ignore him for the moment. 'Remember that story we read—was it Tuesday or Wednesday? The one with the wood sprites and the water nymphs.'

Melly nodded.

'Well, perhaps you could tell them about the wood sprites and water nymphs that live in the Katoomba Cascades.' She nodded her head in the direction of the cascades. 'I'm sure they'd love to hear about that.'

Melly's face lit up. 'Can I go play, Daddy?'

He spread his arms again. It made Jaz gulp. 'Is your name Princess Melly?'

Melly giggled and raced off.

Connor lowered himself to the grass beside Jaz, stretched out on his side. 'Thank you.'

'I…' Her tongue had gone and glued itself to the roof of her mouth again.

'You said exactly the right thing.' He frowned. 'How'd you do that?'

Her tongue unglued itself. 'Why, what would you have said?'

'I'd have probably told her to just play it by ear.'

Jaz shook her head. 'I remember what it was like to be Melanie's age…and shy. I'd have wanted some clear instructions or suggestions about how to get the initial conversation started. You can play it by ear after that.'

Connor watched Melly. 'It seems to be working.'

Warmth wormed through her. 'I'm glad. She's a delightful little girl, Connor. You must be very proud of her.'

He glanced up at her. 'I am.'

She gripped her hands together. 'I'm sorry I came along today,' she blurted out. But it was partly his fault. He'd caught her at a weak moment.

He shot up into a sitting position. 'Why?' he barked. 'Haven't you had a nice time?'

'Yes, of course, but…' She stared back at him

helplessly. 'But you didn't want me as part of Melly's life, remember? I was supposed to keep my distance.' She lifted her hands, then let them fall back to her lap. 'But I didn't know how to say no to her.' She glared. 'And you didn't help.'

She didn't know if it was a grimace or a smile that twisted his lips. 'She wanted you to come along so badly. I didn't know how to say no to her either.'

What about him? Had he really wanted her to come along?

She halted that thought in its tracks. She didn't care what Connor wanted.

'I seem to recall you saying you didn't want me as part of your life either.'

She wrinkled her nose. 'That was just me wanting to say something mean back to you.' It had been about erecting defences.

'It wasn't mean. It was you telling the truth, wasn't it?'

She had no intention of letting him breach those defences. 'Yes.' She pulled in a breath. 'There's a lot of history between us, Connor.'

He nodded.

'And I have no intention of revisiting it.'

'History never repeats?' he asked.

'Something like that.'

'For what it's worth, I think you're right.' He was quiet for a long moment, his eyes on Melly. 'It doesn't mean you and Mel can't be friends, though, does it?'

She blinked. 'But you didn't want me to…'

'For better or worse, Melly likes you, she identifies with you.' He met her gaze head-on. 'But can you promise me that you won't leave again the way you did the last time?'

'Yes, I can promise that.' She'd grown up since those days. 'It's funny, you know, but it's nice to be back.' She gestured to the view spread out before them. 'I've missed all this. When I do get the bookshop back on its feet, I mean to come back for visits.'

She'd promised Gwen.

She'd promise Melly too.

'I have no intention of hurting your little girl, Connor.'

'I know that.'

She turned and stared back out at the view.

CHAPTER SEVEN

THE hunger in Jaz's face as she stared out over the valley made Connor's gut clench.

This was her home. She might not be ready to admit that to herself yet, but the truth was as clear to him as the nose on her face…and the fullness of her lips.

He tried to drag his mind from her lips, from thoughts of kissing her. Jaz had made her position clear—there would be no him and her again.

He didn't know why that should make him scowl. It was what he wanted too.

No, he wanted to kiss her. He was honest enough to admit that much. But she was right. There was no future for them.

But now that she was back in Clara Falls, she shouldn't have to leave in twelve months' time. Not if she didn't want to.

He thought back to Mac—the cheek kisser; Mac of the tattoo parlour. He rolled his shoulders.

'You're good with kids.' Did she plan to have children of her own?

She turned back. He could tell she was trying to hold back a grin. 'You sound surprised.'

'Guess I've never really thought about it before.' He paused. 'You and Mac seem close.'

Her lips twisted. She all but cocked an eyebrow. 'We are. He and his wife Bonnie are my best friends.'

He felt like a transparent fool. He rushed on before she could chide him for getting too personal. 'What are your plans for when you return to your real life in the city?'

She blinked and he shrugged, suddenly and strangely self-conscious—like Mel in her attempts to make new friends. 'You said that returning to run the bookshop was a temporary glitch.'

'It is.'

She eased back on her hands, shifted so she no longer sat on her knees, so she could stretch the long length of her legs out in front of her. Without thinking, he reached out to swipe the leaves from her trouser legs.

She stiffened. He pulled his hand back with a muttered, 'Sorry.'

'Not a problem.'

Her voice came out all tight and strangled. Oh, yeah, there was a problem all right. The same problem there had always been between them— that heat. But it hadn't solved things between them eight years ago and it wouldn't solve anything now.

He just had to remember not to touch her.

'Your plans?' he prompted when she didn't unstiffen.

'Oh, yes.' She relaxed. She waved to Melly on the slippery dip. She didn't look at him; she stared out at the view—it was a spectacular view. He didn't know if her nonchalance was feigned or not, but it helped ease the tenseness inside him a little—enough for him to catch his breath.

He made himself stare out at the view too. It *was* spectacular.

Not as spectacular—

Don't go there.

'I mean to open an art gallery.'

He stared at her. Every muscle in his body tensed up again. 'An art gallery?' An ache stretched through him. He ignored it. 'But don't you run a tattoo parlour?'

'And a bookshop,' she reminded him.

She smiled. Not at him but at something she saw in the middle distance. 'Mac and I financed the tattoo parlour together, but Mac is the one in charge of its day-to-day running. I'm more of a…guest artist.'

The thought made him smile.

'I'm pretty much a silent partner these days.'

'Perhaps that's what you need at the bookshop—a partner?'

She swung around. 'I hadn't thought of that.' Then, 'No.' She gave a decisive shake of her head. 'The bookshop is all I have left of my mother.'

'And you don't want to share?'

Her eyes became hooded. 'It's my responsibility, that's all.' She turned back to the view.

'So the art gallery, that would be your real baby?'

She lifted one shoulder. 'I guess.'

'Where are planning to set it up?'

'I'd only just started looking for premises when Mum—'

She broke off. His heart burned in sympathy.

'I found wonderful premises at Bondi Beach.'

Despite the brightness of her voice, her pain slid in beneath his skin like a splinter of polished hardwood. He wanted to reach for her, only he knew she wouldn't accept his comfort.

He clenched his hands. 'Bondi?' He tried to match her brightness.

'Yes, but I'm afraid the rent went well beyond my budget.'

'I bet.' It suddenly occurred to him that the rents in the Blue Mountains weren't anywhere near as exorbitant as those in the city.

'An art gallery…' He couldn't finish the sentence. All the brightness had drained from his voice. He could see her running this hypothetical gallery, could almost taste her enthusiasm and drive. He could see her paintings hanging on the walls. He could—

'Which brings me to another point.' She turned. Her eyes burned in her face as she fixed him with a glare. 'You!'

He stared back. Somewhere in the background he heard Melly's laughter, registered that she was safe and happy at the moment. 'Me?' What had he done?

She dragged her duffel bag towards her. The bag she'd refused to leave in the car. The one she hadn't allowed him to carry for her on their walk. She'd treated it as if it contained something precious. He'd thought it must hold her tattooing gear. He blinked when she slapped something down on his knees.

A sketch pad!

Bile rose up through him when she pushed a pencil into his hand. 'Draw, Connor.'

Panic gripped him.

She opened the sketch pad. 'Draw,' she ordered again.

She reached over and shook his hand, the one that held the pencil, and he went cold all over.

'No!'

He tried to rise, but she grabbed hold of his arm and wouldn't let it go.

'I don't draw any more,' he ground out, trying to beat back the darkness that threatened him.

'Nonsense!'

'For pity's sake, Jaz, I—'

'You're scared.'

It was a taunt, a challenge. It made him grit his

teeth together in frustration. His fingers around the pencil felt as fat and useless as sausages. 'I gave it up,' he ground out.

'Then it's time you took it back up again.'

Anger shot through him. 'You want to see how bad I've become, is that what this is about?' Did she want some kind of sick triumph over him?

Her eyes travelled across his face. Her chin lifted. 'If that's what it takes.'

Then her eyes became gentle and it was like a punch to the gut. 'Please?' she whispered.

All he could smell was the sweet scent of wattle.

He gripped the pencil so hard it should've snapped. If she wanted him to draw, then he'd draw. Maybe when she saw how ham-fisted he'd become she'd finally leave him in peace. 'What do you want me to draw?'

'That tree.' She pointed.

Connor studied it for a moment—its scale, the dimensions. They settled automatically into his mind. That quick summing up, it was one of the things that made him such a good builder. But he didn't deceive himself. He had no hope of being a halfway decent artist any more.

It didn't mean he wanted Jaz forcing that evidence in front of him. She sat beside him, arms folded, and an air of expectation hung about her. He knew he could shake her off with ease and simply walk away, but such an action would betray the importance he placed on this simple act of drawing.

He dragged a hand down his face. Failure now meant the death of something good deep down inside him. If Jaz sensed how much it meant—and he had the distinct impression she knew exactly what it meant—he had no intention of revealing it by storming away from her. He'd face failure with grace.

Maybe, when this vain attempt was over, the restlessness that plagued him on bright, still days would disappear. His lips twisted. They said there was a silver lining in every cloud, didn't they?

Just when he sensed Jaz's impatience had become too much for her, he set pencil to paper.

And failed.

He couldn't draw any more. The lines he made were too heavy, the sense of balance and perspective all wrong…no flow. He tried to tell himself he'd expected it, but darkness pressed against the backs of his eyes. Jaz peered across at what he'd done and he had to fight the urge to hunch over it and hide it from her sight.

She tore the page from the sketch pad, screwed it into a ball and set it on the ground beside her. Sourness filled his mouth. He'd tried to tell her.

'Draw the playground.'

He gaped at her.

She shrugged. 'Well…what are you waiting for?' She waved to Melly again.

Was she being deliberately obtuse? He stared at the playground, with all its primary colours. The shriek of Melly's laughter filled the air, and that ache pressed against him harder. In a former life he'd have painted that in such brilliant colours it would steal one's breath.

But that was then.

He set pencil to paper again but his fingers refused to follow the dictates of his brain. He'd turned his back on art to become a carpenter. It only seemed right that his fingers had turned into blocks of wood. Nevertheless, he kept trying because he knew Jaz didn't want to triumph over him. She wanted him to draw again—to know its joys, its freedoms once more…to bow to its demands and feel whole.

When she discovered he could no longer draw, she would mourn that loss as deeply as he did.

When he finally put the pencil down, she peeled the page from the sketch pad…and that drawing followed the same fate as its predecessor—screwed up and set down beside her.

'Draw that rock with the clump of grass growing around it.'

He had to turn ninety degrees but it didn't matter. A different position did not bring any latent talent to the fore.

She screwed that picture up too when he was finished with it. Frustration started to oust his sense of defeat. 'Look, Jaz, I—'

'Draw the skyway.'

It meant turning another ninety degrees. 'What's the point?' he burst out. 'I—'

She pushed him—physically. Anger balled in the pit of his stomach.

'Stop your whining,' she snapped.

His hands clenched. 'You push me again…'

'And you'll what?' she taunted.

He flung the sketch pad aside. 'I've had enough!'

'Well, I haven't!' She retrieved the sketch pad and slapped it back on his knees. 'Draw the skyway, Connor!'

Draw the skyway? He wished he were out on that darn skyway right now!

His fingers flew across the page. The sooner this was over, the better. He didn't glance at the drawing when he'd finished. He just tossed the sketch pad at Jaz, not caring if she caught it or not.

She did catch it. And she stared at it for a long, long time. Bile rose from his stomach to burn his throat.

'Better,' she finally said. She didn't tear it from the sketch pad. She didn't screw it up into a ball.

'Don't humour me, Jaz.' The words scraped out of his throat, raw with emotion, but he didn't care. He could deal with defeat but he would not stand for her pity.

In answer, she gave him one of the balled rejects. 'Look at it.'

He was too tired to argue. He smoothed it out and

grimaced. It was the picture of the playground. It was dreadful, horrible…a travesty.

'No,' she said when he went to ball it up again. 'Look at it.'

He looked at it.

'Now look at this.' She stood up and held his drawing of the skyway in front of her.

Everything inside him stilled. It was flawed, vitally flawed in a lot of respects, and yet… He'd captured something there—a sense of freedom and escape. Jaz was right. It was better.

Was it enough of an improvement to count, though?

He glanced up into her face. She pursed her lips and surveyed where he sat. 'This is all wrong.' She tapped a finger against her chin for a moment, then her face cleared. She seized her duffel bag. 'Come with me.'

She led him to a nearby stand of trees. He followed her. His heart thudded in his chest, part of him wanted to turn tail and run, but he followed.

'Sit there.'

She pointed to the base of a tree. Its position would still give him a good, clear view of Melly playing. Melly waved. He waved back.

He settled himself against the tree.

'Good.' She handed him the sketch pad and pencil again. She pulled a second sketch pad and more pencils from her bag and settled herself on the ground to his left, legs crossed. She looked so familiar, hunched over like that, Connor thought he'd been transported back eight years in time.

She glanced across at him. 'Bend your knees like you used to do…as if you're sitting against that old tree at our lookout.'

Our lookout. Richardson's Peak—out of the way and rarely visited. They'd always called it *their lookout.* He tried to hold back the memories.

Jaz touched a hand to the ground. 'See, I'm sitting on the nearby rock.'

It wasn't rock. It was grass, but Connor gave in, adjusted his back and legs, and let the memories flood through him. 'What do you want me to draw?'

'The view.'

Panoramas had always been his speciality, but he wasn't quite sure where to start now.

He wasn't convinced that this wasn't a waste of time.

'Close your eyes.'

She whispered the command. She closed her eyes so he closed his eyes too. It might shut out the ache that gripped him whenever he looked at her.

It didn't, but her voice washed over him, soft and low, soothing him. 'Remember what it was like at the lookout?' she murmured. 'The grand vista spread out in front of us and the calls of the birds…the scent of eucalyptus in the air…'

All Connor could smell was wattle, and he loved it, dragged it into his lungs greedily.

'Remember how the sun glinted off the leaves, how it warmed us in our sheltered little spot, even when the wind played havoc with everything else around us?'

His skin grew warm, his fingers relaxed around the pencil.

'Now draw,' she whispered.

He opened his eyes and drew.

On the few occasions he glanced across at her, he found her hunched over her sketch pad, her fingers moving with the same slow deliberation he remembered from his dreams.

Time passed. Connor had no idea how long they drew but, when he finally set aside his pencil, he glanced up to find the shadows had lengthened and Jaz waiting for him. He searched the picnic ground for Melly.

'Just over there.' Jaz nodded and he found Melly sitting on the grass with her new friends.

'Finished?' she asked.

He nodded.

'May I see?'

She asked in the same shy way she'd have asked eight years ago. He smiled. He felt tired and alive and…free. 'If you want.'

She was by his side in a second. She turned back to the first page in the sketch pad. He'd lost count of how many pictures he'd drawn. His fingers had flown as if they'd had to make up for the past eight years of shackled inactivity.

Jaz sighed and chuckled and teased him, just like she used to do. She pointed to one of the drawings and laughed. 'Is that supposed to be a bird?'

'I was trying to give the impression of time flying.'

'It needs work,' she said with a grin.

He returned her grin. 'So do my slippery dips.'

'Yep, they do.'

The laughter in her voice lifted him.

'But look at how you've captured the way the light shines through the trees here. It's beautiful.'

She turned her face to meet his gaze fully and light trembled in her eyes. 'You can draw again, Connor.'

Her exultation reached out and wrapped around him. *He could draw again.*

He couldn't help himself. He cupped one hand around the back of her head, threaded his fingers through her hair and drew her lips down to his and kissed her—warm, firm…brief. Then he released her because he knew he couldn't take too much of that. 'Thank you. If you hadn't badgered me…' He gestured to the sketch pad.

She drew back, her eyes wide and dazed. 'You're welcome, but—' she moistened her lips '—I didn't do much.'

Didn't do much.

'You had it in you all the time. You just had to let it out, that's all.' She reached up, touched her fingers to her lips. She pulled them away again when she realised he watched her. Her breathing had quickened, grown shallow. She lifted her chin and glared at him. 'If you ever turn your back on your gift again, it will desert you. For ever!'

He knew she was right.

He knew he wanted to kiss her again.

As if she'd read that thought in his face, Jaz drew back. 'It's getting late. We'd better start thinking about making tracks.'

She didn't want him to kiss her.

He remembered all the reasons why he shouldn't kiss her.

'You're right.'

He tried to tell himself it was for the best.

Jaz found Connor sitting on the sales counter munching what looked like a Danish pastry when she let herself into the bookshop at eight o'clock on Monday morning.

'Hey, Jaz.'

She blinked. 'Hello.'

What was he doing here? Shouldn't he be upstairs working on her flat? The absence of hammering and sawing suddenly registered. Her heart gave a funny little leap. 'Is my flat ready?'

'We're completing the final touches today and tomorrow, and then it'll be ready for the painters and carpet layers.'

She'd already decided to paint it herself. It'd give her something to do. Funnily enough, though, considering how she'd expected her time in Clara Falls to drag, this last week had flown.

She'd have the carpet laid in double-quick time. She wasn't spending winter in the mountains on bare floorboards. Once her furniture was delivered from Connor's, she could paint and decorate the flat in her own good time.

She edged around behind the counter to place her handbag in one of the drawers and tried to keep Connor's scent from addling her brain. Handbag taken care of, she edged back out again—his scent too evocative, too tempting. It reminded her of that kiss. That brief thank you of a kiss that had seared her senses.

Forget about the kiss.

'Did you want me for something?'

His eyes darkened at her words and her mouth went dry. He slid off the counter and moved towards her—a hunter stalking its prey. He wore such a look of naked intensity that… Good Lord! He didn't mean to kiss her again, did he? She wanted to turn and flee but her legs wouldn't work. He reached out…took her hand…and…

And plonked a paper bag into it.

'I thought you might like one.'

Like one…? She glanced into the bag. A pastry—he'd given her a pastry. In fact, he'd handed her a whole bag full of them. 'There's at least a dozen pastries in here.'

'Couldn't remember what filling you preferred.'

She almost called him a liar. Then remembered her manners. And her common sense. Who knew how much he'd forgotten in eight years?

But once upon a time he'd teased her about her apple pie tastes.

She wished she could forget.

Her hand inched into the bag for an apple Danish. She pulled it back at the last moment. 'I don't want a pastry!'

She wanted Connor and his disturbing presence and soul-aching scent out of her shop. She tossed the bag of Danishes onto the counter with an insouciance that would've made Mr Sears blanch. 'Why are you here, Connor? What do you want?'

'I want to thank you.'

'For?'

'For your advice to me about Melly. For making me draw again.'

He'd already thanked her for that—*with a kiss!*

She didn't want that kind of thanks, thank you very much. Her heart thud-thudded at the thought of a repeat performance, calling her a liar.

'I think I've made a start on winning back Mel's trust.'

'If Saturday's evidence is anything to go by, I think you're right.' And she was glad for him.

Glad for Melly, she amended.

Okay—she shifted her weight from one foot to the other, slid her hands into the pockets of her trousers—she was glad for both of them, but she was gladder for Melly.

'Look, Jaz, I've been thinking…'

Her mouth went dry. Something in his tone… 'About?'

'What if you didn't leave Clara Falls at the end of this twelve months?'

Her jaw dropped.

He raised both hands. 'Now hear me out before you start arguing.'

She supposed she'd have to because she appeared to have lost all power of speech.

'What if you opened your art gallery in the mountains? It has two advantages over the city. One— lower rents. And two—you'd get the passing tourist trade.' He spread his arms in *that* way. 'Surely that has to be good.'

Of course it was good, but—

'There's an even bigger tourist trade in Sydney,' she pointed out.

'And you'll only attract them if you find premises on or around the harbour.'

She could never afford that.

'What's more, if you settle around here you'll be close to the bookshop if you're needed, and it's an easy commute to the city on the days you're needed in at the tattoo parlour.'

He spread his arms again. 'If you think about it, it makes perfect sense.'

'No, it doesn't!'

He didn't look the least fazed by her outburst. 'Sure it does. And, Jaz, Clara Falls needs people like you.'

She gaped at him then. 'It's official—Connor Reed has rocks in his head.' She stalked through the shop to the kitchenette. 'People like me?' She snorted. 'Get real!'

'People who aren't afraid of hard work,' Connor said right behind her. 'People who care.'

'You're pinning the wrong traits on the wrong girl.' She seized the jug and filled it.

He leant his hip against the sink. 'I don't think so. In fact, I know I'm not.'

She would not look into those autumn-tinted eyes. After a moment's hesitation, she lifted a mug in his direction in a silent question. Common courtesy demanded she at least offer him coffee. After all, he had supplied the pastries.

'Love one,' he said with that infuriating cheerfulness that set her teeth on edge.

He didn't speak while she made the coffees. She handed him one and made the mistake of glancing into those eyes. Things inside her heated up and melted down, turned to mush.

No mush, she ordered.

That didn't work so she dragged her gaze away to stare out of the window.

'Clara Falls needs you, Jaz.'

'But I don't need Clara Falls.'

He remained silent for so long that she finally turned and met his gaze. The gentleness in his eyes made her swallow.

'That's where I think you're wrong. I think you need Clara Falls as much as you ever did. I think you're still searching for the same security, the same acceptance now as you did when you were a teenager.'

Very carefully, she set her coffee down because throwing it all over Connor would be very poor form…and dangerous. The coffee was hot. Very hot. 'You have no idea what you're talking about.'

'You might not want to admit it, but you know I'm right.'

'Garbage! You're the guy with rocks in his head, remember?'

'Frieda knew it too. It's why she wanted you to come back.'

Her mother's name was like a punch to the solar plexus. She wanted to swing away but there wasn't much swinging room in the kitchenette, and to leave meant walking—squeezing—past Connor. If he tried to prevent her from leaving, it would bring them slam-bang up against each other—chest-to-chest, thigh-to-thigh. She wasn't risking that.

She tossed her head. 'How do you know what my mother thought?'

He glanced down into his coffee and it hit her

then. 'You…the pair of you talked about me… behind my back?'

'We'd have been happy to do it to your face, Jaz, if you'd ever bothered to come back.'

Guilt swamped her. And regret. How could she have put her mother through so much? Frieda had only ever wanted Jaz's happiness. Jaz had returned that love by refusing to set foot back in Clara Falls. She'd returned that love by breaking her mother's heart.

Connor swore at whatever he saw in her face. He set his mug down and took a step towards her. Jaz seized her coffee, held it in a gesture that warned him he'd wear it if he took another step. 'Don't even think about it!' If he touched her, she'd cry. She would not cry in front of him.

He settled back against the sink.

'I know I am responsible for my mother's death, Connor. Rubbing my nose in that fact, though, hardly seems the friendly thing to do.'

Frown lines dug furrows into his forehead, drew his eyebrows down low over his eyes. 'What the hell…! You are not responsible for Frieda's suicide.'

He believed that, she could tell. She lifted her chin. He could believe what he liked. She knew the truth.

He straightened. 'Jaz, I—'

'I don't particularly want to talk about this, Connor. And, frankly, no offence intended, but nothing you say will make the slightest scrap of difference.'

'How big are you going to let that chip on your shoulder grow before you let it bury you?'

'Chip?' Her mouth opened and closed but no other words would emerge.

'Fine, we won't talk about your mother, but we will talk about Clara Falls and the possibility of you staying on.'

'There is no possibility. It's not going to happen so just give it a rest.'

'You're not giving yourself or the town the slightest chance on this, Jaz. How fair is that?'

Fair? This had nothing to do with fair. This had to do with putting the past behind her.

'Have you come back to save your mother's shop? Or to damn it?'

How could he even ask her that?

'You need to start getting involved in the local community if you mean to save it. Even if you are only here for twelve months.'

She didn't have to do any such thing.

'The book fair is a start.'

He knew about—?

'You've done a great job on the posters.'

Oh, yes.

'But you need to let the local people see that you're not still the rebel Goth girl.'

Darn it! He had a point. She didn't want to admit it but he did have a point.

'You need to show people that you're all grown

up, that you're a confident and capable business-woman now.'

Was that how he saw her?

She dragged her hands back through her hair to help her think, but as Connor followed that action she wished she'd left her hands exactly where they were. Memories pounded at her. She remembered the way he used to run his fingers through her hair, the way he'd massaged her scalp, how it had soothed and seduced at the same time. And being a confident and capable businesswoman didn't seem any defence at all.

'The annual Harvest Ball is next Saturday night. I dare you to come as my date.'

He folded his arms. His eyes twinkled. He looked good enough to eat. She tried to focus her mind on what he'd said rather than...other things. 'Why?' Why did he want to take her to the ball?

'It'll reintroduce you to the local community, for a start, but also...it occurred to me that while it's all well and good for me to preach to you about staying here in Clara Falls and making it a better place, I should be doing that too. I think it's time Mr Sears had some competition for that councillor's spot, don't you?'

She stared at him. 'You're going to run for town councillor?'

'Yep.'

Being seen with her, taking her to the ball, would

make a definite statement about what he believed in, about the kind of town he wanted Clara Falls to be. Going to the ball would help her quash nasty rumours about drugs and whatnot too.

'Our going to the ball…' she moistened her lips '…that would be business, right?'

She'd made her position clear on Saturday during the picnic. He'd agreed—history didn't repeat. For some reason, though, she needed to double-check.

'That's right.' He frowned. 'What else would it be?'

'N…nothing.'

The picture of Frieda she'd started on the bookshop's wall grew large in her mind. The darn picture she couldn't seem to finish. *Have you come back to save your mother's shop? Or to damn it?*

She wanted to save it. She had to save it.

She shot out her hand. 'I'll take you up on that dare.'

He clasped her hand in warm work-roughened fingers. Then he bent down and kissed her cheek, drenched her in his scent and his heat. 'Good,' he said softly. 'I'll pick you up at seven next Saturday evening.'

'Well—' she reclaimed her hand, smoothed down the front of her trousers '—I guess that's settled, then. Oh! Except I'm going to need more of my things.' Something formal to wear for a start and her strappy heels.

'Why don't I run you around to my place after work this afternoon and you can pick out what you need?'

'Are you sure?' She wasn't a hundred per cent certain what she meant by that only…she remembered the way he hadn't wanted her at his home last week. She added a quick, 'You're not busy?'

'No. And I've arranged for Carmen to mind Mel for a couple of hours this afternoon.'

Had he been so certain she'd say yes?

You did say yes.

She moistened her lips again. 'Thank you, I'd appreciate that.'

She didn't bother trying to stifle the curiosity that balled inside her. She just hoped it didn't show. It didn't make any sense, but she was dying to know where Connor lived now. Not that it had anything to do with her, of course.

Of course it didn't.

'I'll pick you up about five-fifteen this afternoon.'

Then he was gone.

Jaz reached up and touched her cheek. The imprint of his lips still burned there. A business arrangement, she told herself. That was all this was—a business arrangement.

Jaz slipped into the car the moment Connor pulled it to a halt outside the bookshop. At precisely five-fifteen.

'Hi.'

'Hi.'

That was the sum total of their conversation.

Until he swung the car into the drive of Rose Cottage approximately three minutes later and turned off the ignition. 'Here we are,' he finally said.

She gaped at him. She turned back to stare at the house. 'You bought Rose Cottage?'

Most old towns had a Rose Cottage, and as a teenager Jaz had coveted this one. Single-storey sandstone, wide verandas, established gardens, roses lining the drive, picket fence—it had been her ideal of the perfect family home.

It still was.

And now it belonged to Connor? A low whistle left her. Business must be booming if he could afford this. 'You bought Rose Cottage,' she repeated. He'd known how she'd felt about it.

'That's right.' His face had shuttered, closed.

Had he bought it because of her or in spite of her?

'Your things are in there.'

She dragged her gaze from the house to follow the line of his finger to an enormous garage.

He wasn't going to invite her inside the house?

She glanced into his face and her anticipation faded. He had no intention of inviting her inside, of giving her the grand tour. She swallowed back a lump of disappointment…and a bigger lump of hurt. The disappointment she could explain. She did what she could to ignore the hurt.

'Shall we go find what you need?'

'Yes, thank you, that would be lovely.'

She followed him into the garage, blinked when he flicked a switch and flooded the cavernous space with stark white light. Her things stood on the left and hardly took up any space at all. 'All I need is—'

She stopped short. Then veered off in the opposite direction.

'Jaz, your stuff is over here!'

She heard him, but she couldn't heed his unspoken command. She couldn't stop.

Her feet did slow, though, as she moved along the aisle of handmade wood-turned furniture that stood there—writing desks, coffee tables, chests. She marvelled at their craftsmanship, at the attention paid to detail, at the absolute perfection of each piece.

'You made these?'

'Yes.'

The word left him, clipped and short.

He didn't need to explain. Jaz understood immediately. This was what he'd thrown himself into when he'd given up his drawing and painting.

'Connor, you didn't give up your art. You just… redirected it.'

He didn't say anything.

'These pieces are amazing, beautiful.' She knelt down in front of a wine rack, reached out and trailed her fingers across the wood. 'You've been selling some of these pieces to boutiques in Sydney, haven't you?'

'Yes.'

'I came across a piece similar to this a couple of years back.' She forced herself upright. If she'd known then that Connor had made it she'd have moved heaven and earth to buy it.

'I went into that shop in my lunch hour every day for a week just to look at it.'

His face lost some of its hardness. 'Did you buy it?'

'No.' It had been beyond her budget. 'I couldn't justify the expense at the time.'

She sensed his disappointment, though she couldn't say how—the set of his shoulders or his lips, perhaps?

'Mind you,' she started conversationally, 'it did take a whole week of lecturing myself to be sensible…and if it had been that gorgeous book-case—' she motioned across to the next piece '—I'd have been lost…and horrendously in debt. Which is why I'm going to back away from it now, nice and slow.'

Finally he smiled back at her.

'My things!' She suddenly remembered why they were here. 'I'll just grab them and get out of your hair.'

He didn't urge her to take her time. He didn't offer to show her any of the other marvels lined up in the garage. She told herself she was a fool for hoping that he would.

CHAPTER EIGHT

WHEN Jaz opened the door to him on Saturday evening, Connor's jaw nearly hit the ground. She stood there in a floor-length purple dress and he swore he'd never seen anything more perfect in his life. The dress draped the lines of her body in Grecian style folds to fasten between her breasts with a diamanté brooch. It oozed elegance and sex appeal. It suited the confident, capable business-woman she'd become.

Ha! No, it didn't. Not in this lifetime. That dress did not scream professional businesswoman. The material flowed and ran over her body in a way that had his hands itching and his skin growing too tight for the rest of his body. It definitely wasn't business-like. What he wanted to do to Jaz in that dress def-initely wasn't businesslike.

He had to remind himself that the only kind of relationship Jaz wanted with him these days was businesslike.

He had to remind himself that that was what he wanted too.

'Hi, Connor.'

Gwen waved to him from the end of the hallway. It made him realise that he and Jaz hadn't spoken a word to each other yet. He took in Jaz's heightened colour, noted how her eyes glittered with an awareness that matched his own, and desire fire-balled in his groin. If they were alone, he'd back her up against a wall, mould each one of her delectable curves to the angles of his body and slake his hunger in the wet shine of her lips.

No, he wouldn't!

Bloody hell. *Get a grip, man. This is a business arrangement.* He tried to spell out the word in his head—B-U-S... It was a sort of business arrangement, he amended. He wanted to help Jaz the way she'd helped him. He wanted to prove to her that Clara Falls was more than Mr Sears and his pointed conservatism. He wanted her to see the good here— the way Frieda had. Instinct told him Jaz needed to do at least that much. If she wanted to leave at the end of twelve months after that, then all power to her.

He glanced down into her face and tried to harden himself against the soft promise of her lips...and the lush promise of her body.

Gwen strode down the hallway. 'Are you okay, Connor?'

He realised he still hadn't uttered a word.

'Uh…' He cleared his throat, ran a finger around the inside collar of his dress shirt. 'These things cut a man's windpipe in two. I feel as trussed up as a Sunday roast.'

'You look damn fine in it, though.'

'You're looking pretty stunning yourself,' manners made him shoot back at her. In truth, with Jaz in the same room he barely saw Gwen. He had a vague impression of red and that was about it.

Jaz folded her arms and glared at him. Man, what had he done now? He turned back to Gwen. 'Who's your date tonight, then?'

Gwen shook her head. 'I'm going stag this year. I don't want to be shackled to any man. Not when there'll be so many eligible males to choose from this evening.'

Fair enough. 'Need a lift?'

'No, thank you. I mean to be fashionably late.'

'Do you expect me to be shackled to you all evening?' Jaz demanded.

He stiffened. Yes, dammit!

He rolled his shoulders. No, dammit.

So much for relaxation. 'We arrive together. We leave together. We eat together. First dance and last dance.' He rattled each item off. They were non-negotiable as far as he was concerned. 'Fair enough?' he barked at her. They'd settle this before they left.

She didn't bat an eye. 'Fair enough,' she agreed.

The pulse at the base of his throat started to slow.

He found he could breathe again. He meant to negotiate more than two dances out of her, come hell or high water. He meant to hold her in his arms, enjoy the feel of her, safe in the knowledge that nothing could happen in such a public place.

He turned to find Gwen staring at him with narrowed eyes. He gulped. 'I…er…want her to schmooze,' he tried to explain.

'I just bet you do,' she returned with evil knowingness.

'I…' He couldn't think of a damn thing to say.

Jaz jumped in. 'Did you know that Connor is planning to challenge Gordon Sears for the town councillor position at the next election?'

Gwen's jaw dropped. 'Are you serious? But you're not some power-hungry nob.'

'No, he's not.' Satisfaction threaded through Jaz's voice. 'Which should make him the perfect candidate, don't you think?'

He stood a little straighter at her praise, pushed his shoulders back.

'It at least makes him better than Gordon Sears, but enough of that.' Gwen dismissed the subject with a wave of her hand. 'Make Jaz's day and tell her the move is complete.'

'It's all done.' His men had moved Jaz's things out of his garage and into her flat today. He hadn't helped move those things. Whenever he'd driven into the garage, walked through the garage, walked past the garage, and saw her things there, he'd had an insane urge to go through them to try and discover a clue as to how she'd spent the last eight years. He hadn't. He wouldn't. But he'd put himself out of temptation's way today and had taken Mel for a hot chocolate and another skyway ride instead. 'You can move in and start unpacking as early as tomorrow if you want.'

When he'd driven the van into the garage this afternoon and found all her things gone, it had left a hole inside him as big as the Jamison Valley. Why?

Because you're an idiot, that's why. Because you still want her.

He ground his teeth together. He'd made a lot of mistakes in the last eight years, but he wasn't making that one. Not again. He would not kiss Jaz. He would not make love to Jaz. He would not get involved with Jaz.

Never again.

He had to think of Mel. His daughter already adored Jaz more than he thought wise. He didn't want Mel thinking of Jaz as anything other than a friend.

It would be hard enough for Mel to cope with Jaz leaving in twelve months' time, let alone…

He ran a finger around the inside of his collar again. Let alone anything more. End of story.

'I'll move into the flat on Monday,' he heard Jaz tell Gwen. 'I'm hoping business will be brisk in the bookshop tomorrow.'

She was working tomorrow? They'd better not make it a late night then. His jaw tightened. Not that he'd intended on making it a late night.

He tried to get his brain onto business and away from the personal. 'How are the new staff members working out?' She'd spent the last four days training staff the recruitment agency in Katoomba had sent her.

'So well that I'm planning on taking Monday and Tuesday off to unpack and set the flat up properly. I'll only be a shout away if needed.'

'Good. It's about time you stopped working so hard and took a couple of days off. If you're not careful you'll make yourself ill.'

Her eyes widened and he thrust his hands in his pockets with a scowl. That comment had been way too personal. He started to spell *businesslike* out in his mind again.

Speculation fired to life in Gwen's face. She raised an eyebrow at Jaz. Jaz pressed her lips together and gave one tight shake of her head. Connor adjusted his tie. It seemed a whole lot tighter now than it had when he'd left home.

Gwen laughed. 'You two give off as much heat as you ever did.'

His collar tightened until he thought he'd choke. Jaz's eyes all but started from her head.

Jaz swung to him. 'Speaking of heat…'

He wondered if he'd ever breathe again.

'…is the town hall still heated? Or should I change into something warmer? Something with longer sleeves?'

'Don't change!' The words burst out of him with revealing rapidity.

He coughed and quickly overrode Gwen's triumphant 'Aha!'

He rapped out, 'It gets uncomfortably warm in the town hall. You'll be grateful for those short sleeves once the dancing starts.'

'Okay.' She gazed at him expectantly for a moment, then finally sighed. 'I'll get my handbag and wrap and then we can leave.'

The town hall was festooned with ribbons and pine cones, with fragrant boughs of eucalyptus. Beneath it all, Connor could smell the tantalising scent of wattle. He and Jaz paused as they crossed the threshold, and Connor had to bite back a grin when one section of the hall—Gordon Sears and his set—broke off their conversation around a table of hors d'oeuvres to turn and stare.

Actually…gaped summed it up more accurately.

Beside him, Jaz stiffened and he drew her hand into the crook of his arm, folded his hand over it and tried to convey to her that she wasn't alone. He hadn't brought her here to feed her to the lions. Her hand trembled beneath his, but she lifted her chin and planted a smile on her face, held herself tall and erect. That simple act of courage warmed him, made him stand taller and prouder too.

'I think it's safe to say that we've given them something to talk about for the rest of the night,' she quipped.

He released her hand to seize two glasses of champagne from the tray of a passing waiter and handed her one. 'Whereas we won't spare them another thought for the rest of the evening.'

She touched her glass to his. 'I'll drink to that.'

Her hair framed her face in a feathery style that highlighted high cheekbones and long-lashed eyes. He wanted to reach out and touch that hair, to run his fingers through it, cup a hand around the back of her head and draw her in close to—

He snapped upright, glanced around the room.

'Who should we schmooze with first?' she asked.

'This way.' With his hand in the small of her back, he turned her towards a knot of people on the opposite side of the room and tried to ignore the way the heat from her body branded his fingertips as it seeped through the thin material of her dress. With half a growl, he dragged his gaze from the seductive sway of her hips. That was when he saw Sam Hancock.

Sam Hancock without a date!

Sam and his sister hadn't sold the family home when their father had died, although neither one of them lived in Clara Falls now. They used the house as a weekender. Obviously Sam had decided to grace Clara Falls with his presence this particular weekend.

'Connor?'

Jaz's soft query drew him back, her blue-green eyes fathomless.

'I just saw your old friend Sam Hancock.' The observation didn't come out anywhere near as casual as he meant it to.

She stared at him. 'Did you want to go over and say hello?'

She'd promised to leave with him at the end of the night. He held fast to that. He tried to relax his hold on his champagne flute. She didn't crane her neck over his shoulder to catch a glimpse of Sam. She didn't push her glass of champagne into his hand and rush off to embrace her former lover. The tightness in his chest eased a fraction.

Which sent warning bells clanging through him. He didn't want Jaz for himself, but he didn't want other men having her either?

Or was it just Sam Hancock?

He tested the theory, tried to imagine Jaz with some other man in the room—any man. His teeth ground together. No, it wasn't just Sam Hancock.

Charming. He was a dog in the manger.

Only…he did want her for himself, didn't he?

'Connor!'

He snapped to.

'I thought we were supposed to be schmoozing.

Stop glaring around the room like that. You won't win any votes with that look on your face.'

He laughed. He didn't mean to, but her words—the scolding—the warmth deep down in her eyes eased his tension. 'Come and meet the Barries.' He'd enjoy the night for what it was and nothing more.

Connor found that he did enjoy the evening. Jaz conversed easily with everyone he introduced her to. The Jaz of old hadn't had that kind of confidence or social poise. The Jaz of old would've held back and spent most of the night hiding behind him. The Jaz of old had been nothing more than a girl. This Jaz—the here and now version—was a strong, confident woman. Something told him she'd earned that self-possession.

It made her ten times more potent.

She ate dinner at the table beside him. They danced the first dance…and the second…and Connor almost breathed a sigh of relief when she excused herself to go and powder her nose. He needed oxygen—big time.

It didn't stop him from watching her as she made a circuit around the room, though. Along the way, people stopped her. Here and there, she stopped of her own accord. Then she stopped by Sam Hancock, who was sitting on his own, and Connor gripped a handful of linen tablecloth. Sam leapt to his feet and said something that made her laugh. She said something back that made him laugh. Then she kept walking.

She kept walking.

He released the tablecloth. If he hadn't been sitting he'd have fallen.

It hit him then—Jaz hadn't flirted with a single man here tonight. Frieda would've flirted with every man in the room. He saw the defence behind that tactic now too—by flirting with every man present, Frieda had managed to keep them all at arm's length. About the only man she hadn't flirted with was Gordon Sears.

His heart started to burn. Jaz was not made in the same mould as her mother. Had he got it wrong eight years ago?

He remembered the sight of her in Sam Hancock's arms, the words she'd uttered that had damned her. They still proved her guilt, her infidelity.

But, suddenly, he found he wasn't quite so sure of anything.

Jaz returned from the powder room to take her seat at the table beside Connor again. All the other couples from their table were dancing. She gulped. She prayed Connor wouldn't ask her to dance again. She wasn't sure how much more of that she could take, especially now they'd dimmed the lights.

'Enjoying yourself?'

'Yes.' And she meant it. 'It's been lovely meeting up with people again.'

He set a glass of punch down in front of her. 'Nonalcoholic,' he said before she could ask. 'I know you're working tomorrow.'

'Thank you.'

She didn't reach out for the drink because her fingers had gone suddenly boneless. He looked so sure and…male in his dinner suit. His body had grown harder in the eight years she'd been away. His shoulders had become broader, his thighs more powerful. And he still created an ache of need deep down inside her like he'd always done.

She hoped he wouldn't push the stay-in-Clara-Falls-for-ever-and-make-it-your-home thing again. She couldn't stay for ever in the same town as Connor Reed. It just wouldn't work.

One corner of his mouth kinked up but it didn't warm his eyes. 'You've schmoozed beautifully.'

She raised her eyes at the edge in his voice. 'Is that supposed to be a compliment?' she asked warily.

He frowned. 'Yes.'

'Sorry.' She hadn't meant to misinterpret his mood. 'I am having fun, but this really isn't my favourite kind of do.'

'What is?'

'Beer and pizza nights.' She sighed in longing. A beer and pizza night with a bunch of her friends would go down a treat at the moment.

Connor grinned and this time the gold flecks in his eyes came out to play. 'Well, there's not a soul in this room who'd sense you'd rather be anywhere else this evening. You've charmed everyone you've met.'

She smiled at that. 'Wonders will never cease, huh? The rebel Goth girl developing a few social graces after all.'

'It's quite a change, Jaz, even you have to admit that. Where did you go when you decided not to come back to Clara Falls? What did you do? How did you manage the…transformation?'

Jaz realised she'd been waiting for him to ask that question all night. 'After I left my aunt's I went to the airport, directly to the airport, I didn't pass go and I didn't collect two hundred dollars.'

He stared at her. Jaz shrugged. 'I went to America.'

He leant forward. 'Why America?'

She'd wanted to run as far away as possible. She'd wanted to start over in a place that didn't know her. And she'd needed to make a grand gesture. 'Would you believe me if I said—because I was young and stupid?'

He smiled. 'Young, yes, but never stupid.'

He was wrong about that. 'I strode into the airport and decided I was going to Europe or America. The travel agent must've thought me mad…or a criminal. I just asked for the first flight out. And that's how I ended up in LA with next to no money, no job and nowhere to stay. Believe me, that makes a girl start thinking on her feet pretty fast.'

'What did you do?'

'Rented a dingy hotel room for a week, bought a sketch pad and charcoals and spent the week drawing portraits of tourists on the beach and charging them five dollars a pop. That's where Carroll Carson found me. He's *the* big-name tattoo artist on the west coast.' She shrugged. 'He took me under his wing, offered me an apprenticeship. I was lucky.'

She glanced across at him and something inside her shifted. Perhaps Mrs Lavender had been right and Jaz had done the right thing leaving Clara Falls all those years ago. If she hadn't left, she'd have spent her life living in Connor's shadow, grateful to him for loving a misfit like her.

She wasn't a misfit. She'd earned her place in the world. She didn't need any man to make that right.

'Faye was a one-night stand.'

The admission shot out of Connor like bullets from a gun, and with as much impact. All Jaz could do was stare. She wanted to tell him it wasn't any of her business.

'A one-night stand?' Her voice came out hoarse and raspy.

He scratched a hand back through his hair. 'Faye was the one who told me about you and Sam Hancock.'

Her jaw dropped. Surely Faye hadn't thought—

'You'd left. We both missed you like the blazes. We drank too much and…'

He trailed off with a shrug. She was glad he didn't go into details.

'The next day I told her that it had been a mistake. That it couldn't happen again.'

Jaz stared at him, shook her head, tried to comprehend what he was telling her. 'How did she take that?'

'Not well.'

Had Faye been in love with Connor all along? The thought made her feel suddenly ill. 'Why are you telling me this?' She found herself on her feet, shaking with…she wasn't sure what—more regrets? She didn't have room for any more of those.

Connor stood too. 'I just wanted you to know the truth, that's all.'

The gold sparks in Connor's eyes, their concern, reached out and wrapped her in their warmth. The same way his arms had wrapped around her when they'd danced. It had near sent her pulse sky-rocketing off the charts.

She pulled back. There was no future for her and Connor. There was no point wondering what it would be like to rest her head against his shoulder or to nuzzle her face against his neck, to slip her hand beneath his shirt and trace the contours of muscle and sinew honed by hard physical labour.

There might not be any point to it, but she couldn't seem to stop imagining it.

'Hey, guys, having fun?'

Gwen, cheeks flushed from dancing, bore down on them.

'Absolutely,' Jaz managed.

'You bet,' Connor said. 'You look as if you're slaying them in the aisles.'

Jaz ground her teeth together.

'Are you drinking that?' Gwen pointed to the glass of punch.

Jaz handed it to her. 'Help yourself.'

'Thanks.' She drained it dry. 'Ooh, look, there's Tim Wilder. I'll catch you both later.'

'You bet. Go knock him dead.'

That was Connor again.

'Are you okay?' he asked when he turned back to Jaz.

She slammed her hands to her hips. Connor backed up a step. 'You have that itching for a fight look plastered all over your face. What have I done this time?'

'It's what you haven't done. Or, more precisely, what you haven't said. Is there something wrong with my appearance?' she demanded.

He shoved his hands in his pockets. 'No.' He shifted his feet. 'Why?'

'Because you've told every woman you've met this evening how lovely or stunning or wonderful she looks. Every woman, that is, except me!'

A grin spread across his face, slow and sure. His shoulders lost their tightness. He moved in closer, crowding her with his heat, his scent…their history. He angled his body towards hers in a blatant invitation she wanted to accept.

'Does my opinion matter so much to you, Jaz?'

'No, of course not,' she snapped, angry with herself. 'Put it down to a moment of feminine insecurity.'

She tried to move past him but his arm snaked out and caught her around the waist, drew her back against his heat and his hardness. With agonising slowness and thoroughness, he splayed his hand across her stomach. Low down across her stomach. She bit back a whimper. If he moved that hand, if he moved so much as his little finger, she'd melt in his arms where she stood.

'You don't have any reason whatsoever for insecurity, Jazmin.'

His breath touched her ear. She closed her eyes. He'd only ever called her Jazmin when they'd made love. And in the eight long years since she'd left here, she'd never had another lover. Not one. Trembling shivers that started at her knees and moved upwards shook her body, betraying her need.

'But if I start telling you how sexy you look in that dress, how wearing your hair like that highlights your eyes and how the gloss on your lips makes my mouth water…then that might lead to me telling you how I want to tear that dress from your body and make love to you all night long— fast and frantic the first time, slow and sensual the second time, watching every nuance in your face the third time.'

She couldn't find her voice. Her breath came in short shallow gulps.

'But, given the circumstances, that might not be wise.'

No, not wise at all.

He pulled her more firmly against him until she couldn't mistake the hardness pressing against the small of her back. 'I burn for you as much as I ever did, Jazmin.'

His teeth grazed her ear. She moaned.

'I can feel that same need burning in you. I can feel your body trembling for me. I want to take you home and make love to you. Now. Just say the word,' he murmured against her ear, 'and we're out of here. Say it!' he ordered.

Yes! To spend a glorious night of pleasure and freedom in Connor's arms. Yes! To touch him as her fingers and lips burned to do, to scale the heights with him and…

No.

Her heart dropped. She gulped. She peeled his fingers from her stomach, one by one, and stepped away. 'And what happens tomorrow, Connor?' She turned to face him. 'And the day after that?' Did he think they could just pick up where they'd left off?

The flush of desire in his eyes didn't abate. 'We—'

'What happens the next time you find me with another man in a situation you can't account for? Are you going to fly off the handle and accuse me of cheating on you again?'

His head snapped back.

'You didn't trust me then and you don't trust me now.' More importantly, she didn't trust herself. Who would she hurt the next time he broke her heart?

There wouldn't be a next time!

She had no intention of losing her heart to him ever again. No man was worth that kind of pain. 'If you'll excuse me, I'm in serious need of a glass of punch.'

She turned and stalked off in the direction of the refreshments table and she didn't wait to see if he followed. From the evidence she'd seen, he'd need a moment to himself.

She helped herself to punch, started to raise the glass to her lips, when Gordon Sears bore down on her.

'I've been looking for you everywhere, Jaz.'

She loathed his fake jovial tone, the smirk on his face. She ignored the headache pounding at her temples to inject a false brightness of her own. 'Why's that, Mr S? Did you want to ask me to dance?'

'No, just wanted to give you advance warning that I'll be serving papers on your solicitor come Monday morning.'

Her stomach started to churn. 'What kind of papers?'

'No doubt you're aware that I lent your mother fifty thousand dollars?'

Punch sloshed over the side of her glass.

Satisfaction settled over his face. 'No?' he said. 'That was remiss of her.'

'I don't believe you,' she whispered. Why would Frieda borrow money from this man?

'She needed it to buy the bookshop.' He rubbed his hands together, his smile widening. 'And now I'm calling in that debt. Pay up within seven days or the bookshop is mine.'

Fifty thousand dollars! She didn't have that kind of money. He had to be bluffing.

He had to be bluffing!

Oh, Mum. Why? To lure me back to Clara Falls? I wasn't worth it.

'Is there a problem?' Connor demanded, striding up and placing himself between Jaz and Mr Sears.

Mr Sears threw his head back and laughed. 'Not for much longer.' With that, he swaggered off.

Connor's brows drew down low over his eyes. 'What was that all about?'

'Just Mr Sears trying to cause trouble as usual.' But her voice shook.

His eyes narrowed. 'Has he succeeded?'

She lifted her chin, forced her shoulders back. 'Of course not.' She glared at him. 'But why couldn't this have just been a beer and pizza night, huh?' She could do with a fat-laden pepperoni pizza right now, washed down with an ice-cold beer. It might help her think.

It might help her sleep.

Connor frowned. 'Are you feeling okay, Jaz?'

'I'm perfect,' she snapped.

He stared down at her for a long moment. 'You look beat. Are you ready to leave?'

She gave a fervent nod. 'Yes, please.'

CHAPTER NINE

JAZ stood outside the door of her upstairs flat and turned the key over and over in her hand. She tried to regulate her breathing, her heart rate.

With an impatient movement, she shoved the key in the lock, but she didn't turn it. She drew back again to twist her hands together. *Jeez Louise!*

She'd made excuses whenever Connor had asked her if she wanted to inspect the flat. Same with the carpet-layers. And the men who'd fitted the blinds and light-fittings. She couldn't make any more excuses. What on earth would she say to Gwen if she delayed moving into the flat any longer—*I don't want to enter the place where my mother lost all of her hope?*

It wouldn't do.

But she still didn't move forward to open the door.

'Hello, Jaz.'

She jumped and swung around, clutching her heart. 'Connor!' She gulped. 'I…um…didn't hear you.'

He stood two steps below the landing. Wooden

steps. *Rickety* wooden steps. She had a feeling that she really ought to have heard him.

He didn't point out that his work boots must've made plenty of noise. He stared at the closed door and then at her. 'Are you okay?'

'Of course I am.'

'Then what are you doing?'

'I was just about to go into the flat, that's all.'

In one hand he held a large parcel wrapped in brown paper. She wondered what it was. She wondered what he could be doing here with it. She brightened. Perhaps he hadn't finished work on the flat after all and still had one or two things to install? It'd give her a legitimate excuse to race back to Gwen's B&B.

'Housewarming gift,' he explained, gesturing to it. Darn!

Then she remembered her manners. 'That's nice of you, Connor. But you certainly didn't have to go to any trouble.'

'No trouble.'

He glanced at the door again, then back at her. 'Besides, I wanted to.'

For a moment his eyes burned and she recalled with more clarity than she could've thought possible the feel of his hand on her abdomen when it had rested there on Saturday night, his breath against her neck.

'Are you going to open the door?'

She gulped and swung back to the door. 'Yes, of course I am.' But she didn't reach out and unlock it.

Connor moved up the final two steps with a grace she'd have appreciated all the more if her heart hadn't tried to dash itself against her ribs.

'I knew there was a problem when you kept making excuses not to inspect the flat.'

'No problem. I just trusted your workmanship. That's all.'

'Your mother didn't die inside there, you know, Jaz.'

'I know that!' Her mother had died later at the hospital. 'Like I said, there's no problem.'

He ignored that. 'Okay, the way I see it, I can either pick you up and physically carry you inside…'

Good Lord, no. Bad, bad idea. She didn't want him touching her.

Yes, you do, a little voice whispered through her.

Fine, then. She didn't want what it might lead to.

Are you so sure?

She ignored that. 'Or?'

'Or I can watch your back while you go first.'

That didn't fill her with a great deal of enthusiasm either.

'Or I can go first.'

She met the amber and gold flecks in his eyes. He hadn't stated the obvious—that he could leave. She should tell him to go.

'If I go first I can give you the grand tour. I can

point out the work the guys and I have done. You can ooh and ahh over all the improvements.'

She moistened her lips, then nodded. 'I'd… um…appreciate that.'

'I want you to be the one to unlock the door, Jaz.'

She gulped again. His eyes held hers—steady… patient. She didn't glance at the door again. She kept her gaze on his face and soaked up all his warmth and strength. With fingers that shook, she reached out and unlocked the door.

Connor smiled. She wished she could smile back, but she couldn't. He moved past her, gathered her hand inside his and led her into the flat.

'As you can see, the flat is a gun-barrel affair.'

His matter-of-fact tone soothed her.

'This door is the only entrance and exit to the flat. So if a fire ever starts down this end and you're at the other end, you'll need to climb out the front windows onto the shop awning and swing down to the street from there.'

'Just call me Tarzan,' she muttered.

He grinned and, although she couldn't grin back, it eased some of the tightness in her chest.

He gestured to the left. 'We ripped the old bathroom out and replaced it.'

She stuck her head around the door—black and white tiles. 'Nice.'

'This is the kitchen. Another rip-out-and-replace job.'

The hallway opened out into a neat kitchen. Connor and his men had done a nice job. She ran her free hand across a kitchen cupboard, a countertop. Her other hand felt warm and secure in Connor's.

'Very nice,' she managed.

They didn't stop to study it any further. Connor tugged her up the three steps that led into the enormous combined dining and living area, towed her into the centre of the room and then dropped her hand. Jaz turned on the spot. Even with all her boxes piled up in here, she could make out that the proportions of the room were generous.

Perfect for dinner parties.

And beer and pizza evenings.

Some more of that soul-sickening tension eased out of her.

'Why don't you go explore further?'

He smiled that steady, patient smile and his strength arced across the space between them to flood her. With a nod, she followed a short passageway to the two bedrooms—a small one on the left and a large bright one at the front that held her bed, wardrobe and dressing table. Light poured in at two large windows. She leant on the nearest windowsill and stared out at the vista spread before her—a glorious view of Clara Falls' main street, framed by the mountains in the background.

Her mother had lived in this flat without proper heating, without a working gas stove and with rotting floorboards in one section of the living room because of a leak in the roof, not to mention the wood rot in the kitchen and bathroom. Yet…

Jaz's lips curved up. Her mother would've thought that a small price to pay for this view.

Frieda would also have loved the wood-panelled walls and pressed tin ceilings. She'd have been happy here.

Relief hit Jaz then—lovely, glorious relief. She dropped to her knees by the window, lifted her face to the sun and murmured a prayer of thanks. She hadn't come upstairs once in the last two weeks, afraid that the despair that must've enveloped her mother would still hang heavy and grim in these rooms. She'd expected it to taunt her, berate her… sap her of her energy and her determination.

She'd welcomed every delay—first by the carpet layers, then by the firm who'd measured the flat for blinds and curtains, and then the gas board. Even this morning—after she'd rung Richard to warn him of Mr Sears's threats—she'd hung around and dithered in the shop until her staff had shooed her out with promises to call her if she was needed.

But the air didn't press down on her with suffocating heaviness, punishing her for not coming home sooner. It didn't silently and darkly berate her for abandoning her mother. She opened her eyes. The mid-morning sunlight twinkled in at the windows and the flat smelt fresh and clean and full of promise.

She pushed herself to her feet and glanced out of the window at Mr Sears's 'baked-fresh-daily' country bakery and resolve settled over her shoulders.

She had boxes to unpack.

'Connor?'

He hadn't followed her into the bedroom, and the click of the front door told her he'd just left.

She stared down the empty corridor and her heart burned. He'd sensed the demons that had overtaken her. He'd helped her face them…and then he'd left? Just like that? He hadn't let her thank him.

The housewarming gift!

She raced back out to the living room and tugged off the brown paper wrapping. She sat back on her heels and stared. Her throat thickened and she had to swallow.

He'd given her the handmade wine rack she'd admired so much that day in his garage.

With a hand that shook, she reached out and ran a finger across the smooth wood. 'Thank you,' she whispered into the silence.

Jaz hadn't thought to check if the electricity had been connected to the flat until shadows started to lengthen around her. She glared at the light switch on the wall, but she didn't reach out to switch it on and see. She glared around the kitchen. She'd made progress today—good progress.

For all the good it would do her.

Richard had called her an hour ago—Mr Sears's claim was legitimate. Jaz had to find fifty thousand dollars in the next seven days or lose the bookshop.

A knock sounded on the door and Jaz raced to answer it, welcoming the interruption. 'Mrs Lavender! What are you doing here? Come in.'

Mrs Lavender tsk-tsked. 'You'll ruin your eyesight, Jazmin Harper!' She moved past Jaz, flicked on the light and bathed the kitchen in a warm glow. 'That's better. Now, I can't stay. I just wanted to bring you up some supplies.'

The older woman's thoughtfulness touched her. 'You didn't need to go to any trouble.'

'No trouble, dear. It's just some coffee, a carton of milk and a loaf of bread. Oh, and some eggs,' she said, pulling the items out of a muslin bag. 'Now, don't work too late and don't forget to eat.'

'I won't,' Jaz promised. On impulse, she reached out and hugged the older woman. 'Thank you.'

She saw Mrs Lavender out, then came back in and stared up at the kitchen light sending out its golden glow.

'It's a good sign,' she announced to a pile of empty boxes in the corner. 'It's a good sign,' she said to the jug, filling it. She needed all the good signs she could get.

'Oh, stop talking to yourself and go make your bed!'

She flicked on every light as she went. She made her bed, straightened the bedside tables. She hunted out her bedside clock, a couple of paperbacks and a framed photograph of Frieda.

Now it looked as if someone lived here.

Hands on hips, she surveyed the room and decided the dressing table would look better on the opposite wall. She set her shoulder against it, out-of-all-proportion grateful for castor wheels. The dressing table moved an inch, then stuck fast. She tried hauling it towards her instead. Same result. With a grunt she managed to pull it out from the wall, and reached behind to investigate.

'Darn.' A panel of wood was wedged between wall and dressing table. It must've fallen off the wall. Biting back a very rude word, she pulled it out and set it aside, shoved her dressing table into its new location with more speed than grace, then turned to assess the damage.

Connor had said the bedrooms in the flat were structurally sound. That all they'd need was a coat of paint…and new carpet…and new blinds and curtains. 'What do you call this?' she grumbled. Then remembered she wasn't supposed to be talking to herself.

She tried to fit the panel back to the wall.

She didn't try biting back that very rude word when the panel fell off the wall again.

She seized it in both hands and held it like a club. She could tattoo big, burly men without batting an eyelash. She could do a pretty good Carly Simon rendition on karaoke nights, but home maintenance?

Very carefully she set the panel of wood on the floor, hauled in a deep breath and massaged her temples. For reasons of personal pride, it had become important to fix this slim panel of wood back to the wall. She needed to work out how piece A fitted into piece B. It took her all of five seconds to realise she'd need a torch.

'At least I have one of those.'

She rushed out to the living room to rifle through boxes, and forgot to berate herself for talking out loud. 'Aha!' She held the torch aloft in triumph. 'Yes!' The battery even worked.

She raced back to the bedroom and studied the piece of wood panelling thoroughly, and then the wall. What she needed to do was—

Something glittered in the gap in the wall. Jaz squinted, adjusted the torch. An old Christmas shortbread tin?

She hesitated for only a moment before pushing her hand through the hole. 'But if anything black and hairy so much as touches me…'

Her fingers closed around the tin and she drew it out. She set it on the floor and stared at it. 'Wouldn't I love to find fifty thousand dollars inside you,' she murmured.

She reached out, ran her fingers across the tin's lid—remarkably dust-free. She shone her torch into the wall cavity—*not* remarkably dust-free.

She clambered to her feet, tucked the tin under her arm and went to make herself a cup of coffee.

She sipped her coffee on the steps between the kitchen and living room and surveyed the tin. 'If this were a novel, I really would find fifty thousand dollars in you, you know? And, as we are sitting above a bookshop…' She lifted a hand, then let it fall. 'All I'm trying to say is, if you'd like to come to the party I don't have any complaints.'

She set her mug down and pulled the tin towards her. 'With my luck it'll be a bomb,' she grumbled.

She hauled the lid off.

She stared.

And then she smiled.

Letters. Letters addressed to Frieda Harper, tied in pink ribbon and scented with rose petals. 'Oh, Mum—' she sighed '—who'd have guessed you had such a romantic streak?'

She untied the ribbon, lifted the first letter from the pile, eased it out of its envelope and unfolded it.

My beloved Frieda.

Oh, how beautiful. Jaz's hand went to her chest. She turned the letter over, searching for the signature, the name of her mother's admirer, and—

No!

She abandoned the letter to tear open the next

one…and the one after that…until she'd checked them all. They all bore the same signature.

She pinched herself. She started to laugh. She leapt to her feet and danced around the room. 'We've saved the bookshop, Mum!'

The tin didn't hold fifty thousand dollars. It held love letters addressed to her mother from Gordon Sears.

Gordon Sears!

If the contents of these letters became public, his credibility would be ruined in Clara Falls for ever.

She swept the letters and the tin up, along with her still-warm cup of coffee, and raced out of the flat and downstairs to the bookshop to address the portrait of Frieda on the wall. The one she hadn't finished yet. Couldn't finish.

That didn't stop her talking to it. 'Look!' She held the letters up for Frieda to see. 'I don't know if you meant for me to find these, Mum, but you didn't destroy them so…' She hauled in a breath and tried to contain her excitement. 'They couldn't have come at a better time. I can save the bookshop with these.'

For the first time she found she could smile back at the laughing eyes in Frieda's portrait.

She set her mug on the floor, opened the tin and started reading the letters out loud to her mother. 'I would've only been eleven when you received this one.'

But, as she continued to read, her elation started

to fade. 'Oh, Mum…' She finished reading the third letter, folded it and slipped it back into its envelope. She settled herself on the floor beneath her mother's portrait. 'He must've loved you so very much.'

Her triumph turned to pity then, and compassion. Very slowly she eased the tin's lid back into place, pulled it up to her chest and hugged it.

That was how Connor found her half an hour later.

'Am I interrupting anything?'

'No.' She eased the tin back down to her lap.

'I saw the light on and it reminded me that I hadn't returned your key.'

She studied his face as he settled on the floor beside her. She snorted her disbelief at his excuse. 'Richard's spoken to you, hasn't he? Isn't there such a thing as a professional code of privacy in this town?'

'All he said was that you might need a friend this evening, nothing else.'

'Oh.'

'You haven't finished Frieda's portrait yet.'

She couldn't. She didn't know why, but she just couldn't. 'I've been busy.'

She had a feeling he saw through the lie.

'Want to tell me what's going on?'

'Why not?' She didn't bother playing dumb. 'It'll be common knowledge around town soon enough.' She leant her head against the wall. 'My mother borrowed fifty thousand dollars from Gordon Sears. He's calling the debt in.'

'Fifty thousand dollars!' Connor shot forward. 'Are you serious?'

She nodded. 'And no,' she added, answering the next question in his eyes, 'I don't have access to that kind of money. But I do have an appointment with the bank manager first thing tomorrow.'

She dragged a hand down her face. She didn't want to think what would happen if the bank refused her the loan.

Sympathy and concern blazed from Connor's eyes. It bathed her in a warmth she hadn't expected. If felt nice having him sit here on the floor beside her like this—comforting. Perhaps Richard was right and she did need a friend. Maybe, given enough time—and with a concerted effort on her part to ignore the attraction that simmered through her whenever she saw him—she and Connor could be friends.

'Thank you for stopping by and making sure I was okay. I do appreciate it.' Perhaps they were friends already?

'You're welcome.'

She met his eyes. Their gold sparks flashed and glittered and tension coiled through her—that tight, gut-busting yearning she needed to find a way to control. Finally, as if he too could no longer bear it, his gaze dropped to the tin in her lap and she could breathe again.

He nodded towards it. 'What have you got there?'

Without a word, she passed the tin across to him, watched the expressions that chased themselves across his face as he opened it and read the top letter.

'Bloody hell, Jaz! Do you know what this means?' He held the letter up in his long work-roughened fingers, leaning forward in his excitement. 'This is your bargaining chip. Show these to Gordon Sears and he will definitely come to some agreement with you about paying back the loan. They're pure gold!'

'Yes.'

He stilled, studied her face. 'You're not going to use them, are you?'

'No.'

'But…'

She sympathised with the way the air left his lungs, the way he sagged back against the wall to stare at her as if he couldn't possibly have heard her properly.

'I'm not going to use these letters to blackmail Mr Sears.' She couldn't use them.

She tried to haul her mind back from thoughts of dragging Connor's mouth down to hers and kissing him until neither one of them could think straight. Which would be a whole lot easier to do if the scent of autumn hadn't settled all around her, making her yearn for the impossible.

'Why not?'

She took a letter from the tin. '*My beloved Frieda,*' she read. '*All my love…forever yours.*' She dropped it back into the tin. The action sent his scent swirling around her all the more. She breathed it in. She couldn't do anything else. 'To use that as blackmail would be to desecrate something very beautiful. I won't do it.'

She gestured to the unfinished portrait above them. 'My mother wouldn't want me to do it.' She wanted to make Frieda proud of her, not ashamed.

Connor stared at her for a long time and those beautiful broad shoulders of his bowed as if a sudden weight had dropped onto them. His mouth tightened, the lines around it and his eyes became deeper and more pronounced. His skin lost its colour. His autumn eyes turned as bleak as winter.

Her heart thudded in sudden fear. 'Connor?'

'You didn't cheat on me eight years ago, did you, Jaz? I got it wrong. I got it all wrong.'

Her skin went cold, then hot. She hunched her knees up towards her chest and wrapped her arms around them. 'No, I didn't cheat on you.'

She hadn't thought he could go any paler. She'd been wrong. She wanted to reach out a hand and offer him some kind of comfort but she was too afraid to. She'd always known it would rock him to his foundations if he ever discovered the truth. She recognised the regret, the guilt, the sorrow that stretched through his eyes. Recognised too the self-condemnation, the belief in the inadequacy of any apology he tried to offer now.

She should've stayed eight years ago. She should've stayed and fought for him.

She couldn't change the past but…

'What time is it?'

He glanced at his watch, stared at it for an eternity, then shook himself. 'It's only half past six.'

'Is your car out the back?'

He nodded.

'C'mon then.' She rose. 'There's something I want to show you.'

He followed her outside, waited for her to lock the bookshop, then led her to his car. 'Where to?' he asked, starting the engine.

'Sam Hancock's.'

He swung to face her but he didn't say anything. Did he think she meant to punish him? He set his shoulders, his mouth a grim line and she could almost see a mantle of resolve settle over him as he started the car. He intended to endure whatever she threw at him.

Oh, Connor. I don't want to hurt you any more. I want you to understand and find peace, that's all.

They didn't speak as he drove the short distance to Sam's house. Nor did they speak as she led the way to the front door. Sam had told her on Saturday night that he was here for the next week.

'Hi, Sam,' she said when he answered the door. 'You told me the other night that I was welcome to come around and view my handiwork if I wanted. Is now a convenient time?'

'Absolutely.' With a smile, he ushered them into the house and led them through to the main bedroom, gestured to the life-size painting on the wall. 'I'll leave you to it. Yell if you need anything.'

Jaz murmured her thanks but barely managed to drag her gaze away from Connor as he studied the picture she'd painted of Lenore Hancock eight years ago. 'This is Sam's mother,' she said because she had to say something.

'Yes.' He moved closer to it to study it more carefully.

'This is where I first understood the power of my talent.'

He turned to meet her gaze and she shrugged. 'I hadn't fully comprehended the effect something like this could have. It frightened me.'

He gestured to the wall too, but he didn't glance back at the picture. His eyes remained glued to her face. 'How did this come about?'

'Sam's dad developed dementia and started walking the streets at all times of the day and night searching for Lenore. She'd died a couple of years before him, you see.'

'So you drew her on the wall for him?'

'Yes.'

'Why didn't you tell me?'

'Because Sam and his sister asked me to keep it a secret.'

His hands clenched. 'Even from me?'

She wanted to reach out and wipe the anguish from his eyes. 'Sam and his sister didn't want to put their father into a nursing home, but they both had to work and the nurse who came for a few hours every day was finding him harder and harder to deal with. The fewer people who knew, the fewer people who could interfere.'

She pulled in a breath. She owed him the whole truth. 'What I felt for you, Connor…it scared me too. Some days I thought you would swallow me whole. I needed to find my own place in the world that was separate from yours.' And she'd found it in the worst way possible. 'Though it never occurred to me that you could misconstrue…'

He stepped back, his lips pressed together so tightly they almost turned blue. Her stomach turned to ash. Could he even begin to understand her insecurity back then?

He swung away to stare at the picture again. 'Did it work? Did they have to put Mr Hancock into a nursing home?'

'It worked better than any of us had dreamed.' She bit her lip, remembering the evening they'd unveiled the finished portrait to Mr Hancock. 'When he saw the picture, he pulled up a chair and started talking to her. I'll never forget his first words. He said—*Lenore, I've been looking for you everywhere, love. And now I've found you.*' It had damn near broken her heart. She'd had to back out of the room and race outside.

Connor swung around as if he sensed that emotion close to the surface in her now. 'That's the same night I found you with Sam, isn't it?'

She hesitated, then nodded.

'Mr Hancock's reaction, it freaked you out, didn't it? It wore you out the same way that tattoo you did for Jeff wore you out.'

'Yes.' The word whispered out of her.

'And Sam was trying to comfort you.'

Her throat closed over. She managed a nod.

'When you said—*I loathe this thing and I love it too, but whatever I do I can't give it up*—you were talking about your ability to draw people so well, so accurately, and not about your relationship with Sam.'

Her head snapped up. 'Is that what you thought?' She stared at him in shock.

'I should have believed in you.'

Yes, he should've. 'I should have stayed and made you listen.'

Eight years ago, she'd been too afraid to stay and fight for him.

'God, Jaz, I'm sorry!' He reached out one hand towards her, but he let it drop before it could touch her. 'Is it too late to apologise?'

She smiled then. 'It's never too late to apologise.' She had to believe that.

'Then I'm sorry I jumped to conclusions eight years ago. I'm sorry I accused you of cheating on me. I'm sorry for hurting you.'

A weight lifted from her. 'Thank you.'

He reached for her then and she knew he meant to fold her in his arms and kiss her.

She wanted that. She wanted that more than she'd ever wanted anything.

She took a step back. Her heart burned. Her eyes burned. 'It's not too late for apologies, but it is too late for hope. We can't turn time back. I'm sorry, Connor, but it's too late for us.'

He stilled. He dragged a hand back through his hair, his mouth grim. 'Do you really believe that?'

The words rasped out of his throat, raw, and Jaz wanted to close her eyes and rest her head against his shoulder. She stiffened her spine and forced herself to meet his gaze. 'Yes, I do.' Because it was true.

His mouth became even grimmer. 'Does this mean we can't be friends?' she whispered. She could at least have that much, couldn't she?

The mouth didn't soften. The gold highlights in his eyes didn't sparkle. 'Is that what you want?'

'Yes.' For the life of her, though, she couldn't manage a smile.

'Friends it is.'

He didn't smile either.

'C'mon.' He took her arm. 'I'll take you home.'

CHAPTER TEN

CONNOR showed up the next day for her appointment at the bank.

'What on earth…' she started.

'Friends?' he cut in, his mouth as grim as it had been last night.

'Yes, but—'

'Then trust me.'

Something about his grimness made her nod and back down. She didn't need a knight in shining armour, but it was nice knowing Connor was on her side all the same.

She got the loan. Connor told the bank manager he'd take his business—his not inconsiderable business—elsewhere if they refused her the loan. He'd have even gone guarantor for her but she put her foot down at that. The terms of the loan would stretch her resources, the bookshop would need to make a profit—and soon—all plans for an art gallery had to go on hold… But she got the loan.

'Anything else I can help with?' Connor asked once they were standing out on the footpath again.

'Well, now, let me see…' She smiled. She wanted to see the golden highlights in his eyes sparkling. She wanted to see him smile back. 'I don't have anyone lined up to man the sausage sizzle on Saturday.'

This Saturday. The Saturday of the book fair.

The book fair that now had to do well.

Very well.

'Done. I'll be there.'

He turned and strode away. No sparkling. No smiling.

She spent the rest of the week trying to lose herself in the preparations for the book fair. She double-checked that the authors and poets lined up for the Saturday afternoon readings were still available. She double-checked that the fairy she'd hired to read stories to the children hadn't come down with the flu, and that the pirates she'd hired to face-paint said children hadn't walked the plank and disappeared.

She double-checked that the enormous barbecue she'd hired would still arrive first thing Saturday morning, and that the butcher had her order for the umpteen dozen sausages she'd estimated they'd need for the sausage sizzle.

She would not let anything go wrong.

She couldn't afford to.

She didn't double-check that Connor would still man the sausage sizzle, though.

That didn't mean she could get him out of her mind.

Alone in her flat each night, she ached to ring him.

To say what?

Just to find out if he's okay.

Oh, for heaven's sake. Get over yourself. Connor has not spent the last eight years living in the past…or fleeing from it. Of course he's okay.

His men finished work on the bookshop in double-quick time…and Connor was so okay he didn't even bother coming around to check up on it.

Gritting her teeth, she wrote a cheque and posted it.

She tried to sleep but, as usual, insomnia plagued her.

By closing time on Friday afternoon, she was so wound up she didn't know if she wanted to bounce off walls or collapse into a heap.

'You're driving your staff insane, you know that?' Mrs Lavender observed.

'I'm not meaning to.' Jaz twisted her hands together and glanced out of the window. She was always glancing out of the window. What for? Was she hoping for a sight of Connor? She dragged her gaze back.

Mrs Lavender's eyes narrowed. 'What happened to the woman who strode down the street with purpose and determination?'

'I'm still that same woman.'

'Are you? It seems to me you spend more time hand-wringing and…and mooning, these days.'

Jaz exhaled sharply. 'I'll wear the hand-wringing, but not the mooning!'

She wasn't mooning.

Was she?

She gulped. Had she let her feelings for Connor undermine her purpose?

A pulse behind her eyes hammered in time with the heart that beat against her ribs. She could not let anyone, not even Connor—especially not Connor—distract her from making her mother's dream a reality.

She nodded slowly. The hammering eased. 'You're right.' She glanced out of the window, not looking for Connor, but towards Mr Sears's bakery. As if on cue, Connor drove past with Melly in the car. Jaz refused to follow the car's progress. She didn't speak again until the car was lost from her line of sight.

'There's something I need to do,' she said with sudden decision. She didn't want to put it off any longer.

'I'll close the shop for you.'

'Thank you.'

Jaz raced upstairs, grabbed the tin of letters. Then she set off across the road to Mr Sears's 'baked-fresh-daily' country bakery.

She didn't enter the shop with a booming, Howdy, Mr S. She waited quietly to one side until he'd served the two customers in front of her, and only when they were alone did she approach the counter.

'I found something that belongs to you.' She handed him the tin, then stepped back.

Mr Sears frowned, glowered...lifted the lid of the tin...and his face went grey. The skin around his eyes, his mouth, bagged. Some force in his shoulders left him. Jaz wondered if she should race around the counter and lead him to a chair.

'What do you want?' The words rasped out of him, old-sounding and wooden. With both hands clasped around the tin, he leant his arms against the counter. Not to get closer to her, but to support himself.

'Peace,' she whispered.

He met her gaze then. He nodded. Finally he said, 'How much?'

It took her a moment to decipher his meaning. Her head snapped back when she did. He thought she wanted money?

'Or have you already given copies to the local newspapers?'

'I am my mother's daughter, Mr Sears.' She lifted her chin. 'Did my mother ever *once* threaten you with those?'

She nodded towards the letters. He didn't say anything.

'I haven't made copies, I haven't photographed them and I haven't shown them to any gossip columnists.'

She watched the way his lips twisted in disbelief and swore she would never let love tear her up, screw up her thinking, twist her, like it had in the past. Like it was doing now to Mr Sears.

'Once upon a time you loved my mother a great deal. She kept your letters, which tells me she must've loved you too. Now that she's dead they belong to you, not to anybody else.' She took a step back from the counter. 'I did not come back to Clara Falls to make my mother ashamed of me, Mr Sears.'

She turned around and walked away, knowing he didn't believe her. For the next month…three months…perhaps for the rest of his life, Gordon Sears would pick up the local paper with the taste of fear in his mouth. He'd watch for thinly disguised snickers and people falling silent whenever he walked into a room.

Until he let go of his fear, he would find no peace.

Until she let go of her fear, neither would she.

Her feet slowed to a halt outside the bookshop's brightly lit window with its colourful display of hardbacks, the posters advertising tomorrow's book fair.

Her fear.

It wasn't the fear of the bookshop failing—though, with all her heart, she needed to make that dream a reality for her mother. No, it was the fear that a true, passionate love—like the love she and Connor had once shared—would go wrong and once again she'd become bitter and destructive, hurting, even destroying, the people she most loved.

She rested her head against the cold glass. Once she'd reconciled herself to the fact that love was closed to her—love, marriage…and children. Once she'd managed that, then perhaps she'd find peace.

Jaz was awake long before she heard the tapping on the front door of her flat at seven-thirty the next morning.

At six o'clock, and over her first cup of coffee, she'd pored over the day's programme. Even though she'd memorised it earlier in the week. Then she'd started chopping onions and buttering bread rolls for the sausage sizzle. She was counting on the smell of frying onions to swell the crowd at the book fair by at least twenty per cent. Who could resist the smell of frying onions?

And who could be tapping so discreetly on her front door, as if they were worried about disturbing her, this early in the morning?

Unless the barbecue and hotplate had arrived already.

She wondered if Connor would show up and man the sausage sizzle as he'd promised.

Of course he would. Connor always kept his promises.

She tried to push all thoughts of him out of her head as she rushed to answer the door.

'Melly!'

Melly stood there, hopping from one foot to the

other as if her small frame could hardly contain her excitement. 'Did I wake you up?'

'No, I've been up for ages and ages.'

Jaz ushered her into the flat, patted a stool at the breakfast bar and poured her a glass of orange juice. 'What are you doing here?'

Melly clutched a crisp white envelope in one hand and she held it out to Jaz now. 'I had to show you this.' She grinned. She bounced in her seat.

Jaz took the envelope and read the enclosed card, and had a feeling that her grin had grown as wide as Melly's. 'This is an invitation to Yvonne Walker's slumber party tonight!'

Melly nodded so vigorously she almost fell off her stool. Jaz swooped down and hugged her. 'Sweetheart, I'm so happy for you.'

'I knew you would be. I wanted to come over yesterday to tell you, but Daddy said you were busy.'

Did he? 'I…er…see.'

Melly bit her lip. 'Are you busy now?'

'Not too busy for you,' she returned promptly.

Melly's autumn-brown eyes grew so wide with wonder Jaz found herself blinking madly.

'Then…then can you do my hair up in a ponytail bun this afternoon? I…I want to look pretty.'

'Absolutely, and you'll knock their socks off,' Jaz promised. But…

'Daddy knows you're here now, though, doesn't he?'

Melly shook her head. 'He was sleeping and I didn't want to wake him up. He was awake most of last night.'

Jaz wondered why. Then she stiffened. Good Lord! If Connor woke and found Melly gone…

Melly bit her lip again. 'Are you cross with me?'

'No, of course not, Melly, it's just… How would you feel if you woke up and couldn't find Daddy anywhere in the house?'

'I'd be scared.'

'How do you think Daddy will feel if he wakes up and he can't find you?'

Melly's eyes went wide again. 'Will he be scared too?'

Jaz nodded gravely. 'He'll be very, very worried.'

Melly leapt down from her stool. 'Maybe he's not awake yet and if I run home really, really fast…'

Jaz prayed Connor hadn't woken yet. She grabbed her car keys. 'It'll be quicker if I drive you.'

She cast a glance around at all the preparations she'd started, then shook her head. It'd only take a minute or two to see Melly home safe. She had plenty of time before the book fair kicked off at ten.

She gulped. Lord, if Connor woke and couldn't find Melly…

'Hurry, Jaz! I don't want to worry Daddy.'

Jaz stopped trying to moderate her pace. She grabbed Melly's hand and raced for the door. She released Melly to lock the door behind them and, when she turned back, Melly had already started down the stairs. Jaz had almost caught up with her when a voice boomed out, 'Melanie Linda Reed, you are in so much trouble!'

Connor! He'd woken up.

At the sound of his voice Melly swung around and Jaz could see the child's foot start to fly out from beneath her. It would send her hurtling head first down the rest of the stairs. Jaz lunged forward to grab the back of Melly's jumper, pulling the child in close to her chest. She tried to regain her balance but couldn't quite manage it and her left arm and side crashed into the railing, taking the brunt of the impact.

She gritted her teeth at the sound of her shirt sleeve tearing. Exhaled sharply as pain ripped her arm from elbow to shoulder. Struggled to her feet again.

Connor was there in seconds, lifting Melly from her arms and checking the child for injury.

'Is she okay?' Jaz managed.

He nodded.

'We were trying to get home really fast,' Melly said with a sob. 'Jaz said you'd be really, really worried if you woke up and couldn't find me. I'm sorry, Daddy.'

Jaz wanted to tell him to go easy on Melly, but her arm was on fire and it took all her strength to stay upright.

'We'll talk about it later, Mel, but you have to promise me you'll never do that again.'

'I promise.'

'Good. Now I want to make sure Jaz didn't hurt herself.'

Jaz gave up trying to stay upright and sat.

Connor set Melly back down and they turned to her as one.

As one, their eyes widened.

Jaz tried to smile. 'I think I scratched my arm.' She couldn't look at it. She could do other people's blood, but her own made her feel a bit wobbly.

And she knew there was blood. She could feel it.

'You're bleeding, Jaz.' Melly's eyes filled with tears. 'Lots!'

It didn't mean she wanted it confirmed.

'What was it, Connor? A rusty nail?'

He glanced at the railing above, narrowed his eyes, then nodded.

'Brilliant! So now I'll have to go and get a tetanus shot.' It was the day of the book fair. She didn't have time for tetanus shots. *Oh, Mum, I'm sorry.*

Connor kicked the railing. 'I'm going to replace this whole damn structure! It's a safety hazard.' Then he took her arm in gentle fingers and surveyed it.

Melly sat down beside Jaz and stroked her right hand. 'You saved my life,' she whispered in awe.

That made Jaz smile. She squeezed the child's hand gently. 'No, I didn't, sweetheart. I saved you from a nasty tumble, that's all.'

'I'm sorry, Jaz, but I think you're going to need more than a tetanus shot.'

She gulped. 'Stitches?'

He nodded.

'But…but I don't have time for all this today.' The book fair! 'Can't we put it off till tomorrow? Please?'

'It'll take no time at all,' he soothed as if to a frightened child. He brushed her hair back from her face. 'Mel and I will take you to the hospital in Katoomba and they'll have you fixed up within two shakes of a lamb's tail, I promise.'

He looked so strong and male. Jaz wanted to snuggle against his chest and stay there.

'Daddy is a really good hand holder, Jaz. You will hold Jaz's hand, won't you, Daddy?'

'I will,' he promised.

It reminded Jaz that she should at least look brave for Melly's sake. 'No time at all, you say?'

'That's right.' He slipped an arm around her waist. 'Come on, I'll help you to the car.'

She had no choice but to submit. *Oh, Mum, I'm sorry.*

They were at the hospital for four hours.

Four hours!

Connor wanted to roar at the staff, he wanted to tear his hair out…he wanted to take away Jaz's pain.

He paced. He called his father to come and collect

Melly. He rang Mrs Lavender to tell her what had happened. He held Jaz's hand.

Until they took her away and wouldn't let him go with her.

He replayed over and over in his mind that moment when Jaz had thrown herself forward to save Mel from harm. He'd been a bloody fool to roar at Mel like that, but he'd been so darn relieved to find her...

Over and over he relived his fear of that moment when he'd thought both Mel and Jaz would fall headlong down those stairs together.

One certainty crystallised in his mind with a clarity that made his hands clench. From now on, he wanted to keep Jaz from all harm. For ever.

It wasn't too late for them. It couldn't be!

Finally Jaz reappeared. She had some colour in her cheeks again and a bandage around her upper arm. She smiled at him as if she sensed his worry and wanted to allay it. 'Right as rain again, see.' She held up a piece of paper. 'I just need to get this prescription filled and then we can go.'

The nurse accompanying Jaz folded her arms. 'And what else did the doctor say, Ms Harper?'

'I'll have something to eat when I get home, I promise.'

'You'll do no such thing.' The nurse transferred her glare to Connor. 'You will take her down to the cafeteria and you won't let her leave until she's had a sandwich and an orange juice, you hear?'

'Yes, ma'am.'

'But the book fair—'

'No arguments,' he told Jaz. They'd follow the doctor's orders. 'You've been here four hours; another twenty or so minutes won't make any difference.'

She glared at him. 'You said two shakes of a lamb's tail.' She snorted. He couldn't really blame her. When her shoulders slumped he wanted to gather her in close and hold her.

He didn't. He took her for a sandwich and an orange juice.

They sat outside at a table in the sun because Jaz said she'd had enough of being cooped up indoors. He pulled his sweater over his head and settled it around her shoulders. A bolt of warmth shot through him when she pulled the sweater around her more securely and huddled down into its warmth. He found himself fighting the urge to warm her up in a far more primitive manner.

'How are you feeling?' he asked when she'd finished her sandwich.

'Actually, as good as new.'

He raised a sceptical eyebrow.

'It's true! I mean, the arm is a bit sore, but other than that…I'm relieved, if the truth be told.'

'Relieved!'

'From the looks on your and Melly's faces, I thought at the very least I was going to need twenty stitches.'

'How many did you get?'

'Three.'

'Three! I thought—'

'You thought I was going to lose my arm.'

He threw his head back and laughed with sheer relief. 'You really are feeling all right?'

'I am.'

'Good. Then I can do this.'

He leaned over and kissed her, savoured all of her sweet goodness with a slowness designed to give as much pleasure as it received. When her lips trembled beneath his, it tested all of his powers of control.

He drew back and touched a finger to her cheek, smiled at the way her breath hitched in her throat. 'I love you, Jaz.'

The words slid out of him as natural as breathing. Then he bent his head and touched his lips to hers again.

CHAPTER ELEVEN

'WHAT on earth…?'

Jaz pushed against him so violently she'd have fallen off her seat if he hadn't grabbed her around the waist to hold her steady.

'What do you think you're doing?' She leapt right out of his arms and stood trembling, facing him.

He'd have laughed out loud at her words if the expression on her face hadn't sliced him to the marrow. 'I thought that was kind of obvious.' He tried to grin that grin—the one that she'd told him eight years ago could make her knees weak. The grin that kicked up one corner of his mouth and said he couldn't think of anything better on this earth than making love with her.

The grin wasn't a lie. He couldn't think of anything he'd rather do.

She stared at his mouth and took a step back, gripped her hands together. 'This can't happen!'

He rose too, planted his feet. He wanted to fill her field of vision the way she filled his. 'Why not?'

'What do you mean, why not? You… I…' She snapped her mouth shut, dragged in a breath and glared. 'You know why not.'

Her voice trembled. It made him want to smile, to haul her into his arms…to cry.

'Nope, can't say I do.' He shook his head. 'I loved the girl you were eight years ago, and I love the woman you are now even more. I don't get why we can't be together.'

Her eyes grew wide and round. For a brief moment her whole body swayed towards him and a fierce joy gripped him. He'd win her round yet. 'There's nothing to stop us from being together, Jaz. Nothing at all.' He'd prove it to her. He took a step towards her, reached out his hands…

Jaz snapped back, away from him. 'I already told you. It's too late!'

Frustration balled through him. And fear. He couldn't lose her a second time. He couldn't.

'When are you going to stop running?'

'Running?' She snorted. 'I'm not running. I came back to Clara Falls, didn't I? And I'm not leaving until my mother's bookshop is back on its feet. Doesn't seem to me that there's much running away involved in any of that.'

At the mention of the bookshop, though, a spasm of pain contracted her nostrils, twisted her mouth. The bookshop. He thought back to the darn loan with its outrageous interest rate that she'd lumbered herself with. He'd have given her the money if she'd let him. He'd have offered to lend it to her, but he'd known she'd have refused that too.

Something told him she would not survive the closure of the bookshop. Financially, she couldn't afford it. Emotionally…a cold chill raised the hairs on the back of his neck.

'Why is the bookshop so important, Jaz?'

Her eyes darkened. Not for the first time, he noticed the circles beneath them. 'Making it a success…it's the only thing left that I can do for my mother.'

It all clicked into place then. He should've realised it right from the start. Her return to Clara Falls; it wasn't about pride or revenge. It wasn't about showing the town she was better than they'd ever given her credit for. It was about love. This woman standing in front of him had only ever been about love.

And yet she held herself responsible for her mother's death.

She'd healed all the dark places inside him. He wanted to heal the dark places inside her too. 'When are you going to stop punishing yourself and let yourself be happy?'

'I can't,' she whispered.

The pain in her voice tore at him. 'Why not?' He kept his voice low, but something in her eyes frightened him. He wanted to reach for her but he knew that would only make her retreat further. He clenched his hands and forced them to remain by his sides.

'When you thought I'd cheated on you, it broke my heart, Connor.'

A weight pressed down on his chest, thinning his soul. He deserved her resentment. He sure as hell didn't deserve her forgiveness. And yet he'd thought… 'I've tried to apologise, Jaz. I'm sorrier for that mistake than I can find the words for. If I could turn time back…'

'I know, and it's not what I mean. We both made mistakes we're sorry for. It's…' She broke off to pull his sweater more tightly around her body as if she were cold and couldn't get warm, no matter how hard she tried. 'I became a different person after-wards, that's what I'm trying to tell you. I became bitter and hard, destructive.'

She met his eyes, her own bleak but determined. Bile filled his mouth, his soul.

'I'm not saying I blame you for that because I don't. It wasn't your fault. It was mine. I turned into the kind of person who refused to come back to Clara Falls even though my mother begged me to, even when I knew how much it would mean to her. Can you believe that?'

She gave a harsh laugh. He closed his eyes.

'I may as well have handed my mother that bottle of sleeping pills with my own hands.'

His eyes snapped open. 'You can't believe that!'

Her hands shook. 'But I do.'

'You can't hold yourself responsible for another person's actions like that, Jaz.'

'If I'd come home, I'd have seen how things were. I could've helped. I could've saved her.' She whispered the last sentence.

Then she threw her head back and her eyes blazed. 'But I didn't because I'd turned into some unfeeling monster. That's why there's no future for me and you, Connor. I can't risk loving like that ever again. Who will I hurt or destroy the next time love fails me, huh?'

His mouth had gone dry. 'Who says it will fail?'

She stared back at him—wounded, tired... resolute. 'I'm sorry, Connor, but that's one gamble I'm not prepared to take.'

His stomach...his heart...his whole life, dropped to his feet at the note of finality in her voice. She was wrong, so wrong to exile herself from love like this.

To exile him!

He'd imagined her in his arms so fully and completely, and for all of time. To have her snatched back out of them now was too much to bear. This woman standing in front of him was all about love...but she'd exempted herself. And that meant she'd barred him from love too because he would never settle for second best again. For him, anyone but Jaz Harper was second best.

'According to your philosophy then, I'd better not have the gall to go falling in love again.'

Her jaw dropped, but then she pressed her lips together into a tight line. Pain rolled off her in waves. It took all of his strength not to reach for her and do what he could to wipe that pain away.

'I mean, what if I let jealousy get the better of me again for even half a second? Given my past form, I quite obviously have no right messing with women's hearts.'

She pressed the heels of her hands to her eyes. He hated the defeated slope of her shoulders, the way she seemed unable to throw her head back when she pulled her hands away. 'That's not what I meant and you know it.'

'You said the only thing left that you could do for your mother was to save the bookshop. You're wrong. The best gift you could give Frieda is to live your life fully and without fear…to finally let love back into your life. You don't get it, do you, Jaz? Frieda never wanted you to come back to Clara Falls for her own comfort or peace of mind. She wanted you to come back for yours!'

He watched her try to take in the meaning of his words.

'Do you think she'd be pleased by what you are doing to yourself now?'

She paled.

'Do you think she'd be proud of you?'

She just stared back at him, frozen, and he wondered if he'd pushed her too far. All he wanted to do was drop to his knees in front of her and beg her to be happy.

She took a step away from him. 'Take me home, please, Connor.'

She wouldn't meet his eyes and his heart froze over. 'I'm supposed to be running a book fair. I need to see if I can manage to salvage something from this day.'

And then she turned away and Connor knew that was her final word. His words hadn't breached the walls she had erected around herself.

He'd failed.

They made the fifteen-minute journey from Katoomba hospital to Clara Falls in silence. Jaz's heart hurt with every beat it took, as if someone had taken a baseball bat to it. A pain stretched behind her eyes and into eternity.

The force of Connor's words still pounded at her and she could barely make sense of anything. She'd thought she'd started to put things right, to make things better. Except...

Connor loved her.

One part of her gave a wild, joyful leap. She grabbed it and pulled it back into line. She and Connor?

No.

She forced herself to swallow, to straighten in her seat. They'd reach Clara Falls' main street any moment now.

She realised she still clutched Connor's sweater around her like an offer of comfort. She inhaled one last autumn-scented breath, then folded it neatly and set it on the seat beside her.

She tried to ready herself for the sight of a closed bookshop and no customers, for fairies and pirates who would rightly demand payment anyway. She tried to push to the back of her mind how much money she'd plugged into advertising, on orders for sausages and hiring barbecue plates. She tried to think of ways she could allay the disappointment of the authors and poets who'd promised her their time free of charge this afternoon as a favour to their community.

From the corner of her eye, she saw Connor glance at her. 'You think that Mrs Lavender and co have had to cancel the book fair, don't you?'

She ached to reach out and touch his shoulder, to tell him she'd never meant to hurt him. She didn't. It wouldn't help. 'Yes.'

He frowned. 'Why? Do you think you're that indispensable?'

'Of course not!'

She didn't think she was indispensable to him at all. He'd find someone else to love. One day. And she wanted him to. She gritted her teeth. She meant it. She did. He deserved to be happy.

She reminded herself they were talking about the bookshop. 'Mr Sears will have found a way to sabotage the fair.' And without her there to run the gauntlet…

Her stomach roiled and churned as they turned into Clara Falls' main street.

There weren't as many tourists down this end of the street as usual. Even though the day was disgustingly bright and sunny. Her mouth turned down. She wished for grey skies and hail. Somehow that would make her feel better.

But the sun didn't magically stop shining and rain and huge balls of ice didn't pour down from the sky. She bit back a sigh and kept her eyes doggedly on the streetscape directly beside her.

As they moved closer towards the bookshop, Jaz wanted to close her eyes. She didn't. But she didn't move her eyes past the streetscape directly beside her either. She would not look ahead. She didn't have the heart for that.

She didn't have the heart to glance again at Connor either.

She wished the car would break down. She wished it would come to a clunking halt and just strand her here in the middle of the road, where she wouldn't have to move until it was closing time in Clara Falls.

It didn't happen. The car kept moving forward. Jaz kept her eyes on the view beside her. A few more tourists appeared. At least it wasn't only her shop that was doing poorly today.

Then the scent of frying onions hit her.

Onions!

She slid forward to stare out through the front windscreen.

People.

Oodles and oodles of people. All mingling and laughing out the front of her bookshop.

Connor pulled the car to a halt and a cheer went up when the townsfolk saw her.

A cheer? For her?

Her jaw went slack when she saw who led the cheer.

Mr Sears!

Not only did he lead the cheer but he manned the barbecue hotplate full of sausages too. Carmen grinned and waved from her station beside him. Somehow, Jaz managed to lift her hand and wave back.

Just as many people—perhaps more—were crammed inside the bookshop. It was so full it had almost developed a pulse of its own. She recognised two staff members amid all the chaos, caught sight of a fairy and couldn't help wondering where the pirates had set up for the face painting.

She turned to stare at Connor. 'But what…?'

He didn't smile. He just shrugged. 'Why don't you hop out here? I'll park the car around the back.'

She didn't want to get out of the car. She didn't want to leave him like this. She'd hurt him and…

And she couldn't help him now.

She slid out of the car and stood on the footpath, watched as the car drew away. Only then did she turn back to the crowd and wondered what she should tackle first.

Not what, but who. With a sense of unreality, she made her way through the crowd to Mr Sears. 'I…' She lifted her hands, then let them drop. 'Thank you.' Somehow that seemed completely inadequate.

'No.' He shook his head. 'Thank you.'

And then he smiled. She wondered if she'd ever really seen him smile before.

'In this town, Jaz, we pull together.'

'I… It means a lot.' She found herself smiling back and that didn't seem completely inadequate. It felt right.

She glanced around and what she saw fired hope in her heart. *Oh, Mum, if you could only see this.* She swung back to him. 'What can I do?'

'Carmen and I have things sorted out here for the moment, don't we, Carmen?'

The teenager's eyes danced. 'Aye, aye, Captain.' She saluted her father with the tongs and her sense of fun tugged at Jaz.

He pointed to the door. 'You'll find Audra Lavender and Boyd Longbottom directing proceedings inside.'

She went to turn away, then swung back. 'Did I just hear you say Mrs Lavender *and* Boyd Longbottom?'

'That's right.' He winked. 'I think you'll find it's a day for miracles.'

She started to grin. 'I think you must be right.' She turned and headed for the door.

'Jaz, dear.' Mrs Lavender beamed when she saw her. 'I hope your poor arm is okay.'

'Yes, thank you. It's fine.'

Mrs Lavender had set up two sturdy card tables against the back wall in preparation for the cheese and wine Jaz had ordered for the afternoon readings. She'd pushed the leatherette cubes against the walls and into the spaces between the bookcases. It would leave a circle of space around the authors as they gave their readings. Perfect.

'And the authors can use these tables for signings afterwards, you know, dear. I mean, once the crowd hears our three guests, they're going to want to buy the books. And yes, we do have plenty in stock,' she added when Jaz opened her mouth.

Jaz closed it again, noticed Boyd Longbottom sorting bottles of wine in the stockroom and nodded towards him. 'How?' she whispered.

'I said to him this morning—"Boyd Longbottom, I need help with our Jazmin's book fair and I don't know who else I can ask."'

Jaz's eyes widened. 'It was that easy?'

'Well, now, he did say—"If you agree to have dinner with me tonight then I'm all yours, Audra Lavender." And he said it so nice like. A lady shouldn't turn down a nice offer like that, should she?'

'Of course not.'

Jaz couldn't help thinking back to the way Connor had told her he loved her—as if he couldn't help but say it; as if there hadn't been another thought in his head.

Jaz leant forward and clasped Mrs Lavender's hand. 'I'm pleased for you.'

The older woman's eyes turned misty. 'Thank you, dear. Boyd and I, we've wasted enough time now, I think.'

Jaz straightened and her heart started to thump, but she wasn't sure why. She searched the room for Connor but couldn't see him anywhere. He was the usual reason her heart rate went haywire.

'Mrs Lavender, thank you for everything you've done today. I...'

'Did you really think we'd leave you in the lurch?'

'I certainly didn't expect you to take so much upon yourselves.'

'Why not?'

Jaz stared, and then didn't know quite what to say.

'You've given an old woman a new lease of life. You've given your staff a fun and harmonious working environment. This book fair, it's galvanised us, made us work together. You've made us feel as if we matter.'

'But you do!'

'Precisely, Jazmin Harper. We all matter. Even you.'

Before Jaz could respond, Mrs Lavender rushed on, 'And I don't know what you did to charm Mr

Sears, but it was well done. The moment he saw Boyd and I wrestling with the barbecue, he was across the road like buckshot. He started directing and things just fell into place.'

'I'm very grateful.'

'Jazmin, dear, you're one of us. We look after our own.'

Jaz felt the walls of the community wrap around her and it felt as good as she'd always imagined it would.

'I…well, now that I'm here, what can I do?'

'Mingle. Chat and charm. Bask in the glow of the fair's success. And take care of that arm. Everything else has been taken care of. We know where to find you,' she added when Jaz opened her mouth to argue. 'If we need to.'

Jaz had to content herself with that. She mingled. She chatted. As she moved about the room, it occurred to her that she felt comfortable here—here in Clara Falls, of all places. More comfortable than she had ever felt anywhere in her life before.

'Your mother would've enjoyed this,' Mr Sears said, coming up beside her as the guest authors prepared themselves for the readings.

The scent of frying onions still seasoned the air. She glanced out of the window behind her. Connor had taken over the sausage sizzle. A pulse fluttered in her throat. She had to swallow before she could speak. 'Yes, she would've had a ball.'

Mr Sears followed her gaze. He turned back to her. 'Don't make the same mistakes Frieda and I made.'

'Which was?' She held her breath. It was none of her business but…

He stared back at her. 'I loved your mother from the first moment I clapped eyes on her.' His lips tightened briefly. 'I understood why she wouldn't get involved with me when I was married. But when my wife died…'

Mrs Sears had died over ten years ago, when Carmen and her brother were just small children.

'I didn't understand why she wouldn't take a chance on us then. I knew she loved me.'

'Didn't she ever tell you why?'

He was quiet for a long moment. 'She said we couldn't be together until all the children were grown up. She said her reputation would make things too difficult for them.'

Jaz's jaw dropped.

'And I took that to mean that she cared more about what people thought than she cared about me.'

He broke off for a moment, then pulled in a breath. 'I wanted the bookshop so badly because I suspected the letters were in the building somewhere. And I wanted it because it was part of her. I treated you very badly, Jazmin. I'm sorry.'

'Apology accepted,' she said without hesitation. 'But, speaking of the bookshop, I am looking for a business partner.'

His eyes suddenly gleamed. 'The two of us could make Frieda's dream a reality.'

She nodded.

'We'll talk about this further.'

She smiled. 'That's what I was hoping you'd say.'

He sobered again. 'I let my disappointment that Frieda wouldn't marry me turn my love into something ugly and twisted.' He reached out, touched her hand briefly. 'Don't you go and make the same mistake.'

Then he was gone.

Jaz's heart pounded and burned. She turned to the partially completed portrait of Frieda on the back wall for guidance. *Oh, Mum, what do I do?*

The partially completed portrait didn't give her so much as a hint or clue.

Perhaps if Jaz could finish it…but she couldn't seem to bear to.

It wasn't that she couldn't bear to. She simply couldn't do it—it was as plain as that. Something blocked her, something stood between her and her ability to find and execute that final essence of Frieda.

Would Frieda want her to take a chance on Connor?

She glanced out of the window again. Sun glinted off his hair and yearning gripped her. But…

No! Fear filled her soul. She couldn't risk it; she just couldn't. She'd won more today than she had ever expected. She had to content herself with that. It would have to do.

The rest of the afternoon breezed along without so much as the tiniest push from Jaz. Everyone agreed that the author readings were a huge hit—not least the authors, who must've sold dozens of their books between them.

Connor packed up the sausage sizzle and disappeared. Jaz did her best not to notice.

Just when she thought the day was starting to wind down, a new buzz started up. Connor stood at the back of the room, in the same spot the guest authors had, calling for everyone's attention.

Jaz blinked and straightened. She chafed her arms and tried to look nonchalant.

'As most of you know, today wouldn't have been possible if it wasn't for one special lady—Jaz Harper.'

She gulped, tried to smile at the applause that broke out around her.

'Jaz returned to Clara Falls to honour her mother's memory, and to make her mother's final dream a reality. I can't tell you all how glad I am to see the town come out in such numbers to support her.'

Jaz noticed then that most of the tourists had wandered off—they'd probably left after the readings. The people who were left were almost all locals.

Connor gestured to the partially completed portrait on the wall behind him. 'As you can see, Jaz means to leave a lasting memorial of her mother here in Clara Falls. It only seems fitting that the grand finale to the day should be Jaz putting the finishing touches to her mother's portrait. If you agree, put your hands together and we'll get her up here to do exactly that.'

No way! He couldn't force her hand this way. She wouldn't do it. She *couldn't* do it.

But a path had opened up between her and Connor and everyone was clapping. Some people cheered, yet others stomped their feet, and Jaz had no choice but to move forward.

'What is this?' she hissed when she reached him. 'Payback?'

'Just finish the damn picture, Jaz.'

His voice was hard, unrelenting, but when she glanced into his face the gold highlights in his eyes gleamed out at her. 'Connor, I can't.' She was ashamed at the way her voice wobbled, but she couldn't help it.

He took her hands in his. 'What is it you focus on in the photographs that you turn into tattoos? What is it that you see in those photographs of people you don't know, but capture so completely that you bring tears to the eyes of their loved ones?'

She searched his eyes. 'Details,' she finally whispered. She focused on the details—one thing at a time, utterly and completely.

'Will you trust me on this?'

She stared at him for a long moment, then nodded. 'Yes.'

He wouldn't lead her astray on something so important. Even though she had hurt him. She knew that with her whole heart. He would try to help her the way she'd helped him.

He handed her the photograph of her mother. 'Forget that she's your mother, forget that you ever knew her, and focus only on the details.'

She stared at the photograph. The details. Right.

Then he handed her a paintbrush. 'Paint, Jaz.' Only then did she notice that he'd already arranged her paints about her.

Jaz painted. The scent of autumn engulfed her and she painted.

She'd finished the eyes and nose, the brow and the wild hair already. Now she focused on the mouth—the lips wide open in laughter, creases and laughter lines fanning out from the corners. She focused on the strong, square jaw with its beauty spot, then the neck and the shoulders.

She lost herself in details.

As always happened, when Jaz finished the last stroke she had no idea how much time had passed. She set her paintbrush down and stepped back, and the room gave a collective gasp. Jaz heard it for what it was—awe. It meant she'd done a good job.

She couldn't look yet. She needed all those details to fade from her mind first.

She pressed the heels of her hands to her eyes, unutterably weary. Strong arms went around her and drew her in close, soaking her in their warmth and strength. She wanted to shelter in those arms— Connor's arms—for ever. He'd remained standing behind her the entire time she'd painted, his presence urging her on, ordering her to stay focused. And she had.

But she couldn't stay here in his arms. At least, not for ever. She'd already made that decision—she couldn't afford to let the worst of her nature free in the world again.

But, before she was ready to let him go, he was putting her from him. 'Are you ready to see it?'

She pulled in a shaky breath, managed a nod. He eased her back towards the crowd, then slowly turned her around to face her finished artwork.

Jaz stared. And then she staggered as the impact of the portrait hit her. She'd have fallen flat on her face if Connor hadn't kept an arm around her.

Frieda laughing in the sun.

Her mother stood in front of her laughing, filled with happiness and goodwill and her own unique brand of fun, and Jaz ached to reach out and touch her. *This* was how Frieda would want Jaz to remember her. *This* was how Frieda would want everyone to remember her.

Oh, Mum, I loved you. You did know that, didn't you?

Yes. The word drifted to her on an autumn-scented breeze and suddenly her cheeks were wet with all the tears she hadn't yet shed. The tightness in her chest started to ease.

Oh, Mum, what do I do?

No answer came back to her on a breeze—autumn-scented or otherwise, but the answer started to grow in Jaz's heart the longer she stared at Frieda's portrait.

Be happy. That was what her mother would say. It was all that Frieda had ever wanted for her.

Did she dare?

She scrubbed the tears from her cheeks with hands that shook, then turned to face the hushed crowd that stood at her back. 'I want to thank you all for coming here today—for supporting me and Frieda and the bookshop. If she could, I know my mother would thank you too.' She paused, dragged in a breath. 'I came back to Clara Falls with a grudge in my heart, but it's gone now. I've finally realised my true home is here in Clara Falls and—' she found herself smiling '—it's good to be back.'

The crowd broke into a loud round of applause. Mr Sears brought it back under control after what seemed like an age. 'Okay, folks, that's officially the end to the book fair…' he sent Jaz a sly look '…for this year, at least.'

Good Lord!

She thought about it. An annual event? The idea had merit.

'Now, there's still plenty of cleaning up to be done,' Mr Sears continued, 'so those of you who are willing to stick around…'

Jaz couldn't help but grin as he took control.

Connor touched her arm. 'Jaz. I… It's time I headed off.'

The golden lights in his eyes had disappeared. Leaving? But…no! She didn't want him to go.

Her mouth went dry. *She didn't want him to go.* It hit her then. Denying herself the chance of building a life with Connor, of being with him—that was hurting her just as much as his lack of faith in her had eight years ago.

Did that mean she'd turn back into that desperate, destructive person she feared so much?

She all but stopped breathing. Her fingernails bit into her palms. She hunched into herself and waited for the blackness, the anger, to engulf her again… and kept waiting.

She lifted her head a little, dragged in a shaky breath, and counted to three. She lifted her head a little higher, and slowly it dawned on her. The blackness—it wasn't coming back.

She'd learned from the mistakes of the past.

She was stronger, older, wiser.

She wasn't afraid any more!

She wanted to dance. To sing and dance and—

She glanced into Connor's face and the singing and dancing inside her abruptly stopped. Had she left it too late? Had Connor finally run out of patience…and love?

She glanced at Frieda's portrait, then back at Connor.

'I love you.' She said the words as simply and plainly as he had to her earlier in the day. She didn't know if it was too late to say them or not. She only knew she had to say them.

Connor froze. He backed up a step. 'What did you just say?'

She grew aware that the people nearest to them had turned to stare. She leaned in close to him and whispered the words again. 'I love you, Connor.'

He threw his head back, his eyes blazed. 'Are you ashamed of your feelings or something?'

'No, I'm not ashamed that I love you, Connor.' She said the words, loud and proud. 'It's just that guys aren't as gushy-gushy as girls and I thought you might like to have this conversation in private, that's all.'

He just stared at her. He didn't move. He didn't say anything. He had to have heard her. She'd said it three times!

'It's customary for the boy to kiss the girl at this point,' Mrs Lavender pointed out. 'And if that is your intention, Connor Reed, then I definitely suggest you find yourself some privacy.'

Her words acted on him like magic. He grabbed Jaz's hand, pulled her through the stockroom, out through the kitchenette and all the way outside. He dropped her hand again and swung around to stare at her.

'You're not kissing me yet,' Jaz couldn't help but point out.

'Not yet.' He pointed a finger at her. It shook. 'You say that you love me.'

'Yes.'

'Why the change of heart?'

'It's not really a change of heart. I've always loved you.' The way she sensed he'd always loved her.

'What made you change your mind about taking the risk?'

'Frieda.' She said her mother's name simply. 'I couldn't finish her portrait because I was blocked. I was blocked because you were right. I wasn't living my life the way she'd have wanted. When I looked at the finished portrait I finally realised what she'd want me to do.'

He frowned. 'To tell me you love me?'

'To be happy,' she corrected softly. 'And being with you is what makes me the happiest.'

His eyes darkened with intent then. Her pulse leapt. He moved towards her…

It started to rain.

'I don't believe this,' Jaz murmured under her breath. 'Not now!'

She glanced from the sky with its lowering clouds to Connor. 'We could…er…always go up to my flat.'

The gold highlights in his eyes glittered. He reached out and captured her chin in his strong callused fingers. 'If you invite me up there, Jaz, I won't be leaving any time soon.'

A thrill shot through her. The rain continued to fall around them. 'Where's Melly?' she managed.

'With my parents. My father is going to drop her off at Yvonne's party tonight.'

Jaz stared up at the rain again, then back at Connor. 'So you don't have anywhere you need to be tonight?'

'No.'

'Then…'

'Then…?' he mimicked.

Jaz groaned. 'Kiss me, Connor.'

He did.

When he lifted his head, long moments later, she could hardly breathe let alone stand. 'Come on.' When the strength returned to her limbs, she grabbed his hand and headed up the stairs and to her flat.

Connor took the keys from her fingers and turned her to face him, heedless of the rain. 'I'm not prepared to lose you a second time, Jaz. I want you to know that this—' he nodded at the door '—is for keeps. I need to know that you feel the same way.'

Her heart expanded until she thought it might burst. 'For keeps,' she whispered. She'd never been surer of anything in her life. It made a mockery of all her previous doubts.

'For ever?' he demanded.

'And ever,' she agreed.

He rested his forehead against hers. 'I love you with all that's in me, Jaz Harper. Promise me you will never run away again. I don't think I could bear it.'

His eyes darkened with remembered pain. She reached up and brushed his hair from his forehead. 'I promise.' Then she kissed him with all the love in her heart.

They were both breathing hard when she drew back.

'In return,' he rasped, holding her gaze, 'I swear to you that I will always listen to you. I won't jump to stupid conclusions.'

'I know,' she said. But it suddenly occurred to her that, even if he did, they were both stronger now. Together, they could overcome anything.

She didn't know why, but she found herself suddenly laughing in his arms, so glad to be near him and loving him, revelling in the freedom of it.

'What do you young people think you're doing up there?' Mrs Lavender called from below, her voice tart with outrage. 'Don't you know it's raining? Get inside with you before you catch your deaths!'

'Better do what the lady says,' Connor said with a lazy grin, unlocking the door.

Jaz's heart leapt. 'Absolutely,' she agreed, the breath catching in her throat.

He held his hand out to her. She placed hers in it. Together they stepped over the threshold.

2 FREE BOOKS
AND A SURPRISE GIFT

We would like to take this opportunity to thank you for reading this Mills & Boon® book by offering you the chance to take TWO more specially selected titles from the Romance series absolutely FREE! We're also making this offer to introduce you to the benefits of the Mills & Boon® Book Club™—

- **FREE home delivery**
- **FREE gifts and competitions**
- **FREE monthly Newsletter**
- **Exclusive Mills & Boon Book Club offers**
- **Books available before they're in the shops**

Accepting these FREE books and gift places you under no obligation to buy, you may cancel at any time, even after receiving your free shipment. Simply complete your details below and return the entire page to the address below. You don't even need a stamp!

YES Please send me 2 free Romance books and a surprise gift. I understand that unless you hear from me, I will receive 5 superb new stories every month including two 2-in-1 titles priced at £4.99 each and a single title priced at £3.19, postage and packing free. I am under no obligation to purchase any books and may cancel my subscription at any time. The free books and gift will be mine to keep in any case.

Ms/Mrs/Miss/Mr_____ initials _____

Surname _____

address _____

_____

_____ postcode _____

Send this whole page to: Mills & Boon Book Club, Free Book Offer, FREEPOST NAT 10298, Richmond, TW9 1BR